D0897616

W. STANFORD REID

Professor of history at the University of
Guelph in Ontario, W. Stanford Reid
is also a Presbyterian minister and
author of, among other works, *Skipper
from Leith* and *The Economic History
of Great Britain*.

TRUMPETER OF GOD

W. Stanford Reid

TRUMPETER
OF
GOD

A Biography of John Knox

Charles Scribner's Sons
New York

Copyright © 1974 W. Stanford Reid

Library of Congress Cataloging in Publication Data
Reid, William Stanford,
   Trumpeter of God.

   Bibliography: p.
   1. Knox, John, 1505–1572. I. Title.
BX9223.R4   285′.2′0924 [B]   73-1356
ISBN 0-684-13782-8

1 3 5 7 9 11 13 15 17 19 C|C 20 18 16 14 12 10 8 6 4 2

Printed in the United States of America

TO *Professor J. D. Mackie,*
HISTORIOGRAPHER OF SCOTLAND

CONTENTS

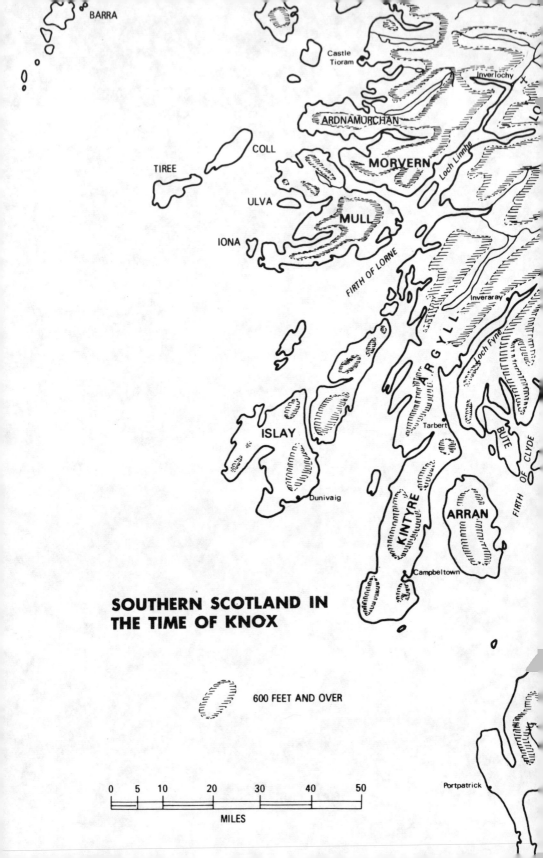

SOUTHERN SCOTLAND IN
THE TIME OF KNOX

600 FEET AND OVER

0   5   10   20   30   40   50

MILES

PREFACE

WHY ANOTHER BIOGRAPHY of John Knox? This will probably be the question of some who are confronted with this book. Since Dr. Thomas M'Crie published his first edition of his biography of Knox, a considerable number have appeared, the number increasing most rapidly in the past few years. Why then add to them? Indeed, some historians feel that Knox is really a subject completely unworthy of any further consideration. Since they do not like him, either because they do not understand him or because his views and theirs are poles apart, they feel that he should descend into a well-deserved oblivion. Neverthless, the fact that new biographies of different types are still appearing quite regularly in publishers' lists, and that they are being reviewed with vigor, if not animosity, indicates that Knox does speak relevantly out of an age very similar to our own.

The present work, however, is not a complete story of John Knox's life. It could not be within a book of this size. Rather it is a biographical study which seeks to interpret Knox in order to provide a better understanding of one who has not infrequently been misrepresented both by his adulators and his critics.

Few biographies of Knox have been genuinely interpretative. Either they have tended to assemble and retail large masses of facts, sometimes interestingly, sometimes dully, but often without understanding, or they have taken up specific aspects of his work or thought which they have stressed, indeed overstressed, to the detriment of the subject as a whole. There have also been those who, like Andrew Lang, have written to denigrate as far as possible Knox's role in the Reformation. But despite all the writing, not many have dug down to the well-springs of the man's dynamism, which all, whether *pro* or *con*, admit that he possessed. The present work endeavors in part to compensate for this lack.

Basic to Knox's motivation and action was his conversion to Protestantism. We do not know exactly how or when that took place, but that it did and that it influenced the rest of his life is very evident. True, it did not make him perfect, or indeed always consistent, a fact that he himself was quite prepared to admit, but it did result in his having a specifically Protestant-biblical point of view of himself and the world in which he lived. This perspective dominated his thinking on all matters.

A second element in Knox's thought was his concept of his calling. It runs throughout his life and his work from the time he entered the ministry at the insistence of the congregation in St. Andrews until his death some twenty-five years later. He believed that he was called in the same way that Jeremiah and Amos, his two favorite prophets, were commissioned to bring God's word to Israel. He was to blow the trumpet in Zion, summoning men back to repentance and faith in Jesus Christ as Saviour and Lord. This he felt was his chief purpose in life.

The "trumpeter theme" thus became central to his thinking. While he might play variations on it from time to time, he always returned to it. Most people who know anything about him have heard of his *First Blast of the Trumpet Against the Monstrous Regiment of Women*, but few realize that his idea of blowing the trumpet was one to which he had already referred frequently in his early ministry in Berwick. And through the rest of his life he repeatedly describes his preaching as "blowing the master's trumpet." This idea which he appropriated from Old Testament prophets such as Jeremiah summed up his own view of his work and at the same time expressed the martial spirit that he believed necessary for the Church of Christ in his own day.

The third major influence on Knox was the social milieu out of which he came. Although the son of a farmer's family in East Lothian, from his early days he associated with a group of local lairds who although by no means wealthy were independent, often violent, and closely bound together by blood and feudal relationships. Their lands formed an arc extending from North Berwick and Haddington on the east, south of Edinburgh through Dalkeith to Calder on the west.

His influence, however, extended beyond the lairds for they were closely linked to the rising burgesses of the towns. Not infrequently pressed for money because of rising costs, fixed rents, and constant lawsuits, the gentry turned to the merchants of the burghs for financial assistance. The result was often close business relations. Furthermore, to meet their obligations the lairds found it convenient to marry a son or a daughter to a merchant's offspring who would bring the cancelled debt as a dowry or marriage portion. At the same time, many of the wealthier burgesses were also buying estates which gave them the position of at least "part–time" gentry. In this way the burgesses and lairds were tending to coalesce.

Out of these people of "the middling sort" in the population, Knox spoke of matters that concerned them and in terms that they understood; and from them he received most of his support: military, financial and spiritual. This also explains why he appealed to the same elements in the population in England and France, and to leaders such as John Calvin in Geneva. It would also indicate why he was not usually on good terms with either the Scottish or English aristocracy, whom he frequently offended by his rather blunt, down-to-earth, "business-like" talk. He was no diplomat in the aristocratic sense and he knew it. His social background made him too middle class for their liking or their ways of thinking.

These three aspects: his conversion, his idea of his calling, and his social milieu should be kept in view as we follow his story, if we are to gain a deeper comprehension of Knox, his problems, and his endeavours to solve them, and also a more sympathetic appreciation of the man himself.

The author thanks his many undergraduate and graduate students who have worked in this field and who in so doing have at times brought forth new insights and understanding that have been of help. He is also deeply grateful to the foundations and granting agencies who have from time to time financed research trips which have made possible the collection of material for this study as well as for other articles and books. He would mention especially the Canada Council, the American Philosophical Society of Philadelphia, the Government of the Republic of France, the Institute for Advanced Christian

Studies, and McGill University. He would also thank the personnel of various libraries and archives who have assisted him: the Redpath Library, McGill University, Montreal; the British Museum and the Public Record Office, London, England; the Scottish Record Office and the National Library of Scotland, Edinburgh, Scotland; the Bibliothèque National and the Archives Nationales, Paris, France; and the MacLaughlin Library, University of Guelph, Guelph, Ontario.

Equally important has been the work of Mrs. Pat Law and Mrs. Donna Pollard who despite the difficulty of interpreting the many corrections in the original typescript have typed the work in its final form.

Finally, the author would thank his wife who read the work over and made corrections, and who has prepared both the bibliography and the index, a monotonous and time consuming task.

W.S.R.
Guelph, Ont., Canada

TRUMPETER OF GOD

CHAPTER I

The Orchestral Background

A MUSICAL VIRTUOSO who plays a concerto must always have an orchestral accompaniment if he is truly to display his artistry as a musician. In much the same way John Knox sounded his metaphorical trumpet against the background of the society and culture of his own day. Consequently to understand him properly we must first look at the world in which he lived. Although we cannot do so in great detail, we should have at least some knowledge of his environment, even if we describe the orchestral score only in somewhat broad and impressionistic terms.

In attempting such a description we must remember that Knox was by no means a simple Scot who spent his life in the northern end of an island off the coast of Europe. Like many of his compatriots of his own day, he was very much a European: a man who travelled and who lived for considerable lengths of time in Germany, France, England and Switzerland. Moreover, wherever he went he exercised no little influence upon both those who favored and those who opposed him. Therefore, if we would see Knox in his total environment we have to think in terms of the whole European setting, with Scotland as its center. While to some this may seem a distortion of the European situation, for an understanding of Knox it is absolutely necessary. Consequently before we look at Knox directly, we must turn to take a quick glance at Europe and Scotland in the early part of the sixteenth century.

Some biographers of Knox have tended to ignore his European, if not his Scottish environment, for apparently they consider that these were of little importance, since he was above all else a religious reformer. One may never, however, separate the religious developments of an age from their social context, for those involved in any religious movement always see their beliefs in terms of their own situation in the world and in terms of the ideas of their own day. Furthermore, these same devout people very often wield an effective influence on their environment as a result of their religious convictions. While the economic and religious developments of a period may be largely independent of each other, they have functional relationships that make for mutual and reciprocal influences.[1] We must see Knox therefore in terms of the world in which he lived.

Society in the sixteenth century was, like twentieth-century society, changing, expanding, and revolutionary. Old medieval patterns of thought were being discarded, not only by the intelligentsia but by the ordinary folk, particularly those of "middling sort," the merchants, the master craftsmen, and the lesser nobility who were now beginning to come into places of influence. Advances and developments in trade, industry, politics and social organization already under way in the fifteenth century went forward at an ever accelerating pace throughout Knox's life.[2]

Economic changes were among the most important. With a general rise in population beginning in the third quarter of the fifteenth century and continuing throughout the sixteenth, the demand for goods and services increased rapidly. This demand received further stimulus from the growth of European silver production and from the introduction of treasure from the New World; both increased the quantity of bullion available as a medium of exchange. New methods of business, including the development of a more flexible credit system, also helped stimulate the economy. The result was an expansion of industry and trade, and inflation. The effect was a series of business cycles or rises and falls in the economy, the low point being reached in the late '50s.[3]

These economic developments inevitably made an impact upon the whole fabric of society. The aristocracy, frequently wealthy in land but short in cash, were greatly affected. No longer required by their national governments as soldiers or as officials, they had to seek incomes elsewhere. This the upper nobility could do by obtaining remunerative but often honorific positions at court, or by dipping by one means or another, into the coffers of the church. The gentry or lower aristocracy, on the other hand, faced a more difficult situation which often led them into competition with the aristocracy, who were vying with them for lucrative positions, and into conflict with their tenants and serfs who resisted their demands for increased rents and services. Their one hope was frequently the bourgeoisie or wealthy element in the towns, who could provide them with loans and often with well-dowered wives or well-endowed husbands for their children.

The wealthy bourgeoisie, on the other hand, with the increase in trade, craft production, and finance were assuming a new position in European society. Affluent in cash or credit, but frequently possessing little in the way of land or social prestige they usually sought to improve their social position and stabilize their investments by marriage alliances with the nobility, by purchasing landed estates, or by winning titles and lands by performing services of various kinds for their own or foreign governments. This rise of the business element in society was to have broad implications for the whole of western European culture and civilization.[4]

One of the most obvious developments accompanying the evolution of a middle class, if we can employ this term broadly, was the growth of urban life. Fifteenth century Italy had already seen Florence, Venice and other cities rise to new heights of both economic and cultural activity; this phenomenon became common in Europe north of the Alps in the following century. Paris of course still retained its dominant position in some respects, but cities such as Augsburg, Frankfurt and Nuremberg in southern Germany, Antwerp in the Netherlands, and London in England, all grew so rapidly in economic importance that they threatened to outstrip Paris commercially and even culturally. The center of life had now moved from the castle and the court to the important urban areas, which meant that city and town dwellers were exercising a much greater influence upon thought and action than heretofore.[5]

All of these changes were summed up in the rise of the so-called "new monarchies." Throughout the fifteenth century, the kings of Spain, France, England, and some of the Scandinavian countries, under various pressures, had gradually assumed greater and greater powers, which tended to change the political structures of Europe. These monarchs labored to free themselves from the old feudal restrictions which curtailed the exercise of their royal prerogatives. At the same time, centralization meant a much greater need for money to meet rising administrative costs. Sixteenth century Spain and Portugal were in the happy position of having wealth in one form or another flow in from the Far East or the Far West. The rulers of France and England, on the other hand, without colonies, had to look elsewhere for funds, which meant that they had to depend increasingly upon their own citizens to provide either taxes or loans. As trade was expanding this should not have been too much of a problem but, since war was endemic throughout much of the century, most governments constantly found themselves in debt, sometimes to such an extent that no one was prepared to loan them money. It was really this situation that brought the fighting between France, England, and Spain to a close with the Treaty of Cateau–Cambrésis in 1558.[6] The new monarchies of the Hapsburgs, the Valois and the Tudors, therefore, despite their apparent ascendency often found their ways beset with many difficulties.

The reason for the constant warfare was the perennial rivalry between the Valois, the ruling family of France, and the Hapsburgs, who, in the person of Charles V united Spain and her dominions with the Holy Roman Empire. Countries such as England and Scotland generally remained on the periphery of this conflict. On the occasions, however, when they joined the fray, England usually took the Spanish side because of her age-old conflicts with France, and Scotland by reason of her "auld alliance" with France and her fear of English designs, automatically joined the other side.[7]

In all of this the Roman Catholic Church also played an important part. As the wealthiest international corporation in Europe headed by the pope who not only held the eternal welfare of all men in his hands, but was a temporal ruler as well, it possessed very great international political influence. Yet it was suffering at this time from internal troubles. For one thing its wealth and power often attracted unworthy people into clerical ranks. Having become very conservative and rigid in its ideas and practices, it appeared increasingly irrelevant to many, especially the rising bourgeoisie of the towns and cities. The result was a growing alienation of many from the church.[8] Although reformers within the church attempted to solve this problem by effecting certain changes during the fifteenth and early sixteenth centuries, they did not have any wide impact. Consequently, when on October 31, 1517 Dr. Martin Luther in Wittenberg, Saxony, set forth his Ninety-Five Theses denying the efficacy of indulgences and expounding the doctrine of justification by faith alone, the ecclesiastical authorities paid little attention to his action. But the new ideas sparked by both the religious and social discontent of the time, spread rapidly throughout Germany and eventually spilled over into neighboring lands. No matter what the church did, it could not stem the Lutheran tide. The German Reformation, centering upon the biblical doctrine of man's reconciliation to God through faith alone in Jesus Christ, swept aside most obstacles.[9]

The new beliefs found important supporters and amplifiers in Switzerland where the situation was parallel and to some extent stimulated by events in Germany. In Zurich Ulrich Zwingli and his successor, Henry Bullinger, holding to Luther's doctrine of justification by faith carried Luther's beliefs to what they felt were their logical conclusions, resulting in new developments in both faith and practice. This movement in turn became allied to the Reformation which was taking place in Geneva, at first under William Farel and then under John Calvin, with the result that the Swiss Reformation provided another dimension to Protestantism.[10]

The importance of Calvin to Knox and the whole Scottish Reformation was such that we must keep in mind certain facts. Calvin, trained as both a humanist and lawyer, developed in his commentaries and his *Institutes of the Christian Religion* a clear and well-defined system of theology and piety that seemed to meet the spiritual needs of many of his contemporaries, particularly those of "the middling sort." At the same time he worked out in Geneva a system of church government and a pattern of church-state relationships which fitted in with bourgeois ideas, becoming the model for many reformers in other lands, including Scotland.[11]

The Reformation split Europe, dividing it into Protestant and Roman Catholic camps. Nevertheless because of dynastic and other rivalries the Roman Catholic powers did not unite to suppress it. Consequently the Reformation succeeded in establishing within

Europe a new concept of Christianity; and in so doing it exercised a major intellectual influence on subsequent European cultural evolution.[12]

In all of these movements Scotland was involved although, because of her geographic position, she usually remained on the periphery. Economically a poor land with few natural advantages either of geographic position or physical resources, she certainly could not make any claim to great prosperity during the sixteenth century. Yet because of growing demand on the continent she was able to carry on an export trade of wool, along with large quantities of fish and a few other items, with the French ports of Dieppe, Rouen and Bordeaux, and the Netherlands ports of Veere and Middleburgh. The eastern Baltic towns also took some of her produce. At the same time, since her industry was relatively small and undeveloped, almost all her manufactured goods, particularly her luxuries, were imported from the Continent.[13]

Notwithstanding this industrial weakness, the sixteenth century saw a slow growth of the trading burghs. Those on the south–west: Ayr, Irvine and Wigtown dealt principally with Ireland or the southern French ports whence came claret, the staple Scottish drink at that time. Much more important were the east coast ports: Aberdeen, Dundee, Perth and Edinburgh. They were all involved in wool and fish export, the northern burghs dealing principally with the Netherlands and the Baltic, while Edinburgh, the wealthiest of them all, though sharing in the commerce with the Netherlands, concentrated primarily on the French market.[14] Foreign trade was the principal sphere in which money, so necessary for power and prestige, was to be made.

As on the Continent the nobles in Scotland were being challenged by the changing economic situation. Most of the earls and lords owned wide lands but suffered from a shortage of ready money. Yet they had the influence that enabled them to obtain profitable positions at court or the provision of their offspring, legitimate and illegitimate, to wealthy ecclesiastical benefices. The lower nobility, or lairds, on the other hand, faced with the same difficulties as their continental counterparts, usually succeeded in keeping their heads above the economic floods by forming marriage or financial alliances with the wealthy merchants in the principal burghs.[15]

The individual in the most difficult position of all during the latter part of the fifteenth and the first half of the sixteenth centuries was probably the monarch. From the accession of James I in 1406 to that of Mary in 1542 every Scottish ruler came to the throne as a minor. One can easily imagine what this meant in terms of aristocratic squabbling and fighting, the squandering of royal revenues and the general breakdown of organized government. The result is shown by the fact that the crown, in the mid-sixteenth century, received no more than a pathetic £17,000 (Scots) in annual revenue, while at the same time it was faced with a turbulent and much more powerful nobility linked to an extremely wealthy and almost as turbulent church.[16]

To add further to the government's problems, neither Scotland's friends nor her enemies would leave her alone. France was forever trying to embroil her with England, to the decided detriment of the Scots, while Henry VIII and later Protector Somerset sought by bribery and, when that failed, by force, to bring her under English control. Furthermore, as the Reformation began to exercise an influence in both England and Scotland, religion became another cause of contention that both England and France sought to use for their own advantage.[17]

The reason for the political importance of the Reformation in which Knox was so deeply involved stems from the position of the church within the state. During the welter of events that took place between 1500 and 1560, the church stood out as the dominant segment of society, largely because of its wealth. It has been estimated that, owning more than half the real estate in the country, it received an annual income of some £300,000 in contrast to the meagre £17,000 of the crown.[18] These revenues, partially derived from lands feued to nobles and wealthy merchants, and partially from tithes and other ecclesiastical dues, excited both the cupidity and dislike of much of the population.

The outcome was a widespread and blatant attempt on the part of the top echelons of society to obtain control of church revenues by any means possible. In this James V derived certain natural advantages from his royal position. For one thing he was able to persuade the pope to allow him to levy a clerical tax to help pay for the setting up of his newly created supreme court, the Court of Session. For another, he was able to gain papal consent to the appointment of his own illegitimate offspring to some of the wealthiest abbacies in the country. To achieve all this more easily he succeeded in having David Beaton, Archbishop of St. Andrews, appointed *legatus a latere,* a position which enabled the latter to ratify such ecclesiastical provisions, as well as to feu church lands to the nobility, without the necessity of resorting to the papal court at Rome. And James gained these privileges because of his constantly implied threat that if the Scottish clergy and the pope refused to accede to his wishes, he could always follow the example of his Uncle Henry of England who had broken with the papacy and suppressed the monasteries.[19] The resultant misgivings of the clergy and the pope persuaded them to listen sympathetically to James's demands in the hope that he would follow their advice and stay away from Henry. The king was thus able to act as a true patron of the church to his own profit.[20]

Naturally the upper aristocracy supported James in his ecclesiastical policies since they relieved the nobles of a heavy load of taxation, and also enabled them to lay hands upon ecclesiastical positions and lands.[21] Moreover, by the king's grace they were able to place the scions of their own houses in important ecclesiastical offices through which they too could both influence the church and mulct it of its wealth. This aristocratic intervention in the church's affairs also had another effect. In the family rivalries and political maneuverings of the day, the upper clergy, as members of "the church militant," usually played as important a part as did the nobles themselves. It was no accident that Gavin Douglas, Bishop of Dunkeld, and Archbishop James Beaton of Glasgow were involved in the notorious "Cleanse the Causeway" of 1520, when the Douglases chased the Hamiltons out of Edinburgh.[22] The aristocracy and upper ranks of the hierarchy were in a close alliance which involved the ecclesiastics in both the financial and political problems of the country, very often more fully than in their religious duties.

Another influence on the state of the church was its low moral condition. Most bishops and abbots were appointed either because they were the king's or the nobles' sons, or because they themselves had proved to be faithful servants of the crown. This did not help maintain a high level of clerical morality. Even at the apex of the hierarchy, virtue was at a low ebb. One Roman Catholic writer has put it somewhat mildly: "Cardinal Beaton's private life was irregular and as a prelate he did not adorn the spiritual estate." He then goes on to point out that Beaton had two daughters and one son legitimated while he was Abbot of Arbroath, three sons before he became cardinal, and four sons after his elevation to that dignity, although he adds, that there may be some duplication in the records.[23] Other Scottish prelates were not far behind in their sexual activities. Of the seventeen bishops at the time of the Reformation, twelve had illegitimate children while many of the abbots, who themselves seem to have been the illegitimate offspring of the king or the nobles, also had plenty of their own.[24] In the light of this situation it is not surprising that the lower clergy too were not generally noted for their puritanical lives, a fact that was not lost on the laity.[25]

More important than the worldliness of the clergy, however, was their apparent failure to meet the spiritual needs of the people, particularly of those who had received any education. With the new pressures of an economic upsurge resulting in an increasing demand for hard work and diligence, many felt that life was a serious matter for which they needed spiritual help and guidance. True there were more than 1,000 churches in Scotland, but of these over 900 were appropriated to monasteries, cathedrals and collegiate churches which either drew the revenues or farmed them out while leaving the care of souls to some starveling, poorly-educated vicar who acted as chaplain. We can well believe that frequently the local flock as "hungry sheep looked up and were not fed." [26] Neither intellectually nor religiously was the church speaking relevantly to the energetic burgesses or the somewhat insecure lairds. Therefore, when Lutheran and later Calvinistic views began to seep over from the Continent, they received a rather warm welcome from this middle group in society.

The first person we can identify as a missionary was a French soldier, de la Tour, one of the Duke of Albany's men-at-arms who was burned in October, 1527 in Paris for his religious activities in Scotland.[27] At the same time, Scots too were bringing in the heretical doctrines. Knox points out that merchants and mariners who encountered the new views in Europe propagated them on their return home.[28] Scholars who studied in Germany did the same thing in St. Andrews and the other Scottish universities. Even repatriated mercenary soldiers such as Sir John Borthwick of Cineray, became missionaries for the Protestant cause.[29] As Cardinal Beaton, himself, testified in the 1530's, heresy was increasing apace.[30]

Such a spread of "heresy" naturally called forth efforts to suppress the movement. By 1525 and 1527, statutes had been passed forbidding the importation of Lutheran books or the teaching of Lutheran doctrines. Then in 1528 in St. Andrews, Patrick Hamilton was burned at the stake for heresy. But it was all to no effect. During the next decade more men and women, many of them from the ranks of the lower nobility or from among the indwellers of the port towns, suffered death or left the country because of their faith. Although the mid-'30s saw a lull in persecution, at the time of James V's marriage to Mary of Guise, when he was pressing for David Beaton's elevation to the cardinalate, persecution recommenced with the execution of a number of clergy and gentry. Others saved themselves by recanting, while a number fled abroad.[31]

Again in 1540 the clergy succeeded in having parliament pass a series of laws against heresy and against those who held heretical views. Among these measures, the most revealing was that forbidding private conventicles. These were prayer meetings and study groups, later known as "Privy Kirks," established on the French pattern, which greatly assisted the spread of Protestantism. While such statutes revealed the determination of Beaton and his cohorts to root out the heretical plague, it also showed their fears of what might take place, and they had some reason for their uncertainty since parliament enacted at the same time a law calling upon the churchmen to correct their own "unhonesty and misrule." [32]

The reactions of Scots in general to the persecution cannot be estimated, but it appears that a substantial number of the nobility opposed it. James's increasing subservience to clerical advisers had alienated the nobles who maintained that they, not the priests, were the proper and constitutional councillors of the monarch. On this point they were very insistent not only for constitutional reasons, but also because a number had either turned Protestant already or were inclining in that direction. Consequently when Cardinal Beaton suggested to James that he might replenish the royal coffers by indicting all the heretical nobles and taking over their lands, he did not gain many friends. Although James did order Sir James Hamilton of Finnart, his Principal Steward, to investigate those designated as heretics, the latter accomplished nothing. According to some accounts William Kirkcaldy of Grange and Sir James Learmonth of Dairsie, both Protestants, even persuaded James to execute Hamilton on an old charge of treason. This settled the matter for the moment.[33]

There remained, however, a feeling of mutual suspicion between clergy and nobles which was further intensified when the King, contrary to the wishes of many nobles but on the advice of the clergy, refused to meet Henry VIII for a conference at York.[34]

The ecclesiastics, however, were by no means satisfied with even these successes, for they knew that as long as England carried on its heretical way they would never be truly safe. Hence they favored organizing a crusade along with France and Spain to overthrow Henry. Since, however, those two continental powers were in continual conflict, there was little chance that anything would be done. Meanwhile Scotland, having angered Henry by the failure of James V to keep his tryst at York, found itself in a precarious position. James, still influenced by the clerics, decided to take direct action to forestall an attack by invading England, albeit without the support of any allies. The outcome was the disaster of Solway Moss in 1542 where a Scottish army of 10,000 mishandled and misled, was defeated by an English force about one fifth its size. The ensuing loss of prestige as well as the loss of arms and men, many of them nobles whom the English captured, brought on the moral collapse of James V, who literally willing himself to death, passed away on December 14th at the age of thirty, leaving as successor his week-old daughter Mary.[35]

The person who now took control of the country was James Hamilton, Earl of Arran, next in line to the throne, if he was legitimate, after the baby queen herself. Beaton had sought to have a commission of regency established with himself as chairman, but this the nobles defeated. Arran's assumption of the regency indicated that a new era had arrived, for he was regarded as being favorable to, if he had not already accepted, Protestantism. A change in policies was imminent.

Immediately after taking over the direction of the government Arran showed his colors. He began by appointing as his chaplains two Protestant preachers, Thomas Gwilliam, a former Black Friar, and John Rough, both of whom were to have a great influence upon Knox.[36] Like a good many nobles and others who had Protestant convictions or leanings, he seems to have felt that the eventual unification of the English and Scottish crowns was the only possible solution to many of Scotland's problems. Therefore, with the approval of parliament, he dispatched a delegation to England to discuss the possible marriage of the English heir, Prince Edward, son of Henry VIII by Jane Seymour, to the Scottish Queen Mary. Although some Roman Catholics supported this move, it is interesting to note that the delegation was made up primarily of Protestants: Sir William Hamilton, Sir James Learmonth of Dairsie, and Henry Balnaves, who were joined later by the Earl of Glencairn and Sir George Douglas of Pittendreich, brother of the Earl of Angus. At the same time Henry sent Sir Ralph Sadler, an able English negotiator, to Scotland to make sure that Arran would go through with the plan. The outcome was the Treaties of Greenwich duly concluded on July 1, 1543, and ratified by Arran in August.[37] Another step had been taken which would strengthen the Protestant cause.

Meanwhile, the situation in Scotland had been changing further in the Protestants' favor. Robert Lord Maxwell, and William Lord Ruthven, supported by Henry Balnaves and others of that group, had presented to the governor and the Lords of the Articles, who prepared legislation for the parliament, a proposal to make reading the Old and New Testaments in the vernacular legal, as long as people did not dispute about them. The representative of the clergy, Gavin Dunbar, Archbishop of Glasgow, objected stating that nothing should be decided until a council of the clergy could be held to pass on the matter. Since the Lords of the Articles, however, said they could find no law forbidding such a practice, they agreed that parliament should grant this permission. Of the twenty-eight Lords of the Articles present, ten were clergy, ten were earls or lords and eight were representatives of the burghs. While approved by Arran, this statute was in fact enacted on the insistence of the lords and burgesses.[38] It looked as though Protestantism had already won the day.

Appearances were, however, deceiving, for the old church was by no means finished. The very terror invoked by the thought of Henry gaining control of Scotland through the marriage of the young queen stimulated the clergy to feverish activity. They declared themselves ready at any cost to provide the regent with money for an army to resist Henry should he attempt to attack Scotland in the event that the Treaties of Greenwich were abrogated.[39] At the same time the Abbot of Paisley, Arran's half brother, returned from France to persuade him to change his policies. But the greatest help to the hierarchy came from Henry himself, who, notwithstanding the warnings of his ambassador, had failed to ratify the treaties within the allotted time but still insisted that the Franco-Scottish alliance should be dissolved and that Mary should be turned over to him immediately. His stupid arrogance drove even many of his erstwhile Protestant supporters into the pro-French, Roman Catholic camp of the Queen Mother, Mary of Guise, and the cardinal. Even Arran, never a very stable individual, after he had ratified the treaties suddenly changed sides to ally himself with Mary and Beaton. When the coronation of the young queen in September 1543 was quickly followed by the confirmation of the "auld alliance" with France it was the Protestants' turn to be apprehensive.[40]

Mary of Guise and the cardinal were now firmly in the saddle, although Arran still held the title of governor. Henry's attempt to dictate to Scotland had failed. Parliament was persuaded to denounce the agreements with England and the English marriage was off for good.[41]

But the religious struggle was by no means over. The cardinal and his party still faced serious problems, for as both he and Mary of Guise reported to Rome, heresy was spreading throughout the country.[42] To arrest this disease all Protestants including Arran's chaplains, along with advisers such as Kirkcaldy of Grange, Henry Balnaves, Thomas Ballantyne, and Sir David Lindsay of the Mount, were ousted from their positions and persecution began once again.[43] The renewed attack upon the Protestants seems to have had its beginning in the governor's declaration of December 15, 1543 in parliament, in which he called upon the clergy to proceed against heretics with vigor and promised to give them his whole-hearted support.[44]

Yet the very success of the Franco-papalist party raised up enemies against it. Many of the merchants suffered by the seizure of their ships by the English because of the change of Scottish policy, while at home those nobles who had opposed Beaton were arrested and imprisoned. Consequently, many Scots whether Roman Catholic or Protestant, became uneasy over Beaton's increasing power. As Knox pointed out, unless men consented to play the valet to the cardinal they were in serious trouble. In confirmation of this judgment we find the Earl of Angus writing to Arran on February 27, 1545 that he should stop paying attention to priests who know nothing about warfare or politics, and should heed the proper councillors of the realm, the nobles.[45] The tide was once again beginning to turn.

It was at this point that Knox found himself actively involved in the conflict that was arising between Protestant and Roman Catholic. We must, therefore, turn back to him.

CHAPTER II

The Preparation

ALTHOUGH WE DO NOT possess any direct evidence as to the date of John Knox's birth, it would seem from references by Theodore Beza and others that he must have been born some time between 1513 and 1515.

This was a difficult time in which to enter the world, particularly in Scotland, for James IV had just died on the Field of Flodden, ushering in fourteen or more years of sorrow, terror and political anarchy as various factions of nobles fought for control of the crown. At the same time both the English and the French monarchs sought by intrigue and subversion to dominate the country for their own aggrandizement.

The exact location of Knox's birthplace is, like his birth date, known only vaguely. Beza in his *Icones* referred to him as of Gifford, the name of a small village not far from Haddington in East Lothian. When Knox became a burgess of Geneva, however, he termed himself a native of Haddington, which was undoubtedly the case. His family may have lived on the Gifford Road or Giffordgate, which might explain Beza's designation.[1]

But wherever his parents may have lived, he came from one of the leading towns of Lothian. Its importance is testified to by the fact that it had three chapels, two monasteries, one abbey, and three churches, one of which was considered so magnificent that it was known as the "Lamp of Lothian." Yet while situated in one of the most pleasant and fertile areas of Scotland, it lay under the shadow of the Hepburn Earls of Bothwell who held nearby Hailes Castle.[2] And because of the easy access to the area both from the south and from Edinburgh, it lay athwart the usual English invasion route. This fact, coupled with the early Protestantism of the local lairds ensured that most of them were also inclined to be pro-English in their outlook, a point of view expressed forcibly by another son of Haddington, John Major, the theologian and historian, in his *History of Greater Britain.*[3]

The Knox family seems to have been of no great importance in the area. In 1564 Knox referred to the fact that some of his ancestors had fought under the standard of the Earls of Bothwell, but it would not seem that his father was more than an upcoming yeoman farmer, who may have had connections with some of the local lairds. We know that he had married a Sinclair through whom he may have been related to Ker of Samuelston whose wife was also a Sinclair.[4] But whatever the status of Knox's father, it would seem that he had at least enough money to set his eldest son William up in business, and send another son, John, to the schools.[5]

It has been suggested that John's mother may have died while he was in his infancy. Although we have no documentary evidence, it is reasonable to suppose that he attended the local school in Haddington, the same as that which had commenced John Major's education some years earlier.[6] From Haddington he probably went to St. Andrews where Major had been teaching since 1531. Unfortunately we are again left at this point without documentary evidence since Knox's name does not appear on the St. Andrews University roll of graduates. Either he may not have finished his course or what is perhaps more likely, since the university records were not always well kept at this time, the record of his graduation may simply have disappeared. George Buchanan, however, states that he attended St. Andrews University while Major taught there, a fact that we can easily credit when we take into account the dates of both Major's professorship and Knox's education, as well as the similarity which appeared later in the two men's views on a number of important subjects.[7]

Major undoubtedly wielded an important influence on St. Andrews. When he returned from Paris he came with the reputation of an important scholar having made a name for himself at the Collège de Montaigu as both an acute reasoner and a prolific writer. Furthermore, as the last of the great advocates of church government by councils and a New Testament commentator, his point of view was hardly favorable to the conditions prevalent in the church of the day. This comes out clearly in Knox's description of the support from Major at St. Andrews for William Arth, who vigorously attacked the clergy for both their lives and their teachings. From Knox's detailed account of Arth's speech it would seem that he too had been present at the time. Consequently one cannot but suspect that under Major the atmosphere at St. Andrews was such that a young man would be constrained to take a very critical look at the ecclesiastical and political "establishment" of his own day.[8]

It was not, however, just a matter of being critical. Although by European standards the Scottish universities were quite small and inclined to be very conservative in their outlook, new ideas were beginning to seep in. As Knox points out, Gavin Logie of St. Leonard's College and the novices of the Abbey under the Sub-Prior, probably John Winram, were beginning "to smell somewhat of the verity, and to espy the vanity of the received superstitions." [9] These were aided by vigorous preachers such as Alexander Seton, a former Black Friar, and others like him. Both students and faculty were becoming increasingly open to reformist thought from the Continent.

The conveyors of these new and heretical doctrines were generally Scots who had studied abroad. And these were numerous, since Scottish students favored continental institutions over their own which all told took in probably no more than one hundred entrants a year.[10]

One area to which Scottish students migrated in search of learning was Germany. Knox tells us that Patrick Hamilton, the first Protestant martyr, studied at Wittenberg.[11] Others also studied and often taught in northern institutions. Alexander Alesius, for instance, went to Frankfort-on-Oder in 1540 and taught later at Leipzig. John MacAlpine (Machabaeus) went first to Louvain, later becoming a professor at the University of Copenhagen. Besides MacAlpine, Henry Balnaves, Thomas Forret, and John Lyne were for a time at Louvain. John Erskine of Dun may have studied at Cologne while some went even farther afield to places such as Vienna. After the Reformation had really begun to flow strongly in

Scotland, a number studied at Wittenberg, Griefswald, Frankfort and Leipzig.[12]

The most attractive institution for the Scottish student was, however, the University of Paris, the largest and most influential center of learning of its day. There Scots could usually find compatriots among both the student body and the faculty. Furthermore, it was the gathering place for many nationalities. As members of the German nation, the Scots came under the influence of Dutch, Flemish and German thought. At the same time the Spaniards Vives, Enzinas and Juan Gelida, later a patron of Scottish scholars at Bordeaux, taught in the Paris halls. Similarly Aleandro and Ficino from Italy expounded the classics to audiences in which Scots such as John Major sat.[13]

Usually after a time spent at Paris or one of the northern universities, the Scottish student would head for sunnier climes. Montpellier seems to have been one of his favorite resorts, while Bordeaux was also popular. Others crossed the Alps into Italy to study at Bologna, Pavia, Padua, or Rome. John de Scotia, Thomas Erskine the secretary of James V, and John Row, one of the Protestant reformers, as well as many others, all registered at one or more of these institutions.[14]

As Dr. John Durkan has indicated in his essay on the cultural background of the Scottish Reformation, many of these men eventually returned to Scotland to teach or to take up positions in church or state. Those who came home to act as professors frequently ended up in St. Andrews University as did members of the religious orders, although some such as Hector Boece took up positions at Aberdeen and others went to Glasgow. But whatever their positions they all brought back with them some flavor of the thinking of the humanist Erasmus, of the conservative ecclesiastical reformers Standonck and Lefevre d'Etaples, or of the more radical Protestants of Germany or Switzerland. Their views would be further reinforced by the teaching of a Frenchman such as Jean Charpentier who lectured at St. Andrews in the 1530's and 40's. Thus Girolamo Cardano, the Italian, after his visit to Scotland in 1553 could express his surprise and gratification at the refinement and civilized character of the Scottish academics.[15] It was in this atmosphere that Knox received his university training.

Since we do not know the exact date of his graduation, we cannot

say precisely when he left the university. That he had done so by
1540 would seem to be quite clear from the fact that in that year he
appears as "Sir John Knox" and as a papal notary. The term "Sir"
seems to indicate that he had been ordained to the priesthood, some
believe as early as 1536, while the fact that he was a papal notary
would show that he was a member in good standing of the
ecclesiastical "establishment." A notary public was an important
person in a parish for he held the position of a kind of lawyer. Besides
doing parish duties as a chaplain and/or a schoolmaster, after being
examined and duly installed with pen and case by a prothonotary, he
could authenticate legal documents with his docquet and sign manual.
He was also registered by the bishop for whom he could act as
commissary to induct into benefices and prepare various types of
ecclesiastical papers.[16]

From 1540 to 1543 Knox served in his legal capacity for Ker of
Samuelston, to whom, as mentioned above, he may have been related
through his mother. At the same time he acted as the tutor of a
certain William Brounefield. Since Samuelston was in the heart of
Lothian not far from the properties of Cockburn of Ormiston and
Douglas of Longniddry, he may at the same time have begun to teach
the sons of those two lairds. In this situation he undoubtedly enjoyed
a comfortable and protected existence. Yet it could not continue for
long, for in the last extant document that he notarized, dated March
27, 1543, one finds an interesting attestation: *"Testis per Christum
fidelis, cui gloria,"* (The faithful witness through Christ, to whom be
the glory), words that may indicate that he had by now become a
Protestant. Thomas Thomson who printed all his notarial documents
believes that it does, stating also that Knox had sought refuge from
persecution with his relatives at Samuelston. But whether Knox had
already become a Protestant or was just on the way we cannot say
for certain, although the area of Lothian in which he found himself
was by 1543 becoming a hot-bed of those who favored drastic reform
within the church.[17]

If, however, we are to grasp the significance of what was taking
place during the last half of the forties we must pause to look more
closely at the social and geographic patterns of the Protestant
movement. Only then shall we be able to understand Knox's position
in the whole sequence of events.

From what we can gather concerning the beginnings of Protestantism in Scotland, it seems to have entered by way of the north, imported by merchants from the Baltic area. As early as August 1525 James V was sending word to the sheriffs of Aberdeenshire that the Bishop of Aberdeen had complained about foreigners who had brought in Lutheran books. He commanded them to take immediate steps to arrest such heretics and to confiscate their goods to the use of the crown.[18] This, however, did not stop the spread of the new ideas. The Aberdeen burgh council seems to have taken little or no action during the 1530's to restrain the growth of Protestantism with the result that by 1543 some of the citizens were attacking the persons of friars and had even been guilty of the "hanging of the image of St. Francis." [19] It is probable that only the proximity of the Earl of Huntly, one of the staunchest Roman Catholic nobles, restrained the Protestants from becoming even bolder.

To the south of Aberdeen, in the burghs of the Tay Valley, Protestantism seems to have spread without any inhibiting influence from outside. Perhaps the first indication of what was taking place is to be found in the failure of a number of the burgesses of Perth in 1527–28 to pay their annuals to the local clergy.[20] By 1540 the Protestants had gained a foothold in the burgh council, the result being a Protestant-Romanist conflict that James V in vain tried to stop by appointing his own nominees. Subsequently Arran and Beaton tried the same policy which led to a major battle in which Patrick, Master of Ruthven, son of the Protestant provost and supported by the burgesses of Perth routed with a loss of sixty men, the invading forces of Lord Gray, Norman Leslie, Master of Rothes, and John Charteris of Kinfauns, the last being the government's nominee for the provostship.[21] According to Knox, the cardinal then laid charges of heresy against a number of the citizens who had manifested strong Protestant sympathies by eating meat on Friday or by interrupting the preaching of a friar, and had them executed.[22]

Down the River Tay from Perth lay the burgh of Dundee, second only to Edinburgh as a commercial entrepot and, because of its relative remoteness from the capital, the real center of the Reformation movement before 1555. With its trade lines running out to the Baltic, Holland, and France, continental Protestant ideas soon appeared among its merchants and sailors. One of the best known of the early Protestant families was that of the Wedderburns who some time in the thirties seem to have gone over to the Lutheran faith. One of them, John, who had returned from the Continent to Scotland, published in 1540 a collection of Protestant hymns, many of them translations from German, which came to be known as *The Gude and Godlie Ballattis*, a work that played a considerable part in the extension of the Reformation. The author, however, soon found it expedient to move to England. For the same reason his brother James, also a poet, joined the Scottish colony in Dieppe. Not only did the Wedderburns seek to inspire people to true faith, but used popular songs, rhymes and tunes to lampoon Roman Catholic doctrines, particularly the Mass.[23] Other burgess families such as the Scrimgeours likewise gave their adherence to the Protestant cause. The outcome of this growth of heresy was that sometime in 1543 a group of the Dundee burgesses broke down the doors of the Black Friars' house and carried off chalices, vestments and the Eucharist. Although all Dundonians did not favor such action, this was but a foretaste of things to come.[24]

In Edinburgh the new beliefs gained ground more slowly. Although the burgh's port of Leith seems to have harbored a considerable number of those holding heretical views, Knox tells us that in 1542 the town "for the most part, was drowned in superstition." [25] Yet even under the guns of the Castle and the eyes of the government, some burgesses had accepted Protestantism. Knox, himself, refers to Edward Hope, William Adamson, Sibilla Lindsay, Patrick Lindsay, and Francis Aikman as holding the new doctrines.[26] Another Protestant, John Henryson, in 1544 found it advisable to retire with the English forces that had attacked Edinburgh to England, where he spent his time writing pamphlets against the French and the Romanists.[27] Yet in the final count, Knox's estimate must have been about right for when some of the governor's troops decided to follow the Dundonian example and raid the Black Friars' Priory, the citizens rallied to its defense and drove them off.[28] Edinburgh was not yet a center of Protestantism.

While the east coast burghs were becoming increasingly Protestant, the same trend was manifesting itself among the gentry and, to a lesser extent, among the nobles. Some of the earls, such as Glencairn and Rothes, and lords such as Ruthven, Gray, and Maxwell had moved into the Protestant camp, but most of the upper ranks of the aristocracy, who were doing very well out of church revenues, seemed uninterested in reform. Much more important for the cause of the Reformation was the growing adherence of the lairds, many of whom were closely connected with the burgesses who had already moved in this direction. These men were of great significance for the whole movement, not only because many of them were strongly attached to Protestantism, but also because they could help to provide the military forces and leadership necessary to overthrow the politico-ecclesiastical establishment. Owing to the weakness of the central government they were able to build up a force that could not be crushed except with external aid.[29]

As one attempts to gain some idea of the geographical distribution of the lairds and lords who were favorable to Protestantism, one discovers that as in the case of the burghs a definite pattern emerges.

In the southwest, in Dumfriesshire and Galloway, the area where Wycliffite Lollardy had been strong in the fifteenth century, Protestantism gained an early following both in burghs such as Ayr and Irvine and among the nobles and gentry. Some of those who had quickly accepted Lutheran teachings were the Campbells of Kinzeancleuch and of New Mylns, the Shaws of Polkemmet and the Chalmers of Gadgirth.[30] Somewhat to the north of these lairds lay the lands of the Cunningham Earl of Glencairn, who also at an early date became a Protestant to play an important part later in the movement of reform as one of Knox's most devoted supporters. Then in the late forties or early fifties when the fourth Earl of Argyll was converted, Argyllshire and the west Highlands began to feel the influence of Protestantism.[31]

Of greater importance for our immediate interest was the group of lairds and nobles on the east coast. In the northeast, in the hinterland of Aberdeen, we do not find many Protestant nobles, probably because of the opposition of the Earl of Huntly who controlled and even at times held the position of the provost of the "toun." [32]

Stretching south from Aberdeenshire to the River Tay, however, in Angus, the Mearns, and south of the Tay in Fife, the new teachings had been embraced by many of the gentry and nobles, who as subsequent events proved, were ready to fight for them. Among the most influential in this group was the Earl of Rothes, who held lands in various parts of Angus, the Mearns, and Fife. That he was on the Protestant side by 1543 is indicated by his arrest, along with two well-known Protestants, Lord Gray and Henry Balnaves, at the instigation of Cardinal Beaton.[33] Coupled with these names we often find those of William Lord Ruthven, Provost of Perth in 1546, his son, Patrick, who became third Lord Ruthven in 1552, and John Erskine, Laird of Dun. The latter was one of the first of the gentry to join the Reformation cause, probably about 1534, for which reason he spent some time as a prisoner in Blackness Castle with Sir James Learmonth of Dairsie, the Protestant provost of St. Andrews.[34] In the same group were Sir James Kirkcaldy of Grange, Lord High Treasurer, and Sir John Melville of Raith.[35] Frequently linked to each other by blood or by marriage, and all owning property and often holding offices within a burgh close to, if not on, their land, they formed a close-knit Protestant phalanx that was difficult to pierce.

Yet if we think that lairds and nobles of Angus and the Mearns were a tightly knit group, they were nothing to the Protestant lairds of Lothian, the hinterland of Edinburgh. How Protestantism gained entry to this "clutch" of gentry we do not know, but it is probable that some became Protestants while in France as soldiers, for a number of them did serve as mercenaries in the French army. Yet Protestantism was not the sole bond that held them together. Related by marriage or blood, they all held lands that lay on the route of an invading English army, a fact that repeatedly impressed them, as it had John Major of Haddington, with the ultimate necessity of some tie between England and Scotland. Moreover, because of their exposed geographic position they found it necessary to keep on good terms with the English, particularly in such times as the 1540's when they could expect little or no protection from the weak Scottish government. The only way in which they could survive was to become "assured" to the English. By taking an oath to forward the marriage of Prince Edward to the infant Queen Mary and to root out Romanism, they could protect themselves from the vengeance Henry unleashed on Scotland after the Scots' repudiation of the Treaties of Greenwich in 1543. Some, no doubt became "assured" solely to protect their own personal interests, but quite a number also had religious motives, for they faced persecution by their own government because of their Protestant views.[36] Consequently those who were "assured" for religious as well as political reasons usually proved to be the more reliable allies of the English.

More important to Knox at this time were the lairds whose lands lay to the east somewhat closer to Haddington than to Edinburgh. As we have seen already, he had secured himself a living under the wing of Ker of Samuelston, about whom we know little except that he was probably related to the Cockburns of Langton.[37] There were, however, others in the area who were of equal if not more importance such as the Hamiltons of Preston, the Cockburns of Ormiston and Langton, the Douglases of Longiddry and the Crichtons of Brunston. By 1540 this whole group of lairds had become Protestant and by 1543 were actively supporting the idea of a close Anglo–Scottish alliance.[38]

Although precise dating is impossible, it looks as though some time in 1543, Knox left Samuelston to become the tutor for Francis and George, the two sons of Hugh Douglas of Longniddry, and Alexander, son of John Cockburn of Ormiston, taking up his residence at Longniddry on the coast road running from Leith to Haddington.[39] This move put him firmly in the midst of the Anglo-Protestant group with all their inter-relationships and connections.

Why Knox made this move he does not say. It may be that having tired of his notarial work at Samuelston, with the opportunity to devote himself to private tutoring, he felt that a new career had offered itself. It may also have been that Knox had finally decided to come out on the Protestant side, but that the Kers of Samuelston were by no means sympathetic to his taking a public stand on the matter. Whatever the reason, he had decided to move into an environment that would be more congenial.

But when did Knox's conversion to the Protestant faith take place? He gives us no clear statement as to how or when he experienced this radical alteration in his views. It may have happened very gradually. His experiences at St. Andrews University undoubtedly helped to prepare the way. His references to the sermons of Alexander Seton and the teachings of others such as John Major would all indicate that he had listened to, and had been very much impressed by, their views. Calderwood, on the other hand, tells us that it was Thomas Gwilliam, one of the Black Friars whom Arran had appointed as his chaplains when he became governor, who "was the first man frome whome Mr. Knox receaved anie taste of the truthe." [40] This is possible since Gwilliam came from Athelstaneford three miles northeast of Haddington. Perhaps Gwilliam and Knox had known each other for some time with the result that when Gwilliam was free to preach before the governor, he took the opportunity to approach his acquaintances and friends with the Gospel.[41]

Knox like many of the other reformers tells us nothing about his conversion, his servant, Richard Bannatyne, reported that on his deathbed when asked what portions of Scripture he would have read, one of those he requested was the seventeenth chapter of the Gospel of John where, he said, "I first cast my anchor." While this may not seem to be a very significant statement at first, it does indicate one or two things. First of all it shows that Knox's conversion was not something into which he drifted, but was the result of a definite decision—apparently on the basis of what he read in John 17. Furthermore, this chapter which contains Christ's "High Priestly Prayer" for his disciples and those who believe through their testimony, lays great stress on the Christian's salvation through faith in Christ, his calling to Christ's service, the consequent enmity of the world, but also his assurance of eternal life. These all became themes which Knox continuously sounded in his letters, his pamphlets and his preaching. It may have been these elements in Gwilliam's teaching that finally persuaded him to cast his anchor on this rock. Some have also suggested that it was Knox's feeling of dependence and of a need for assistance that ultimately led to his decision. And in the light of his reference to John 17, this may have been the case. Yet he would insist that ultimately it was the result of the Holy Spirit's moving which finally brought him to faith. But however we interpret his conversion, we cannot doubt that it made a radical change in the whole course of his life.[42]

Conversion would ultimately force a man of his temperament into active support of the Reformation, a move, however, which was to take place only gradually, for in 1543 he filled a very small space in a much larger movement. With the alliance of the governor and the cardinal, who was really in the driver's seat, conflict was bound to come within the country. Scotland was now so divided that neither cardinal, Queen mother, nor governor could be sure of who would obey their orders. As the French ambassador Jacques de la Brosse reported, everyone so mistrusted everyone else that all went armed to the teeth. Even the clergy, the friars and the peasants travelled only in companies armed with pikes, swords and bucklers. A year later, according to the *Diurnal of Remarkable Occurrents* the same state of affairs still prevailed for "there was na credit amang the nobilitie." [43]

Then to add to the chaos, the English began to prepare for "the rough wooing" of the Scottish princess. This move brought about a polarization of the parties within the kingdom.

Fearful that the Douglases, who had long held a very equivocal position in Anglo-Scottish relations, would side with Henry in case of war, in October of 1543 Arran and the cardinal made a sudden attack upon the friends of the Douglases in Edinburgh whom they threw into prison. Crichton of Brunston in reporting this to Ralph Sadler the English ambassador, stated as the reason that the Douglas group wished for peace and concord with England, but the cardinal sought for war.[44] For this he did not have long to wait. In May of the next year the English army led by Edward Seymour, Earl of Hertford, made a devastating raid upon the Lowlands culminating in the burning of Edinburgh, Leith, Haddington and Dunbar.[45] As neither the governor nor the cardinal had taken any effective steps to meet this invasion, the lairds of Lothian who were caught in the line of fire either had to submit to the English or face the loss, not only of their property but even of their lives. There seemed to be no alternative. As Knox put it, the country was thus divided between the French and the English parties, with the former looking to France for financial and military help and the latter to England for peace, security and perhaps ultimate union.[46]

Another element in this polarization was religion. Writers have frequently condemned the "assured lords" for cooperating with the English invaders, and one cannot doubt that such slippery characters as George Douglas of Pittendreich sought always to play both ends against the middle. It would seem, however, that the Lothian lairds, along with the Earl of Glencairn and some of the Ayrshire lairds in the west, were forced into an alliance with the English because of their Protestantism. If they had refused to "assure" and had attempted to fight off the English, with the Scottish government in its state of chronic anarchy, they would have undoubtedly been crushed by the invading forces. At the same time, in view of the religious policies of Beaton, if they had resisted the English and maintained their Protestant stance they would have faced the danger of persecution, perhaps death at the stake, by their own government. Living in a turbulent land where everyone's hand was against his neighbor, they had to seek the best means of securing their own safety. Since the English were present with superior military power and were also opposed to the Roman church, they had hardly any choice. Therefore, to brand the Lothian lairds as "gangsters" and "thugs" as some have done, scarcely gives a true description of these men.[47]

At this point George Wishart appeared on the scene to give focus to the thinking of the Protestant-Anglophile group, not only in Lothian, but throughout the country. Protestantism had been growing apace, resulting in attacks upon churches and monasteries in Dundee and the surrounding country. To this the ecclesiastical authorities had replied by burning heretical books and heretics, whenever they could lay their hands on them.[48] It would be Wishart's work to bring the disparate Protestant groups into closer contact with each other, and by his martyrdom to provide them with a common cause. Moreover, he held a most important place in Knox's career, for in the final analysis he faced Knox with the responsibility of taking a militant public stand for the Evangel.

Wishart, who was related to the Wisharts of Pitarrow, Aberdeen-shire, and may have been the brother of the justice clerk of James V, graduated from Louvain in 1532, first out of 118 determinants. He then returned to Scotland where he taught Greek in Erskine of Dun's school in Montrose. As his views aroused the opposition of the church authorities he left for England where again he got into trouble by preaching in Bristol against various Roman Catholic practices. Having recanted, he once again took off for the Continent spending some time in Germany and Switzerland where he translated into English the *First Helvetic Confession.* In 1543 he was back in England, a member of Corpus Christi College, Cambridge, and shortly afterwards returned to Scotland with the English ambassadors who had come to arrange the marriage of Queen Mary and Prince Edward.[49]

On April 17, 1544 Hertford along with some others wrote from Newcastle to Henry VIII stating that a certain Scot by the name of Wyssehart had come to them with letters from the Laird of Brunston proposing that James Kirkcaldy, Laird of Grange, Norman Leslie, Master of Rothes, and John Charteris, would waylay the cardinal while passing through Fife and kill him, if Henry approved. And if he did, they asked for asylum should they have to leave Scotland, along with money enough to raise 1,000 to 1,500 men to join with the Earl Marischal and others in razing churchmen's houses in the lands north of the Forth. Henry consented to the assassination and promised them a safe refuge and £1,000 to cover their expenses.[50]

It has usually been agreed among both Protestant and Roman Catholic historians that this could not have been George Wishart, a judgment based largely on the views of two of Wishart's greatest admirers, Emery Tylney and John Knox, who claimed that he was a very gentle and loving soul. Yet the present writer would not be at all sure, for Wishart could, from what we know of his sermons, be quite violent and fiery. Moreover, the fact that he went around with a bodyguard carrying a two-handed sword hardly bespeaks a man wholly devoted to peace.[51] Moreover, even in our own day we have a good example of much the same type of person in Dietrich Bonhœffer, who was implicated in an attempt to kill Adolf Hitler and was executed as a result. Therefore, it would not seem impossible that Wishart should have played the part of an emissary for the anti-Beaton faction. However, the plot, whoever may have been the go-between, did not come to fruition.

Beaton and the governor, on the other hand, realized their precarious position, with English raids devastating the country and growing discontent and conflict among the suffering population whether urban or rural. Consequently they sought to win support by various means such as making grants of land to those who they felt were trustworthy.[52] At the same time they called upon parliament to grant taxes amounting to £26,000 to pay for an army to stop the English depredations. All the arrangements were completed for efficient collection, but there was considerable resistance among the nobles, partially because of lack of funds, and partially because many opposed the governor and Beaton.[53] The only other means of blocking the English and the Protestants was France. Although the "Auld Alliance" had never brought anything but disaster to Scotland, the party in power now felt that France was their one make-weight against the might of England. Yet French money, French troops, and French Roman Catholicism only helped to alienate considerable parts of the people from the government.[54] As a result, the opposition to the rulers continued to grow.

Against this background George Wishart began to preach his fiery sermons of denunciation. Commencing at Montrose where he had previously taught, he moved on to Dundee. In this town, already strongly Protestant in sympathy, he found an immediate response which manifested itself in large attendances at his sermons. The cardinal and governor, however, applied pressure to the burgh officials who persuaded him to leave. Wishart thereupon went to the west where he received a hearty welcome from the Earl of Glencairn, Campbell of Kinzeancleuch, and others of the gentry and common people who at times sought, contrary to his own wishes, to use force to open the churches to his preaching. While busily employed in this work, he suddenly received a call to return to Dundee which was being ravaged by the plague. Much to the disappointment of the western lairds he left immediately since he felt it was his duty to be with those who were suffering and dying.

As the virulence of the plague gradually declined, probably towards the end of the summer, the western lairds wrote suggesting that he might meet them at Edinburgh where he could have a debate with the bishops and their minions. To this Wishart agreed with alacrity, apparently feeling that with the support and protection of the western lairds combined with that which he could expect from gentry around Edinburgh, he would be quite safe. Erskine of Dun and others opposed this move, but he insisted although he was beginning to have fears as to what might happen. By the time he arrived at Leith he had even more cause for uncertainty since the western lairds had not arrived. Therefore, Crichton of Brunston, Douglas of Longniddry, and Cockburn of Ormiston took him under their wings by having him live with them and moving him around from house to house in order that he would not be seized by the authorities. Nevertheless, Wishart, not happy with this development, insisted that he should be allowed to preach in Leith, then in Inveresk, Tranent, and finally in Haddington. In all except the last mentioned, he had large congregations and even won over, at least temporarily, such chronic turncoats as Sir George Douglas of Pittendreich.

Throughout Wishart's five weeks in Lothian, Knox accompanied him as his bodyguard, carrying a two-handed sword. When Wishart came to Haddington at the beginning of January 1545, he expected to find a large crowd awaiting him, but the Earl of Bothwell had apparently warned the inhabitants of the area not to attend on pain of his displeasure—and knowing the earl's ways of dealing with opponents, most did not come. On the fourth day after his arrival, probably Wednesday, a letter came from the western lairds saying that they would not meet Wishart as they had promised. This naturally threw him into such a state of depression that after the service he bade farewell to Douglas of Longniddry and told Knox, who wished to remain with him, to return with Douglas to his "bairns," since "one is sufficient for a sacrifice." He then walked with Cockburn of Ormiston, Crichton of Brunston, and John Sandilands of Calder, and a few others to Ormiston for the night.

About midnight Bothwell arrived at Ormiston with some 500 men. Although the earl might have had trouble forcing his way into Ormiston House, he persuaded Cockburn and the others that he would not hand Wishart over to the cardinal, but would keep him safe and sound, although he does not seem to have indicated what other reason he had for arresting him. The three lairds mistakenly believed Bothwell who promptly carried Wishart off to Elphinstone about a mile away where Beaton and Arran lay with another 500 soldiers. Beaton thereupon ordered that the three lairds also be seized. Ormiston and Calder, fearing nothing, submitted, but Brunston, already involved in the plot against Beaton, escaped into Ormiston Wood whence he fled to the safety of the Douglas stronghold of Tantallon Castle. The two arrested lairds were then conveyed to Edinburgh for imprisonment.

The one person to suffer the ultimate penalty was Wishart. Held by Bothwell, he was carried to Hailes Castle whence after considerable bargaining between the earl, Beaton, and Mary of Guise, he was turned over to the ecclesiastical authorities. Arran reportedly opposed his execution, but the cardinal insisted on a trial that took place in St. Andrews at the end of February. The verdict, as one might expect, was "guilty" and on March 1st Wishart was brought out to the place of execution before the castle, while Beaton looked on from an upper window. After he had prayed, Wishart was strangled and burned.[55]

The execution of Wishart had a deep and lasting effect on Knox. Both men were of about the same age, but Wishart had travelled widely and had received a continental theological training. Added to this he was, from all testimony, a winsome character who attracted the rougher types such as Knox. As one reads Knox's account of Wishart's last five weeks in Lothian, one cannot but feel that he is almost thinking in terms of Elija's commissioning of Elisha to take up the prophetic task after him. The fact that Knox only avoided arrest with Wishart by the space of about five hours may also have impressed him forcibly. All agree, however, that his time with Wishart for those important five weeks probably set his future course as a reformer. He had taken his stand for the Gospel, two-handed sword and all, and would not look back.

A further effect of Wishart's death upon Knox was that it stirred up a great hate of both the cardinal and everything for which he stood. Partially because his family had served the Earls of Bothwell in arms in the past, and partially because he felt that Bothwell was a weak man, Knox is lenient with him and also with the governor in his account of these events. But he does pour forth all his venom against the prelate responsible for Wishart's execution. His antagonism towards the Roman Church, however, did not disappear with Beaton's death, for he undoubtedly felt that the Cardinal was but the product of the teaching and the practice of the Church itself. One only has to read some of Knox's pamphlets written later to see the abhorrence he bore to all things related to "the whore of Babylon." [56]

CHAPTER III

St. Andrews Castle:
The Call

THE SHORT PERIOD OF four months from April to August 1547 brought radical change to Knox's life. From the time he left St. Andrews University until the end of March of that year, he had lived a rather sheltered existence, first with Ker of Samuelston and then with Douglas of Longniddry and the other Lothian lairds. Among them he had not only found security and peace, but also a certain amount of Christian fellowship, although how much he never reveals. The effect on him of the arrest and martyrdom of Wishart had been powerful, but the real change took place when he left East Lothian around Easter of 1547. This constituted a turning point in his life, for not only did he face new circumstances but he also heard a clear call to become a leader in the Reformation.

Around thirty-three years of age, Knox was a man of considerable physical strength. The fact that he stood up to the rigors of galley-slave life a little later on would seem to bear this out. Although no pictures actually painted during his lifetime exist, from contemporary descriptions he must have been stocky in build, not particularly tall, and dark in complexion. Two different portraits have come down to us, one a painting that still hangs in Calder House and another in Theodore Beza's *Icones of the Reformers*, but both have come under fire as not being authentic. Consequently we do not have an accurate knowledge of his appearance. But even had we a portrait, if he wore a full beard as many of his contemporaries did, we would still not know what he looked like.[1]

As to Knox's personality, one finds that considerable disagreement exists among his biographers. Some think of him as "the thundering Scot," while others declare that he was basically timid, if not actually cowardly. His late successor in St. Giles Kirk, Dr. Charles L. Warr, Dean of the Thistle, declared that "there ran through his complex character a yellow streak of enervating cowardice . . ."[2] It might be nearer the truth to say that Knox was typically human with his ups and downs of emotion, although we do gain the impression that in situations where he was unsure of himself, he was inclined to be rather timorous and hesitant.

Of one thing we can be certain: Knox had a strong sense of humor. Even in the midst of describing the persecution of Wishart he pauses to tell "the merry tale" of the violent confrontation between the archbishops of St. Andrews and Glasgow in the doorway of the latter's cathedral. His account of the murder of Beaton also has some rather wry humor, while at times his descriptions of the cardinal, Mary of Guise, and others are in much the same vein. His satirical approach was akin to the somewhat acrid humor of John Calvin. Whether we appreciate it or not in our own day, we cannot but feel that such humor betokened a strong strain of hard-headed realism in his make-up that kept him from taking himself too seriously even on his deathbed, and enabled him to evaluate situations accurately.[3] This in turn resulted in realistic actions that might at times be taken for cowardice, but were in fact simply common sense moves.

As a product of St. Andrews University and a notary public, Knox had been trained in the academic disciplines of his day and had likely developed a strong bent towards abstract and legalistic thinking. Some writers have commented on the fact that he showed these characteristics markedly in the sermons and hortatory epistles that he wrote during his life. But we should hardly be surprised at this when we remember that his training took place under the supervision of scholastics such as John Major. Furthermore, the Scot through the ages has usually been surrounded by what Robert Louis Stevenson termed "a hum of metaphysical divinity."[4] Yet while displaying this tendency, he never lost his practicality, perhaps as the result of his sense of humor. He was the typical hard-headed Lowlander.

His religious views as far as we can know them at this time seem to have been quite firmly settled. Basic to his whole theology was the final authority of the Scriptures of the Old and New Testaments as the inspired record of God's revelation of his redeeming purpose in Jesus Christ. In religious matters the Bible was, therefore, the final authority which overrode all church tradition and theologizing. Such a point of view naturally brought him into direct opposition to the church of his day, leading to innumerable confrontations. Yet his theological battles never seemed to divert him from his principal interest in bringing men to a mature faith in Christ as Saviour and Lord. In all of this we see, at least in his early years, the constant influence of the man who seems to have been his example and inspiration: George Wishart.[5]

Knox, at the beginning of his career, gave no indication that he would become a leader of a reform movement. In the presence of Wishart he had been quite content to carry a sword as the armor-bearer of a Jonathan. When Wishart told him to go back to his "bairns," he was ready to return to the quiet of Longniddry where he could continue to fulfill his duties as a tutor. At this point in his life, he enjoyed the relative obscurity of a member of a laird's household where he could study and expound the Bible, teach grammar and encourage intellectually two or three teen-agers, without having to face the hurly-burly of the violent world around him. He had probably carried the sword for Wishart on the suggestion of the lairds, but he soon surrendered it in favor of his academic pursuits, which were his real interest.

It was not possible for Knox, however, to continue in this unreal situation. Since he had obviously become known as one of Wishart's followers during the latter's sojourn in Lothian, he could be sure that the ecclesiastical authorities would soon be hot on his trail to make him recant or else. Exactly when the pressure actually became heavy on him, we do not know, but it is likely that once Wishart had paid the penalty for his heresy and the lairds Calder, Ormiston, and Brunston had been charged with sheltering the heretic, Knox realized that his turn would be next.[6] The question then was: what should he do? The answer seemed to come from events taking place in Fife, where on May 29, 1546 a group of gentry had murdered Cardinal Beaton and taken possession of his Castle of St. Andrews. This might well provide a haven for him in view of the fact that even the landed gentry of Lothian were not safe from the ecclesiastical authorities.

Such a move, however, would mean a considerable change in Knox's situation and way of life. Consequently, in order to understand what was involved, we must turn aside for a moment to look at events in Fife.

Since the untimely death of James V, as we have noted, one of the principal figures in Scotland had been Cardinal David Beaton, Archbishop of St. Andrews, who represented the Roman Catholic and pro-French faction in Scottish politics. Closely allied with him was the queen mother, Mary of Guise, who in some quarters was said to have been his mistress, although he seemed to have had plenty of mistresses without her. One of the wealthiest men in Scotland by virtue of his control of various ecclesiastical benefices, Beaton sought to dominate the country with the assistance of those who agreed with him. Those whom he suspected of opposition he forced, whenever possible, to sign bonds of manrent, or to give him hostages. He even persuaded the governor to hand over his eldest son, ostensibly for his education, but in fact as a pledge of cooperation.[7]

A complicating factor in this situation, however, was Protestantism. While it had been for some time spreading quietly, the execution of Wishart brought opposition to him to a head in a number of quarters. Since Wishart had been better known throughout the country than most of those calling for reformation, his death in St. Andrews had far wider repercussions than the executions of any other heretics who had passed through the fire. Moreover, many Protestants, no matter how highly placed, were, no doubt wondering where the persecution would end. With the governor, who had earlier shown himself sympathetic to Protestant views, now under the cardinal's thumb, no one could feel secure.[8]

The natural result of this growing feeling of suspicion and uncertainty was the hatching of plots to remove the cardinal by force. We have already mentioned the abortive plot by Kirkcaldy of Grange and some of the other Fife lairds in 1544. Undoubtedly, Beaton knew of some of these moves on the part of his opponents, but was so confident that he did not seem to worry. According to Knox he expressed his assurance in saying: "Tush, a fig for the feud, and a button for the bragging of all the heretics and their assistance in Scotland. Is not my lord Governor mine? Witness his eldest son there, pledge at my table? Have I not the Queen at my own devotion? . . . Is not France my friend, and I friend to France? What danger should I fear?" [9] But as George Buchanan points out in his history, fear, hatred and frustration were building up to a violent outburst. [10]

The person who led in the final and successful conspiracy was Norman Leslie, Master of Rothes, son and heir of the Earl of Rothes, once a loyal and obedient henchman of the cardinal who had decided that Beaton was to blame for the loss of some of his property. [11]

From what we know of Leslie and the other conspirators, we cannot label their action against the cardinal as simply a "Protestant desire to avenge Wishart," as has been done so frequently. To say the least, the motivation was very mixed, with the predominant element purely secular. Some may have felt that it would be well to put "the loon," as a contemporary song called him, away in order to protect themselves and others from persecution for their faith, but a good many had a much more worldly desire for revenge for economic losses they felt they had sustained through Beaton's machinations. [12]

The plan that the conspirators worked out resembled a number of others devised by Scots as far back as Robert the Bruce. Beaton had for some years been working at strengthening his stronghold of St. Andrews and the renovations were now in full swing. Consequently, the small group of conspirators numbering between twelve and twenty (Knox puts the figure at sixteen), had to use guile rather than force to take over the castle, if they were not to end as some had already done, in the Bottle Dungeon, a "bourne" from which few inmates returned. Furthermore, to enter the castle by any but the main gate would be extremely difficult for its walls ran close to the edge of the cliffs that looked eastward across the North Sea, while the landward side was protected by both a moat and high bastion provided with only a small postern which was well secured. It was therefore decided that a small group entering as though to enquire for the cardinal, would seize the gate. The others would then appear, and after expelling the hundred or so workmen and the fifty or more staff, they would be free to deal with the cardinal as they wished. To prevent his possible escape William Kirkcaldy was given the responsibility of seizing the postern as soon as they had gained control.

Everything worked according to plan. The cardinal, as Knox relates, "had been busy at his accounts with Mistress Marion Ogilvy that night, who was espied to depart from him by the privy postern that morning: and therefore quietness after the rules of physic, and a morning sleep was requisite for my Lord." Consequently when William Kirkcaldy approached the gate and asked if the archbishop was yet awake, he received a negative answer from the sentry. While he stood and chatted with the man, Norman Leslie of Parkhill with a few others came up, followed by John Leslie with another group. At this point the guard, becoming suspicious, attempted to raise the drawbridge but was seized, his keys taken, and he himself tossed into the moat. The conspirators, having chased out the workmen and the staff, headed for Beaton's apartment.

He in the meantime had realized that something strange was taking place for when he had called from his window to ask the cause of the noise, he had been told that Norman Leslie had taken the castle. He then thought to escape by the postern, but as he found this held by Kirkcaldy he returned to his bedroom where he and a servant piled chests and furniture against the door. When John Leslie along with some of the others demanded admittance, Beaton refused, until they threatened to burn down the door. Faced with this, Beaton removed the barricade, and Leslie with Melville of Carnbee and Carmichael of Balmedy rushed in to find him sitting in a chair, crying that they should not kill him since he was a priest. Leslie and Carmichael both struck him, probably with their daggers, but Melville, according to Knox "a man of nature most gentle and most modest," (one wonders if his sense of humor did not get the better of him here) restrained the other two, declaring that everything should be done "with gravity." He thereupon presented the point of his sword to Beaton calling upon him to repent of his wickedness, particularly the death of Wishart, but without giving him further time to follow this advice, stabbed him twice. Beaton fell to the ground saying: "I am a priest, I am a priest: fye, fye, all is gone," and expired.

Meanwhile, word had been carried to the town that something was amiss in the castle. Sir James Learmonth of Dairsie, the provost and a Protestant whose name was on Beaton's list for seizure the following day, promptly hurried with some three to four hundred men to the castle and demanded to know what was going on. When Norman Leslie, from the wall, replied that Beaton had been killed, the citizens required proof, whereupon the Castilians (for such they came to be called) hung his body over the wall with a sheet attached to a leg and an arm. As Knox put it: "How miserably lay David Beaton, careful cardinal!" Whether sickened or satisfied with this sight, the burgesses of St. Andrews returned to their homes, while Beaton's remains were placed in a lead coffin with salt and lowered into the Bottle Dungeon, "a place," Knox comments, "where many of God's children had been imprisoned before." [13]

"These things we write merrily." So comments Knox, but then goes on to point out that this is what happens to those who trust in their own strength and not in God. For this statement he has been attacked vigorously from many sides. Various writers have accused him of condoning murder and assassination, but in fact on other occasions he insisted that such actions were wrong and subject to God's wrath and punishment.[14] It would seem that in this case, however, because of the martyrdom of Wishart and the probable threats to his own life, he was too emotionally involved to be dispassionate. Furthermore, he believed that although the perpetrators of this deed may have been guilty of a very serious crime, and he later reveals his estimate of their characters, the whole event took place in the providence of God to accomplish His purpose for the protection of His people. Censure of Knox for his levity in this matter is a little hard to swallow in the light of so many contemporary reformers' willingness to term policemen and others "pigs" to be shot without compunction. Knox's position was probably very close to that of the popular dittie:

> As for the Cardinal I grant
> He was a man we weel could want,
> And we'll forget him soon.
> And yet I think that, sooth to say,
> Although the Loon be well away,
> The deed was foully done.

Once the deed was done the immediate question facing the conspirators was what should be their next move. They had murdered not only a cardinal and an archbishop, but the chancellor of the realm. They had compounded sacrilege with the crime of treason. All the legal thunderbolts available, ecclesiastical and civil, for here and hereafter, could, therefore, descend upon their heads.

The only sensible course appeared to be to hold the castle which was well fortified and well supplied. They had one further advantage in that they had found the governor's son in the castle which meant that they had a valuable hostage. Moreover, since they had murdered Arran's principal rival for power he was not likely to feel any personal animus against them. Therefore, they closed the gate and manned the walls in defiance of all authority.

Had they been left entirely on their own, the few men involved would not have been able to hold out for very long. But it looks as though the conspiracy had been known to others than those who actually participated in the action. Before the day of the murder came to a close, Sir James Kirkcaldy of Grange along with a number of his sons and retainers, entered the castle to take part in its defense. A day or so later Sir John Melville of Raith rode into St. Andrews with a considerable retinue to add more men to the garrison. And shortly afterwards, John Rough, one of the two chaplains of Arran when he was leaning towards Protestantism, appeared on the scene to become chaplain to the garrison, a greatly needed addition. Within a short time the total had risen to something between 120 and 150 men.[15]

If the Castilians hoped that this betokened a general rising on their behalf against the government, they were soon disillusioned. Although we have some evidence that in a few isolated places zealous Protestants knocked down images or seized the property of kirkmen, they by no means constituted a general movement of revolt and were easily crushed.[16] Individuals such as Lord Gray and his brother-in-law Andrew Whitelaw, friends of Norman Leslie, indeed gave some encouragement and supplies, as did the Balfour Laird of Montquhanny whose four sons were within the walls; but no concerted or effective support came from any quarter.[17]

That the executioners of Beaton received so little backing outside of Fife, may at first appear strange. Angus which lay just to the north across the Firth of Tay had long been known as a hotbed of Protestantism. Although John Erskine, Laird of Dun, had been one of the first to turn Protestant and later became one of the leaders in the Reformed Church, he seems to have made no move to assist the garrison of St. Andrews. He spent his time seeing to the well-being of his own lands and those of the burgh of Montrose.[18] Lord William Ruthven and his son and heir, Patrick, did not merely remain aloof, they actually took the side of Arran and the Queen mother. Indeed,

Ruthven, who acted as one of the governor's negotiators with the Castilians, a little later was appointed to go to England to persuade the English to refrain from assisting the rebels. He probably could not forget Norman Leslie's participation in the attempt to remove his son from the provostship of Perth. His commission was recalled, however, before he had commenced his journey.[19]

The western nobles were no more cooperative. Although the Earl of Glencairn had long been a Protestant, not until April of 1547 did he show particular interest in those holding St. Andrews. Nor did any of the others such as Campbell of Kinzeancleuch, the Maxwells, or the Earl of Cassillis take steps to help the Castilians. Many of them, on the contrary, no doubt rejoiced that the man who had marked them down for prosecution as heretics had been effectively removed.

Of all those expected to flock to the assistance of Norman Leslie and his supporters, the lairds of Lothian might well have been considered the strongest candidates. They, however, were themselves in difficulties. The Sandilands of Calder were under a shadow for their support of Wishart. John, the son and heir, on pain of a fine of £10,000, was obliged to stay at Corstorphine until summoned to turn himself in at Edinburgh Castle. At the same time, he had become surety for the appearance of Cockburn of Ormiston at his trial on charges of supporting Wishart.[20] Both Cockburn and Crichton of Brunston were summoned to stand trial for treason on July 3, 1546, but the case dragged on well into the next year.[21] This made it impossible for them to take action on behalf of the rebels in St. Andrews Castle, nor does it appear that they were interested in so doing. Cockburn of Langton, a relative of Ormiston, a vassal of Bothwell, and another leader of the Lothian Protestants, spent his time raiding some church lands, notably those of the priory of Coldingham, while at the same time he looked to England for protection against retribution by the governor and his forces.[22] Since we can find no evidence that any of the Lothian lairds supported either the Castilians or the governor in the siege of St. Andrews, it would seem that they simply ignored the whole episode.

From all this, it looks very much as though the seizure of St. Andrews and the murder of Beaton was solely the project of a number of Fife lairds. No one outside Fife, at least at first, seems to have been involved and even after some time only a very few from other parts seem to have joined them. From this we may well conclude that the Protestants in general hardly considered the move to originate so much from religious zeal and fervor as from a desire for vengeance or for personal advantage. Only later, as circumstances changed and persecution against Protestants began to intensify did some of the Protestants look with greater favor on the St. Andrews' venture.

This in turn bears upon the story of Wishart's martyrdom. In some of the later accounts of this event, we are told that Wishart at the time of his execution made a prophecy that Beaton would, within a few months, be killed. Despite the fact that neither Knox nor any of the other contemporary historians record such words, they have often been taken as true. Wishart has been linked with the conspiracy for Beaton's murder, partially because of this report and partially because of the earlier reference to a Wishart being involved in another anti-Beaton plot. As one looks at what happened in St. Andrews, however, it appears that the coup took place as the result of a sudden decision, perhaps to forestall a plan of Beaton to seize the conspirators a day or so later. Furthermore, as it was entirely a Fife move and Wishart had had little contact with Fife, except to travel through it from Dundee to Leith, his involvement is very doubtful. Consequently, without further evidence, it looks as though the whole story and the deductions from it are a later fabrication.

The first move of the governor in attempting to deal with the Castilians was to apply the sanctions of the law. On July 30th the Privy Council issued a summons for treason against thirty-four persons held responsible for the murder of Beaton and the occupation of his castle. These included not only those who had actually participated in the deed, but also those who had joined them subsequently. In order to make this summons applicable to the whole group, parliament decreed at the opening of the trial on August 14th that all those assisting the holders of the castle should be treated as if they themselves had participated in the murder of Beaton.[23] With this extension of the net, the authorities were able to include Lord Gray as well as some of the burgesses of St. Andrews itself.[24] At the same time, some of the wives of the Castilians intervened to have themselves freed from the consequences of the action which might involve the loss of marriage portions, since they had not been involved in the conspiracy. George, Earl of Rothes, was also particularly insistent that his property, temporarily feued to his son Norman, should not be forfeited.[25]

While the legal action was being taken, Arran had sent the Bishop of Dunkeld and Lord Ruthven to the Castilians with a blank remission, in the hope of negotiating the surrender of the castle. The two emissaries reported on August 14th, however, that the Castilians would not adhere to their own conditions. Therefore although the stipulations of the conspirators were kept on the books, the remission was ordered destroyed. A sentence of treason requiring forfeiture of life, goods and lands was then passed against all those named in the summons of July 30th, except Carmichael of Balmady and Norman Leslie. The names of these two were crossed out with the information added that for certain reasons Norman Leslie's sentence was postponed to August 16th. On that date he received the same sentence as his co-conspirators, although Carmichael's name does not again appear.[26] Judgment had now been given against the Castilians, and the governor could proceed forthwith to deal with them.

Since the Castilians apparently held all the winning cards: St. Andrews Castle, the governor's son and probably English support, the governor's only hope was that he could capture the stronghold quickly and without difficulty. Consequently plans were formulated, according to the *Diurnal of Remarkable Occurrents*, by August 10th to divide Scotland into four parts each of which was to provide troops to besiege St. Andrews for a specified time. The first contingent was to be that from Lothian which was supposed to arrive on September 1st.[27] This proposal became a formal act of parliament on August 14th once the two negotiators reported that they could do nothing with Norman Leslie and his company. Apparently because a cleric had been the victim, the clergy were to pay up to £3,000 per month to help finance the siege, although the Archbishop of Glasgow protested that the clergy would not judge concerning blood or on the lives of those who might be captured.[28]

Despite all these well laid plans, however, the siege got nowhere. The Castilians were well supplied with munitions and food, and when the latter began to run low they were able to obtain supplies by boat from Balfour of Montquhanny and other supporters. Added to this, many of those summoned to come to the siege failed to appear. The governor, on the other hand, lacking adequate support and always fearing for the safety of his son, did not push his attack on the castle with any vigor.

Both sides were playing for time. The governor hoped that he would be able to starve out the Castilians, while they looked to England to bail them out, either by sending in needed supplies or by taking over the castle itself. To this end they dispatched William Kirkcaldy to England in October, 1547 to press for aid. He succeeded in persuading the English to send a fleet with supplies which were transferred to the castle with some difficulty. When the fleet left on November 20th it took two more negotiators with it, Norman Leslie and Henry Balnaves of Halhill, who had the Castilians' authorization to enter into a firm alliance with Henry VIII.[29]

That Balnaves was now among those who were in the castle was of the greatest importance to them. Having arisen from an obscure background, he had come under the patronage of Melville of Raith. After studying in Germany he had returned to Scotland where he became secretary to James V and a member of the newly formed Court of Session. Although he had been one of those to pronounce a sentence of treason against the Castilians in August of 1546, because of his close connection with Melville of Raith and also probably because of his known Protestantism, he found his situation at the Session becoming uncomfortable. Consequently, some time in September or early October, he was either deprived of, or abandoned, his judicial office and entered St. Andrews.[30] His adherence to the rebel group was a significant addition to their strength, for he was an experienced administrator and an able diplomat. It is not surprising, therefore, that they appointed him to go with their leader to negotiate with the King of England.

While Balnaves and Leslie were in England, however, the governor, pressed by Mary of Guise and Henri Cleutin, Seigneur d'Oysel, her French adviser, decided to reopen talks with the Castilians in the hope of bringing them to terms. Knox believed that the real objective was to persuade the Castilians to lower their guard so that they might be overcome by subterfuge. To this end, he tells us, George Durie, Abbot of Dunfermline and Balfour of Montquhanny acted as the go–betweens. Eventually the discussions that had been commenced about the beginning of December were brought to a conclusion on the 17th of the month when it was agreed that the governor would send to Rome for a papal absolution for their murder of Beaton; meanwhile they would hold the castle and the governor's son as pledges. Once the absolution was delivered they would hand over the castle and the governor would restore their property and offices.[31]

The truth was, however, that neither side intended to fulfill the terms of the agreement. While Knox accuses the governor and his party of double-dealing, there is little doubt that the Castilians were no more trustworthy, for they promptly dispatched a representative to Henry VIII to ask that through the emperor he block any possibility of the pope's granting the requested absolution.[32] Indeed the proposal of a papal absolution sounds strange in the light of the fact that a considerable number of those in the castle were Protestants. They may have made the move, of course, for political reasons, or it may have been that the nominal Roman Catholics in the garrison hoped that this would be a means of extricating themselves from a difficulty. Perhaps the Balfours' influence was the predominant force here. But however dubious the honesty of the respective parties, the truce brought a temporary cessation to hostilities in St. Andrews.

While this state of affairs prevailed, the Castilians felt safe. The only problem was that there seemed to be a growing division within their own ranks. Once the truce was agreed upon, those who had entered into the plot primarily for personal revenge on the archbishiop or for personal gain behaved in the typical style of mercenary soldiers, raiding, robbing and raping in all directions.[33] Others who had taken part mainly for religious reasons seem to have had different attitudes. Among this group were men such as Henry Balnaves, Melville of Carnbee and some of the clergy who having thrown in their lot with the Castilians had been deprived of their benefices.[34] Of the latter John Rough, the erstwhile chaplain of the governor, now began preaching Protestant doctrine in the parish church of St. Andrews.[35] Thus the Castilians, like the government, seem to have been divided among themselves.

It was at this stage in the country's affairs that after Easter (April 10, 1547) John Knox and his three pupils appeared at the gate of St. Andrews Castle to seek entrance. Tired of having to be continually on the move in order to escape the minions of Archbishop Hamilton

who were apparently on his trail, he had at first thought of leaving
Scotland for the academic fields of Germany. England did not attract
him as he felt that the English Reformation was no real reformation
but only the displacement of the pope by the king, as head of the
church.[36] Therefore, when he had complained of his precarious
position to his employers, Douglas of Longniddry and Cockburn of
Ormiston, they had advised him to take his three charges to St.
Andrews. There, safe from ecclesiastical censures, he would undoubtedly find spiritual fellowship.

Why they made this suggestion and why Knox accepted it is not
entirely clear. From what he intimates his employers did not wish to
lose him as the tutor for their sons since he was apparently doing well
in training them.[37] Pierre Janton feels that he did not wish to go to
St. Andrews, but that the influence of the two lairds pushed him in
that direction.[38] From the way in which Knox speaks about the castle
and the situation in it, however, it is clear that neither he nor the
lairds knew very much about it. They may have felt that it was held
by a body of "the godly" with whom Knox would have true
fellowship as well as peace of mind. At the same time, since St.
Andrews was Knox's *alma mater* still under the leadership of his old
teacher John Major, we can imagine that he may have felt he would
have an opportunity to take more academic training, since with the
truce established, the Castilians were free to come and to go as they
saw fit.

Knox must have received something of a shock, when he entered
the precincts of the castle. He did not find "a perfect school of
Christ" as he did later at Geneva. Instead, he found a military
garrison with all its usual characteristics, most of which were hardly
conducive to Christian fellowship. For this reason, no doubt, he
decided that the best thing for him to do was to concentrate on his
tutoring while leaving other matters, including preaching, to those
called to such duties.

He tells us that he continued, as had been his custom, to teach the
three boys grammar and "other humane authors." At the same time
he also read to them a catechism of which they had to give an account
publicly in the parish Kirk. Last of all, he lectured to them on the
Gospel of John in the chapel within the castle. One would like to
know more about this course of study. What was the grammar and
who were the "humane authors"? The fact that he called them

"humane" probably points to Cicero, Seneca and similar writers. The nature of the catechism is also a matter of curiosity. Was it Luther's work or some of the earlier catechetical materials of his followers? [39] Unfortunately Knox gives no indication. Nor does he tell much about his lessons on the Fourth Gospel. We would also like to know something of his audiences. For instance, did young Lord Hamilton, who later founded Protestant churches in Poitou and aided the reformers in Scotland, receive his first knowledge of Protestantism in the chapel of the castle? He was about ten years old at this time, and being about the same age as Knox's charges, probably shared in their instruction. We do not know, however, what effect Knox had on any of these boys except that Alexander Cockburn, who later studied abroad, wrote a number of works, but died at the age of twenty-eight in 1564.[40]

Meanwhile, Balnaves had come back from England with a subsidy of £1,180 and promises of military succor for the garrison. In return, the leaders of the Castilians signed an agreement, later adhered to also by some of their friends outside such as Lord Gray, in which they promised to hand over to the English the son of the governor, and promote the marriage of Edward VI and Mary. The Castilians who subscribed were Norman Leslie, Henry Balnaves, James Kirkcaldy of Grange, David Monypenny of Pitmilly and William Kirkcaldy.[41] Following the signing which took place about the time of Knox's arrival, Balnaves, Captain John Borthwick and John Leslie of Parkhill left again to confirm the alliance with England and to urge immediate action on behalf of the garrison. When Balnaves returned we do not know, but that he did was to be of the utmost importance to Knox.[42]

During Balnaves' absence in England John Rough had been preaching in the local parish church, but had been meeting stiff opposition from Dean John Annand ("a rotten papist"), opposition which he had not been able to overcome. He had, therefore, turned for help to Knox who wrote out arguments that he could use on behalf of the Protestant cause. These seem to have impressed him as did Knox's public instruction of his scholars. Consequently when Balnaves returned, he and Rough came to the decision that Knox should become Rough's colleague. As Rough soon afterwards left St. Andrews for England, it may have been that, already desirous of retiring, he was seeking a successor. The two men thereupon

approached Knox privately with the request that he take over the
spiritual leadership of the garrison.

According to Knox's account, he turned down the request
"alleging 'That he could not run where God had not called him':
meaning, that he would do nothing without a lawful vocation." The
two men then arranged some sort of meeting with Sir David Lindsay
of the Mount, Lord Lyon King at Arms (who although not a
Castilian favored ecclesiastical reform) to determine what should be
done. After some consideration they reached the decision that Knox
should be called to the office of minister publicly, so that he would
have no conscientious grounds for refusing. This would clearly place
him in the awkward position of having to take his stand or retire from
the scene. Rough, therefore, probably at the end of April, preached a
sermon on the election of ministers, and when he had finished
summoned Knox to accept a call from the congregation to the
ministerial office. With this action the members signified their hearty
concurrence.

Knox's immediate reaction to this call was neither to accept nor
refuse but to break into tears and to become very depressed. C. L.
Warr declares that he did so because of the basic "yellow streak" in
his make-up. He was afraid that such a position would mark him out
for martyrdom. Naturally in his particular situation at that time he
might well fear the consequences of taking on such a responsibility.
Yet other factors also were involved. It would mean that he would
have to change his whole life style from that of a family chaplain and
tutor to that of a man in the public ministry of the Gospel. This in
itself would cause something of a personal upheaval. But what was
probably even more difficult for him was that he would be faced with
the necessity of taking up the work of Wishart, where the latter had
laid it down. In times past he had thought of himself as Wishart's
"squire," but now he would have to carry on as his successor, and the
question that naturally would arise in his mind was: "Could he do
it?" Nevertheless, publicly called, he had to make up his mind,
although he did not do so at once.

The decisive moment came soon after when Rough, using Knox's
arguments, drove Dean Annand in a public debate to claim that,
since the authority of the church was final and since it had damned all
Lutherans and heretics, there was no further need of discussion. As
one of the congregation at this service, Knox spoke out against

Annand's claim for the Church of Rome, offering to prove that she was "further degenerate from the purity which was in the days of the Apostles than was the Church of the Jews from the ordinance given by Moses, when they consented to the innocent death of Jesus Christ." On hearing this challenge, those present called upon him to make good his words.

That Knox was very nervous about this first sermon goes without saying. For one thing, he had involved himself in a major task by his blast at Annand. But what was even more nerve-racking was the fact that he would have to prove his case, not to a group of ignorant bumpkins, nor even to the rough soldiers of the garrison, but to the intellectual elite of the land: the faculty of St. Andrews University. Added to all this, what was most difficult, he would face some of his former teachers such as John Major. This ordeal would oblige him to screw up his courage to the tightest pitch which may explain some of the violence of his language. On the other hand, he now felt that he had been clearly called by God through the voice of the congregation, to take this step so he could preach his sermon with complete freedom from the fear of what men might think. Such ambivalence of thought could not but result in great mental and emotional tension.

For his sermon Knox took his text from Daniel 7:24 and 25, concerning the little horn or kingdom which would arise after the ten horns or kingdoms had grown from the head of the fourth apocalyptic beast. He maintained that the Roman Church which had arisen out of the wreckage of the Roman Empire was the Antichrist spoken of in the New Testament. He then proceeded to deal with the lives of various popes and with the doctrines of the Roman Church which conflicted with the New Testament teaching of justification by faith alone. He ended by challenging anyone present who disagreed with his interpretation of Scripture to discuss the matter with him afterwards when he would prove that his views were those intended by the biblical writers.

Knox's sermon and the reaction to it reveals much concerning the man, himself. In the first place, his total reliance on the Bible as the Word of God gave him an assurance that he was speaking the truth, while his interpretation of contemporary events by biblical prophecy made him feel that he had his feet on firm ground. Then, too, his stress upon the doctrine of justification by faith alone gave him the confidence that he required in the face of opposition, for he spoke as

one of God's people. He retained these two elements in his thought
for the rest of his life. But equally important, he believed that God
confirmed his call to the ministry by the reaction of his hearers, some
of whom declared that while other preachers lopped off the branches,
Knox struck at the very roots of papistry. He went out of the Parish
Church of St. Andrews convinced that he had, in truth, been called
to become "the Trumpeter of God." [43]

Yet while he gained the support of a considerable number of his
hearers, opposition quickly manifested itself. Unfortunately, we do
not know the reaction of John Major or of some of the other leading
academics. They seem to have listened but to have made no move
either to support or to oppose his views. None of them seems to have
taken up his challenge to query his biblical exegesis or to question his
conclusions. Those who manifested an adverse reaction came more
from the clergy or from the Black and Grey Friars. That he had
"sned" at the roots of Romanism stirred up a hornets' nest within
these bodies. The outcome was a public debate in St. Leonard's yard
at the university.

According to Knox, this confrontation took place before Dean
John Winram, the subprior of the Augustinian priory which formed
the chapter of the cathedral, as the result of Archbishop Hamilton's
reprimand of Winram for permitting Knox to preach his sermon in
the parish church without at the same time opposing his teaching.
Winram's difficulty was that he undoubtedly agreed with much that
Knox had said, for he had already begun to move in the direction of
Protestantism, although he had not yet taken any overt step.
Therefore, to protect himself he decided that a public summons
should be issued to Rough and Knox to answer for their erroneous
views.

Nine articles were prepared setting forth their doctrines and
Rough was called first to hear the statement and answer whether it
expressed his beliefs. Then Knox was brought in. The articles as
reproduced by Knox indicate that the person who had drawn them
knew very well the teachings of the reformers. They contained a
denial of the pope as head of the church, terming him Antichrist, and
a rejection of any religion not based exclusively on the Bible,
declaring the Mass to be an abomination, purgatory non-existent and
prayers for the dead vanity and idolatry. Finally they asserted that
only preaching bishops were true bishops and that the tithe did not

necessarily belong to ecclesiastics.[44] In affirming these articles Knox
showed himself much less belligerent than he had been in the pulpit.
He obviously knew the direction in which Winram was moving and
did not wish to attack him. With this approach Winram cooperated
by explaining at the commencement of the meeting that he had
summoned him not for judgement, but for discussion.

The dialogue then commenced with the dean's raising the question
of the lawfulness of ceremonies being added to those required by the
Scriptures. With the intervention, however, of a Grey Friar,
Arbuckle, who seems to have been a fool, the whole discussion
turned into a silly argument in which Knox finally forced the friar to
claim that the Apostles had received inspiration by the Holy Spirit
only after they had completed the writings contained in the New
Testament. When even Winram could not stand this, Knox was able
to employ his humorous approach to the full in making fun of the
hapless mendicant. So the debate broke up. But the clergy, in order
to keep Rough and Knox from preaching in the parish kirk on
Sundays, summoned all those in the Abbey and the university who
were capable of preaching to take turns. Knox, however, countered
by preaching in the kirk on the weekdays, with the intention of
replying to any statements made on Sundays. To this end he urged
his hearers to accept nothing from the clergy until they had heard
from him on the subject.

The preaching of Rough and Knox bore such fruit that they
decided to hold a communion service in which not only the garrison
but also some of the townspeople joined. One would give a good deal
to know exactly who participated, for in the manuscript of Knox's
History where he originally stated that *all* the garrison partook, the
all has been scored out. Despite this a number of writers on the
subject of Knox, Andrew Lang, Jasper Ridley and others have made
critical remarks about Knox permitting murderers and the like to
take the sacrament.[45] Of this, however, we have no clear evidence. A
number of the garrison may not have bothered, since it would mean
nothing to them, and the preachers may have excluded others.

Ridley, without any proof claims that the form of the Lord's
Supper followed by Knox was that devised by Wishart and Rough,
based upon the Strasburg service. This would mean that the form
used was either that of Martin Bucer or of Valerian Poullain, who
used a liturgy derived from one prepared by Calvin, his predecessor

as pastor of the French church. As we have no evidence of this at all, it would seem more probable that Knox and Rough simply worked out their own form of service on the basis of the New Testament.

Lord Eustace Percy believes that the holding of the Lord's Supper indicated that Knox was attempting to replace the Mass with a true form of the sacrament by which he differentiated the Church of Scotland from all other Protestant communions and made it, "in the strict sense of the term, a Eucharistic Church." Such a conclusion would seem to be gratuitous, for as Andrew Lang points out, Knox felt that preaching, not the sacrament, was at the heart of any service. Moreover, we never find him battling with the civil authorities, as did Calvin, in order to have the sacrament celebrated every Sunday. He regarded the Lord's Supper as necessary but not as central as the exposition of the Word of God. This is quite clear from the Scots Confession of 1560 which we shall examine later, but it is well to note that Knox always lays much more stress on his call to preach, than upon any appointment to dispense the sacraments which, he believed, automatically came to the expositor of God's Word.[46]

It must have been shortly after this, probably about the middle of June, that John Rough left St. Andrews Castle. From a letter of the Earl of Lennox and Lord Wharton in September it looks as though he had intended to be away only temporarily, but the re-imposition of the siege prevented his return. He then went to Carlisle to carry on his ministry, but eventually paid for his beliefs with his life during the reign of Mary Tudor.[47] As a result of Rough's departure, Knox found himself in charge of the religious life of the garrison, an unenviable task if we can believe his reports on their behavior; and from what we know of them from other sources, he was probably quite accurate in his estimate. From the time of his call to preach he warned them repeatedly that unless they repented because of their sinful ways they would come under the severe judgment of God, who would certainly allow them to be overcome and taken captive to France.[48] Nevertheless, his strictures had little or no effect upon their ungodliness.

It may, however, have been something else than divine justice that convinced Knox of the Castilians' ultimate defeat. Balnaves on his return, no doubt, had brought back word of the problems faced by Protector Somerset in attempting to establish the government of Edward VI. Moreover, Knox never seems to have had too much confidence in the help of the English administration. Consequently he may well have come to the conclusion that the French would act before the English, with disastrous results for the occupants of St. Andrews Castle. He realized only too clearly that if the French did arrive first, they could easily capture the castle, for it was extremely vulnerable to heavy artillery.

Meanwhile matters had not been going well with the government forces, for the governor and the Queen mother were by no means of one mind. Arran seems to have still leaned towards negotiating an accommodation with England while Mary looked to France for the force necessary to crush the rebels. In this she was encouraged by d'Oysel, with whom Knox hints she had illicit relations.[49] Arran apparently hoped that by some deal with the Castilians he might gain control of the castle, while Mary, convinced that this could not be done, dispatched the Archbishop of St. Andrews to France to spur Henry II to action. Division of counsel thus hindered and weakened the government. At the same time, English incursions into the southwest, resulting in the occupation of the Castle of Langholme and other strongholds, tended to divert attention from the problem of St. Andrews.[50]

Although we are not told exactly when, the papal absolution for the Castilians had arrived in St. Andrews prior to April 2, 1547, but the authorities did not present it to them at that time. James Stewart of Cardonald reported on that date that the governor had the absolution in hand, but that the Castilians, still holding his son, had told him that "if he would keep to them they would keep to him," apparently against Mary of Guise. Furthermore, confident that the English would soon send them aid, they said on the quiet that "thai wald lever hayf ane boll of quhet nor all the popes remysshones." [51] Both sides were sitting tight hoping that their foreign allies would come to their rescue.

Before his departure for the siege of Langholme, probably early in July, the governor, in order to protect himself from charges of double-dealing presented the Castilians with the papal absolution. It, however, contained the statement *remittimus irremissibile* (we remit the irremissible) which the Castilians rejected as this did not meet their case.[52] They felt that they could take a hard line since the English would undoubtedly come to their rescue. The governor, on the other hand, apparently knowing that the French forces were on the way, offered the Castilians this document in the assurance that if they accepted it they would fall into his hands, and if they did not, the French would bring them to heel in short order.[53]

When the fleet of some twenty French galleys under Leon Strozzi arrived, about mid-July, their first action was to summon the Castilians to surrender. The latter, however, still trusting in English assistance refused, and when the galleys attempted to bombard the castle from the sea, they administered to the French such a drubbing with the castle's cannon that the French found it advisable to retire with one ship badly damaged to Dundee. At this point the governor returned from the siege of Langholme to assist Strozzi in his efforts. The latter now decided to resort to the usual siege operations. He placed cannon in the towers of St. Salvator's College and in the Abbey Church, to command the courtyard of the castle. Then he proceeded to blow a breach in the curtain wall. At this point the Castilians realized that the game was up. The house party was over. Plague had broken out and the walls no longer protected them. They therefore sent William Kirkcaldy of Grange to negotiate with the French commander; and on July 31st the castle surrendered.[54]

What Knox's feelings were as the siege drew to a close he does not reveal in his history. We can hardly doubt, however, that while he may have experienced a grim satisfaction that his warnings to the garrison had turned out to be true, the uncertainty of his own future must have caused him some misgivings. He had been clearly called by the congregation of St. Andrews Castle to the ministry, but what would be the outcome of it all? If he were handed over to the governor and Queen mother he would probably end his days at the stake. If, on the other hand, he were carried to France his future might be equally dim. He must also have wondered what would happen to his three young pupils. Altogether it was a time of great uncertainty and perplexity.

CHAPTER IV

The Galley Slave

ONCE ST. ANDREWS CASTLE had capitulated, the French moved in. The prisoners, numbering some 120 men, were herded into the galleys while the victors completed the sacking of the fort, which according to the *Diurnal of Remarkable Occurrents* yielded loot worth some £100,000.[1] What the reaction of the prisoners during these days of waiting was, we can only imagine. Most were, no doubt, thankful that they had not fallen into the hands of the governor and Mary of Guise, for if they had, they would have received short shrift before being executed. At the same time, their position with regard to the French was anomalous to say the least. They were neither prisoners of war nor rebels against the King of France. Consequently if the French commander were to take them back to France, there would be no legal reason to keep them in captivity. No doubt this gave them a feeling of confidence which was not, however, entirely warranted.

According to Knox, although no one else gives the same report, by the terms of surrender Strozzi had promised that once in France they would be set at liberty to go where they wished, except back to Scotland.[2] This provision would be quite in accord with their legal position under French law, and the gentlemen no doubt planned, as Norman Leslie and William Kirkcaldy did later, to take service under the French crown. Such was the normal procedure of Scots nobles, many of whom were at the time serving in the French forces.[3] Consequently, when they sailed into Fécamp, near Dieppe they thought that freedom was now theirs.

They were soon disillusioned, however, for the fleet sailed on to Rouen. In Scotland the popular ballad ran:

> Preasts content you now; Preasts content you now
> For Normond and his company has filled the galleys fow,

and the French gave the Scottish authorities further reason for joy. Acting, according to Knox on the requests of both pope and governor, they condemned all the prisoners to perpetual captivity, the gentry in various castles, and those of the lower orders in the galleys. Thus all hopes of freedom were dashed.[4]

Of the gentry, Norman Leslie, James Kirkcaldy of Grange, and David Monypenny were sent to Cherbourg, where attempts were made to have them attend Mass. But when they threatened to cause trouble at the church services they were left alone and in December, presumably because regarded as dangerous, were transferred to Mont St. Michel. There they found William Kirkcaldy, Peter Carmichael, and Robert and William Leslie, who had adopted the same intransigent religious attitude. James Melville of Carnbee who was sent to Brest died soon afterwards, while Henry Balnaves was kept in the Old Palace at Rouen.[5] Some names, such as Sir John Melville of Raith and Patrick Kirkcaldy, are missing from those referred to as imprisoned, and we know that Melville of Raith was in Scotland in 1549.[6] Consequently, we may conclude that some of those in the castle had, before the arrival of the French, returned to their homes, perhaps realizing that the Castilians had little chance of success. Those gentry, however, who were taken by Strozzi all landed in French prisons.

As for the "lower orders," which included Knox and the three Balfour brothers, they were condemned to the galleys as common criminals to spend the rest of their lives tugging at oars for the French monarch. At least they had entered French service, albeit unwillingly. They all worked in the same galley, the *Nostre Dame*, which formed part of a fleet, stationed during the summer at Rouen to protect the coast from the raids of English corsairs, but with its winter headquarters in Nantes, to which it departed some time in the autumn of 1547.[7] As a considerable number of the Nantois had by this time accepted Protestant teachings, it is possible that Knox may have made contact with them, particularly since Nantes was the port of origin of many expeditions to Scotland.[8]

The *Nostre Dame* formed a part of the flotilla that sailed to Scotland in 1548. In fact, Knox made the journey twice, as the French sent over more and more troops to help the governor resist the English "wooing." On the second occasion he was so desperately sick, he records, that those with him feared for his life. But not so Knox. When James Balfour told him to look ashore, to see if he recognized the port off which they were lying, he replied: "Yes: I know it well, for I see the steeple of that place where God first in public opened my mouth to his glory, and I am fully persuaded, how weak that ever I now appear, that I shall not depart this life, till that my tongue shall glorify his godly name in the same place." [9] He had not forgotten that he had received a dramatic call to the ministry, despite his apparently hopeless position at the time.

In the French galley Knox found himself in a situation unlike anything he had experienced before. He does not dwell on his life as a galley slave, regarding it more as a trial sent to him by God, than anything else. Nevertheless, one cannot but recognize that it did leave a deep impression on him.

The average galley was one hundred and fifty feet long with a beam of fifty feet. At the stern was a small cabin for the captain and another for the stores. Down the length of the center of the ship ran a raised walk between the slaves benches for the overseer who could urge on by word and blows those lagging in the rowing. Usually propelled by twenty-five oars to a side, the galley would carry about three hundred slaves who worked six to an oar, each chained to his bench. At night on shipboard they slept either on the benches or on the floor, while during the day, since the galleys were only partially decked, they either roasted in the sun or shivered in the rain or cold winds. At times, presumably when the galleys were laid up for the winter or for cleaning and repairs, the slaves were lodged on shore in barracks.[10] But even there life was arduous and difficult.

The mental and spiritual conditions were probably equally hard to bear. Although the procedure did not become law until 1561, from 1532 on the custom had developed of sending felons to the galleys. This meant that Knox and his companions found themselves mixed with some of the worst criminals of France, an experience that must have shaken them considerably.[11] At the same time, the officers of the galley sought to convert, or at least make the prisoners conform, to Roman Catholicism. To this, the Scots replied by simply putting on their hats or hoods when forced to go to Mass, showing that they were not willing to submit in such matters. In this they felt that they were following the example of the faithful Israelites in Babylon, despite the fact that their "obduracy in error," as it was termed, often brought them more hard blows from those in charge. It was little wonder that Knox could speak of the "torment I sustained in the galleys, which brought forth sobs of my heart." [12]

Yet despite his extremely difficult situation, he seems to have maintained a position of leadership among the Scottish galley slaves, buoyed up by his faith coupled with his sense of humor. This comes out in his account of the attempt, soon after the *Nostre Dame*'s arrival at Nantes, to make the Protestants kiss a painted image of the Virgin Mary. Knox relates that one of the Scots, probably himself, refused, whereupon the officers forced the image into the hands of the objector who "advisedly looking about," threw it into the river saying: "Let our Lady now save herself: she is light enough: let her learn to swim." This has all the earmarks of a typical Knoxian action. After that episode, he informs us, the officers made no further attempts to have the Scots participate in such idolatry.[13]

Meanwhile, the French ecclesiastical authorities sought to convert the gentlemen who were in the various prisons, but they soon abandoned their attempts. They seem to have felt, on the other hand, that a man such as Henry Balnaves of Halhill, a scholar and a lawyer, might provide more fertile soil for their seed. This may have been the reason for his imprisonment in the Old Palace in Rouen. According to Knox, they labored assiduously with him in the hope of bringing him back to the church, but without success for he won all the debates which he had with the Romanist advocates.[14]

It may well have been that in order to strengthen himself against the Roman Catholic arguments, or indeed to clarify his own thinking, Balnaves at this time wrote a treatise on justification by faith. Under such pressure as he would have to sustain, a clear and concise statement of his views on the subject would be essential to him in maintaining his position. Furthermore, such a document might well be useful as a piece of propagandist literature if read by his inquisitors. It is interesting to note that a Scottish Archer of the

Guard, Robert Norvell, while imprisoned in the Bastille in 1555 for his Protestantism, wrote a similar work, *The Miroure of ane Christiane composed and drawn from Holy Scripture*, which was published in Edinburgh in 1561.[15] Such an opportunity for meditation provided by some French prisons seems to have been conducive to literary production.

Balnaves arranged to have the manuscript of his treatise transmitted to Knox for his perusal and editing. Although, as Knox points out in his introduction, he was at that time "lying in irons and sore troubled by corporall infirmitie" in the galley at Rouen, he took the trouble, "as imbecillitie of ingine [genius] and incommoditie of place would permit," to divide it into chapters, to write a prefatory letter to the congregation of the Castle of St. Andrews, to make a summary and to annotate it in the margin for unlearned readers. He then sent the whole to Scotland for publication. What happened to it at that time we do not know. It disappeared to be found later in the papers of Lady Alison Sandilands, widow of Cockburn of Ormiston, by Knox's secretary, Richard Bannatyne, who first published it in 1584. It may be, however, that although it was too "hot" an item to publish in 1548 that it circulated in manuscript among the Protestants in Lothian.[16]

This raises a problem, however, for one cannot but ask how such a document could be sent by a prisoner in the Old Palace to a slave in chains on a galley and thence to Scotland. Andrew Lang believes that Knox's situation was obviously not all that difficult, when such things could take place. This, however, still does not answer the question of how such a Protestant manifesto could pass safely through two systems of security. The answer would seem to be that Rouen, like Dieppe, had a considerable colony of Scots, some of whom were undoubtedly Protestants. These men would naturally interest themselves in the fates of their Protestant fellow countrymen whom they would visit to comfort and encourage. That this was quite a common practice we learn from the activities of such a man as Robert Stuart of Vezines who about this time was doing the same thing for Protestants in Paris.[17] It would have been relatively easy for these visitors to smuggle a short manuscript from Balnaves to Knox in the galley. After its revision they could then obtain it and send it off to Scotland with their merchandise. This seems to be the most likely explanation.

Another fact which we must take into consideration was that Balnaves and Knox were imprisoned, neither as malefactors, nor as heretics. This placed them in a somewhat peculiar position. Furthermore, from the correspondence of de Selve, the French ambassador in London, it is quite evident that Protector Somerset was negotiating to have their condition ameliorated, if he could not actually have them released. Indeed, it was through the instrumentality of Sir John Mason, the English ambassador to France, that the prisoners were finally set free. Consequently it may have been that Knox and Balnaves both received more lenient treatment than that accorded to ordinary prisoners either in jail or in the galleys.[18]

Knox addressed his prefatory letter to the treatise to "his best beloved brethern of the congregation of the Castle of St. Andrews." Whether he meant those who were imprisoned with him or those who remained in Scotland, he does not state. His theme, however, is quite clear: although Satan constantly attempts to destroy the people of God by persecution, God in the end always gives them the victory, to his own glory. To prove his case he cites the examples of Joseph, Israel in Egypt and Babylon, but above all that of Christ in his death. This has also been the experience of the Church down through the ages. He then goes on to point out that he has revised and digested Balnaves' treatise, not merely to "illustrate" it, but "to give my Confession of the article of Justification therein conteined." This confession, he insists, shows that he has not changed his views from the time he was in St. Andrews Castle, when some said that he was bold because he was behind solid walls. Furthermore, his work is not that of some speculative academic theologian, but of one who is actually suffering under Satan's persecution. Therefore, since the readers know that victory will shortly be theirs, they are to study it diligently rejoicing in the fact that even those in prison are seeking the "utilitie and salvation of others." [19]

What then did the treatise say, that Knox should take it for his own confession? James MacKinnon states that it is basically Lutheran, particularly in its references to the civil government.[20] But is it? Knox's summary of Balnaves' work gives us quite a clear view of a part of his theology, but not all, for after all he is dealing here primarily with the doctrine of Justification by Faith.

Following Balnaves, Knox commences his digest most appropriately by raising the question of the Christian's tribulations. He points

out that persecutions bring the Christian closer to God and are a sign
of divine love for which he gives thanks since in them he participates
in the passion of Christ. The Christian has this attitude to tribulation,
however, only if he is possessed of the Spirit and justified by faith.
And, "the substance of justification is, to cleave fast unto God by
Jesus Christ, and not by our selfe, nor yet by our workes." [21] All
other methods of justification are of the devil whose plans God
frustrates by bringing out a faithful seed who, believing, do not seek
their own justification by the law. It was this desire for self-justifica-
tion by the law that had led to the invention of man-made methods of
salvation in the Church of Rome.

Knox then proceeds with Balnaves to consider the question of
good works. "Justice" he holds, is, on the one hand, an outward
obedience and honesty which a man performs of his own power, as
for instance in fulfilling political and ceremonial requirements, and
on the other hand, in obeying the Law of God. While he may fulfill
the first, he cannot, because of his sin, meet God's just requirements
of holiness. Therefore, he must turn to Jesus Christ for justification.
Man may conform to the outward requirements of the Law in
political or ceremonial matters, because the Fall has not entirely
destroyed his original knowledge and power, but for acceptance
before God, committal to Jesus Christ alone meets the sinner's
requirements. He then points out that in both Old and New
Testaments those who are justified are always required to bring forth
good works as fruits of justification and as a proof of their faith. Yet
these good works are not human inventions but the fruits of the
Spirit, the primary good work being belief in Christ as Saviour.

The fundamental method of doing good works is, therefore, the
fulfilling of one's calling. He points out, no doubt with his own
recent call in St. Andrews still fresh in his mind, that Christians
know of two types of calling: the direct call of God as in the cases of
the apostles and prophets, and the indirect call through the
instrumentality of men, as Timothy and Titus were called through
Paul. Besides these, there is the general effective vocation of men
who are called to Christ and who believe. On the other hand, there
are special vocations in life, *i.e.* those of prince and subject, pastor and
flock, father and son, lord and servant. He then brings his summary
to a conclusion by outlining the duties, responsibilities and privileges
of these various occupations in life.[22]

This statement is the first manifesto, the preliminary blast of the trumpet blown by Knox as the "Trumpeter of God." It is hardly Lutheran. Of course, we must recognize the fact that Luther wielded a strong influence on the Protestant movement all through this period, but one cannot call it specifically the product of his thought. Indeed, in some ways, it more closely resembles some of the views expressed by Calvin in the second edition of the *Institutes of the Christian Religion.*[23] It is interesting that neither Knox nor Balnaves attempted to deal with the question of the sacraments, except to manifest a negative attitude towards the Mass. By this omission they would seem to indicate that they regarded the sacraments as secondary to the true doctrine of justification and the proper exposition of a theology of good works.

Here we see Knox's basic beliefs. He himself pointed out in 1566, when writing the first book of his *History*, that it contained "the sum of his doctrine, and confession of his faith." [24] He would later develop many of the ideas adumbrated in this document, but always justification by faith formed the foundation of all his thinking. One might even call it the base continuo of his trumpeting to which he continually reverted in order to expand and develop various other themes as the occasion and the need arose. His anchor still held in John 17 of which this confession is very much an elaboration and the key to much that follows.

Knox hoped that his epistle would both comfort and stimulate his former comrades in arms who were still in Scotland. As noted above, certain occupants of the castle do not appear to have been taken to France. Rough had left the castle before the arrival of the French and could not return because of the siege. This may have been true also of some of the others such as Patrick Leslie and Sir John Melville of Raith. What happened to Leslie is not known, but in 1549 Melville was accused of treason because of a letter he had written to his son in England describing the situation among the Scots. After being tried hastily he was executed, as Knox pointed out, probably more because of his Protestantism and his friendship to the Castilians, than owing to anything treasonable that he had done.[25] Another member of the castle garrison was Ninian Cockburn whom Knox accuses of providing the evidence against Melville, and whom the Earl of Glencairn had already labelled as a spy for the governor. We may well doubt that he would take to heart Knox's admonitions.[26] That there were still in Scotland, however, a considerable number of those who had listened to Knox preaching in St. Andrews would make it well worthwhile sending them such an exposition.

Meanwhile changes were taking place in Scotland, England and France with the result that after nineteen months Knox and a companion, probably Alexander Clerk, found themselves restored to freedom. How this came about is related to events that had been taking place not only in Scotland, but in western Europe as well.

Although the French, with their capture of St. Andrews Castle, had won the first round of the struggle for control of Scotland, the English had been laying their own plans with the result that early in September 1547, an army of about 12,000 men, supported by a fleet off the coast, crossed the borders. Protector Somerset published on September 4th a proclamation declaring that he had come with his forces only to ensure that the Treaties of Greenwich would be faithfully carried out. The Governor and his supporters bluntly refused to accede to the English demands, preferring to fight. The Scottish forces, however, proved to be no match for the experienced English veterans who on September 11th virtually destroyed the Scots' army at Pinkie Cleuch in Lothian. They then advanced to Leith which they sacked and quickly returned to England.[27] But this was not the end for soon afterwards the English fleet appearing off Dundee on the Tay, seized Broughty Crag which it fortified, much to the discomfiture of the governor's supporters, but apparently with the approval of the Protestants in the city and the surrounding area. Shortly afterwards Inchcolm on the Forth fell to the English who followed this by seizing Haddington and the castles of Home and Roxburgh.[28] In this way Lothian largely became "assured" to the English and those who refused to cooperate soon felt the weight of the invaders' wrath.

The councils of the Scots in all of this conflict continued to be very much divided. Yet it seemed to most of those out of the actual reach of English arms that the only hope was France. In this the "rough wooing" of Henry VIII and Somerset was essentially wrong-headed and stupid, for instead of trying to win over the Scots to their way of thinking by persuasion, they mistakenly thought that they could force the Scots into submission, an error of arrogance made frequently both before and since by English politicians. The outcome was that by October 1547 the Scots had dispatched emissaries to France with pleas for help. To these the French replied by sending a fleet with more troops to assist in resisting the English advances.[29]

The one group that did not go along with this appeal to France was that made up of Protestants, whether lairds or burgesses. Living in constant fear of Roman Catholicism, they could not see the French in the light of true deliverers. For one thing, they undoubtedly knew of Henry II's attacks upon the Protestants in his own kingdom. Furthermore, they saw examples of persecution in Scotland, such as the execution of Melville of Raith on what they regarded as trumped-up charges.[30] Consequently they viewed the English not as enemies, but rather as deliverers from both the persecuting authorities and the French troops. For this reason they were prepared to give their "assurance" to the English in opposition to their own government.[31]

In Angus (Forfarshire), the Mearns (Kincardineshire), and Dundee, this Protestant attitude to the English came out very clearly. On October 27th Sir Andrew Dudley, the commander of Broughty Castle and the leading burgesses of Dundee, most of whom were Protestants, entered into a treaty in which the latter promised that they would be faithful setters forth of God's Word and loyal to King Edward VI. They also guaranteed that they would supply the garrison with its necessities at reasonable prices, and that they would resist the governor in his attempts to capture Broughty. This document was signed by John Scrimgeour, constable and provost, the baillies and other prominent citizens.[32] Dudley reported on November 1st that most of the "honest and substantial men" of Angus and the Mearns also favored the Gospel desiring to obtain Bibles and testaments as well as other English books by Tyndale and Firth. He also stated that "St. Johnstown [Perth] has abbeys and religious houses to be taken and that the gentlemen of the neighborhood are ready to help in such Godly work!" On December 20th he said in a further report that the Master of Ruthven, who was constable (provost) of Perth, along with others was prepared to aid the English against the Governor. The great need, however, was for effective preachers and good books "which would do more good than fire or sword." [33] Lord Gray and Erskine of Dun both indicated that they would consider the possibility of becoming "assured," although Dun found this impossible, not so much because of Mary of Guise's offer of a pension, as stated by Merriman, but because of her threat of the use of force against him. He even found it necessary to allow a French garrison to take over his town of Montrose.[34] Despite these minor difficulties, we can see that the English had many allies north of the Firth of Tay.

Although the lairds of Fife were quiescent at this time, probably because most of their leaders were in French prisons, the Protestants of Lothian were in close touch with the English commanders, at first with Somerset himself, and after his departure with the Earl of Warwick and Lord Grey of Wilton. The Cockburns of Ormiston and Langton, Crichton of Brunston and Douglas of Longniddry all appear to have been quite willing to act as English agents and spies on the ground that the marriage of Mary and Edward was a truly "godly" affair.[35] George Douglas of Pittendreich, brother of the Earl of Angus, also made certain professions of support for the English, but as both sides knew, he always turned as a weather vane with the stronger wind.[36] In spite of any losses that they had suffered through the English invasion, the Protestant lairds of Lothian for the most part seem never to have swerved from their support of the English efforts to bring together the two countries.[37]

One exception to this was the Earl of Bothwell, whom Knox characterized as "an effeminate man." He apparently agreed to become assured to the English and to hand over to them the Hermitage Castle. The intermediary in the negotiations was Cockburn of Langton, one of his vassals. Bothwell, however, playing one side against the other, dickered first with the English and then with the governor. Langton, becoming very much angered with this type of bargaining, refused to have any more dealing with the earl who continued to hesitate until March 1548, when he finally became "assured" promising to surrender the Hermitage to the English in return for 3,000 crowns and 100 lances "à la mode." But the conditions of the bargain seem never to have been carried out.[38]

By April 1548 it looked very much as though the English would soon control the whole of Scotland. As Knox points out, they had fortified Haddington and the lairds in the surrounding area had either submitted or had been attacked by the English who wasted their lands. The French, however, had now decided that help must be sent to their allies, despite the fact that they were not officially at war with the English. A fleet was fitted out and an army under André

Montalembert, Sieur d'Essé, dispatched from Nantes and arriving in Scotland towards the end of May.[39]

The English, naturally very worried at this sudden threat to their dominant position, took steps to secure it by increasing their offers of bribes to Argyll, Huntly, Gray and others. Mary of Guise and the governor, on the other hand, were now in a much improved position. They called a parliament which met in the Abbey of Haddington in the shadow of the English guns. This body, according to Knox, under French pressure and bought by French bribes, ratified an agreement with France whereby Mary, the young Queen of Scots, would be sent to France to be betrothed to Francis, the Dauphin. With this decision made, Mary was promptly dispatched to France, landing in Roscoff on the north coast of Brittany on August 13th.[40] France had by this move acquired a trump card in the diplomatic game she was playing.

Yet all was not easy going for either side. On the one hand, the French adopted the attitude that Scotland had become a sort of French province in which they could do very much as they pleased. They attempted to tax the Scots to support their forces, while at the same time treating the ordinary Scot as the Frenchman's servant. The result was opposition which often erupted into open rioting and fighting.[41] The English, on the other hand, were no more diplomatic. In their anger and frustration at the arrival of the French, they hit out in all directions, not only raiding the lands of those who opposed them, but even of those supposed to be "assured" to them and on their side.[42] Furthermore, they were now finding that many of the "assured" lairds had come in not because of love but only because of their fear of reprisals if they resisted. The strongly Protestant lairds, particularly Ormiston, Brunston and Langton seem to have been the only individuals who remained conscientiously loyal to their engagements.[43]

The country was threatened with chaos. With fighting going on in various areas no one could ever feel quite sure who was his enemy and who his ally. The Earl of Rothes was borrowing money to help defend Fife against the English, while Argyll was endeavoring to raise troops in the west to help with the siege of Haddington, the focal point of English action. On the other side, the Lothian lairds, Brunston, Ormiston and Langton, very much in the line of fire because of their geographical location, were strongly supporting the

English forces attempting to relieve the town. Langton was particularly active in these operations, capturing stragglers from the Scottish
army and seeking to obtain the release of English soldiers captured
by the governor.[44] Such was the state of anarchy to which the
country was reduced, and it continued even after the Franco-Scottish
forces withdrew from Haddington to Edinburgh.

This was all part of a much larger picture. In 1544 the Earl of
Suffolk had captured Boulogne, which the English still held by the
Treaty of Campe (1546), despite all French attempts to dislodge
them. French strategists, however, felt that one way to regain the
city would be to so involve England's forces in Scotland that she
would be unable to do much to ward off effectively a sudden attack
that might recapture this important port. Simultaneously both sides
were seeking a truly permanent peace for they had major internal
political and financial troubles with which their respective governments had to contend. Consequently while making warlike noises
and while stirring up the Scots to fight each other and their mutual
enemies, they also carried on negotiations which eventually ended in
1550 in the Treaty of Boulogne.

Sir John Mason and Odette de Selve were the ambassadors
accredited to Paris and London respectively. While endeavoring to
negotiate a definitive peace, they also dealt with other matters, one of
which was the fate of the prisoners from St. Andrews Castle in
French hands. Since the English government claimed these men
were in fact English subjects, the French had no right to hold them.
But because they had imprisoned them or placed them in galleys, the
English asserted the right on their part to take Frenchmen prisoners,
which they proceeded to do. Indeed, Somerset actually threatened to
order all French prisoners to be strangled unless the garrison of St.
Andrews received better treatment.[45] At the same time, Sir John
Mason in Paris was pushing for their release and dispatch to England
but without much success. The French demanded that the prisoners
held by England be released first, since the two countries were not at
war. This Somerset refused on the ground that he had the better
quality of prisoner.[46] The result was a stalemate, each country hoping
to force the other to make the first concession—and all at the expense
of the prisoners.

The prisoners, or at least some of them, however, were not
prepared to await the slow-moving negotiations of the two govern-

ments. In a letter written probably in December of 1547 William Kirkcaldy, Peter Carmichael and Robert and William Leslie asked Knox if they could "with safe conscience" escape from prison. To this query he replied from his galley that if they could do so without shedding blood they *should* do so. He emphasized this because, as he pointed out, Sir James Kirkcaldy and others not willing to make the attempt opposed a break-out on the ground that if the four did escape, those left would be treated more harshly. Knox maintained that "such fear proceeded not from God's Spirit, but only from a blind love of the self; and therefore, that no good purpose was to be stayed for things that were in the hands and power of God." As God did not always save all men in the same way or at the same time, those who chose not to make a try for liberty should await God's pleasure.[47]

Knox's reference to the objections of James Kirkcaldy indicates that this letter was sent to him after the transfer of Kirkcaldy, Carmichael, and Norman Leslie to Mont St. Michel in December 1547.[48] It is interesting to note, however, that Norman Leslie did not participate in the ensuing "prison break." It may have been that he decided to await the granting of freedom by the French king, whose service he wished to enter, rather than to take the risk of going to England. How these letters were transmitted between the two parties remains a mystery. Most likely soldiers, perhaps some of them Scots, may have been bribed to act as intermediaries.

Once Knox had given Kirkcaldy and his group clearance for their escape they laid their plans carefully. On the night of Epiphany (January 6, 1549) when "Frenchmen commonly use to drink liberally," the conspirators, with the help of a boy in the house, bound the guards whom they locked in different rooms, and after relieving the captain, who was also drunk, of his keys escaped across the causeway that linked the castle with the shore. One problem arose, however, when the boy who had assisted them, decamped with their small supply of money. Moreover, knowing that there would be an immediate hue and cry after them, they decided to divide into two groups. The two Leslies headed north to Rouen where they had landed and where they might obtain help from Scottish merchants. Kirkcaldy and Carmichael set off for the west, in search of a Scottish ship which would take them home. Dressed as beggars they travelled as far west as le Conquet which was also well-known to Scots' sailors.

After some thirteen weeks they found a vessel which met their needs. Although they landed on the west coast of Scotland, they soon made their way to England, since the situation in their homeland was by no means inviting.

Meanwhile, Knox and Alexander Clerk had been released. This probably took place in March 1549 some two months subsequent to the escape of Kirkcaldy and the others, which he says they accomplished in the "same winter." [49] Why or how Knox and Clerk gained their freedom we are not told. There have been many conjectures, the most likely being that some of his friends made representations, perhaps through Sir John Mason, to the French king, claiming that since Knox had not been guilty of participation in the cardinal's murder, he should not be kept in the galleys. Some of the Scottish officers in the Archers of the French king's Body-Guard may even have taken a hand in this matter, but be that as it may, the important thing was that he was set free.

A few of the prisoners were allowed to go shortly afterwards. The majority of the gentlemen did not obtain their release, however, until July of 1550, when they were set at liberty at the request of Mary of Guise who felt that if she were instrumental in their liberation they would support her in her efforts to supplant the governor. The men of the lower orders had to wait in the galleys until the signing of the Treaty of Boulogne later in the year. Thus, as Knox points out, with the exception of Melville of Carnbee, who died during the imprisonment, all eventually regained their freedom. [50]

On being freed, Knox had to decide on his next move. He could return home, but at that time it hardly seemed wise, since the French and the English were still battling in Lothian. The latter, however, hung on grimly despite the gradual loss of their hold on the country, evacuating Haddington only in September. If Knox returned at this time he would undoubtedly be accused of heresy and perhaps faced with the necessity of confessing his faith even at the stake. He could of course go to one of the European universities, but the situation in both Germany and France was likewise very uncertain. Consequently he felt that the best place to light would be England, where Archbishop Cranmer was seeking to gather together a body of international reformers who, under his leadership, would help with the work of remaking the Church of England.

The reunion of Knox with his former comrades in arms in

England was a time for great rejoicing. After all they had been through together they had much to discuss and many things to recount to each other. Yet a change had taken place in their relations. During his time in the galleys, Knox had emerged as the leader of the group involved in the St. Andrews Castle episode. The appeals to him on various matters all through the nineteen months indicate that he had established a moral dominance that continued for many years afterwards. Consequently, in order to understand his later influence we must constantly think back to the galleys, where he first seems to have assumed this role.

The reasons for his assuming such a position during this period are not far to seek. He had already shown his mettle in St. Andrews Castle and continued to do so in the galleys. In his introduction to Balnaves *Treatise* he pointed out that although some had said that he spoke boldly in St. Andrews because he was behind strong stone walls, he had maintained an equally forthright testimony as a prisoner of the French. In so doing he had been a means of strengthening and emboldening his fellow slaves. Furthermore, he had never lost his optimism, which he had demonstrated by his assurance, when lying sick in the galley off St. Andrews that he would preach again in the parish church, thus indicating his confidence that the Protestants would ultimately gain the victory.

Knox, however, was able to fill the role of leader because he himself became much stronger as a result of his experiences. No longer was there any weeping when he had to face a difficult decision. He had come to hate and fear Roman Catholicism not only because he had suffered under the slave-driver's lash for his Protestant beliefs, but because he was convinced that it destroyed men's souls by its idolatry. His sense of calling and mission from this time on was directed not just to an academic desire to refute Romanism, but to destroy it as the Israelites did when they blew the trumpets around the walls of Jericho. This fervency and relentless-ness of purpose made him an effective leader of a religious revolution.

CHAPTER V

The First Notes Sound

SOME TIME EARLY IN 1549, perhaps late in January or in the first days of February, Knox landed in England. Although the Duke of Somerset, the Lord Protector, who had used his good offices with the French government on behalf of the imprisoned Scots, was no doubt pleased with his release, the immediate question was, what should he do with Knox now that he was free.[1] He could not go back to Scotland, but at the same time, as he probably spoke with a broad Lowland Scottish accent, he would be of very little use in southern England and the North was still strongly Roman Catholic. Here was something of a problem. Coupled with this, the religious situation in England at the time made the future look a little uncertain.

In the 1520's Henry VIII as "Defender of the Faith" had instituted a rigorous persecution of English Lutherans, forcing many of them, among whom was William Tyndale, to flee to the Continent where they found refuge not in Lutheran centers but in cities which had come under the influences of Ulrich Zwingli and Martin Bucer: Zurich, Strasbourg and Antwerp. Supported financially by anticlerical London merchants they had imbibed more of the new ideas, particularly the belief that the Bible is the final authority in all matters relating to Christian faith and worship.[2] When Henry's views changed with his desire to have his marriage to Catherine annulled, he tended to become more tolerant of the reformers with the result that many of the exiles now returned home to be welcomed by Thomas Cromwell, the pro-Protestant chancellor.[3] The honeymoon, however, was short, for with the fall of Cromwell and the passing of the Six Acts in 1539, many of the Protestants, including John Hooper and Miles Coverdale, found it wise to take off for continental centers, while those who remained: Cranmer, Latimer, and others, were silenced.[4]

With the accession of Edward VI, conditions changed once again. Henry had left his crown and kingdom to his son under the direction of a council that was ostensibly equally divided between Henrician Catholics and Protestants. It soon became clear, however, that the Protestants were in control.[5] The boy-king's uncle, Edward Seymour, Earl of Hertford, who became Lord Protector and Duke of Somerset, leaned towards the thinking of John Calvin in Geneva, but was by no means "a rank Calvinist" as some have thought. He did, however, believe strongly in the responsibility and authority of the state to govern the church. In this he was supported both by Archbishop Cranmer and even by such radicals as John Hooper.[6] At the same time, it was very difficult always to know what Somerset sought to accomplish, for although undoubtedly an idealist, he was not prepared to force his views on others, at crucial moments seeming to hesitate and waver, very often with disastrous results for himself and his followers.[7] On the other hand, he and Cranmer, as Conyers Read has pointed out, were the only two members of the Council who really had any zeal for both social and ecclesiastical reform.[8]

The reforming interests of these two men, one the head of the state and the other the head of the church, soon became apparent when Somerset was firmly in the saddle. Although earlier, under Bishop Stephen Gardiner, who in 1540 had succeeded Cromwell as Henry VIII's first minister, the supremacy of the pope had not been restored, all the old ceremonies and doctrines had been brought back and those who disagreed had been persecuted vigorously. With Gardiner now removed from power, tentative advances began towards a more Protestant position. Cranmer's *Book of Homilies*, prepared during Henry's lifetime, appeared in print along with the *Injunctions* that ordered the clergy both to read them publicly and to celebrate the Eucharist with less of the Roman Catholic ceremonial (July, 1547). These were followed in the autumn of 1548 by parliament's move to introduce a new *Book of Common Prayer* in English with a much greater Protestant bias than anything heretofore in use in the Church of England. At the same time, the advocates of the old system found themselves increasingly pressed to accept the innovations, even to the extent that Gardiner, Bonner of London, and other recalcitrants were sent to prison for a season. The pro-Protestant lines were being drawn more tightly than ever before.[9]

The conflict was not, however, merely a matter of differences between Protestant and Catholic, although that was always present, leading even to armed rebellions against the first Edwardian Prayer Book. More important, conflict came within the Protestant ranks themselves, between what one might call the "Continentals" led by John Hooper, Bartholomew Traheron, and others who had spent some time in Zurich and/or Geneva on one side, and the "little Englanders" of the current "establishment," headed by Cranmer, Ridley, Sir William Cecil and their supporters on the other.[10] The "Continentals" wished to push for complete reform as quickly as possible while those of the "establishment" around Somerset felt that the move should come more slowly and gradually and perhaps not go as far.[11] At the same time, even more radical reformist ideas were finding expression among the "lower classes" who were being influenced by an influx of European Anabaptists.[12] While this latter group could with relative ease be persecuted and forced under-ground, "the establishment" found the more thoroughgoing upper-class reformers somewhat harder to control.

The conflict over the question of how far and how fast the reform movement should go, was linked to the problem of the socio-eco-nomic condition of the country. At this time, rising prices and unemployment resulted in much economic distress among the common people; it was generally blamed, although probably erro-neously, on the rural landowners' attempts to engross and enclose land for sheep-raising.[13] To seek a remedy for this evil condition many, particularly among the clergy and some of the gentry, began to speak out against enclosures and the oppression of the poor commons by the nobility. Although Somerset, Cranmer and others of "the establishment" were sympathetic, a more radical "ginger group" consisting of Hugh Latimer, the martyr, Thomas Lever,

Robert Crowley, Sir John Hales, and a little later, John Hooper, came into being under the title of the "Commonwealth men." [14] Made up of non-Londoners who were both strongly Protestant in their theology and compassionate and conservative in their economic thinking, this group became the focal point for social reform propaganda both in parliament and outside. Not only did Latimer, Hooper and Lever in their sermons attack the oppressive practices of the landlords and the money-grabbing techniques of the Londoners, but Sir John Hales was largely responsible for a number of statutes which sought by commission investigations and by taxation to stop enclosure in order that the land might be handed back to the yeoman and the copyholder.[15] These agitators worried and aroused the opposition of the landed classes who, seeking to increase their holdings and their profits, were not too enthusiastic over the more restrictive ideas of the social reformers.[16] Here was another cause of trouble within the country.

When Knox landed in England, therefore, he found a country that was sorely divided within itself. Roman Catholic opposed Protestant innovation, while at the same time the Protestants carried on an internal battle among themselves over the character of the Reformation. This was in turn further complicated by a cleavage over social and economic issues that led eventually to a political *coup d'etat* which cost Somerset his head. Had this been all, Knox would probably have found little trouble in accommodating himself to his situation, particularly as his natural tendency would be to ally himself to the Commonwealth party. A further complication arose, however, out of English policy in Scotland.

Somerset had inherited from Henry VIII the idea that the only way to deal with the Scots, Catholic or Protestant, was at the point of the sword or the mouth of the cannon, a policy he proceeded to follow ruthlessly.[17] Yet all he accomplished by this murderous action was to force the Scots into the arms of France, and to oblige his Scottish Protestant allies to leave their homes and migrate south with the retreating armies.[18] Somerset's failure to exploit the sentiments of the nobles and burgesses who favored the Reformation by following a conciliatory policy, had destroyed all English hope of victory. Consequently Henry II of France was not far wrong when in September 1550 he wrote to his ambassador at Constantinople that he had completely pacified Scotland which had now become a French province. Eventually, he said, he would do the same to England and be king of all three countries.[19]

It was around April 1549, while the conflict in Scotland was coming to its climax that Knox, probably after he had talked with Kirkcaldy of Grange about the situation in Scotland, was appointed pastor of the parish of Berwick. The Privy Council licensed him to preach and gave him money before he headed north.[20] One can well imagine what his feelings were as he rode out of London for the unknown future of a preacher in a typical rough, tough, border town. He had already learned much about the seemier side of life in St. Andrews Castle and in the French galleys. Now he was faced with the prospect of preaching in a town whose normal population would be largely augmented by soldiers recently returned from Haddington or on their way to attempt to break through the besiegers' lines. These men hated Scots, regarding them as vermin whom they could kill with impunity. How would they regard the preachings of a Scottish preacher with a strong burr on his tongue?[21]

Added to the problems that he would have to solve in a garrison town which provided a staging point for forays and attacks upon his homeland, Knox also had to deal with a difficult religious situation. So far the Reformation had achieved little success in the north of England. Tunstall, Bishop of Durham, was a rather typical Catholic prelate of the day. Well educated, an effective negotiator and a determined conservative religiously, he had little use for Knox and his beliefs.[22] Moreover, most of the people in the Berwick parish were probably strongly committed to the old ways. On the other hand, considerable numbers of Scottish Protestant refugees, perhaps even some of his old friends: Cockburn of Ormiston, Crichton of Brunston, Sandy Whitelaw and others, who at this time were receiving pensions from the English government, may have been in the town.[23] In considering all these factors, Somerset may have felt that Knox, who had been through the mill, would be the one man able to appeal to all the various groups in this inflammable frontier environment.

Although it is true that Knox probably was a good man for the situation, Berwick presented him with a very different kind of challenge from any he had experienced before. Consequently, the time he spent there and a little later in Newcastle, was of great importance to his own development. For one thing, it probably gave him time to recover from the physical effects of the galleys. Apparently he had contracted some infection of the kidneys as well as stomach ulcers which kept him in such constant pain that he found it difficult to sleep at night and to carry out his various pastoral duties during the day.[24] The period of relative quiet in northern England helped him to recover from these disabilities. Equally important, however, he was now for the first time the pastor of a settled congregation, and would face new situations that would force him to grow mentally and spiritually. In the galley he had become very much a man of prayer; in Berwick and Newcastle new challenges and opportunities would develop other aspects of his character.

Probably the most immediate benefit of being settled in one place was that he had time for study, something he had not known since his departure from Longniddry. That he occupied himself as much as possible in both Berwick and Newcastle studying the Bible with the aid of various commentaries may be gathered from some of his passing remarks. On one occasion he reports in a letter that a communication had reached him as he was reading Chrysostom on "the seed," presumably the parable of the "Sower and the seed." On another occasion he specifically refers to John Calvin's commentary on Jeremiah 10:11 with reference to the fact that this verse appears in Chaldee instead of Hebrew.[25] It is hardly surprising, therefore, that he continued to stress the Scriptures in all his writing and preaching. As he put it in his *Godly Letter to the Faithful of London, Newcastle and Berwick* (1554), the prophecies he made of the coming troubles were "not the Mervallis of Merlin, nor yit the dark sentences of prophane Prophesies," but the understanding of and application to his own day of the "treuth of God's Word." [26]

The immediate outcome of this study we may see in his preaching, which he referred to as "the blawing of my Maisteris trumpet," a description he frequently applied to all faithful proclamation of the Gospel.[27] As the "trumpeter of God," he undoubtedly began with the basic doctrinal position set forth by Balnaves in his *Treatise*. Yet as we read his account of what he considered to be the full Gospel, set forth in his *Letter to the Congregation of Berwick* in 1552, we cannot escape the impression that we have here a theology of greater depth than that of Balnaves' confession; one that reveals clearly the influence of Calvin. For one thing Knox lays much greater stress upon the objective redemptive work of Christ than he does upon the subjective reaction of the Christian. At the same time, he also emphasizes the doctrine of election out of God's "infinitt goodnesse and meare mercye." While he sets forth the doctrine of justification by faith, his sacramental views are purely Calvinistic.[28] Thus by the autumn of 1552 Knox must have gone over completely to the Reformed position, a development that was to have a determining influence on his work not only in Berwick and Newcastle, but throughout the rest of his life.

The order of service that Knox followed in his two congregations was not that of the first Edwardian Prayer Book, which had not penetrated the northern stronghold of Roman Catholicism by the time of his arrival. Rather he devised his own form of public worship, centered around the sermon which he regarded as the focal point of the service. For this reason he always considered that his most important responsibility was the preaching of the Gospel without either bowing to any man's person or for the purpose of gaining wealth.[29] As he wrote to those of the congregations of Newcastle and Berwick in 1558:

> . . . neither for feare dyd I spare to speake the simple truthe unto you; neither for hope of worldly promotion, dignitie or honour, dyd I willingly adulterate any parte of God's Scriptures, whether it were in exposition, in preaching, contention or writing; . . . Let him amongst you that is farthest declined, convict me if he can, if that he ever dyd perceyve me, by craftie or unlawfull means, to seke the substance or riches of any: . . .

Furthermore, as Lorimer points out, preaching to a congregation probably made up largely of soldiers, he undoubtedly spoke, as was his later custom, in terms of warfare and conflict, particularly when attacking "the idolatry of the mass." [30] His preaching was, in his own thought, truly blowing Joshua's trumpets around the walls of Jericho.

From what we know of Knox's sermons, and we do not know very much seeing that he published only two, he seems to have followed a general pattern in their composition. He chose his topics either as part of a series on some doctrinal subject, such as prayer, or on the basis of a text taken from a biblical book such as the Gospel of John, through which he was preaching verse by verse. He always began with the exposition of the verse or passage, thus having the assurance that he was truly proclaiming God's Word. He then proceeded to draw forth the doctrinal implications of the text, no doubt pointing out the failings of Roman Catholic teachings at this point. Finally he would close with an application of both text and doctrine to his auditors and, if he thought fit, to the state of the world at the time. It was his applications in particular that caused him so much trouble at a later date, although even in Berwick his practice of directing his remarks pointedly to the contemporary situation brought down upon his head the wrath of local magnates and even disturbed the government in London.

Yet while he was careful that the Gospel should be truly preached, he was equally insistent that the sacraments should be properly administered. The final and absolute rule in this was the New Testament, particularly Christ's precept and example. To this end he developed his own form of Communion Service, probably similar to that which he and Rough had instituted in St. Andrews Castle. As we know from a fragment of a liturgical outline of his service, after the preaching of a sermon based on chapters 13 to 16 of the Gospel of John, he offered a prayer for faith followed by the reading of Paul's account of the institution of the Lord's Supper in 1 Corinthians 11:17–31. He then "fenced the tables" by warning unrepentant sinners to refrain, and by calling on true believers to partake. He followed this with a prayer of confession and a promise of forgiveness read from the Bible. Then after praying for the congregation, he presumably distributed the elements to the communicants who sat at tables to receive the ordinary leavened bread and wine.[31] In all of this he insisted strongly that neither the Roman Catholic doctrine of Transubstantiation nor the Lutheran doctrine of Consubstantiation gave the true meaning of the Lord's Supper. As he put it in his tract on the sacrament written while in Berwick, Christ gives himself to the believer "to be receivit with faith, and not with mouth, nor yit by transfusioun of substance. . . . For in the Sacrament we receave Jesus Chryst spirituallie as did the Fathers of the Old Testament, according to St. Paulis saying." [32]

That Knox, as well as a good many of the other reformers, regarded as extremely important the complete change of the Roman Catholic Mass into a properly celebrated Lord's Supper, appears over and over again. He and his fellow prisoners in France had resisted all attempts to make them partake of the Mass, nor had his opinions softened in any way since his arrival in England. In fact, so bold and vigorous was his speech on this matter that by 1550 he was in trouble with Bishop Tunstall.[33]

Because of his public attacks on the doctrine of the Mass, which many Roman Catholics believed could still be read into the *Book of Common Prayer*, Tunstall decided that he should be called before the Council of the North. This body, presided over by the Earl of Shrewsbury had strong Roman Catholics such as Lord Dacre, Lord Wharton and Lord Conyers, in its membership. Instead of the investigation taking place *in camera*, it was held on April 4, 1550 in the parish church of Newcastle where Knox had to give his defense before a large congregation. Whether this was so arranged that he might be publicly humiliated or that his views might be given the greater prominence is hard to say.[34] But whatever the purpose, he came well prepared to meet the Roman Catholics on their own ground.

In good medieval fashion he based his arguments on two syllogisms: 1. That all worshipping of God invented by man without his commands is idolatry: the Mass was invented by man and therefore is idolatry. 2. All service of God to which is added a wicked opinion is abomination: to the Mass is added a wicked opinion, therefore it is an abomination. He then proceeded to show from the Bible that man could worship God only as he had prescribed, but that the Mass made additions which were unbiblical. Although at times he became somewhat picayune and pedantic, his principal argument consisted in an attack upon the doctrine of "the sacrifice of the altar," on the ground that Christ alone could offer himself, and that since his one sacrifice was sufficient those who claimed to repeat the sacrifice were "Christ killers." He concluded by pointing to the fact that not only did the priest wear garments very different from the ordinary garments that Christ had worn, but that he also used many different, but unauthorized actions and genuflections. He himself had refused to bow to or partake of the Mass even in the galleys, and he was not prepared to do so now.[35]

There is little doubt that Knox gained a considerable reputation throughout the north country by this bold and rather dramatic statement of his view of the Mass. At the same time, he also attracted no less attention by constantly warning his hearers that unless they repented and believed the Gospel, it would be taken from them. He was very dubious of the sincerity of many especially among the nobles, who professed to accept the Reformation, insisting that such things as the "sweating sickness" that struck England in August of 1551 with dire results, pointed to God's judgments to come on such hypocrites.[36] He often admonished his congregations that "the last Trumpet was then in blawing within the Realme of England, and thairfoir aucht everie man to prepair himself for battell." And privately he declared that he did not feel that he would long be able to continue in the country.[37]

Yet despite his fears for the future, Knox sought to carry on his work in Berwick and the surrounding area with diligence. As a result his preaching had a powerful impact on the border countries in which he made a number of converts to Protestantism. This success in turn required him to devote more and more time to the pastoral counselling and guiding of those who had but recently taken their stand as believers.[38] One of his most important tasks was that of reassuring the members of his flock that since their sins were forgiven, they themselves were reconciled to God through faith in Christ alone, without the ceremonies and requirements of the Roman Catholic Church. Furthermore, as they ever faced new spiritual problems and doubts, he had to resolve their fears and guide them in their everyday lives.[39] He probably had had some experience of such work in St. Andrews Castle and even in the French galleys, but never before had he faced it in so concentrated a form.

Of all the members of his flock his most important consultant was the wife of the captain of Norham Castle, Elizabeth Bowes of Aske, who later became his mother-in-law. Daughter and co-heir of Sir Roger Aske of Aske, Yorkshire, Mrs. Bowes, who had borne her husband some fifteen children, had accepted the Protestant doctrine of justification by faith alone, probably prior to Knox's arrival. She soon became an important member of the congregation. Nevertheless, her views were not shared by her husband, although her fifth daughter Marjory and her son George seem to have followed her example.[40] While we do not know very much about her, she shows herself to have been a woman with two distinct sides to her nature. On the one, according to Knox she was a person with strong convictions who at times strengthened even him when he was faint. This we may well believe, for she withstood considerable opposition, if not persecution, in her own family because of her faith. On the other hand, she had continual doubts and fears about her own spiritual condition: whether she had true faith, whether she was of the elect, whether she had committed the unpardonable sin. This uncertainty caused her constantly to consult Knox, and when he was not present to write to him. The letters in which he attempted to reply to her questions she kept and these provide us with a good insight not only into her problems, but into Knox, himself.[41]

Although Knox admitted later her constant raising of spiritual concerns was something of a cross to bear, he always did his best to help her.[42] Moreover, he never showed any sense of superiority, constantly acknowledging his own weakness and sinfulness. In fact more than once he admits that her questions have forced him to look at himself critically in the light of the Scriptures. As he expressed it in one of his letters:

> I can wryt to yow be my awn experience. I have sumtymes bene in that securitie that I felt not dolour for syn, nether yit displeasure aganis myslef for any iniquitie in whilk I did offend; but rathr myane hart did thus flatter myself . . . 'Thow hes sufferit great trubill for professing of Chrystis treuth, God has done great thingis for thee, delyvering thee fra that maist cruell bondage. He has placeit thee in a maist honorabill vocatioun, and thy labouris are not without frute; thairfoir thow aucht rejois and gif prais unto God . . .' I drank shortlie efter this flatterie of myself a cup of contra poysone, that whatever I have sufferit, or presentlie dois, I reput as dung, yea and myslef worthie of dampnatioun for my ingratitude towards my God.[43]

In this way he felt himself to be reduced to his proper stature.

In his dealing with Mrs. Bowes, one cannot but be impressed with the mixture of Scriptural principles and hard Lowland common sense that he manifested. As he explained to her, the Devil tries all Christians. "He is a roaring lyon seiking whome he may devour; whome he has devourit alreadie he seikis na mair." Therefore, her very fears indicate that she is truly a Christian, for if she had none, something would be wrong.[44] But even more, as we read his letters we find a warmth, a gentleness, and an understanding that most people do not associate with him. Against Mary of Guise, Catherine de Medici, or Mary Tudor he could blow a "blast of the trumpet," but for troubled souls his notes were soft and comforting. Lorimer is quite right when he says that Mrs. Bowes helped to bring out the elements of humility and sympathy as a counterpoise to the strength and vigor of his nature.[45] In this way Mrs. Bowes and Knox proved to be helpers to each other in their difficulties.

From Knox's letters to Mrs. Bowes, we gather that in his own day snide remarks were made about their friendship, a practice not unknown even in our own time.[46] Writing to her on December 22, 1551, and again the following month, he said that some people were spreading false rumors about them.[47] In February 1552 he states that he has heard from her brother-in-law, Harry Wickliffe, how her "adversarie" has troubled her because he, Knox, had started back from her rehearsing of her infirmities, something he always did when his heart was touched. Then he continues:

> Call to your mynd what I did standing at the copburd in Alnwick: in verie deid I thought that na creature had bene temptit as I was. And when that I heard proceid fra your mouth the verie same wordis that he trubillis me with, I did wonder, and fra my heart lament your sair trubell, knowing in my selfe the dolour thairof.[48]

On the basis of these cryptic remarks some authors have based their innuendos. If we take the first sentence of this quotation in its context, however, whatever his temptation, it seems to have related to Mrs. Bowes's spiritual troubles. (Moreover, from the fact that Mrs. Bowes was considerably older than Knox and had already borne many children, we must conclude that by this time she had lost most of her physical attractiveness.) Reading through all his other letters written to her, they hardly look like the communications of one who had had or was carrying on an illicit love affair with the recipient. What he did "at the copburd in Alnwick," remains a mystery, although it may simply have been that he was startled to discover that she had some of the temptations that he had experienced, or it may have been that he was simply weary of her complaints and was tempted to leave. Many a pastor since Knox's day has had the same reactions.

Perhaps partly as a result of the importunities of Mrs. Bowes, partly as a result of his own experience during his residence in Berwick, Knox wrote *A Confession and Declaration of the Nature of Prayer*. Although the date of publication of the first extant edition is 1554, as Lorimer has pointed out internal evidence indicates earlier composition.[49] If written either in 1550 or 1551 it provides us with a good example of both Knox's preaching and of his counselling of his congregation.

He begins by defining prayer as "ane earnest and familiar talking with God" to whom we declare our miseries, from whom we ask help and to whom we give praise and thanks. He then lays down certain principles of prayer. We should pray with concentration, keeping our mind from wandering and we should understand that for which we are praying, in all things seeking to glorify God. We must recognize that we have no claim upon God, but that he answers only of his mercy through the intercession of Jesus Christ who alone, without saints and similar human creations, is the true mediator. He insists that petitions concerning spiritual matters such as forgiveness of sins, the gifts of the Holy Spirit and deliverance from impiety can always be made unconditionally. With regard to corporeal or temporal things, the Christian must be at peace with God and be willing to leave all things in his hands, for he may defer answering for a season. While private prayer is important, "common prayer" is also necessary:

> I mene not to heir pyping, singing or playing; nor to patter upon beidis, or bukis whairof thai haif no understanding; nor to commit idolatrie, honoring that for God whilk is no God indeid.[50]

On the contrary the people of Christ should gather to praise God, to receive the Lord's Supper without any ceremony other than that which Christ used and to make provision for the support of those in need. Typically Reformed or Calvinistic in approach, the whole tone is practical, obviously directed to those seeking his help.

Some time in the summer of 1551 Knox moved to broader fields. As a result of his effective work in Berwick, his plain speaking on the subject of the Mass in Newcastle in 1550, and also perhaps because he was attracting too many Scots across the border, he was moved to the larger city of Newcastle, although he continued to serve the congregation in Berwick, at least on certain occasions. It may have been that the Marquis of Dorset, who was leading an attack upon the Scottish Lowlands with both cavalry and Protestant preachers, was responsible for his translation to St. Nicholas Church in the hope of drawing farther south the increasing number of Scottish religious refugees in Berwick, a sensitive point.[51]

This new posting not only offered Knox a greater sphere of influence because of the larger congregation, but also extended his preaching to other areas in the north country. Furthermore, while ministering in Newcastle he began to become involved in English public affairs. On November 1st he spoke out against the arrest of the Duke of Somerset by the Earl of Northumberland, blaming the conflict between the nobles on the machinations of the Papists.[52] Yet his forthrightness does not seem to have prevented him from receiving favors from Northumberland's new government. On December 18th the council decided that six royal chaplains should be named, of whom two in turn would be present with the king while the other four would spend their time touring the country as itinerant preachers. Each was to receive £40 per annum as salary. Edward VI's *Chronicle* names only four appointees but since there are two references to the fact that Knox received £40 from the king for his services, it seems very likely that he was one of the select group.[53] If so, this placed him in a new position of eminence and certainly made him a more important personage throughout the north country.

During the spring of 1552, taking full advantage of his newly acquired prestige he preached in various churches that might not have been open to him earlier. The climax of his activity came, however, with the arrival of the Duke of Northumberland who as Warden General of the Northern Marches was on a tour of inspection of the defenses that were his responsibility. Knox preached before him on numerous occasions, but whether the duke appreciated the plain spoken Scot or not we cannot tell. In any case when he returned south, he took Knox along with him to both his own and the preacher's eventual discomfort.[54]

Although Knox must have felt Northumberland's interest and patronage to be an honor, he probably took his journey southward with mixed feelings. From early in 1549 until the late summer of 1552 he had been very much his own master in the north, isolated as he was from the maneuverings, both ecclesiastical and political, in the capital. He had been able to carry on his work in his congregation with complete freedom, happily ignoring the *Book of Common Prayer*. Moreover, the strategic position of Berwick and Newcastle had enabled him to wield a wide influence on both sides of the border. Equally important, he seems to have both recovered physically from the effects of his experience as a galley slave, and to have grown spiritually in his efforts to meet the needs of his congregation. Added to all this, his interest in Marjory Bowes had begun to stir, as may be indicated by his reference in a letter to her that this was "the first letter that ever I wrait you." [55] So all things considered he might be pardoned, if he had some doubts about a future in or around London.

When he arrived in the south, he found a situation very different from that which he had known in 1549. A virtual revolution had taken place in both church and state. Somerset, who had worked diligently to obtain his freedom from the French galleys and who had sent him north to Berwick to preach, was now dead, executed by the Northumberland faction. In his place the power-hungry duke supported by a clique of grasping nobles dominated the scene, forcing all to submit to his ruthless governance. Knox may have felt that he was another Daniel entering the lions' den. No wonder he often looked back to his years in the north with nostalgia.

One of the first things which would strike him would be the great change that had taken place in the whole ecclesiastical situation. Hardly was the ink dry on the pages of the Prayer Book, when those who had experienced the impact of continental Reformed thinking were advocating more radical changes. Both Cranmer and Somerset wished to move slowly, despite the fact that many of the unreformed clergy were using and interpreting the new liturgy in Roman Catholic terms. The archbishop and the protector had been extremely careful in their dealings with both Bishop Gardiner of Winchester and Bishop Bonner of London, whom they had deposed only after their refusal to conform to the new service; therefore, they were not prepared to produce a new prayer book without good reason. The more radical group, on the other hand, led by John Hooper and fortified by the agreement (1549) between Zurich and Geneva on the nature of the Lord's Supper, thus bringing Zwinglians and Calvinists together, were pushing for further reformation. By this they meant that all teachings and ceremonies not actually taught or exemplified in the New Testament should be omitted from a prayer book drawn up for use in the Church of England.[56] The more conservative elements, on the other hand, opposed any further change.

In this conflict the more "thorough" reformers obtained the assistance of some of the continental refugees now in England. When the Emperor Charles V hoping to reverse the trend towards Protestant ecclesiastical reform had established the Interim in May 1548, those who refused to submit found it necessary to leave the

Imperial territories. Cranmer immediately invited various leaders such as Martin Bucer and Peter Martyr Vermigli of Strasbourg, Bernardino Ochino, John à Lasco, and even Melanchthon, to come to England, thereby widening the division already appearing in the English church.[57] Bucer, Martyr, Paul Fagius, and some of the others were inclined to accept the Lutheran doctrine of "consubstantiation" on the Lord's Supper, while à Lasco and those influenced by Heinrich Bullinger of Zurich and Jean Calvin of Geneva adopted the views expressed in the 1549 Zurich Consensus, *i.e.* that the communicant partook of Christ's body and blood only spiritually. Furthermore, Calvin insisted that all matters relating to the doctrine, worship and government of the church must be derived directly from the New Testament, a position he set forth in his letters to Edward VI and to Somerset.[58] Although à Lasco won over Bucer and Martyr to the Reformed view of the sacrament, these two men, one a Regius Professor at Cambridge and the other a Regius Professor at Oxford, were not prepared to take a vigorous stand on any issue, although Bucer did admit to Calvin that much was wrong in the Church of England. While welcoming à Lasco and others of like views, Hooper, disappointed by the compromising attitude of some of the Europeans, began to regard them with suspicion and even hostility.[59] Therefore, despite Cranmer's desire to organize a Protestant counter-council to the Roman Catholic Council of Trent in order to establish agreement upon Protestant doctrine, he could not achieve unity even in his own church.[60] As Richard Hilles explained to Bullinger, Cranmer had to compromise on every issue:

> For the preservation of the public peace they afford no cause of offence to the Lutherans, pay attention to your very learned German divines, submit their judgment to them, and also retain some popish ceremonies.[61]

One means, however, by which Cranmer and the king hoped to influence the Church of England and bring it gradually into closer conformity to the Reformed position on the Continent, was the introduction of foreign refugee congregations. By 1548 a French congregation had been established in Canterbury under Jan van Utenhove and shortly afterwards John à Lasco brought his group of Polish and German refugees to London, to whom were soon added another group made up of Italians. About the same time, Valerian Poullain, who had succeeded Calvin as pastor of the French church in

Strasbourg, arrived with some Walloon weavers who were settled by Somerset on his lands in Glastonbury.[62] Organizing their churches in the usual continental Reformed fashion with elders and deacons, and following a much simpler liturgy than that prescribed by the *Book of Common Prayer*, they exemplified a pattern of church life and worship very different from that of the Church of England. This brought the London Congregation of Strangers into conflict with Ridley, Bonner's Protestant successor in the see of London, who insisted that à Lasco's congregation must be subject to his authority and must use the Prayer Book. To enforce his wishes he used every possible means of coercion, despite pleas for tolerance from men such as Calvin. Only when Edward VI intervened in person was the bishop forced to concede some freedom to the foreigners.[63] Again Cranmer's plan had not proved entirely successful.

The first stage of the conflict between what Knappen has called "nationalistic Anglicanism" and "international Puritanism" came to its climax in the confrontation between Ridley and Hooper over the latter's ordination as Bishop of Gloucester. Hooper on his return from Zurich had been particularly vocal and belligerent in his criticisms of the Prayer Book. Consequently when on May 15, 1550 he was nominated Bishop of Gloucester, he found himself in trouble, since he was willing neither to take the required oath nor use the episcopal vestments and ceremonies in the ordination.[64] He therefore declined the office. In this stand he was backed by many of the refugee theologians, but especially by à Lasco. Bucer and Martyr, on the other hand, said that since the vestments and ceremonies were matters of indifference, he should accept them. Both Ridley, whom Hooper never seems to have trusted completely, and Cranmer, while accepting the indifferent character of the clothes and rites, quite inconsistently insisted that they must be used. When Hooper refused, they sought and gained the backing of the Privy Council who committed Hooper to the Fleet prison until he submitted to ordination according to the prescribed ceremonies.[65] Although Hooper eventually gave in, the foreign refugee churches thereafter never seem to have trusted either Northumberland or Cecil, both of whom had turned against Hooper in his difficulties; and Knox may well have had the same reaction.[66]

Coupled with these ecclesiastical conflicts were the continuing social and economic problems. While many of the common people and some of the nobles opposed or at least disliked the religious innovations, they were even more affected by the rising prices, unemployment, and the resulting social dislocation that was taking place. Somerset made some attempt to mitigate the changes, but without success. The outcome was constant trouble, stirs and rebellions, with two major uprisings, one in the southwest which combined both Roman Catholic and economic motifs, and another in East Anglia which seems to have been purely economic. Both were crushed, but only after considerable bloodshed, loss of life, and destruction of property.[67]

These uprisings finally brought about Somerset's downfall. Strongly idealistic and influenced by the "Commonwealth Men," he had recognized that the common people had such cause for opposition to the nobility that he would not take drastic action against the rebels. This, however, had not satisfied the nobles who were enclosing lands, or the London merchants who were attempting to put their newly acquired country properties on a profitable basis. The Earl of Warwick, therefore, who had taken the lead in putting down the uprisings, had won the support of the worried upper classes.[68] This had enabled him to achieve the position he had sought all along: his own replacement of Somerset as governor of the realm. On a series of charges, most of them only partially true, Somerset had been arrested on October 11, 1549, but although released somewhat later, he had never been able to regain his power and authority. Warwick, created Duke of Northumberland on October 11, 1551, now in the saddle, foiled Somerset's efforts to oust him by having him again arrested, tried and executed, on January 22, 1552. Northumberland was now truly in control.[69]

The doubts and uncertainty of at least some Protestants on Northumberland's assumption of power soon turned to joy. He raised a number of his protégés to the peerage, knighted several of Somerset's erstwhile supporters such as William Cecil and, most important to the reformers, proceeded to carry along the Reformation more rapidly and more radically than ever before.[70] Although Cranmer may have had doubts about the new ruler, Hooper, ab Ulmis, and Poullain were soon dispatching letters to the Continent praising his faith and life.[71] He stopped Princess Mary from holding Mass in her house.[72] He expressed his admiration for Bullinger and promoted Hooper to the bishopric of Worcester which he united with Gloucester.[73] He also rigorously enforced the laws against both Roman Catholics and Anabaptists. Not only to Hooper but to many others he was indeed "a most fearless instrument of the Word of God." [74] Yet into all of this enthusiasm soon began to creep a note of doubt, for the duke and his friends were constantly seeking to obtain possession of church lands, as when Hooper had to surrender part of the endowments of his new bishopric to the crown in return for the honor.[75] Nevertheless, despite the spoliation, the radical Protestants stiffling their fears, swung, along with *politiques* such as Cecil, to Northumberland's side.

Yet while the duke ostensibly controlled the country he realized that his domestic policies, which involved the appropriation of church lands and the countenancing of enclosure, were bringing him into disrepute with a considerable number of the Reformers.[76] This may have been one reason why he was prepared to favor Archbishop Cranmer's plan to produce a revised and more clearly Protestant *Book of Common Prayer*, along with a confession of faith, that would be in accord with the teachings of Swiss Reformers. He even agreed to a revision of the Canon Law, although he apparently did not see what this would involve.[77] Yet while he was prepared to accept such changes in the hope of bringing unity under his rule, the outcome was in fact a conflict in which Knox took a leading part.

Such was the situation when Knox entered London in Northumberland's train during August 1552. While in the north, he had been out of touch with the movements developing around London, but now he suddenly found himself very much at the center of things. From his subsequent words and actions he seems to have been growing increasingly distrustful of Northumberland from the time of Somerset's second imprisonment, a reaction that could only have been strengthened when he began to see at close range what was going on in both the civil and ecclesiastical governments. Moreover, it looks as though he soon came to regard Cranmer and his lieutenants such as Ridley as compromisers unprepared to go the whole way in bringing about reform in the church, a view already provoked by their dealing with Hooper somewhat earlier.

Knox now took his place squarely on the side of those who wished a reform similar to that advocated in Switzerland, particularly since Calvin and Bullinger had reached an agreement on the doctrine of the Lord's Supper. This radical group included such diverse individuals as Hooper, Martin Bucer, Richard Cox, the king's almoner, and apparently even the king, himself.[78] At the same time, he would also find that he agreed with the economic views of men such as Hooper, Sir John Hales, and others of the "Commonwealth" party, for he was always concerned for the poor and the economically depressed. Even in his letter to the Berwick congregation in November 1552 treating of the second Prayer Book, he stressed the necessity of the faithful's taking care of the "orphanes, widowes and others impotent," among their number.[79] Consequently, not long after his arrival in London he had joined the opposition to the ecclesiastical and political "establishments."

Knox's ecclesiastical position came to light at the beginning of October 1552. Owing to the criticisms of the first *Book of Common Prayer* Cranmer and Ridley, along with others, had been working on a revision which, while making the doctrinal basis more explicitly Protestant, in addition laid down specific requirements for kneeling at the Lord's Supper, a prescription which had been omitted in the first book.[80] This liturgical addition Knox considered to be *ultra vires* since the Lord's Supper should be conducted "as Christ Jesus dyd institute, and as it is evident that Sancte Paule dyd practise." Even royal sanction would not make it right.[81] In this he apparently had the strong endorsement of à Lasco, who about this time wrote a Latin tract on the subject of the proper use of the sacraments. Bucer in his *Censura* on the first Prayer Book took a similar although more irenic line.[82] Consequently, when, early in October Knox preached before the King and Council, a sermon containing a vigorous attack on kneeling at Communion, he had considerable support. Kneeling to receive the elements, he insisted, might well be taken as an act of adoration which the unreformed clergy would use in order to continue the old superstitious and idolatrous use of the sacrament.[83]

Although the new Prayer Book as approved by parliament was already coming off the press, the Council was so impressed by Knox's arguments that at a meeting held on either October 4th or 6th, they decided to have Cranmer and Ridley consider more fully the matter of kneeling. Cranmer complied, perhaps discussing the question with his whole committee, and on October 7th sent a reply to Knox's strictures to the Council. His argument was in essence that the Council should pay no attention to "these glorious and unquiet spirits, which can like nothing but that is after their own fancy, and cease not to make trouble and disquietness when things be most quiet and in good order." They would never be content no matter what was done. Moreover, the view that worship must consist in nothing not in the Scriptures was Anabaptistic.

> I will set my foot by his to be tried by fire, that his doctrine is untrue, and not only untrue, but also seditious, and perilous to be heard of any subjects as a thing breaking the bridel of obedience and loosing them from the bond of all princes' laws.

Finally kneeling fitted most easily into the whole pattern of the service.[84] Here the argument was deadlocked.

At this point another factor entered into the controversy. Perhaps because of the disagreement, the Privy Council on October 21st instructed Messrs. Harley, Bill, Horne, Grindal, Percy, and Knox to examine the Forty-five Articles presented to the King by Cranmer for subscription by all those admitted as preachers, and to report on them.[85] In these, Article 38 stated that the ceremonies of the Prayer Book "are godly, and in no point repugnant to the wholesome doctrines of the Gospel." By October 27th however, just three days before the new Prayer Book was to come into use, a declaration opposed to kneeling at the Communion was presented to the Council. Since the introduction to this document stated that it was being submitted before the other comments on the articles, obviously the writers wished to beat the deadline of the *Book of Common Prayer.* The arguments against kneeling were 1. that kneeling implied adoration and worship; 2. that Papists would, therefore, say that there is really no difference between their views and those of Protestants; 3. that Christ sat at the Last Supper without bringing any disgrace upon it; 4. that sitting was a sign of joy not of fear; 5. that sitting, in contrast to the standing in "the prophetical church" of the Old Testament, was a sign of the completeness of Christ's work which it commemorated. As Lorimer, who edited this declaration points out, all the circumstances as well as the style point to Knox as its author. Others such as Thomas Becon, Professor of Divinity at Cambridge, Roger Hutchison, provost of Eton College, as well as à Lasco and Hooper had publicly set forth this position, but it was Knox who gave the leadership in presenting it to the Council.[86]

The results of these representations appeared very quickly. On the instruction of the Council, Cranmer prepared a statement in which he explained that kneeling at the Lord's Supper was not a superstitious adoration of the sacraments, but simply the showing of reverence in the partaking of the elements. This statement later known to its opponents as "The Black Rubric," printed on a single sheet was then pasted into the already published copies of the Prayer Book. At the same time, the statement in the Forty-five Articles, now reduced to Forty-two, omitted all reference to ceremonies as such by giving only a general commendation to the Prayer Book and the ordinal. Thus the second Edwardian *Book of Common Prayer* came into use with a declaration attached that clearly rejected both the Roman Catholic and the Lutheran doctrines of the Lord's Supper, but at the same time brought it into accord with the views of the Swiss Reformers. For these changes Knox was the individual largely responsible.[87]

What then was Knox's attitude towards the new *Book of Common Prayer* now that it had been significantly altered by the addition of the rubric on kneeling? Some have stated that he accepted it fully, but this is hardly the case. To prepare his congregation in Berwick to receive the book he wrote them, probably in November, a letter which is very revealing. He pointed out that the times were evil and difficult, for although persecution had not broken out against the faithful, he saw signs of what might come out of the contempt of God's truth, the unpunished iniquity and "the away taiking of godlie magistrates"—the latter undoubtedly a reference to Somerset's execution. In the light of this state of affairs he advised them to follow the prescriptions of the Prayer Book, although he, himself, did not agree with all of them, in order that they might not come into conflict with the magistrates. He said that they should obey the injunction to kneel at the Lord's Supper as long as they made it quite clear that they were in no way adoring the elements, that they recognized that kneeling was a purely human requirement, and that no one criticized him for having administered the Communion differently in bygone days. At the same time they should pray that God would bring the magistrates to change their views on worship. But "less offense it is to bear this one thing (with dolour of your hearts daily calling unto God for reformation of the same), than to provoke the magistrates to displeasure, seeing that in principles we agree." [88]

This letter reveals much concerning the man and the reformer. In the first place, it indicates that his primary interest was in basic principles, rather than in outward ceremonies. As long as the principles were quite clear he would go along with the ceremonies, little as he liked them. At the same time, he did not give up his opposition to the outward trappings, but felt called upon constantly to push for further reform while at the same time praying that the magistrates would have their eyes opened to what should be done. He also realized that if the Berwick congregation resisted and came under persecution, they would be doing so because of something that was relatively unimportant. To come into conflict with those with whom they were in basic agreement, would also tend to weaken the reformers in their striving to present a united front against the forces of Romanism and unbelief. In adopting this approach Knox showed a breadth of vision, and one might even say statesmanship, with which he is not always credited. His was a more tolerant attitude than that of Cranmer and Ridley who insisted on absolute conformity to their liturgy. Although disliking aspects of the Prayer Book he was prepared to conform to it for peace, but always in the hope of further improvement.

Even with this compromise on the Prayer Book, however, Knox was not free from problems. The same day on which the declaration against kneeling was presented to the Privy Council, Northumberland wrote to Cecil suggesting that Knox should be made Bishop of Rochester. The reasons he gave were that Knox would be a whetstone to the Archbishop, with whom Knox was arguing over the question of kneeling at the Communion, and would at the same time be a confounder of the Anabaptists who were becoming influential in Kent. Added to these benefits would be his permanent removal from the north, where he had ignored the *Book of Common Prayer* and where he had been attracting Scottish Protestants from across the border which was a constant source of danger.[89]

Knox was apparently summoned to the ducal residence in Chelsea where he received the offer of Rochester. Whether the duke attached certain strings which would have spoiled the see of some of its endowments, we do not know, but Knox turned the offer down flatly. Later he said that he did so because he saw what was coming in England and did not wish to be involved. Whether this was hindsight or not we cannot tell, but Northumberland was clearly put out by the refusal, for he returned to Knox on December 7th with the comment that he loved "not to have to do with men neither grateful nor pleaseable." [90] Knox had spoken plainly and unacceptably, with the result that he and the duke parted on less than friendly terms. Yet no open break took place, for although Knox obviously did not trust Northumberland, the latter may still have felt that he could use him for his own purposes.

Between the time of the appearance of the second Prayer Book and his return to Newcastle shortly after his interview with Northumberland, Knox had been occupied with the revision of the Articles of Religion, to which the committee added a number of statements that clearly sought to make the Church of England Reformed in the Continental or Swiss sense. The new statement of doctrine attempted neither to win over the Lutherans or Anabaptists, nor to find a compromise with Rome. As both articles XVII which dealt with predestination and XXXV which treated of the sacraments were strongly Calvinistic, Knox's hand obviously did much to shape these parts of the credo. [91]

While working with the committee of revision, Knox also was probably preaching at court and in the city, experiences that led him to realize that all was not well in England. In a letter to Mrs. Locke and Mrs. Hickman, written later from the Continent, he reminded them that when he was in London while no trouble was yet visible in the offing, he had warned them that there might well be a reaction involving violent persecution. [92]

For this reason it must have been with considerable joy and anticipation that about the middle of December he headed along the Great North Road towards Newcastle. The Privy Council had given him his salary of £40 and a letter of commendation to Lord Wharton, the deputy Warden of the Marches, thus supplying both his economic and legal needs. [93] But probably even more important he was leaving behind all the petty politicking and scheming of the capital for his Newcastle congregation and more particularly for the friendship and understanding of Mrs. Bowes and her daughter Marjory. For the time being at any rate, the world must have looked very pleasant and attractive.

His joy, however, was not to last for long. On Christmas Sunday he preached a sermon in Newcastle that must have shaken his hearers. Instead of the usual Christmas topic, he told of what he had

seen in London, warning his audience against the resurgent Romanism that he feared was taking over the government. He then went on
to state that

> whosoever in his heart was an enemy to Christ's Gospel and doctrine,
> which then was preached within the realm of England, was enemy also
> to God, and secret traitor to the Crown and Commonwealth of Eng-
> land.[94]

The reaction to this was immediate and violent, for Lord Wharton
and Sir Robert Brandling, the mayor of Newcastle both Roman
Catholics, promptly preferred charges against him before the Earl of
Westmoreland, Lord Lieutenant of the Bishopric of Durham.[95]

Westmoreland seems to have jumped at the opportunity to deal
with Knox, for like Wharton and Brandling he was on the Roman
Catholic side of the fence. He summoned Knox to appear without
delay "as I will answeir at my perrell," not even permitting him to
remain to preach on the next day.[96] What happened at the trial we
do not know, but Knox sent off a letter post haste to Northumberland who immediately instructed Cecil to warn both Wharton and
Brandling to leave Knox alone since he stood high in royal favor. The
duke was particularly annoyed at Brandling for "his greedy accusation of the poor man, wherein he hath . . . uttered his malicious
stomach towards the King's proceedings." From the tone of
Northumberland's description of Knox's letter we cannot but
conclude that this sudden attack had depressed Knox greatly,
especially after the elation of his victories over even Cranmer in
London.[97] The situation was by no means as rosey in the north as he
may earlier have imagined.

It was perhaps this flare-up that persuaded the Privy Council to do
what it could to bring Knox south again where he would have less
freedom by virtue of the fact that he would be under stricter
episcopal supervision. Consequently on February 2, 1553 they issued
instructions to Cranmer to present Knox to Allhallows in Broadstreet
which was in the archbishop's gift and vacant through the elevation
of Thomas Sampson to the Deanery of Chichester.[98] This move
would place Knox under the authority of Nicholas Ridley who was
noted for dealing summarily with non-conformists of all kinds. As
Cranmer agreed with this decision, Knox received a summons to
come south to take up his new duties.

Before leaving Newcastle, however, several important personal events took place that were to have an influence on Knox's subsequent actions. For one thing, his brother William, having received permission to trade with England, had arrived from Scotland and had confessed to John that he had become a Protestant. Naturally this pleased the latter greatly for in it he saw the gracious action of God.[99]

Even more important than his meeting with his brother, was his reopening of communications with Mrs. Bowes. While he had probably corresponded with her from London, when he returned to Newcastle their letter writing increased, for although he was able to visit her occasionally, because of his pastoral duties he was not free to come and go as he pleased. Always he had to deal with the same problems: her doubts, her fears, and one may suspect, sometimes her fantasies. At times he speaks very plainly to her and shows a certain amount of natural impatience, although he was always willing to help as he himself said:

> . . . be sa bold upon me in godliness, as ye wald be upon any flesche, and na uthir labouris save onlie the blawing of my Maisteris trumpet sall impeid me to do the uttermaist of my power.[100]

Yet he felt it unwise to visit her too often as some people, perhaps her husband, were only too ready to spread rumors about them. Sometime in January 1553 his letters suddenly changed, at least in the form of address, for instead of writing to her as "Derlie Belovit Sister," he begins to employ the terms "Derlie Belovit Mother," and on occasion he adds a note to his "deirest Spouse." The change had come as a result of his betrothal, probably in that month, to Marjory Bowes. We could wish that his wife had been as diligent in preserving his letters to her as was her mother, for they would have revealed much concerning the writer. Yet as we read his references to her we see reflected a very deep affection which she undoubtedly reciprocated, and which he was at no pains to hide from Mrs. Bowes, for on more than one occasion while he indicated his affection for her he always put Marjory first, if only in brackets.[101]

Marjory was probably at this time about nineteen years of age and of all the Bowes' children seems to have been the one closest to her mother. Although we do not have any description of her, from Knox's first letter to her he evidently had great confidence in her common sense. We also have the comments of John Calvin who assured Knox, on her death in 1560, that his departed spouse had no equal, referring to her as a "most sweet wife." [102] That she was consistently loyal to Knox is indicated first of all by the fact that despite no little opposition from her father and some of her other relatives, she did become hand-fasted to this penniless refugee preacher. At the time of the actual engagement those who objected may have agreed to it because as a royal chaplain Knox was high in favor at court. Later, however, when Knox was fleeing from the Marian persecution, they did not hesitate to express their true feelings. Nevertheless, Marjory remained firm in her betrothal, prepared even to go abroad with him.

We do not know the exact date of Knox's arrival in London from the north, but it was probably during February, for he was at that time appointed one of the Lenten preachers before the king and the court. Many of the ecclesiastical leaders had now become quite disillusioned with Northumberland and his policies. The spoliation of the church was proceeding apace, law and order was breaking down, and most frightening of all, many felt that Northumberland and some of his henchmen such as Paulet, Marquis of Winchester, and others, were quite prepared to see Romanism restored. The Lenten preachers, therefore, took the opportunity to speak out against the drift of the government's policy. Grindal warned of the king's approaching death and complained of the courtiers' opposition to the Gospel. Lever spoke of the desolation of the commonwealth and coming plagues, while Bradford foretold God's vengeance because of the leaders' disobedience, and Haddon prophesied that worse events than anything hitherto experienced, were about to strike England. As Ridley, writing later from prison while awaiting martyrdom, put it:

> As for Latimer, Lever, Bradford and Knox, their tongues were so sharp, they ripped in so deep in their galled backs, to have purged them no doubt of the filthy matter that was festered in their hearts. . . .

Other godly men did the same in a softer manner, "but, alas all sped in like." [everybody went on as usual] [103]

As noted by Ridley, Knox was involved in this attack upon the establishment. What he actually said we do not know, except that he apparently spoke out strongly against the execution of Somerset and

made direct personal comments about Northumberland and a
number of the members of the Privy Council, whom he accused of
attempting to overthrow the Protestant settlement, warning them of
the dire consequences of such a policy.[104] The reaction of the
courtiers to these attacks were, in Knox's words that:

> They wald heir no mo of their sermonis: they were but indifferent
> fellowis: (yea and sum of thame eschamit not to call thame prating
> knaves).[105]

In the light of all this controversy, it is hardly surprising that Knox
refused to accept the appointment to Allhallows. Therefore, early in
April he was summoned to appear before the Privy Council to
explain why he would not accept the charge selected for him. Did he
think that no Christian might serve in the Church of England
according to the laws of the realm, and was kneeling at the Lord's
Table not a matter indifferent? To these questions Knox replied that
he thought he could be employed more profitably for Christ
otherwise than in a parish church, adding in a letter describing the
interview that Northumberland had told him to refuse. Apparently
after the Lenten sermon the duke felt that he would be no help if
preaching in London. As for service in the Church of England he
stated that he felt it required much greater reformation, particularly
the right of the minister "to divide and separate the lepers from the
heal," *i.e.* to enforce discipline against manifest sinners, which class
presumably included many on the Council. As for kneeling, since
Christ himself did not kneel but sat at the Last Supper, that was all
that was required of a Christian, since he should follow only Christ's
example. A long argument ensued but finally Knox and the Council
parted on friendly terms.[106] However, probably to keep him from
causing any trouble around London he was commissioned to carry
out his duties as a royal chaplain by going to Buckinghamshire to
preach, his headquarters being located at Amersham.[107]

Knox had now turned down two important positions in the
Church of England, the bishopric of Rochester and the rectorship of
Allhallows. One cannot but wonder why. The answer would seem
to be found in the fact that he was perceptive enough to see that the
state of affairs in England could not continue as they were, which
meant almost inevitably that the country would experience a
resurgence of Romanism, particularly since Edward VI's health was

obviously declining. One outcome of this situation could be Mary Tudor's accession and revived persecution of the Protestants. But even if this did not take place he probably did not wish to become part of an establishment that had so many faults. Remaining unhampered by formal responsibilities and duties, he could criticize more freely and more effectively than if he were in an official position. Thus, whatever happened, he did not desire to become tied down by the rules and regulations of a bishopric or of a London parish. This interpretation is borne out by his comments at the beginning of his exposition of the Sixth Psalm written a little later.[108]

Knox may also have concluded that before long Northumberland, particularly after the very plain spoken Lenten sermons, would try to gain increased control over the church for his own purposes and to silence opposition. If this was his expectation, he did not have long to wait to see his fears realized. When in the parliamentary session of March 1553 Cranmer brought in his revision of the Canon Law which would give the church greater independence and increased powers of discipline, the duke bitterly attacked the clergy, particularly the Lenten preachers, declaring that unless they stopped their anti-government propaganda they would suffer for it. Cranmer hastily backed down, but it was quite obvious to many that the courtiers would not stand for ecclesiastics getting in the way of their economic or political ambitions.[109] Northumberland had tried and failed to bribe Knox to support him, but when Cranmer began to attempt to assert the church's independence, the duke found that the best method of attack was the direct, threatening approach, which for the time being worked.

Meanwhile, other forces were moving in the direction of Northumberland's fall. Some time in January King Edward contracted a cold which soon turned to pulmonary tuberculosis. Northumberland, according to W. K. Jordan, now sought to strengthen his hands by allying himself through the marriage of a son and a daughter with the Greys who had some claim to succeed to the throne. Since at this time (May 21st) it did not seem likely that the king would die, he may not have taken this action with the succession in mind but looked only for political support. As the king grew worse, he himself became increasingly determined that his sister Mary, because of her Roman Catholicism, should not succeed him on the throne. He therefore had drawn up a devise that gave the rights to the crown to Lady Jane Grey, daughter-in-law of Northumberland.[110] By this action everything was thrown into such uncertainty that none of the principal actors could foretell what would happen. Such was the state of affairs when Edward passed away on July 6th.

What of Knox during these trying times? It would seem that he spent most of this period in Buckinghamshire, interrupted perhaps by a foray down into Kent. In June he was back in London, probably staying with the Lockes or the Hickmans, and watching closely what was transpiring. But his stay was short, for when Edward died on July 6th he was already back at his post in Amersham, where shortly afterwards he preached a sermon in which he called upon England to repent for her sins lest great and terrible plagues should come upon her and warned her not to ally herself with the Catholic princes of the Continent who would surely lead her astray.[111] This he must have done at no little risk to himself since many of the soldiers raised by Lord Hastings in Mary's favor were at that time in the area. Some may even have been in attendance at the service.

Meanwhile, Northumberland, realizing his own dangerous position in view of the fact that Mary might succeed in gaining the throne, had sought to have Lady Jane Grey made queen, according to the devise of Edward. It was, however, to no avail, for Mary was generally acknowledged as Edward's successor. Thereupon Northumberland turned around completely, declaring himself a loyal subject of the new Tudor monarch. Now firmly in control, Mary proclaimed toleration for all religions views until parliament had had time to consider matters. In the meantime everything was to remain as it had been. Only Northumberland, Lady Jane, and her husband, and one or two others were imprisoned, but for treason, not for heresy.

Yet despite Mary's call for a standstill in matters religious, no one doubted what the outcome would be. Consequently those who had clung to the old beliefs, despite the statutes against Roman Catholicism, now came out into the open to profess their faith, while the Protestants either prepared to leave the country or steeled themselves to withstand pressure, even persecution, which would seek to force them back into the old paths. Although at the beginning the leading Protestant clergy remained at liberty, the former incumbents of ecclesiastical positions who had been ousted because of their

Romanism, such as Gardiner of Winchester, Bonner of London, and others, were restored to their dignities. By the end of July, the push to bring the country back to papal obedience was on. Pressure was being applied for instance to men such as Sir John Cheke who in June had succeeded Cecil as one of Edward VI's principal secretaries. Then came the turn of clergy such as Richard Cox, Miles Coverdale, and John Hooper.[112] No one knew who would be next.

At this point Knox must have found himself in something of a quandary. Although Amersham was strongly Protestant, he would find little safety there if persecution became general. He, therefore, seems to have returned to London about the time of the proclamation of Mary as queen on July 10th, for he reported later that more than once he had warned the people in Westminster and London, when they were celebrating Mary's accession, of what was going to happen.[113] On September 20th he wrote to Mrs. Bowes that he had been preaching in Kent—perhaps against the Anabaptists. Both his actions and his letters at this time indicate his restlessness and uncertainty, for he was fearful as to what might happen both to England and to himself. The turmoil in his soul shows in two pieces of writing upon which he was working at the time: "A Godly Letter of Warning to the Faithful in London, Newcastle and Berwick," and an exposition of the Sixth Psalm. Neither of these works, however, did he complete before leaving England.[114] Life was much too complicated for intensive literary activity.

One wishes that when writing his letters he had been more explicit in dating them, or that the person who copied them early in the seventeenth century had been somewhat more accurate, for as they now stand they are tantalizing in the vagueness of their indication of the exact time of composition. Consequently, various historians and biographers have suggested different hypotheses concerning his activities during the months following Mary's accession to the throne.

The only letter of this period that is properly dated is the one to Mrs. Bowes written on September 20th, from London. In this he reports that he has been so occupied with his labors in Kent that he has not been able to give much thought to the "process" between herself and her husband over his marriage to Marjory. He thanked God for her boldness on his behalf, but urged her not to give too much thought to the matter, since he might have to flee for his life.

He had written to Sir Richard Bowes, her husband, about the marriage and had sent the letter by "our brother Harie" Wickliffe, who would tell her and Marjory what it contained. He expressed a hope to see them soon, but warned them not to depend upon him, as he was but weak flesh and the gifts of God were not bound to any one person, a clear indication of his state of despondency.[115]

In reply to this letter Knox may have received some further communications from Mrs. Bowes by her son George and Roger Widdrington. Perhaps she suggested that Knox might win over to the idea of the marriage her brother-in-law, Sir Robert Bowes, who would then support Knox's suit. In accordance with this thought, Knox journeyed northward to make contact with Sir Robert, which he did on November 4th. Sir Robert, who was a man of considerable importance in the north country, could not, however, see his niece marrying a Scottish Protestant preacher who was on the run from the authorities. His reply to Knox's appeal for assistance was negative. As Knox, himself, reported his "disdanefull, yea dispytfull, words hath sa persit my hart, that my life is bitter unto me." When Knox tried to argue with him he taunted him with being a Protestant and ended by saying: "Away with your rhetorical reasons! for I will not be persuaded with them." From what we can gather from Knox's letter, Bowes accused him and Mrs. Bowes of planning the marriage themselves without reference to Sir Richard. At this point Knox declared that he hoped he would soon die.[116]

Sir Robert had not merely refused to assist Knox, but had failed to let Marjory and Mrs. Bowes know that he was coming north. Consequently they came to the conclusion that he felt that they were no longer of "our noumber." When he learned this he hastened to assure them that this was not so. He explained that the messenger carrying his letters to them had been seized and the letters taken. Then when he, himself, had sought to visit the two women, presumably at Norham Castle, his companions had persuaded him that since this would be much too dangerous he should escape from England while he could. He adds in his sardonic style that he had left London with only ten groats in his purse but that he had been provided for since then. The Queen or Treasurer, on the other hand, would now be £40 richer for his salary had not been paid.[117]

When he wrote this letter Knox was probably at Newcastle, although this must be a matter of speculation. It is likely that he then

decided to return to the south in the hope of being able to escape
overseas, since Mary had begun to take strong measures against
Protestants and Protestantism. Parliament had enacted a law banning
the use of the second *Book of Common Prayer* after December 1st,
most of the Protestant bishops had been imprisoned, and no doubt his
name had been placed on the list of the "most wanted" men in
England. In another letter to Mrs. Bowes, he pointed out that
because he was so well known in the north, he could not move
around with any freedom, lest he be apprehended.[118] His only hope,
therefore, was to leave England, but with Mary of Guise in control
in Scotland, to go home would be certain death. Safety, therefore,
would lie only in escape to the Continent, and in particular to
Switzerland.

While Lorimer believes that he took ship from Newcastle or from
one of the other northeast ports, this seems doubtful, since such a
January sailing would have been extremely hazardous, if not
impossible. It is more likely, therefore, that he went south in the hope
of obtaining passage to Dieppe from Dover or one of the other
Kentish ports. Before leaving, however, it may be while in London,
he completed the first part of his exposition of Psalm 6 for Mrs.
Bowes. In his concluding paragraph he laments that he cannot see her
and others, but hopes that he will do so soon, either in this life or in
the next. This was written on January 6, 1554. By the beginning of
February he had landed in France.

He left England with a heavy heart. Deprived of the many friends
he had made, and separated from Marjory Bowes whom he loved and
whom he hoped to marry, he doubtless felt very depressed as once
again the coast of France hove into sight. His mind must have gone
back to the day in 1547, only seven short years before when he had
watched those self-same cliffs from the French galley in which he
was a prisoner. Now he was free. He had been forced to flee from
England, a land for which he had developed a deep affection. In his
exposition of the Sixth Psalm, his last writing on English soil he had
penned these words:

> Som tyme I have thought that impossible it had bene, so to remove my
> affection from the Realme of Scotland, that eny Realme or Nation could
> have bene equall deare unto me. But God I take to recorde in my
> conscience, that the troubles present (and appearing to be) in the Realme

of England, are double more dolorous unto my hert, than ever were the troubles of Scotland.[119]

Sad though he must have been, Knox had both learned much during the five years he had spent in England and also exercised a considerable influence, not just in a small area, but on the whole development of the English Reformation. It had been for him a time of intellectual and spiritual growth. While working in the north he had had the opportunity to study and to formulate his ideas on many different matters, particularly on those relating to the Christian faith. His Protestantism was now more solidly based than it had been in Scotland.

His faith, however, was not the only thing about him that had developed. As the minister of a congregation first in Berwick and then in Newcastle he had been obliged as never before to come to grips with others' personal problems and difficulties. From these experiences he became in a true sense a "bishop of souls." His letters to Mrs. Bowes, Mrs. Locke, and others as well as the pamphlets that he wrote later on for those who had been under his pastoral care, reveal this aspect of his growth. He had learned "to weep with them that weep and to rejoice with them that do rejoice." Furthermore, his relations with Mrs. Bowes and his love for Marjory point to the considerable change that was wrought in him as he worked among both the English and the Scottish refugees in the north. He could speak firmly and directly on occasion, but he could also show great patience and tenderness with those in spiritual trouble and doubt. This is a point often forgotten by those who criticize him.

Related to this is the fact that he had also learned to distinguish between essentials and matters indifferent. While Hooper would stir up a great storm over some matter and then back down, Knox learned to count the cost before he made a move. He sought to separate principle from outward practice, appearance from basic reality, shaping his course accordingly. Consequently he frequently won his case, but even when he did he insisted that the principle not the appearance was the real question at issue. We shall see further evidence of this in his actions in Frankfort.

Out of all this he had also come to understand the ways and maneuverings of politicians particularly of great lords and high ecclesiastics whom he had come to distrust. From this time on, he was increasingly unwilling to submit blindly to the civil authorities, even though they were truly "the powers ordained of God." The Christian always had the higher obligation to God's law and the court of God's justice to which he could appeal.

Now all was over and he said "Good night to England."

CHAPTER VI

Sour Notes in
Frankfort-am-Main

SOME TIME IN JANUARY 1554 Knox set foot once again on French soil, but this time as an exile, not as a prisoner. Some of his biographers have tended to feel sorry for him, alone and without friends in a strange land. This, however, was hardly the case, for Scottish trade with France had led to the establishment in various French ports such as Bordeaux, LaRochelle, Le Havre, Rouen and Dieppe, of colonies of Scottish merchants and commercial agents.[1] Of these centers, Dieppe, favored by the activities of freebooters and traders such as Jean Ango (*c.* 1560), was one of the most important. Here a number of Scots thrived on the business opportunities that the town provided.[2] Among these were men such as James Wedderburn, who because of their Protestantism had found it advisable to move to France, particularly to Dieppe where they could live in comparative safety but still keep in constant contact with their homeland.[3] Consequently, although Knox may have felt depressed over the religious situation in England when he left the boat in Dieppe, he would by no means be a friendless outcast on a foreign shore.

He may also have found in Dieppe co-religionists, since Protestantism, contrary to historians' usual statements, had probably reached the town before this date.[4] Although Mary of Guise, when she was met at Dieppe by Henry II in the autumn of 1550, congratulated him that no Huguenots lived in the town, it is doubtful

that her commendations were entirely merited.[5] As various of the
older writers have pointed out, the new doctrines seem to have come
in via the nearby village of Launeray where the weavers and drapers
were reading Calvin's books and singing psalms. The earliest
converts in Dieppe itself were women, perhaps weavers, who would
have contacts with these Protestants. The first person actually named
is Hélène Boucher, a rich bourgeoise involved in the cloth trade, who
is said to have been a correspondent of Calvin and who was the first
Protestant leader in the city. She no doubt received support from
some of her fellow townsmen who participated in the trade with
England as well as from the Scottish Protestant refugees. Knox may
have known some of the Scottish merchants before ever coming to
France.[6]

At this point we have a problem with chronology. Although Knox
has dated some of his writings, they do not always seem to fit
together or agree with other statements. Likewise, his indications of
what he was doing confuse the issue even more. One time reference
which seems to be correct is appended to the conclusion of the first
part of his "Exposition of Psalm 6," in which he states that he
completed it on January 6, 1554 in England, whence he dispatched it
north to Mrs. Bowes. Although he did not date the second part, he
apparently sent it off from Dieppe.[7] The closing sentence of his
"Godly Letter to the Faithful of London, Newcastle and Berwick,"
explains that he finished it on the last of February, as he was leaving
he knew not whither. This letter first appeared in print dated May 8,
1554, purporting to have been printed in Wittenberg by Nicholas
Dorcaster. Only two days later (May 10th) Knox penned a letter of
comfort "to his afflicted brethren in England" from Dieppe after
visiting all the churches in Switzerland.[8] While this may all appear
very straightforward, Calvin wrote to Viret in Lausanne on
February 23rd, a letter of introduction for an unnamed Scot who had
been very active in England under Edward VI and who wished to go
on to Zurich. This no doubt was Knox. But how about the dating?
The English edition of Calvin's letters gives March 9th as the date
which would be a possibility if Knox left Dieppe on February 28th.
In the original Latin, however, the date is clearly "7 Kal. Martius,"
which means February 23rd.[9] What the answer is we do not know,
except that when Knox said he was writing on the last of February,
he may have been using only very general terms.

Apart from the question of dating, the letters, really pamphlets, that Knox wrote from Dieppe, were of considerable importance, since they not only served to encourage and strengthen those undergoing persecution in England, but they also revealed his own state of mind at this time.

In his Exposition of Psalm 6, his sorrow over the situation in England comes out clearly. He reminded Mrs. Bowes that he had frequently predicted troubles were coming even though at the time he could not offer any certain proof of his premonitions. He even added that this was one of his reasons for refusing the bishopric of Rochester. But what troubled him most was that many of those who had made the greatest professions under Edward VI had fallen away and were conforming to Queen Mary's religious changes. He therefore warned Mrs. Bowes against doing the same, reminding her that God had called her and given her courage and strength to resist the enemy: the Devil, her own flesh, and some of her close friends who would have her return to idolatry. She had manifested her fortitude both by the aid that she often gave him when he was faint, and by her ability to reason and speak in such a way that she had also been able to help and comfort others in trouble. He then concluded by saying that although they might never meet again in this life, he would urge her to continue in the faith and never to submit to the idolatry of the Mass. His closing words were "And thairfoir, Mother, be not moveit with any wind, but stick to Chryst Jesus in the day of this his battell." [10] As we read these words, we are brought to a greater realization of the terror and uncertainty of life under which the Protestants both at home and in exile lived from day to day.

"A Godly Letter to the Faithful in London, Newcastle and Berwick," was really an expanded version of his exposition of Psalm 6. Although it appeared first in print on May 8, 1554 professedly published in Wittenberg, we cannot help doubting this attribution. For when it appeared in a second edition on July 2nd, it bore the statement that it had been printed in Rome with papal permission. Knox's sense of humor was apparently coming to the surface once again.[11] Some have held that this letter was sent to England in manuscript where it was published by some clandestine press, but perhaps the simplest explanation is closest to the truth. It may have been published in Dieppe or in nearby Rouen. But as this is also conjecture we shall probably never know for certain.

As in most of his writings Knox based his statements in "The Godly Letter" on Holy Writ, using not only Psalm 6, but also the writings of Jeremiah which he had been studying while in Newcastle with the help of Calvin's commentary. He developed the theme that England was in truth worse than Judah in the days of the prophet, for he, Knox, had warned the Protestants repeatedly of troubles to come, but they had continued in their sinful ways. The same views had been expressed by the Lenten preachers in 1553, but they had had no more effect than Jeremiah. When Edward VI, another King Josiah, had passed away and Mary had come to the throne with Gardiner of Winchester, Bonner of London and Tunstall of Durham as her religious advisers, persecution had commenced, but the nobles unlike those of Judah in Josiah's day had failed to protect the preachers. Instead, they had joined the reactionary forces. Furthermore, few of those who had made great professions before now stood by the preachers, either by open confession or by fleeing into exile. They had apparently paid no attention to his admonitions that "the last Trumpet was then in blawing within the Realme of England, and thairfoir aucht everie man to prepair himself for battell." [12] With this now in view he urged the faithful to refuse to participate in the idolatry of the Mass. As private individuals they could not stop its celebration but they could refuse to attend though it might cost them dearly in worldly goods, even life itself. And he closed with this exhortation:

> O, deare Brethren, remember the dignitie of oure vocation: you haif followit Christ: you haif proclamit warre against ydolatrie: you haif laid hand upon the treuth, and haif communicate with the Lordis Tabill: Will ye now suddenlie slyde back? Will ye refuse Christ and his truth, and mak pactioun with the Devil and his discevable doctrine? Will ye tread the maist precious blude of Chrystis Testament under your feit, and set up an idol befoir the people? Whilk thingis assuredlie ye do as oft as ever ye present your bodies amangis ydolataris befoir that blasphemous ydoll. God, the Father of all mercies, for Chryst his Sonnes sake, preserve you frome that soir temptatioun whose colouris and dangeris verie sorowe will not suffer me to express. . . .[13]

In this letter we must note one or two important points. The first is that while Knox attacks the Mass deploring its reintroduction into England, he blames this reversion on the nobles' infidelity to the Gospel, and above all on the machinations and schemings of the three leading bishops of the old regime. He does not attack Mary, herself, but instead seems to hope that she may experience a change of heart that would turn her towards the Protestant faith so bringing about the confirmation of the Reformation. This conclusion is borne out by "A Confession and Declaration of Prayers," probably written while he was in Newcastle, but now published along with the "Godly Letter." In the "Prayer of Confession" annexed to it, he lamented Edward VI's death, but prayed that Mary and her councillors would be brought to the truth. He was hoping against hope that a change in the Edwardian government's religious policy might not take place. If it did, and England consistently refused to hold to the Gospel, the only answer would be God's wrath and judgment upon both individuals and the nation as a whole.[14]

Some historians and biographers of Knox have criticized him severely for laying down the law to the English Protestants, while he himself had taken care to leave the country. How could he be so apodictical in his statements of what they should do? To understand Knox's position we should note what he said in one of his last letters to Mrs. Bowes before leaving England. He explained that since he was a marked man his friends insisted that he should leave. They felt that his remaining might not only endanger his life, but also theirs.[15] Yet despite his protestations, he does at this time seem to have felt that he had panicked and had run away. In his exposition on Psalm 6 he refers twice to his flight. He insists that it was not the fear of death that had caused him to leave England, and prays that he would soon be restored to the battle that he might once again proclaim the Gospel to his congregation even though it be in the hour of death.[16] In his "Godly Letter" he also urged those who will not submit to the idolatry of the Mass to leave the country, even though it should mean the loss of all worldly goods.[17] Thus he certainly sanctioned the following of his own example. Nevertheless, one can discern in his thinking at this time a certain sense of shame that he had "appeired to play the faynt-heartit and febill souldeour." [18] But this would change as time went by and as he fulfilled his promise to return to the battle.

While writing, and perhaps preparing these pamphlets for the press, Knox had been considering carefully, probably in consultation with his friends in Dieppe, what his next move should be. Word had but recently reached him that Mary of England was contemplating marriage with her cousin Philip of Spain with all that that might entail, including the introduction to England of the Spanish Inquisition. Naturally Knox became very distressed over this possibility. But realizing that at that moment he could do little or nothing concerning events in England, he decided to leave Dieppe for Switzerland, where he could consult the leaders of the Reformation concerning various matters that were troubling him, particularly the right of Mary to hand over her realm to a foreign prince.

As mentioned earlier dating now becomes a problem. If the Latin dating, 7 Kal. Mart., (Feb. 23rd) is correct it is difficult to fit it in with Knox's own statement concerning his date of leaving Dieppe. If, on the other hand, the scribe has inserted the Kalends when the date was really March 7th, all would be clear. Knox could quite easily have travelled by horse from Dieppe to Geneva in a week, as the main roads of France at this time seem to have been in relatively good condition.[19]

Because of the problem of chronology as well as the question of the identity of the anonymous Scot whom Calvin introduced to Viret, some have thought that the person referred to was Christopher Goodman, later a colleague of Knox in Geneva, but he does not fit the picture, for he was English and not Scottish. Moreover, Calvin states that he had played an important part in the Reformation in England under Edward VI, which Goodman certainly had not done. The only Scot who fits the description is Knox, who himself recounted that he spent the period after January 28th travelling through Switzerland reasoning and discussing various matters with the reformed leaders.[20] The date January 28th which he gives as the beginning of his travels, may refer, however, to the date upon which he landed in Dieppe, rather than to the date upon which he left for Geneva.

As far as we can gather, therefore, Knox first arrived in Geneva early in March, and immediately approached Calvin with certain questions, much in the way of a Gallup pollster. Was the son of a king who inherited the throne as a minor to be obeyed as of divine right as a lawful magistrate? Could a woman who bears rule over a country transfer her rights to her husband? Was it obligatory to obey a magistrate who sought to enforce idolatry, and was it lawful for local authorities holding a town by force, to resist such orders? Was it lawful for Christians to support a nobility who were resisting an idolatrous ruler? [21] As we may see, these were leading questions that might apply equally to Scotland, to England, or elsewhere.

Calvin received Knox cordially and gave him verbal answers to his queries.[22] He then passed him on to Viret in Lausanne and finally to Bullinger in Zurich. What Viret had to say we do not know, but Bullinger's answers, which he sent to Calvin, we have in full. They show how cautious he was in all his replies. He agreed that Edward VI was a true and lawful monarch who should be obeyed, a view that by extension would apply also to Mary of Scotland. He was opposed to female rule, but if a woman did come to the throne legitimately she could hand over her rights to her husband if this was according to the law of the land. With regard to resistance to idolatrous rulers, Bullinger insisted that each case would have to be examined on its own merits and action taken prayerfully and with great wisdom. At the same time, he held that death was preferable to idolatry. As for a nobility resisting an idolatrous ruler, circumstances and conscience would have to determine, but above all else hypocrites who would use such rebellion for their own purposes must be removed and all action must be taken in a spirit of repentance always looking unto God. Calvin generally agreed with Bullinger's replies, although he felt that he might have made his views on female rule more explicit. While abhorring it, he admitted that God had given great gifts to Deborah and other women to accomplish his purposes. He added that in case of conflict the only recourse was prayer, since violence blinds those involved in it.[23] In this way the two Swiss leaders sought to avoid any commitment to supporting rebellion which could only harm their cause. Whether Knox received much comfort from their views is doubtful, for he was coming to the conclusion that perhaps only violence could save English Protestantism from destruction.

Having received no great satisfaction from either Calvin or Bullinger, Knox decided to return to Dieppe that he might ascertain how matters were developing in England. What route he followed is difficult to determine. If the imprint on his "Godly Letter" of May 8th is genuine he may have gone via Wittenberg. This would support the contention of Frank Isaac who claims to have proved that Knox's "Faithful Admonition," published after his return to Dieppe and said to have been printed in "Kalykow," was published by Egidius van der Erve in Emden. Knox could easily have passed through Emden on the way to or from Wittenberg.[24] Yet it is strange that he should not have mentioned visiting Germany when reporting to his "afflicted brethren" what he had been doing during the late winter and early spring of the year.[25] The only information that seems certain about his movements after his departure from Zurich, is that he arrived back in Dieppe some time, probably early in April.

The news awaiting him was anything but cheering. Matters had definitely taken a turn for the worse in England. Despite the general support that Mary had received from the Anglican bishops, she obviously had no intention of allowing them to continue in office. Ridley had been ousted as Bishop of London in favor of the previous incumbent, Bonner. Gardiner had returned to his former see of Winchester as had Tunstall to Durham. The Edwardian bishops were at this point confined to their houses or were in jail awaiting trial, on what charges they knew not. What was even more disturbing was the turn around of so many of the laity, particularly the nobles, who were now conforming to the old religion with great enthusiasm.[26]

While these developments naturally discouraged Knox, he also received the comforting news that many of those who had professed conversion during the sunnier days of Edward's reign were remaining true to the Gospel. As in so many continental countries, they were holding meetings in secret for prayer, Bible study and mutual exhortation and comfort, the beginnings of the later Puritan prophecyings. Suffolk and Essex apparently had numerous such informal gatherings, but London seemed to be the center of the underground church, one of whose leaders was John Rough, Knox's former colleague in St. Andrews Castle.[27] Unwilling to submit to government orders concerning matters of religion, these people were prepared to risk persecution for their faith. Others, who had been somewhat prominent in the Edwardian church but who had not been placed under surveillance or arrest, were beginning to flee the country. This sad state of English Protestantism could not but stir the heart of Knox to attempt some form of help and comfort.

The outcome of Knox's concern were "Two Comfortable Epistles to his Afflicted Brethren in England," written in Dieppe on May 10th and 31st. Since the second seems to have been an expanded version of the first, written for a larger audience, they are both alike in their approach and argument. The theme is that both before and after Christ's resurrection the church was in a state of great depression by virtue of persecution, yet God eventually gave the victory. In the same way, the Protestants in England should look forward to ultimate triumph.

> . . . Thairfoir beloved in the Lord, hoip now against all warldlie appeirance, the power of oure God salbe knawin unto his awin glorie in dispyt of theis conjured enemys, whais judgment sall not sleip, but suddanlie sall fall upon them to their perpetuall confusion.[28]

Apparently to strengthen them against charges that because they did not submit to the queen's religious policy they were traitors, he pointed out that all is not lawful or just that is established by civil law, nor is everything sin that ungodly people allege to be treason. Knox's views on political matters were beginning to take shape; although, perhaps under the influence of Calvin and Bullinger, he hastened to add that they could not take the law into their own hands, but must resign their case to God in prayers for deliverance. At the same time, they were not to have a carnal hatred towards the Roman Catholics, but must pray for their repentance, for if the latter did not turn from their evil ways God's judgment would fall upon them, and that very soon. With this note of confidence Knox sought to encourage those who were depressed and uncertain as to what the future might hold.[29]

Having delivered himself of these two exhortations, Knox stayed on in Dieppe for several months, perhaps in the hope that he would find an opportunity to return to England, or at least in order to keep in touch with what was happening to his former congregations. He may well have lived with William Aikman, a Protestant merchant from Edinburgh, who apparently thought it wiser to stay in France than to try to survive in Scotland. As news from England, however, became increasingly dark, Knox soon realized that any plan to recross the Channel was simply out of the question. Not only would he be risking his life, but he would also put those whom he might visit in danger. It was then that he began to write another longer and more vigorous pamphlet under the title of "A Faithful Admonition to the Professors of God's Truth in England." [30] Published on July 20th, it indicates clearly that the six weeks which intervened between his second "Comfortable Epistle" and the "Faithful Admonition" had brought a radical change in his thinking. His reaction to the persecution in England was becoming increasingly violent as he realized that Mary would do everything possible to blot out what she considered to be heresy. One might even say that the publication of the latter pamphlet represented a turning point in his religio-political views.

One of the longest of his publications up to this time, the "Faithful Admonition" was undoubtedly the most important. A preface written by a "banished man from Leicestershire," probably Anthony Gilby, who may also have been in Dieppe at that time and who later served with Knox in the English congregation in Geneva, urged the readers to heed the author's warnings. Knox opens his pamphlet as he does so often by introducing a biblical situation, in this case that of Christ walking on the water, with which he draws a contemporary parallel. He points out that Christ sent away the crowd when it sought to make him, as the English Protestants had done with Edward, a purely secular king. He then likens the storm which caused the disciples to fear to the current persecution, since both were caused by the Devil, working in Knox's day through evil counsellors such as William Paulet, Marquis of Winchester, who changed with every political wind that blew, and through the Bishops of Winchester, London, and Durham who were compulsive persecutors. Nevertheless, the Protestants should realize from Peter's failure to walk on the water through lack of faith that this trouble has come upon them for the same reason. Therefore, if they would but repent and turn to Christ with only a small spark of faith they would be saved, even though persecution should grow hotter as the day of redemption drew nigh.

Up to this point Knox really says nothing particularly new. However, he then goes on to state what he believes to be the basic reasons for the present evil situation. His first charge is against the preachers, including himself, who did not plainly and directly rebuke men's sins as they should. He confesses that he had not moved around the country preaching but had tended to stay in one place, and had even wasted time in taking bodily exercise. He then goes on to castigate the political leaders who had failed in their duties, particularly "miserable Northumberlande" who could not be satisfied until he had taken Somerset's life. He had foreseen all these events as well as Northumberland's eventual overthrow, for many like the duke had supported the Reformation only for their own profit. Even the doctrine of transubstantiation was not demolished until "that reverend father in God, Thomas Cranmer," had cut the devilish sophistry worked out by Gardiner and "his blynd buzzards." Then parliament took away most of the superstitions, except kneeling at the Lord's Table.[31] As we read the pamphlet today, we can feel the mounting tension in Knox's thought as he reviews the situation that had developed in England since Edward VI's death.

He next turns to specific instances from the past. He reminds his readers that in his last sermon before the young king, presumably in Lent, 1553, he had raised the question of why princes retain unfaithful councillors. Some, he had explained, do so because the councillors veil their anti-God attitudes, as did Achitophel, Shebna and Judas in the Bible. Others believe that they cannot rule without them. Although his references to Shebna in his Lenten sermon indicated quite clearly that he was referring to Paulet, he now believes that he should have named names in order to give a clear warning. Yet, despite the Satanic motivation of "wyly Winchester, dreaming Duresme [Durham] and bloudy Bonnar, with the rest of their bloudy, butcherly broode," they will not overcome. Consequently he urges the Protestants to hold up their hands to rejoice in God's mercy and promises of victory.[32]

All this, however, was but an introduction to the final blast, for he next turns his attention to Queen Mary. If, he says, she and Winchester had been executed as they deserved for their idolatry, the present situation would never have arisen. But as they were not, Mary is now referred to as "the most blessed Virgin" by the Archdeacon of London, and she has handed over the country to the pope and to Philip of Spain. By these acts she has dishonored her father who rejected the papacy, and has broken her promises, "to the utter subversion of the whole publicke estate and common wealth of England."[33] Later he adds: "But the saying is too true, that the usurped government of an affectionate [emotional] woman is a rage without reason."[34] He then adds that in all of this she was aided and abetted by Gardiner and Tunstall, who, although they had taken oaths that they would never let the country fall into the hands of a foreign ruler, had done so because Spain would maintain them in power. He also taunts Winchester, who wrote a book defending Henry VIII's ecclesiastical policies, with once again recognizing papal supremacy and with seeking the blood of Cranmer, Latimer and Ridley whose blameless lives are well known and who protected him when he was in danger of execution. Nevertheless, in spite of Mary's and the bishops' apparent success, God will save his elect to give them the victory. The Protestants do not need to strive, but should leave all things in God's hands doing nothing that might divide them from the fellowship of Christ.[35]

In this pamphlet, Knox sounded the trumpet with a harsher note than he had ever done before. Moreover, he now entered more directly into the political arena, but it must be noted, not as a political scientist or even as a political reformer, but as one speaking out against the persecution of God's elect people. Nevertheless, his readers could not but recognize the political implications of what he said. His regret that Mary had not been executed and a violent attack also upon her allies, Charles V and Philip of Spain, as worthy successors of Nero, was virtually a call to rebellion. This he would not deny, for earlier in his "Godly Letter to the Faithful," he had pointed out that this was what Jeremiah had done:

> Lat a thing be heir notit, that the Prophetis of God sumtymes may teache treasone aganis Kings, and yit neither he, nor sic as obeyis the word spokin in the Lordis name be him, offendis God.[36]

Although this sentence does not appear in the printed edition, it seems to have been in the original manuscript letter sent to England. Consequently, while he still taught that the removal of an unfaithful monarch was not the right or duty of a private citizen, he had now moved to a position diametrically opposed to that of the Swiss reformers. He even rejected that of his old friend Balnaves, who in his *Confession* which he had edited, had said:

> Disobey him not; howbeit he bee evill and doe the wrong (which becometh not of his office); grudge not thereat, but pray for him, and commit thy cause to God.[37]

His views on the magistrate expressed in the "Faithful Admonition," were to have an important influence upon much of his future conduct, and upon the development of the Reformation in both England and Scotland.

At the same time, Knox also held firmly to the need for Christian unity in the face of the Devil's opposition. He knew only too well that a church divided within itself would be ineffectual. Therefore,

Christians should avoid conflict with their brethren. While they are required to separate themselves from all such error as that set forth in the Mass, they must also strive to keep the "unity of the Spirit," even though they do not see eye to eye on all details. While this was good Calvinism, it was also the position that Knox had adopted some years earlier when he wrote to his congregations in the north concerning the second *Book of Common Prayer.*[38]

Once he had seen his "Faithful Admonition" through the press, concluding that he could do nothing more for England, Knox decided to leave Dieppe for Geneva. There he planned to spend his time studying Greek and Hebrew which would give him a greater understanding of the Scriptures.[39] In so doing he was following the example of other refugees such as Lever, later his colleague in Frankfort, who likewise sought to study under the guidance of the eminent leaders of the Swiss Reformation.[40] Moreover, considering the direction affairs were now taking in England, he probably felt that he would soon have many companions in exile. About the beginning of August, therefore, he bade Dieppe farewell.

At the same time that Knox was setting out for Geneva, the Marian government in England was putting in motion the machinery that would eventually light the fires of Oxford, Gloucester, and Smithfield. Cranmer, Latimer and Ridley were already under arrest; Miles Coverdale and John Hooper had both been summoned to appear before the Privy Council which committed Hooper to the Fleet prison and commanded Coverdale to await the Lords' pleasure. Coverdale knew, however, that their pleasure would not bring him any, so he promptly fled to the Continent.[41] Shortly afterwards Mary and Philip of Spain were united in marriage which served to alarm the Protestants even more. Some, such as Sir William Cecil, conformed, retaining their offices and positions. Many others, however, of a more courageous and radical character, refusing to submit, suffered martyrdom. Most important for Knox, however, were the 800 or more who packed up and left for Germany and Switzerland.[42]

One question that arises in connection with the Protestant migrants from England is were they organized, or was this movement the spontaneous action of a large number of individuals? Christina H. Garrett in *The Marian Exiles* (1938) insists that the migration was the concerted and planned action of a defeated political party. with religious commitments, who went abroad to preserve themselves and to better resist Mary's government. She believes that Sir William Knollys visited the Continent in September 1553 to spy out the land, and that the continental Protestants who had found refuge in England went on in advance to prepare the way in Zurich, Wesel, Emden, Strasbourg, and Frankfort. Once the continental refugees were settled, Cecil, with the help of merchants and bankers, organized various groups of Englishmen who then left the country some five months before persecution really commenced. The students went to Zurich, while the merchants, artisans, and gentry located themselves in the other cities where they established churches "upon the Genevan model." [43]

Although this is a very interesting hypothesis since little hard evidence seems to be forthcoming in its support, most of the proof is circumstantial. Furthermore, much of the ascertainable information seems to run counter to Miss Garrett's reconstruction. For one thing, as Southgate has pointed out, the refugees were by no means all Puritans, and what is more, it is strange that if they had indeed set up churches "upon the Genevan model," they should all at first have avoided Geneva.[44] Added to this, as Conyers Read has shown, no evidence exists to indicate that Cecil organized the movement. Indeed, some of the exiles felt that he had compromised his Protestant position seriously in order to retain his government offices.[45] Most important of all, however, the Marian exiles were themselves very much divided on ecclesiastical, social and political issues. Consequently the idea of an underlying "conspiracy" to set up a "government-in-exile" seems to have been far from their minds.[46]

The most that we can say about the movement of the refugees is that we have no evidence of any long distance group planning. Peter Martyr and Heinrich Bullinger reported from Zurich that a number of students had been financed by some merchants to reside there in order to continue their education in preparation for returning to England. These did not even form an English colony, but lived in the homes of some of the citizens.[47] The only other group that seems to have followed any predetermined plan was the one at Strasbourg,[48] made up of men who had been leaders in the Protestant "Establishment" under Northumberland, and who generally had supported Northumberland's take over. They sought to maintain the organizational structure and form of worship by law established in order that they might have a truly English church in exile. We cannot go as far as Southgate in calling them "a virtual centre of opposition to the Calvinists" since many agreed with Calvin in doctrine.[49] Strongly "Anglican" in their outlook, they felt that they should supervise and direct the groups of exiles living in the four or five other centers in Germany and Switzerland.[50] To maintain "the face of an English church," however, was not easy, for the refugees, now free from any coercive governmental control, were at liberty to accept or reject what had been established under Edward VI. It was at this point that trouble arose.[51]

Among the exiles were men who had not been happy with the ecclesiastical, social or political developments in Edwardian England. Some who had sympathized with the "Commonwealth Men" in social policy, or who had supported Somerset against Northumberland, or who had favored Hooper and Knox in their struggles against the authoritarianism of Cranmer and Ridley, did not head for Strasbourg, but set themselves up in cities such as Emden, Wesel, or other places where they hoped to worship as they pleased. Usually, however, because of Lutheran intolerance they soon found it necessary once again to move. They could of course settle in Strasbourg, but since the views of the "Establishment" element did not appeal to them, they tended instead to gravitate to Frankfort-am-Main.[52] Then came a struggle as to whether the congregation in Frankfort or the congregation in Strasbourg would dominate the English refugee colonies. At this time Knox became involved with important results both for himself and for the English Reformation as a whole.

On Mary's accession to the throne, the foreign Protestant congregations had promptly decided that they should leave England for they had already tasted something of life under a Roman Catholic ruler. The members of the Flemish and German congregation in London went to Germany, eventually settling in Emden. The Walloon weavers who had been living on Somerset's lands in Gloucestershire having received a passport from Mary early in September 1553 left, and eventually, after some difficulties with Lutherans in other cities arrived in Frankfort under the leadership of Vauville.[53] Their acceptance in this city they owed to the support given them by Melanchthon and one of the city councillors, Johann von Glauberg, who had studied at Wittenberg, but was also on good

terms with the Strasbourg reformers.[54] Valerian Poullain, the
minister of the congregation, who had waited to take part in a
disputation on the eucharist held in Westminster in October,
subsequently joined his flock in their new location. When he
presented to the city authorities the congregation's confession of faith
and form of worship, they granted him the use of the former White
Nun's Church. At the same time he also obtained permission for any
English refugees who wished to, to join his church if they would
conform to his doctrine and polity. Significantly five Englishmen
signed the original request, and Anne Hooper, the wife of the
imprisoned bishop, who had come over with the Walloons, was a
member of the congregation.[55] The way was now open for the
advent of any Englishmen who did not care for the rule of the
"Establishment" in Strasbourg.

That Frankfort should appeal to the English exiles as a refuge is
hardly surprising. It was the location of some of the most important
fairs in Europe, especially the book-fair, whence had come a good
portion of the literature that had brought Protestantism to England.
In such an international center, the refugees would meet other
Protestants from all over Europe. Furthermore, its economic position
would offer them opportunities for employment by which they could
support themselves, a very necessary consideration. Probably of equal
importance, however, was the fact that the Englishmen already
established there as merchants or factors would be more tolerant of
deviation from the established forms of worship and church organization which the exiles in Strasbourg wished to maintain. Consequently
the more radical English reformers tended to move to Frankfort
where, under the aegis of the Walloon congregation, they found
what they believed to be a more thoroughly reformed church.

The reason for their belief that Poullain's congregation was more
truly reformed stemmed from the order of service and confession he
had used in England and was now following in Frankfort.[56] Based on,
and in many ways similar to the simple order devised by Calvin
when he was pastor in Strasbourg, it allowed much freedom to the
minister, although the heart of the service remained the preaching of
the Gospel.[57] Some have attempted to claim that Poullain's liturgy
and the other early Reformed service books were based upon the
eucharistic service of the Roman Catholic Church. But in view of the
separation in all their liturgies of the Lord's Supper from the regular

service of worship, the emphasis on the central position of the sermon and the belief that the Mass was idolatrous, this interpretation of Poullain's, Calvin's, or Knox's forms of service has little in its favor.[58] One cannot but suspect that much of the desire on the part of some modern interpreters to show that the Medieval and the Reformed churches' worship was not too far apart arises from the wish to foster present day ecumenical projects. Poullain's form of service certainly did not fit into the pattern prescribed by the English prayer book.

Although some of the English Protestants who signed the original documents submitted to the Frankfort city council were present probably on business, the first considerable group of recognized exiles arrived in June of 1554 led by William Whittingham, Edmund Sutton, William Williams, and Thomas Wood and their households. These could have joined the French-speaking congregation, but since many of them, in typical English fashion, knew no French, they felt that they should organize their own church. To this the Frankfort authorities agreed, as long as they did not deviate materially from the doctrine and practices of the Walloons. Quite content with such limitations, the English having drawn up a simple form of common prayer similar to, but not exactly the same as Poullain's, began services in July.[59]

Jeremy Collier, representing the Anglican point of view, explains that "the English gave in to the German and French novelties and refined to a considerable alteration upon their own Common Prayer-book. . . . The reason was, because the reformed in those countries would be somewhat shocked with these ceremonies." [60] The members, however, had another explanation. Once they had settled matters to their own satisfaction, they sent off letters to the other exile congregations pointing out the privileges they had been granted and inviting them to come to Frankfort where "they might heare gods worde truly preached, the Sacraments rightly ministered and Discipline used, which in their owne countrie could never be obtained." [61]

From this statement we can draw some conclusions that shed light on later events. Whittingham and the other leaders of the congregation in Frankfort had never been prominent in the church before leaving England. Indeed, a number of them had spent part of the reign of Edward VI studying on the Continent, for generally they were younger men. In Geneva in 1552 Whittingham himself had become a disciple of Calvin, so that his sympathies would clearly be with the preachers of the Lenten sermons in 1553, and with Knox in his desire to change the Prayer Book.[62]

This conclusion receives support from the form of service drawn up by the Frankfort congregation. Many of the practices prescribed in the *Book of Common Prayer*: answering aloud to the minister and the use of the Litany, surplices and other vestments, were all abolished, while in the Lord's Supper kneeling to receive the elements was removed. The new service provided that the minister would commence by repeating a confession, followed by a psalm sung by the congregation in a plain tune, according to the Genevan custom. He would then pray for the enlightenment of the Holy Spirit and proceed to preach. Following the sermon the minister would pray for all men, particularly for England. The service would conclude with the congregation singing another psalm, followed by the benediction.[63] Although Pocok erroneously regards this as the culmination of a foul Calvinist plot originated at the beginning of Edward VI's reign by Somerset, "a rank Calvinist," to set up a Calvinistic church in England, we can hardly doubt that those responsible for this order of worship, did indeed hope that if ever they should return home it would replace the second *Book of Common Prayer*.[64] Consequently, with the establishment of this congregation under the leadership of John MacBray, a Scottish refugee who was elected minister for the time being, a new form of English Reformed church came into existence.[65]

The plan of the Frankfort congregation appears to have been first to set up a church that conformed to their views of the Reformation, and then to invite all the other English refugees to come to Frankfort to join with them. Like the Puritans at the end of the century, they wished for a Reformation "without tarrying for any." In this way they hoped to create a unity which might bring about a complete change in the church in England if ever they should return.

The letter that they dispatched on November 15th to the students at Zurich made this clear. It urged them to move to Frankfort where they would have great liberty, assuring them that the new form of service removed from the Prayer Book only those things that might cause scandal in a foreign land and which were clearly unscriptural. In so doing the exiles in Frankfort had not in any way hurt the people imprisoned for the faith in England, nor had they done despite to Edward VI's ordinances, since even Cranmer and Ridley themselves had already altered the first Prayer Book. To the congregation at Strasbourg they presented much the same argument at the beginning of December, urging unity and insisting that they had altered the *Book of Common Prayer* only as far as circumstances and the Bible required.[66]

To these arguments, however, neither the students at Zurich nor the bishops at Strasbourg would give their assent. Both groups insisted that the Prayer Book must be retained, as it was biblical in most matters. Chambers who came over to Frankfort from Strasbourg early in the autumn consented to the removal of those ceremonies that did not seem quite politic—presumably some that were not exactly in harmony with Poullain's liturgy. But he was not prepared to accept the much simplified service devised by Whittingham and his group. Clearly conflict was beginning to develop between the Frankfort congregation and the representatives of the Edwardian "Establishment."[67]

It was into this situation that Knox found himself somewhat suddenly thrust. As soon as the Strasbourg group had heard of developments in Frankfort, Edmund Grindal, had written to John Scory at Emden, asking him to take charge of the newly organized congregation. Thereupon Scory had written offering his services. Some time later, Grindal and his confreres wrote to Frankfort suggesting that Ponet, Scory, Bale, or Cox might take over the direction of the work. Since all these men had either been bishops or high in the hierarchy of the church establishment, the Strasbourg exiles no doubt felt that this would ensure conformity to the established structures and form of worship. Whittingham and his brethren, however, seeing through this move, replied that since the choosing of a minister was a matter for the congregation itself to decide, they had already issued calls to Haddon at Strasbourg, Lever at Zurich, and Knox at Geneva. It would seem, however, that both Haddon and Lever came under pressure from the "establishment," with the result that they declined. Knox would have done likewise, as he was much more interested in staying in Geneva working at his books, had not Calvin pressed him to accept the invitation. After much heart-searching he finally agreed to serve and arrived in Frankfort early in November.[68]

Knox now found himself immediately plunged into controversy.

over the use of the second *Book of Common Prayer.* In this situation
his position was particularly difficult since not only had he been
called to Frankfort without the approval of the "establishment" in
Strasbourg, but he was also known as one who in England had
criticized the liturgy and had called upon his congregations in
Berwick and Newcastle to pray for a change to a different order. As
he stated in 1558 he had employed in his English churches a form of
baptism and Communion:

> prepared, used and ministered in all simplicitie, not as man had devised,
> neither as the King's proceedings dyd alowe, but as Christ Jesus dyd
> institute, and as it is evident that Saincte Paule dyd practise.[69]

He was, however, quite prepared to accept the Frankfort order,
based upon Poullain's *Liturgia*, even if he had some doubts about it,
in the hope of maintaining unity within the body of exiles.

Shortly after Knox's arrival, Edmund Grindal and Richard
Chambers, arrived to discuss the possibility of the Strasbourg and
Zurich groups' uniting in Frankfort with Knox and his congregation.
No agreement, however, could be reached on the subject of the form
of worship, for the two visitors insisted that the Prayer Book was the
only form of service allowable. To this the majority of the
congregation would not agree. The exiles in Strasbourg and Zurich,
therefore, refused to move. The reaction in Frankfort was then to
adopt Calvin's *Forme des Prières*, but Knox opposed this unless the
other exile colonies were prepared to follow suit. It seems to have
been his view that if they could reach agreement on this matter they
would be in a good position to bring about further reform if and
when they should return home. At this point Lever arrived from
Zurich, perhaps sent as a fifth columnist, to work with the
"establishment" element in the congregation, but he failed to win
over the majority to accepting even a somewhat modified Prayer
Book. Knox took the stand that he could not use the Anglican liturgy
because there were more superstitious elements in it than kneeling at
the Communion. Therefore, if the congregation adopted it, he would
let Lever administer the Communion while he contented himself
with preaching. Should the congregation not accept this compromise,
he would leave. This was rejected, however, and on the advice of
Calvin, who had expressed his doubts about the Prayer Book, another
order was drawn up as a compromise, to continue in use until April

of the next year (1555) when it would be reviewed. To this all agreed, and peace seemed assured.[70]

From February 6 to March 13 peace indeed reigned, but on the latter date Dr. Richard Cox and a company arrived from Strasbourg, and immediately made application to join the congregation. Cox, formerly a tutor of Edward VI and Chancellor of Oxford University, had been very much involved in preparing the second Prayer Book. Moreover, he was the typical bureaucratic church official, by no means unknown in our own day.[71] Although he had in 1551 written to Bullinger that he wished "all things in the church should be pure, simple and removed as far as possible from all elements and pomps of this world," he was apparently convinced in 1555 that the Prayer Book must be used in Frankfort.[72] Indeed, it seems likely that he had been dispatched from Strasbourg for the purpose of forcing it on the congregation. At the first service they attended, he and his companions insisted that they should follow the *Prayer Book*, but when this was refused by the elders at the morning service, they carried on anyway, answering the minister with responses. At this point Lever coming out in his true colors, swung over to their side. Despite his promises to maintain the compromise liturgy, he used the Litany from the Prayer Book in the service. The battle was on once more.[73]

At the afternoon service Knox preached the sermon in which he made a frontal attack upon the *Book of Common Prayer*. He pointed out that at first he had thought it had some merit, but had now come to the conclusion that it contained many things improper and wrong, which he was prepared to prove. He then attacked the whole Church of England as being only half reformed since it had no discipline, had insisted that such a man as Hooper should be ordained as a bishop with all kinds of unbiblical trifles and frills, and had condoned pluralism even among the bishops. This outburst naturally brought a violent reaction on the part of Cox and his faction with the result that a congregational meeting was convened to consider the whole matter. Those who demanded that the church must have "an English face," now confronted those who insisted on a Reformed church along what one might call international lines. Yet even at this point Knox did not take a hard stand, perhaps because he believed he had the majority behind him. When the question of the Coxians' right to participate in the meeting was denied by the congregation, Knox

persuaded them to allow Cox's group to become members. He may
have thought that this would make them a little more amenable to
compromise, but he was sadly mistaken.

No sooner were Cox and his company admitted to full membership in the congregation than they linked up with the minority
that followed Lever, to become the majority. Once in power they
immediately forbade Knox to preach. At this point the city council,
apparently surfeited with the squabbling of the Englishmen, sent
Glauberg to tell them that they must adhere strictly to Poullain's
order. To this Cox agreed, but when he, Whittingham, Lever and
Knox met in Poullain's house to give his liturgy an English form,
they promptly locked horns over the introduction of unbiblical
statements and practices. When Knox did not submit to Cox's
pressures he began to receive threats that unless he did, worse would
befall him. This move, however, had little effect, for he replied to
Edward Isaack, former Sheriff of Kent, who made the threat "That I
could wish my name to perish, so that God's book and glory might
only be sought among us." [74] This was a direct challenge to the
Strasbourg group.

Cox and his supporters now determined to run rough-shod over
the objections of the majority of the members of the original
congregation, to have Knox either imprisoned or expelled from
Frankfort. As we read the accounts of the anonymous author of the
Brieff Discourse of the Troubles at Frankfort, of Knox and of various
others involved, we cannot but receive the impression that this
conflict between Cox and Knox also had a personal aspect that
probably went back to their days in England. It may be that Cox was
determined to "get" Knox for his objections in 1552 to the second
Prayer Book. But whatever the cause, we cannot doubt that Cox's
dislike, if not hatred, of Knox went very deep, for he and his
supporters now charged him before the City Council with *lèse-majesté* against Mary of England and Charles and Philip of Spain, citing
as proof statements from his recently published *Faithful Admonition
to England*. When the magistrates, understandably nervous because
of the proximity of Charles and his army in Augsburg, considered
Knox's remarks, they became even more worried, and summoning
Williams and Whittingham, they told them that Knox must leave
immediately.[75]

Knox's reaction to the news of his expulsion was that when

attackers upon true preachers have no other means of silencing them, they use the old cry of, "He is not Caesar's friend." This was the theme of the last sermon that he preached to some fifty of his followers who met with him in his lodging the night before he left Frankfort. The next morning he set out upon his return to Geneva, accompanied for the first few miles by his friends "who with great heaviness of harte and plentie of teares committed him to the Lorde." [76] One may suspect, however, that as Knox travelled towards Switzerland, his heart was considerably lighter than it had been when he reluctantly departed from Geneva to answer the call from Frankfort.

By the time he arrived in Geneva, notice of his coming had already been given by a letter from Whittingham to Calvin explaining what had happened. Shortly afterwards another letter arrived, this time from Cox and his principal supporters, exculpating themselves from any blame, by asserting that while they had abolished everything in the Prayer Book that was superstitious or unbiblical, Knox and his faction had still refused any compromise. At the same time Cox insisted that the actions of the congregational meeting were quite legal. To this communication Calvin replied with a carefully worded letter in which, while he sought to avoid stirring up any further trouble, he clearly stated "that Master Knox was, in my judgment, neither godly nor brotherly dealt withall." The leaders in Frankfort angered by this rebuke replied with some asperity that it was really all Knox's fault not only because he was factious, but even more, because his *Admonition* was responsible for starting the fires of persecution in England. Nobody had been burned until after the appearance of his pamphlet, so apparently *post hoc, propter hoc,* since the one followed on the other they were related as cause and effect, a somewhat dubious inference without any empirical evidence. At the same time, they also admitted that other reasons existed for their wanting to get rid of him, which may point to the true cause of the whole controversy. [77] But what these reasons were, no one anywhere indicates.

And what of Knox's followers who remained in Frankfort? Whittingham and the others apparently hoped that once Knox's personality was out of the picture, they would be able to reach some kind of compromise with the victors. This, however, was simply impossible. Although Cox, as he reported to Calvin, had modified the

Prayer Book to a certain extent, he was not prepared to give it up completely. The outcome was further conflict, in which even Lever became involved on the "nonconformists' " side. The battle eventually reached such a pitch that Whittingham with a number of his supporters sought to set up a separate congregation in connection with Poullain's church, but Cox succeeded in blocking that plan. Whittingham and those with him then decided to move. Even this Cox sought to frustrate but in spite of his efforts the dissidents left in August for Geneva, or, as in the case of John Foxe, the martyrologist, for Basle.[78] Although Whitehead along with Horne took charge of the remaining congregation, they had nothing but trouble, for the majority wished to govern themselves without dictation from Strasbourg, and by February Horne was reporting to Bullinger that the congregation was "almost ruined." [79]

Although some modern historians have, presumably in the interests of "ecumenical understanding," sought to play down the differences between the Coxian and the Knoxian parties in Frankfort, we can hardly escape the conclusion that the conflict over the form of worship, actually grew out of differences of principle.[80] Certainly we can detect personal antagonisms, particularly in the case of Cox towards Knox, which may have exacerbated the dispute. The real issue was, however, whether tradition, albeit of only some three or four years life, should determine forms of church worship and polity, or whether the pattern should come from the New Testament only. With Cox's insistence that the *Book of Common Prayer*, albeit with some modifications, must determine the form of English worship, and with the attempt of the exiled bishops to control the Frankfort congregation, especially in the choice of a minister, a confrontation could not but take place. Therefore, the views of some of the older historians such as P. Hume Brown and P. Lorimer, as well as those of the more recent writers such as P. Collinson and W. M. Southgate, give a somewhat truer picture when they say that out of the Frankfort conflict came the division that led to the rise of a non-conforming Puritanism.[81] As Christopher Goodman put it in 1558 when writing to Peter Martyr, he was sorry for the controversy, but not that he had stood for the truth against

> those who have so pertinaciously endeavoured to load the free consciences of the brethren with unprofitable ceremonies and paltry ordinances of men.[82]

We can see from what happened in Frankfort, that Knox played an important part in laying the groundwork for a movement which has left its mark on English history down to the present time. From our perspective, however, we must also ask what effect this controversy had on him. While he had striven to maintain the unity of the faith, he had found that he could not do this in worship since his modifications and changes in the Prayer Book had been rejected by those who represented the Reformed Church of England. Following on Hooper's failure to change episcopal ordination, and his own only partial success in altering the second *Book of Common Prayer*, he now seems to have realized that he could do nothing more to purge the English church of the "dregs of popery." It may also have been that as a result of his experiences both in England and Frankfort, he had become disenchanted with Englishmen generally. Some have claimed that his attitude to England expressed in the conclusion of the first part of the exposition of Psalm 6 still remained, but this one may well doubt. When Elizabeth ascended the throne in 1558, he did not ask to return to England but only to pass through to Scotland, a request that Elizabeth denied. It would seem, therefore, that he decided to leave the Englishmen to themselves, and when the opportunity came to devote his attention to the reforming of the church in Scotland.

CHAPTER VII

The Most Perfect Schole of Christ

THE TIME THAT KNOX spent in Geneva (1555–1559) after his return from Frankfort was perhaps the most formative in his life. During this period he had the opportunity both to devote himself to study, which increased his understanding of the Scriptures and of theology, and to make contact with Calvin as well as various other Protestant leaders who visited the city, which added much to his knowledge and broadened his horizons. Under these influences many of his own ideas which seem hitherto to have been rather amorphous, began to take more specific form in his mind, with the result that when he returned to Scotland he was prepared to assume a position of leadership in the movement for religious reform.

The year 1555 saw Calvin's final triumph in Geneva. He had been opposed since his return in 1541 by the Libertines who disliked his idea of establishing a strict private and public morality, as well as by others such as Jacques Gruet, Jerome Bolsec and Michael Servetus who had attacked Calvin personally, or, what was more important to him, had rejected his teaching. With the execution of Servetus in 1553 by a Libertine controlled government, most of the opposition had been snowed under. Nevertheless, one last cause of complaint still remained: the influx of Protestant refugees, principally from France, but also from many other countries. The Libertines, led by the strongly anti-refugee Ami Perrin, made the mistake, when a riot broke out on May 16, 1555, of supporting the rioters, with disastrous results for themselves. The city government, now largely composed of Calvin's supporters, cracked down hard. Some of the rebel leaders were executed; others fled for safety to Berne, leaving Calvin's supporters in full control, at which the refugees naturally rejoiced.[1]

Whether Knox paid any attention to the stirring events taking place in Geneva soon after his arrival in town, we do not know, for he makes no mention of them. That they were known within a short time in Strasbourg is indicated by Sir John Cheke's letter to Calvin congratulating him on his victory.[2] Knox, although he could not have been ignorant of what was going on seems to have concentrated on his studies and the cultural side of Geneva, rather than on the political. And despite some statements to the contrary, Geneva did have a blossoming cultural life. Some historians in referring to the city place all their stress on Calvin's efforts to curb vice and immorality, while viewing Geneva as a provincial town with a provincial outlook.[3] This, however, is hardly an accurate description of the city in the 1550's.

For one thing, with the increase of persecution in France after Henry II's accession to the throne in 1547, a considerable number of the leading Huguenots, many of them nobles or gentry moved to Geneva. Along with them went merchants, printers, and scholars of repute. At the same time with mounting attacks on Protestants in Italy, in Lucca, Ferrara, and other places, many Italians also were forced to leave for Geneva.[4] Besides these largest of the groups, smaller bodies made up of English, Dutch, Germans, Spaniards, and Poles all settled under Calvin's aegis. Names such as Budé, Caracciolo, Bodley, Crespin, Estienne, and Marot indicate that Geneva provided a home for a cosmopolitan and cultured body of refugees who fitted in well with the elite of the city itself.[5]

These people welcomed by Calvin, caused a considerable efflorescence of letters and music. Jean Crespin and Henri Estienne set up their printing presses which quickly began producing works of all kinds and in many different languages. Although the main interest was probably theology, books of poetry, satire, history, political theory and similar subjects also appeared in print.[6] Similarly music, under the influence of Louis Bourgeois, Claude Goudimel, and Guillaume Franc, had an important place in the city's life. Calvin's interest in the psalms for congregational singing lay at the basis of this development, but the composers went considerably farther than just producing common meter psalm church tunes. As one author has pointed out the musical developments in Geneva laid the ground-work for a new and fresh approach to popular music.[7] These formed but two areas of the Genevan cultural development.

At the same time the refugees brought with them not only money but also new trades and professions. While a number were shoe-makers, tailors, weavers and the like, others were "great merchants" and many were doctors, lawyers or teachers. Probably most important of all were the printers: the two Estiennes, Crespin, Badius, Hall and others who helped to make Geneva the center of the Reformed publishing trade, competing with Basle and Lyon, the other two centers of Protestant book production. Thus, the refugees were by no means beggars or parasites, but contributed generously to the development of the Genevan economy.[8]

In a city such as this new ideas were continually floating in the air. While theological views might be rather carefully scrutinized at the weekly meeting of the *consistoire,* other ideas seem to have been subject to few controls. Censorship of books or pamphlets was apparently rather loose, as is indicated by the fact that Calvin knew nothing of Knox's *First Blast of the Trumpet* until a year after its publication by Crespin.[9] In this atmosphere of freedom, constant theological debate, discussion with refugees coming to settle or just passing through, Knox experienced a stimulation he had never known before. Yet withal, the stimulus was always within a Christian context. We can understand, therefore, his comment to Mrs. Locke:

> I nether feir nor eschame to say, [it] is the maist perfyte schoole of Chryst that ever was in the erthe since the dayis of the Apostillis. In other places, I confess Chryst to be trewlie preachit; but maneris and religioun so sinceirlie reformat, I have not yit sene in any uther place. . . .[10]

Although Knox enjoyed the new environment free from the bickering of Frankfort, the self-seeking of the nobles of England, and the lawlessness and turmoil of his own native land, he did not savor his peace and quiet for very long. Because of various pressures, after six months in Geneva he decided, apparently quite suddenly, to return to Scotland where he arrived in September 1555. As his activities in that country, however, belong to another part of his story we shall leave them for consideration later.

Meanwhile as we have seen, with his departure from Frankfort "the establishment" party in Strasbourg gained control of the English congregation with the result that William Whittingham and Anthony Gilby along with other more radical Protestants moved to Geneva, where they arrived in October 1555, just after Knox had left for Scotland.[11]

When the Frankfort non-conformists reached Geneva they found some twenty other English refugees already settled there. Among these were even a few who had opposed Knox in Frankfort, but who had left shortly after he had been ousted. For example Thomas Lever and William Amondsham had arrived during the summer to join Sir William Stafford and others who had come directly from England.[12] Therefore, when through Calvin's good offices, Whittingham, Wood, and Gilby obtained permission to set up an English church in Geneva, the congregation began in November 1555 with a membership of about fifty.[13] Once established, they followed the Frankfort example of writing to the other English refugee groups inviting them to move to Geneva. Although no great number immediately rushed to join the new colony, Englishmen began gradually to drift in, some to settle and others to stay for a while and then move on. Altogether the total number of English in Geneva never amounted to more than 213, about 25% of all the Marian exiles. Nevertheless, they were a very dynamic group that later had an important influence upon Protestantism in England and Scotland.[14]

In any attempt to analyze the composition of this body we must depend largely upon the *Livre des Anglois* which records the names of 113 households containing 186 individuals. To this number we should add twenty-seven from the *Régistre des Habitants*, making a total of 213. The economic and social pattern which emerges gives us some understanding both of the development of the congregation in Geneva and of its members' policies and actions after their return home. It is as follows:

	IN GENEVA	TOTAL EXILES
Gentry	30	166
Merchants	10	40
Artisans	13	32
Students	20 (SOME GENTRY)	119
Priests and *ex-religious*	8	67

Besides these we find a few who are denominated "preachers"
without further description and some whose occupations are not
recorded. Only four appear to have had any close connection with
agriculture.[15] One may say, therefore, that the congregation consisted largely of either gentry or city dwellers, representing the two
social classes that tended to be radical in their religious and political
outlooks, and to whom Knox made a special appeal.

From its inception on November 1st, the congregation declared
itself to be "truly reformed." As a number of historians have pointed
out it was indeed the first Puritan church. Christopher Goodman and
Anthony Gilby were elected the acting ministers "in the absence of
John Knox," whom apparently they still regarded as their minister
by virtue of his call to Frankfort. Yet they were not content merely
to have some rather informal organization under the direction of a
minister or two. They believed that they must set up a completely
structured body both for their own benefit and also for the purpose of
preparing for the time when they would return to England. It was
because of this organization and pattern, planned and established in
Geneva, that they wielded such an influence on the other exiles and
upon the English church as a whole after 1558.[16]

Although the working out of a constitution and a form of worship
for the congregation took place while Knox was absent in Scotland,
one cannot doubt that his influence was felt by those who did the
work. As their basic premise they adopted from Poullain's *Liturgia
Sacra*, the statement that the marks of the church were the true
preaching of the Word, the proper administration of the sacraments
and the upright enforcement of discipline. For the effective imple-
mentation of these objectives, both the congregation as a whole and
the civil magistrates in their official capacity, had a God-given
responsibility.[17] Therefore, they sought to draw up an order of
worship, a confession of faith and a system of discipline, by which the
church would not have "the face of an English church" but the marks
of a Christian church, transcending national distinctions.

On February 10, 1556 *The Forme of Prayers and Ministration of
the Sacraments etc.* came from the press of Jean Crespin. It consisted
in a confession of faith, an order of worship, and a form of
government which now at last established a truly Reformed church
such as they had sought both in England and Frankfort. The
character of the whole was summed up in Whittingham's introduc-

tion which laid down the principle that everything in the Christian Church's confession, worship and discipline must be determined by the Word of God. Even the singing in public worship was to be limited to the inspired words of the Psalms. No room was left for custom, tradition or philosophy. The basic motif, therefore, was quite different from that of the *Book of Common Prayer* and of the form of organization established under Edward VI.[18] This the authors of the book wished to make quite clear as they addressed it "to our bretherne in Englande, and elsewhere . . ."

The order of worship followed a very simple pattern with its central point "The Interpretation of Scripture." The liturgy consisted of a confession of sins, the singing of a psalm, the prayer of invocation, the sermon followed by questions and discussion, the pastoral prayer, another psalm, and the benediction. That the service of worship is called "the interpretation of Scripture" indicates clearly the purpose in mind, *i.e.* instruction. Moreover, the fact that at that time "it is lawfull for every man to speake or enquire, as God shall move his harte, and the text occasion," indicates that the service was to be quite informal. This interpretation is supported by the absence of set prayers which, as in the case of the Prayer Book, the minister would have to use. He was at liberty to organize the service very much as he pleased, as long as it was informal and centered on the Bible.[19]

With regard to the administration of the sacraments, the same attitude prevailed. Baptism was to be administered at "the common prayer and preaching." [20] The Lord's Supper, on the other hand, was to be celebrated once a month or as often as the congregation determined. One finds no indication that the authors believed that the Lord's Supper must be celebrated at every service of worship or "common prayer." Moreover, when celebrated, it was to be dispensed to the congregation in as simple a manner as possible. The minister was to sit at the table with the congregation, break the bread, give thanks and distribute to all. The same was to be the action with the wine. A final thanksgiving followed by a psalm and the benediction would conclude the service, "so that without his woorde and warrante, there is nothing in this holy action attempted." [21] In all of this one is reminded of the services of such present day groups as the Plymouth Brethren.

Over the past few decades various efforts have been made in some circles to prove that the *Form of Prayers* of the English Genevan congregation was really based upon the second Edwardian *Book of Common Prayer*, or at least held the same tradition of worship.[22] Indeed it has even been said that the *Form of Prayers* and also Calvin favored the use of set prayers and a fixed liturgy.[23] It would seem, however, that the character of the suggested form of English service hardly warrants such conclusions, particularly when we remember that the reason for Knox's leaving Frankfort, and the subsequent departure of Whittingham and his companions, was the demand that they use the second Edwardian Prayer Book.

The form of worship used in Geneva was, according to the author of the discourse on the troubles in Frankfort, that drawn up in Frankfort in the first attempt to reach an agreement with the supporters of the Prayer Book.[24] Knox probably carried this to Geneva where with a few amendments, including Whittingham's introduction, it became the form of service for the Genevan congregation. Calvin's *Forme des Prières* undoubtedly provided the basis for it, although Poullain's *Liturgia Sacra* also had its influence as we can see from the introduction into the Genevan service book of a translation of his confession of sins as one of those which could be used. Yet in neither case did the authors follow their prototypes slavishly, for they agreed with Poullain that "the faith of Christ is by no means violated by diversity of ceremonies as long as they are such as do not engender superstition." [25]

That this had long been Knox's position all the evidence proves. The service of God's worship, including the administration of the sacraments, was to be determined completely by New Testament precept and example. Biblical simplicity without humanly devised rituals was his objective as early as 1549 when he served the congregation in Berwick. This he stated in his "Declaration of the Christian Belief in the Lord's Supper," probably written around 1550, as well as in the fragment outlining his service of the Lord's Supper of about the same date.[26] He makes it very explicit in his declaration on prayer published in 1554, but written somewhat earlier, and in his letter to the Protestants in London (1554), in both of which he maintains that human inventions in worship are idolatry. These views he kept repeating in later writings during his exile, pointing out that under his ministry the sacraments were celebrated in Berwick and Newcastle in as simple a manner as possible.[27] In

1556 he advised the Scottish Protestants to have "conferences of Scriptures, assemblies of brethren," which were to be conducted very much according to the form which had recently been published in Geneva. And in 1559 he went so far as to refer to the Prayer Book as "a mingle mangle." [28] From this evidence we can conclude, therefore, that he favored the form of service which Whittingham and his collaborators prepared.

As an introduction to the order of worship, the authors of the work placed a confession of faith that was said to be the confession of the whole congregation. It was an expansion of the Apostle's Creed in a clearly Calvinistic direction. That this was the intention is shown by the fact that the twelfth item in the *Form of Prayers* was a translation of Calvin's Genevan catechism, which Whittingham and his collaborators regarded as the most reliable doctrinally and the most easily taught.[29] In all of these doctrinal statements the Genevan church did not come into conflict with their fellow English exiles elsewhere, for they were all agreed on the basic tenets of the Christian faith. Consequently, later there could be doctrinal harmony between the churches of England and Scotland, even though they disagreed strongly on liturgical practices.

In the matter of church government, the *Form of Prayers* followed closely on the pattern established by Calvin in Geneva. The church was to be governed by a threefold structure of ministers, elders and deacons, all elected annually. The ministers were to devote their time to the preaching of the Word and the administration of the sacraments, while the elders were to help govern and admonish the members, and also to advise the ministers on the work of the congregation. The deacons were responsible for the gathering and distribution of alms. Every Thursday the three groups were required to convene in an assembly or consistory for the purpose of discussion and discipline.[30] Since there was no idea of different "orders", as in the medieval church, this all fitted in with the concept of a church governed by Jesus Christ speaking by his Spirit through the whole body of Christians. In this way a democratic organization of a specifically Christian character was to be established.

With regard to discipline, it was laid down that the primary objective was to protect the church and to bring about the repentance and return of the sinner, all to the glory of God. If private admonition failed, public accusation might then be made, the ultimate penalty being excommunication. This final step, however, had to be the action of the whole church, not just of the consistory. Moreover, the standard of judgment was to be the rule of the Scriptures, excluding any idea of punishment for failing to obey man-made injunctions. On the other hand, the Confession of Faith admitted that the civil magistrate had the right to root out all forms of idolatry and heresy and to reform the church.[31] This was a concession that was to trouble the Church of Scotland for many a year, although it had little significance at the moment. The immediate importance was that this form of organization laid the foundation for later "classical" or "presbyterial" movements in the English speaking world.[32]

The reference to the ultimate influence of the *Form of Prayers*, reminds us of the fact that it was drawn up, not merely for a local congregation, but in the hope that it would form the basis for more complete reform in England once the reign of Mary Tudor had come to an end. The view that it "was published merely for the use of a very small congregation in a distant land" hardly seems accurate.[33] Those who prepared the book hoped that they would not have to stay in Geneva all the rest of their days, nor were they prepared, on their return to England, simply to fall into the ecclesiastical pattern established at the end of Edward VI's reign. That Whittingham's introduction was addressed to the Protestants in England, indicates clearly the objective they had in mind.[34] Unfortunately for them, John Knox was the only one who succeeded in carrying out the plan, and that in Scotland.

Knox returned to Geneva on September 13, 1556, after spending almost a year in his homeland, encouraging and strengthening the hands of the growing body of Protestants. It would seem, however, that although much heartened by developments, he had come to the conclusion that the time had not yet arrived for a full and complete reformation. Consequently when the Genevan congregation wrote him calling upon him to return and take up his work among them, he acceded to their summons, bringing with him his wife, Marjory, her mother, James Young, his servant, and Patrick, his pupil. As he explained in a letter to Mrs. Locke, he was "now burdenit with dowbill cairis," to which he was not accustomed, and therefore besought her prayers.[35] His days of freedom to move around as he saw fit had ended for he was not only the head of a family, but the pastor of a congregation that would make many demands upon him.

The latter responsibility undoubtedly took up most of his time. The *Livre des Anglois* records the various people who settled in Geneva, at least for a time, that they might enjoy relative peace in the fellowship of the congregation. They would have to be helped to establish themselves and then be examined for membership in the church. Furthermore we find records of nineteen baptisms, nine marriages and eighteen burials of which seven were children.[36] Although these dry statistics may sound unimportant, any pastor of a congregation knows how much work such responsibilities, coupled with the accompanying counselling and the oversight of the congregation as a whole, would involve. As Knox pointed out to Mrs. Locke in December 1556, his letters were no longer so extensive for

> daylie trubles occurring as weill in my domesticall charge, whair befoir I haif not bene accustomit, and thairfoir ar thay the more feirfull, as in the administratioun of publick thingis aperteaning to the pure flock heir assemblit in Chrystis name, do compell me oftentymes to forget, not onlie my maist special friends, but also my self. . . .[37]

Yet while burdened with the responsibility of his congregation, he now had a home with a wife, described by Calvin as very charming, who in due time presented him with sons Nathaniel and Eleazar. His life was happier and more stable. That Marjory was quite literate, writing a good hand, meant that at times she could take over some of his correspondence, perhaps also the transcribing of his manuscripts, which would be of very great help.[38] What he might lose in time for official matters while taking care of his family, he would gain in peace and tranquility which would enable him to work more effectively and productively. Unfortunately we have no detailed account of his family life, but can only speculate from fragments of evidence what it must have been like.

Yet with all his preoccupation with the problems of his pastoral charge and his family affairs, Knox never lost sight of the much larger issue, which was the situation in England and Scotland. For one thing, a number of individuals were constantly in touch with him concerning their spiritual problems, calling upon him for help and counsel. This kept him busy writing letters, some of which were preserved by the recipients and have come down to us. At the same time, considerable numbers of his letters to individuals must have been lost. On his return to Geneva from Scotland he sent back to the

Scottish Protestants "A Letter of Wholesome Counsel," in which he advised them concerning their services of their "privy kirks," offering to answer any questions concerning portions of Scripture that they might wish to pose to him.[39] No doubt he received a number of requests for this type of service, but neither they nor his answers have survived. The nearest thing to such an exposition is his sermon on Christ's first temptation which he preached while in Scotland, but had published when he returned to Geneva for the benefit of the church as a whole.

In the personal letters to individuals that have survived from this period, one finds him answering a variety of questions, and dealing with a number of different problems. One constant theme that runs through all the communications is his warning against bowing down to idolatry.[40] He also seeks to comfort and encourage those who fear that they have failed as Christians, or who feel that God has deserted them in the midst of their troubles.[41] On one occasion he deals very cannily with the question of how Christian women should dress. Although he refuses to prescribe any rule, he insists that Christians should not dress ostentatiously, nor should women wear men's clothing nor men women's, for then they will be disturbing the proper order established by God, since clothes indicate one's function in life.[42] The problem of social intercourse with unbelievers and the relevance of Paul's statements on the eating of meat offered to idols also arose. Knox points out that the apostolic instructions applied only to the matter of worship, not to social contacts, although the Christian must avoid misleading the weaker brother.[43] Last of all some ladies questioned him on the matter of their unbelieving, or at least luke-warm, husbands. To them he replies by urging obedience, but at the same time encouraging them to pray either for their husbands' conversion or, if necessary, that they might be free to escape from persecution.[44] This was no doubt the advice that he had given Mrs. Bowes before she left England for Geneva.

One person of considerable importance in his correspondence was Mrs. Anne Locke, who has already appeared a number of times in this story. The wife of a merchant of Cheapside in London, she was probably in her early twenties when she and Knox first met in 1552. Both Robert Louis Stevenson and Patrick Collinson feel that she was the only women whom Knox really loved.[45] Although this conclusion is somewhat speculative, whatever their feelings toward each other, one thing is certain, Mrs. Locke was an ardent Protestant. Her husband, on the other hand, while he accepted the new doctrines, was apparently not so enthusiastic. As persecution mounted in London, Knox urged her to come to Geneva if at all possible, advice that she followed, eventually arriving in May 1557 with her son Harie and her daughter Anne, the latter dying within a few days of their entry to the city. During her stay in Geneva, Mrs. Locke translated Calvin's sermons on the song of Hezekiah which she published along with a poetical meditation on Psalm 51, possibly written by Knox himself. Later she returned to England where she acted as the distributing center to "the brethren" for Knox's news concerning the Reformation in Scotland. As Knox seems to have had no contact with her after 1562, however, one cannot but feel that Stevenson's and Collinson's views lack a strong foundation.[46]

This raises the question of Knox's relationship with his women friends. While Stevenson does not say so directly he seems to imply that Knox was overly interested in the opposite sex. Janton inclines to the belief that he was seeking a mother figure to replace his own mother who had died when he was quite young, while Trevor Roper goes further by stating that he should be understood in Freudian terms, presumably desiring sexual relations with his female confidants.[47] Collinson, on the other hand, points out that many Protestant divines of the period such as Cartwright and Wilcox, as well as, one might add, Calvin, Bullinger, and Luther, were constantly consulted by women of high social rank on spiritual problems. One reason for this was that with the abolition of the confessional, they needed some other means of spiritual direction. Furthermore, they were often troubled by some of the new doctrines, particularly that of election and predestination. As the women enjoyed considerable freedom they could travel around, meeting people and discussing problems that they sought to have resolved by spiritual advisers.[48] Webster's Duchess of Malfi might well represent this type. As Knox was not very different from many others, it seems hardly fair to make innuendoes or suggestions about him that cannot be substantiated with factual evidence.

We must at the same time, recognize that Knox, although willing and able to help those women who sought his assistance, was violently opposed to women who attempted to dominate and rule men, and particularly those who persecuted Protestants for their faith. Within this latter group were Mary Tudor, Queen of England, Mary of Guise, Regent of Scotland, Diane of Poitiers, the mistress of Henry II of France, and perhaps Henry's wife, Catherine de Medici. Against these "weaker vessels" who, in his opinion, should not bear rule, he was prepared, as the trumpeter of God, to give a blast with all the strength he could muster. The events of 1557 soon gave him what he thought was the propitious moment.

In the month of May, James Syme, his host during his last stay in Edinburgh, and James Barron, one of the leading merchants of Edinburgh, arrived with a letter signed by the Earl of Glencairn, Lord Lorne, son of the Earl of Argyll, Erskine, whose identity is doubtful, and James Stewart, Prior of St. Andrews and half-brother of Mary Queen of Scots. Because of the relaxation of persecution and the apparent favor the Queen Regent was showing to the Protestants, they felt that this would be a propitious time for his return for a preaching-mission.[49] To this invitation Knox had an ambivalent attitude. His first son had just been born, his congregation needed his help and counsel, the Scottish nobles were none too dependable, and war was about to break out between Spain and France which would make travelling difficult.[50] What should he do?

He did as he had done before. He turned to Calvin and the "other godly ministers" for their advice, which was unanimous that he should obey the summons. He thereupon gave his affirmative answer to Syme and Barron, and set about preparing for his journey. Yet it still does not appear that he was too anxious to be on his way. Nevertheless, in September he set out for Dieppe where he arrived after what must have been a hazardous journey through the war zone. But after all that he had ventured, on his arrival he found awaiting him letters which stated that as the nobles felt that the time was not ripe, he had better postpone his visit.[51]

The reasons for this sudden change of plan we shall consider later, but whatever the cause, it had a radical effect upon Knox. He was suddenly brought face to face with the question of the dependability of the Scottish nobility and the responsibility of the common people before God to bring about a true reformation of religion. The nobles, on the one hand, were apparently trying to work out some kind of compromise with the Queen Regent since they did not feel that they could legitimately or effectively bring about a religious revolution by the use of force. In Knox's eyes, on the other hand, no compromise was possible, for the Queen Regent was a Guise who would stick at nothing to maintain both French and Roman Catholic power intact. The nobles, therefore were toying with both their temporal and eternal salvation. At the same time, he could not help wondering if his own slowness in making his decision to return had not been sinful, for which God was punishing him.[52] He therefore dispatched on October 27th a letter to the nobles, in the hope that they would change their minds and renew the invitation.

While awaiting a reply, he did not spend his time in Dieppe in idleness. As the Protestants were increasing there in number and activity, we cannot doubt that, as he did later, he took part in their secret meetings. Even more important, however, new letters he received from Scotland describing the situation there, gradually forced him to clarify his own thinking on the subject of rebellion for righteousness sake. When he reached his conclusions the results appeared in a number of letters and manifestos.

The first open letter that he dispatched and later published, was dated at Dieppe, December 1, 1557. It was in reply to word that he had received from Scotland concerning a type of perfectionism developing among the congregations, in that some were saying that the sinful lives of the nobles supporting the Reformation discredited the whole movement. To this, Knox replied that while righteousness was required of all Christians, it was not the ultimate test of truth, otherwise a moral reform of the old church would have been enough. The real criterion of the truth of doctrine was that it conformed to the Scriptures, God's Word. False doctrine was much more dangerous than oppression by the government or failure of the ministers to live godly lives.[53] This letter he followed seventeen days later with another, now addressed "To the Professors of the Truth in Scotland," in which he sought to arouse the nobles to a sense of their responsibility. He commenced by pointing out their obligation to carry on the work of reformation trusting only in God, but warned them against rebellion. Nevertheless, if the government refused to reform the church they then should make a public protestation of their obedience to the crown in all things not contrary to the Word of God, and follow that with a demand for the free preaching of the Gospel and the proper administration of the sacraments. At the same time, no matter who opposed, they were to protect their brethren from persecution. He concluded by warning them against cooperating with those who sought only their own profit, against backsliders such as James Hamilton, Duc de Châtelherault, and against persecutors.[54] He had moved a step farther along the road to rebellion, but the same letter also indicates a certain distrust of the aristocracy.

One of the reasons for his moving towards the idea of armed resistance to the government was the news he had received of the continuing persecution in England. Ridley, Latimer, Cranmer, Hooper and others of both high and low degree, many of whom he had known personally, had perished in the flames while others were languishing in rat infested prisons across the land. Many, however, who wished to escape such a fate without fleeing abroad like Sir William Cecil, had submitted, keeping their lives, offices and property intact. Knox could see the true church being decimated by executions and desertions. Even his old congregations, whom he had instructed with so much care, had proven to be unfaithful in face of the threat of royal displeasure. This seems to have worried him more than the actual executions. The situation was very black for English Protestantism.

Even closer to Dieppe was the persecution of the Protestants in France. Their numbers had been growing, not merely in a few main centers or port towns, but right across the country, and persecution had increased correspondingly. The central government under Henry II was determined to wipe out the heretics. Right under his royal nose in Paris, however, *"la religion réformée"* was having its greatest success. On September 4, 1557 an attack had been made upon upwards of three hundred Protestants gathered for a service in a house on Rue St. Jacques behind the Sorbonne. Although some had fought their way out, many had been arrested, imprisoned in the Châtelet, and eventually some executed. The accusation against them was not so much one of heresy as of treason, a cry that gained an immediate response since the French had just suffered a heavy defeat by Spanish forces at St. Quentin. One of the Paris pastors, probably Antoine de Chandieu, wrote a defense of the prisoners, which Knox, while at Dieppe, arranged to have translated with the addition of some of his own comments. Although this document was never published before the nineteenth century, it gives a clear indication of his growing concern and conviction that unless the nobles united for action, the whole movement could be doomed.[55]

As he looked at the situation in Scotland, in France, and

particularly in England, everywhere he saw the malevolent operation of the female of the species. Because woman had usurped the natural authority of the man, she was causing most of the problems now faced by the true believers. In this he had quite general support, for Bishop Ponet, who had recently died in exile in Strasbourg, in his *Treatise of Politick Power* insisted that women should not rule, while a little later the French political theorist, Jean Bodin, in his *De Republica* set forth the same view. An even more disturbing situation existed in England, however, in that Mary Tudor had actually handed the kingdom over to her husband Philip of Spain, thus bringing it under bondage to the most fiercely Roman Catholic power in Europe.[56]

It was little wonder that in his frustration he decided to write on the subject of women's rule and how it should be ended. But he does not appear to have done so "to pander to popular prejudices," as Jasper Ridley maintains, for he was only too well aware of the fact that his views would not be accepted in many quarters. Rather, he felt that since he had struck upon the secret of the trouble that was afflicting both Scotland and England he should make known what the remedy must be. Therefore, he spent the latter part of his stay in Dieppe drawing up what he called *The First Blast of the Trumpet against the Monstrous Regiment of Women* [against the unnatural reign of women]. In the light of all that he knew and feared, in the light of all his frustration, we can well imagine that writing this treaty was truly a dramatic catharsis.

When he had completed this work, as he had received no further encouragement from Scotland, Knox decided to return to Geneva by a roundabout route through the center of France. Perhaps the military situation was such that it would have been extremely dangerous to take the direct route across the north of France. In any case, he headed south for La Rochelle where he found a considerable colony of Protestant Scots and a strong body of Huguenots.[57] According to John Row, writing in the early seventeenth century, Knox preached there at a secret service during which he baptized a child that had been brought a long distance for this sacrament. At that time, according to Row, he also declared that he would be preaching in St. Giles within two or three years, something which the Roman Catholics certainly would never have credited.[58]

From La Rochelle he then crossed the country to Lyon which had earned a growing notoriety for its Protestantism ever since 1524, when with the advent of German Lutheran printers, the new doctrines had begun to win adherents among its citizenry. During the thirties and forties their numbers had increased to such an extent that a strong church had come into existence. The cause, however, had suffered a blow with the arrest and martyrdom of five young Protestant students from Lausanne. Yet Protestantism had survived, and when Knox paid his visit "the Religion" had become strong throughout all ranks of society.[59] Although there do not seem to have been any Scots in Lyon, Knox would undoubtedly find many friends among the Protestant population.

One cannot but wonder if he also visited Poitiers on this tour, either on the road to La Rochelle or on his trip across country to Lyon. Poitiers had a strongly Protestant element also, but equally important just to the north of it was Châtelherault now owned by the former regent of Scotland and occupied by his son the Earl of Arran. It was this young man who had been in St. Andrews Castle at the time of the murder of Beaton, and he undoubtedly had become acquainted with Knox during the siege. As suggested earlier he may have become a Protestant in St. Andrews, so it is not far-fetched to hazard the guess that Knox stopped to see him on his way home. If he did, since Arran was very much involved in the problems of the Protestant church in Poitiers, he may also have become temporarily involved in the conflict that had arisen in the Poitiers congregation and which led to the drawing up of the first French confession and form of church government. These formed the basis for the confession and discipline prepared in Paris in 1559. Having helped to produce a similar document in Frankfort, Knox may even have been consulted on its form and content.[60]

Back in Geneva in the spring of 1558, where he received the gift of burgesship, he settled down once again to his pastoral duties, his preaching and above all to his writing and publishing.[61] The latter was undoubtedly the most important historically, for it was during this short period of about a year that he worked out his theory of "a godly revolution" which was to bear much fruit over the next three centuries. Whether it was good or bad, will depend very much on one's point of view.

The first in his series of revolutionary writings to come off the press was his *First Blast of the Trumpet*. Having worked on it in

Dieppe, he had brought it back to Geneva for publication, a task undertaken by Jean Crespin who must have agreed with his thinking. Since, however, the book appeared anonymously and without either publisher's name or any indication of the place of publication, neither seemed prepared to identify himself with it. At first it was generally attributed to Christopher Goodman for whom Crespin published on January 1, 1558, *How Superior Powers ought to be Obeyd of their Subjects*, the real point of which was how subjects ought to disobey non-Christian or popish rulers.[62] Only after some months did Knox reveal his identity as the author for he had intended to remain unknown until after two more "blasts" of the trumpet.

The principal contention of *The First Blast* is that it is wrong for women to bear rule in the state, or even for a woman ruler to turn over the power of government to her husband, particularly if he is a foreign monarch. Knox had been interested in this subject ever since Mary Tudor had come to the throne—perhaps even before. Concerning it he had queried Calvin, Bullinger and others when he had first arrived in Europe, but had received only rather evasive answers. By 1558 he had finally reached his own conclusion. Therefore, he insisted,

> by the determinations and laws, illuminated only by the light of nature, by the order of God's creation, by the curse and malediction pronounced against woman, by the mouth of St. Paul, who is the interpreter of God's sentence and law, and finally by the minds of those writers, who in God's church have been always holden in greatest reverence that it is a thing most repugnant to nature, to God's will and appointed ordinance; yea that it cannot be without contumely against God, that a woman should be promoted to dominion or empire, to reign over man, be it in realm, nation, province or city.[63]

On these grounds, despite the extraordinary gifts bestowed on women in the Bible such as Deborah and Hulda and any other arguments, the Estates who have allowed women to rule

> ought to remove frome honor and authoritie that monstre in nature: So call I a woman cled in the habit of man, yea, a woman against nature rigning above man.[64]

Mary Tudor was the reward of the English parliament's failure to do so, but she would not long withstand "the fire of God's Word."

> And therefore let all men be advertised, for THE TRUMPET HATH ONES BLOWN.[65]

As we might expect this trumpet note did not by any means harmonize with the thinking of many of Knox's contemporaries. The Roman Catholics were of course very much opposed to the views expressed, for they struck at both Mary Tudor and Mary Stewart. Their reaction, however, was to be expected. Much more important was the criticism voiced by Protestants of all shades. The remnants of the English Congregation in Frankfort being quite upset, instructed one of their number at Strasbourg, John Aylmer, to prepare a reply, which he did. Although he sought to be as diplomatic as possible in dealing with Knox, he was quite sycophantic to Elizabeth who, by the time of the publication of his reply, had come to the throne. He did his utmost to excuse Knox for his ideas and his way of expressing them. Perhaps more important was Calvin's refusal to take any responsibility for the Scottish reformer's opinions. As he explained to Cecil in 1559, he had not seen the book for over a year after its publication, but had some time earlier warned Knox against taking too radical a position with regard to this matter of female rule. Even Francis Hotman who some years later was to write in his *Franco-Gallia* an attack upon female governance, expressed his opposition in 1559 to Knox's point of view.[66]

Yet in all of this storm, Knox seems to have felt little rocking of the boat. He next proceeded to publish a letter to Mary of Guise, the Queen Regent. He had originally written this piece while in Scotland in 1555, but she had made fun of it with the result that he now broadcast it with certain additions that drove his point home even more forcefully. His theme was that the Queen Regent should take in hand the reforming of the Scottish church since it represented "the poisoned cup of Rome." If, however, she would not do this, God's just judgment must eventually fall upon her. While obedience is part of a subject's responsibility, a time may come when because of the unlawful commands of the ruler, the subject must disobey, even to the point of armed resistance. In the case of Scotland, Romanism, oppression, and extortion were so prevalent that God's judgment could not but be near. Furthermore, women cannot rule a country in felicity for they are sent as a punishment. If, however, Mary would reform the church, her position would be confirmed and the country blessed. If not, in the death of her two sons and her husband, she had already been warned that she would suffer the same punishment as did the idolatrous kings of the Old Testament.[67]

Apparently having little hope that he would receive a favorable hearing from Mary of Guise, Knox next turned his attention to the nobles. This pamphlet took the form of an appeal from the sentence of the Scottish bishops who had tried him *in absentia* and had burned him in effigy to the hereditary councillors of the King of Scotland. As one with some knowledge of the law, he based his appeal on technical legal grounds, but then went on to urge the reform of the church. To justify such action, he insisted that the Scriptures, especially the Prophecy of Jeremiah, all supported the idea that the nobles as subordinate magistrates had the duty of suppressing idolatry and of establishing true religion, even against the wishes of the monarch. They had, as the powers that are ordained by God, the right "to remove from honours and to punish with death such as God hath condemned by his owne mouth." Even the clergy did not have exemption from this rule, despite the fact that the papacy always attempted to claim that it possessed the ultimate authority over all men and nations. The nobility, therefore, had the duty of taking action, lest they should suffer the same fate as the English nobility under Mary Tudor.

Not content to leave such matters in the hands of the nobles, who he felt had already let him down once, Knox then proceeded to pen an exhortation to "the Commonalty of Scotland." Commencing with the usual attack on Romanism, he pointed out that subjects were no less bound to believe the Gospel than were the rulers since all were equally sinful and must find salvation alone through faith in Christ. The common people, therefore, had the right to demand reform when error crept in. He offered to come to Scotland to prove from the Scriptures that Romanism was error, asking only that the ecclesiastical authorities be held in check until he had been able to do so. He then went on to point out that subjects might require their rulers to provide them with proper preachers, but if they failed to do so the people could appoint their own whom they could lawfully support with tithes and fruits withheld from unfaithful clergy. If the "commonalty" should take this stand, God would bless them, otherwise he would punish them along with the princes and bishops.[68]

These two letters he published in the volume which contained also an admonition to England and Scotland by Anthony Gilby and an outline of the proposed "Second Blast of the Trumpet." In this latter document Knox acknowledged his authorship of the "First Blast," and proceeded to set forth further propositions: 1. That a king does not rule over a Christian people by birth only, "but in his election must the ordenance, of which God hath established in the election of inferior judges, be observed." 2. No manifest idolator should be given public office in a kingdom that has once acknowledged Jesus Christ. 3. No oath can bind people to obey and maintain tyrants against God and his known truth. 4. If people have elected a ruler who turns out to be an idolator, those who did the electing may remove and punish him.[69]

In these four documents published before August 1558, Knox set forth quite clearly his views on the whole matter of government and of the rights of subjects against oppressive and idolatrous rulers. He had touched upon most of these matters in his *First Blast*, but now spelled them out in these later letters. He first of all called upon the Queen Regent to reform the church, but followed that shortly with an appeal to the nobles to force such a reform and a summons to the commons to apply pressure to the rulers to the same end. He declared that the nobles had a right to remove a recalcitrant monarch while the "commonalty" could proceed if the rulers failed to act to set up their own "reformed church." One other facet of his thought appears in his "An Exhortation to England for the Speedy Embracing of the Gospel," which was published in the autumn of 1558, in that he insisted that England as "a covenanted nation" had the obligation to remove an idolatrous ruler under pain of God's just vengeance.[70]

Such writing was clearly revolutionary, going much farther than Calvin's statements in the last chapter of the *Institutes of the Christian Religion*. Influenced to some extent no doubt by the thinking of John Major, who in both his *History of Greater Britain* and his *Commentary on the Fourth Book of the Sentences*, had held that an oppressive or evil king might be removed, but even more by the contemporary persecutions in France and England, Knox had pushed Calvin's principles to their logical conclusion.[71] He had taken the first step in 1554 in his "Letter to the Faithful in London, Berwick and Newcastle," but with the tremendous increase in persecution he had now made the decision that only revolution could bring about the necessary change.[72] John Ponet in his *A Short Treatise of Politick Power* had already taken much the same stand, as had Christopher

Goodman in his *How Superior Powers Ought to be Obeyed*.[73] Knox now pulled all this thinking together in 1558 in his series of open letters in which he set forth, on the basis of the covenant idea, the first coherent statement of the right to Christian revolution. He was thus the first of the Monarchomachs, for which reason, according to J. W. Allen, "he cannot but be regarded as one of the chief personal factors in the history of political thought in the sixteenth century." [74]

These were not the only writings that Knox produced at this time, for he also carried on an extensive correspondence which reveals much of his thinking. In one of his letters to "his Sisters in Edinburgh," written April 16th, he had explained that one reason for his hesitating to come back to Scotland had been that he did not wish to stir up strife in the country, as it would only impede the preaching of the Gospel. By July such fears had apparently disappeared, for he was then advocating what amounted to revolution.[75]

It would seem that his theories were quickly accepted by the English refugees; in fact he was expressing their already established point of view. This becomes clear when we turn to the English translation of the Bible in which he was participating at this time, under the direction of William Whittingham. Comments on passages such as Exodus 15:19, 2 Chronicles 19:16 and Revelation 9:3 favored the removal and punishment of idolatrous and oppressive rulers.[76] It is little wonder that the Genevan Bible did not find enthusiastic acceptance by the English "establishment" under Elizabeth.

That Knox must have been very busy during his residence in Geneva in 1558 and the early part of 1559 is indicated not only by the amount of pamphlet material he published, by his participation in the translation and annotation of the Geneva Bible, and by his constant writing of letters, but also by the fact that he wrote more than 450 pages in reply to an Anabaptist's book entitled *Careless by Necessity*, which was an attack upon the doctrine of predestination. Although the book was anonymous, Knox apparently was acquainted with the author who may have been Robert Cooke, a figure at the court of Edward VI. In his detailed rebuttal which he had been requested to make by the English refugees in Geneva, Knox set forth as clearly and as fully as possible what he believed to be the biblical doctrine. In some cases he carried Calvin's formulation through to conclusions from which the Genevan reformer had refrained. At the same time, one cannot but be impressed with the fact that the doctrine to Knox was not just a theoretical matter, but was extremely practical, revealing the mainspring of much of his thinking and action. Utterly convinced of the sovereignty of God over all of history, he was prepared to take his stand on God's truth no matter what the consequences. Only when we take this into account do we understand him.[77]

Not until the autumn of 1559, after Knox's departure, however, did the English refugees obtain permission for the book to be printed in Geneva; and even then, only after William Whittingham and John Barron became securities that nothing unorthodox was expressed, and that it would not bear the Genevan imprint, did the city council permit it to appear.[78] After *The First Blast*, they were taking no chances.

Then suddenly everything changed. On November 17, 1558 Queen Mary died to be succeeded by her half-sister Elizabeth. By necessity, if not by conviction, a Protestant because of the Roman Catholic denial of her legitimacy, Elizabeth's accession was a source of great joy to the refugees. Yet the joy must have been tinged with uncertainty as to her future course in ecclesiastical affairs. Therefore, while the Bible translators in Geneva immediately despatched to her a specially prepared volume of the Psalms, the congregation hurriedly sent William Kethe to the other exile groups calling upon them for mutual forgiveness for past wrongs and for the organization of a united front to bring about a complete reform of the new Protestant church that they hoped would now be established.[79]

Knox was doubtless behind this move for he would recognize, after his experiences in Frankfort, the difficulty of making any alterations in the second Prayer Book. Kethe, however, was not successful, for while the congregation at Aarau agreed heartily, as they would, since they had left Frankfort because of the "Troubles," when he arrived in Frankfort he found that all those originally involved in the debate over the Prayer Book, had already set out for England, and that those who remained were busily packing up to return. The exiles seemed more anxious to go back to England as quickly as possible in search of preferment, although the Frankfort group said that they would support the Reformation, whatever that might mean. Kethe, therefore, came back to Geneva empty handed.

Kethe's arrival was the sign for the Genevan congregation also to leave. On January 24th, at their request, the city council granted them permission to depart and wished them well. Only those involved in the printing of the English Bible remained to see it through the press, an operation not completed until 1560.[80]

This rapid change in the situation placed Knox in a somewhat uncertain position. Without a congregation to which to minister he had no valid reason for remaining in Geneva. The question was then, where should he go. Some have held that he really wanted to go back to England, but this is very doubtful.[81] From the time that he visited Scotland in 1555, his eyes seem to have been on his homeland, rather than upon England, for he indicates in some of his letters that he believed that in Scotland existed a greater opportunity for true reform of the church. Furthermore, his experiences in Frankfort had hardly endeared Englishmen, particularly English bishops, to him. Added to this, Elizabeth's known antipathy to his *First Blast* would not encourage him. Scotland, in God's providence, seemed to be the only place.

Therefore, leaving Marjory, his two young sons and Mrs. Bowes in Geneva under the care of Christopher Goodman, he set out for Dieppe in the hope that he would obtain a safe-conduct through England to Scotland. On February 19th he arrived in the French port whence he immediately dispatched a letter to Sir William Cecil requesting a passport. He then turned his attention to the Protestant church of the city. While ministers had been placed there through the instrumentality of Calvin and the Genevan consistory, the congregation had experienced difficult times through persecution, plague and the loss of one of its pastors through death. The man in charge at Knox's arrival was Sieur De la Porte, formerly pastor at Rouen. Knox immediately threw himself into the work of the congregation with such effect that shortly afterwards through his ministry a number of the local gentry and ladies, including some royal officials became Protestants.[82] It was also while he was in Dieppe that the notice of the first French Reformed Synod to be held in Paris in May arrived. Although Knox left the country before these meetings, he undoubtedly saw the proposed confession and form of discipline, which he may well have copied and taken with him to Scotland.[83]

Yet while occupying himself with this congregational work, Knox was extremely anxious to move on, for he could hear that things were stirring in Scotland. Still no passport came. A second letter brought no better results, and finally on April 10th he sent off a third. He pointed out to Cecil that all he wanted to do was go through England to Scotland, visiting his former congregations on the way. Somewhat undiplomatically he warned Cecil that because he had compromised his Christian profession under Mary, unless he repented he would be punished. He then went on to clear the English refugees, who, he had heard, had received a very cool reception from the queen, of any responsibility for his *First Blast*. Finally, he declared that if Elizabeth would acknowledge that she sat on the throne through God's appointment alone and not by man's device, he would be prepared to acknowledge her authority. Even this concession got him nowhere, however, and as a result late in April he set sail in a ship travelling directly to Leith.[84]

Up to this time, Knox in a very real sense had been undergoing training for his principal work in life. While he had already exercised considerable influence upon the Reformation movement in England, Scotland and the Continent, he had also received many hard knocks, usually because of his efforts wherever he had gone to make the Reformation full and complete. His times in England and Geneva, however, had so broadened his outlook on the whole movement, that he now saw the Reformation not just as an effort at religious reform, but as a movement to create a reformed Christian public and private life-style. Therefore, as he sailed from Dieppe for Scotland, he left with the determination that he would now blow the Lord's trumpet in his own homeland more earnestly and effectively than ever before.

John Knox

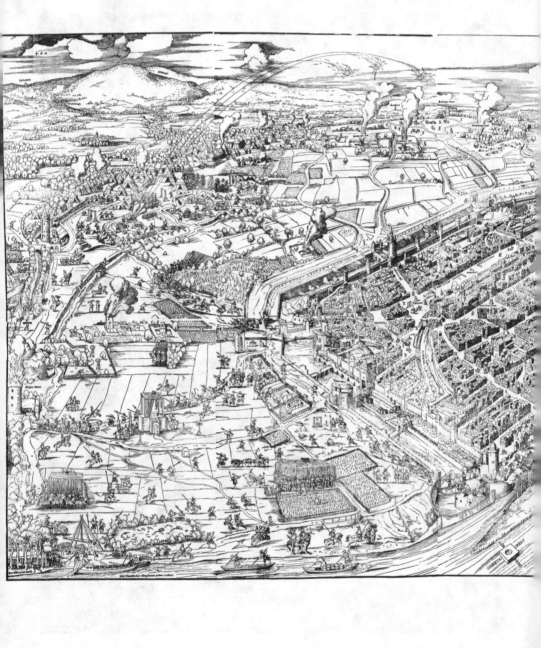

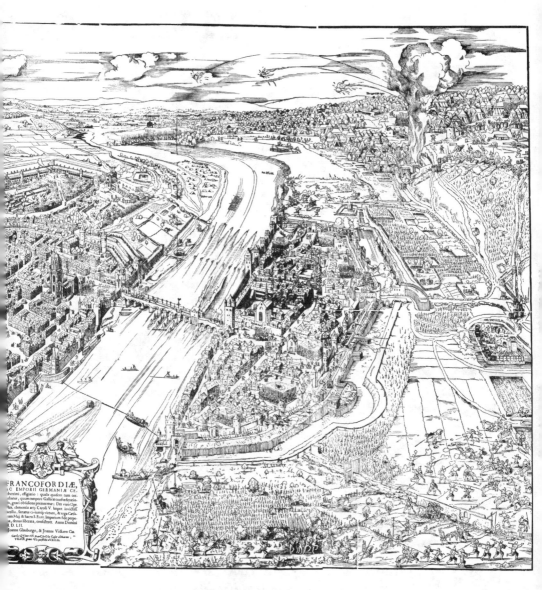

Frankfort, 1552

POST TENE BRAS LVX

N

A

F

B

C

D E

G Eneue eſt vne ville au pays de Sauoye, de merueilleuſe, & grande ancienneté, ↄ
auoit vn pont paſſant oultre le Rhoſne, lequel de ſon temps eſtoit ſoubz la puiſ
force vignes, & aſſeℤ grande abondance de bleds. Du coſté, où le Rhoſne ſort dↄ
haults, ſur vne petite montaigne. Il y a deux villes en icelle encore auiourd'huy,
La grand ville eſt du coſté du Midy, & la petite eſt du coſté de Septentrion. Les hↄ
lée de ſon nom Aurelia, mais elle a retenu ſon nom ancien. Elle eſt preſqu'au mↄ
ↄ ecouuers d'aucuns perſonages touchans Genéue.

eſme que Iules Ceſar en fait mention, au premier liure de la guerre Gallique, affermant qu'il y
les Suyſſes. La ſituation de ceſte ville & eſt plaiſante, & gracieuſe, & la conſrée fertile. Il y à
and Lac, qu'on appelloit anciennement le Lac Leman, elle eſt baſſe, mais depuis elle eſt eſlevée en
millieu deſquelles le Rhoſne paſſe, ſur lequel il y a un pont de bois, qui conioint ces deux villes
ens reciſent, que ceſte ville a eſté refaite par l'empereur Aurelien, qui voulut, qu'elle fut appel-
de tout le pays de Sauoye. Mais pour mieux entendre cecy, i'ay bien voulu icy adiouſter ce que i'ay

Geneva, 1548

Top to bottom:
*James Stewart, Earl of Moray; James Douglas,
Fourth Earl of Morton; John Erskine, First
Lord Erskine and Earl of Mar*

Top to bottom:
James Hamilton, Second Earl of Arran, Duc de Châtelherault; Sir William Kirkcaldy of Grange; William Maitland of Lethington

Castrum puellarum

EDE

EDENBVRGVM.
SCOTIAE
METROPOLIS.

Edinburgh, 1582

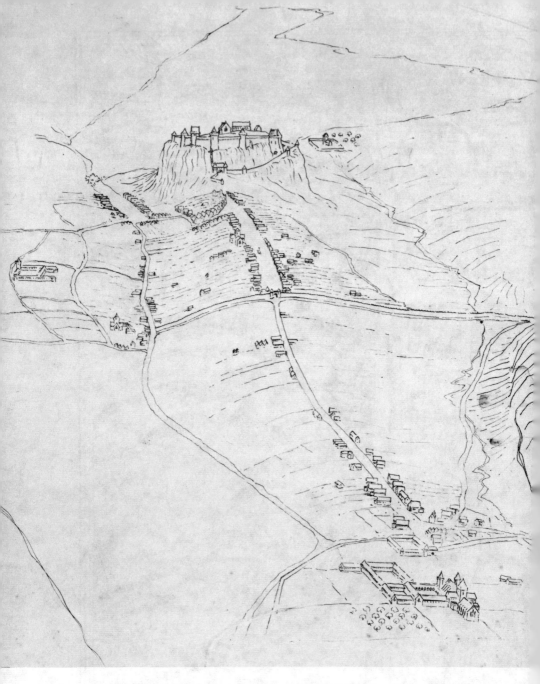

A fifteenth-century drawing of the Edinburgh Castle

CHAPTER VIII

Summons to Battle

ON MAY 2, 1559 KNOX landed at Leith. While he had commenced his journey with great hopes, he arrived with fear in his heart, for on the ship that brought him from Dieppe had travelled also a messenger of Queen Mary who carried a Great Seal engraven with the arms of France, Scotland and England and a staff with the same arms, to be used at the appropriate moment.[1] To Knox who was shown them in secrecy, they represented France's plan, as prophesied earlier by Henry II, to rule all three kingdoms. This knowledge combined with what he knew of French dealings with Protestants, such as those who had been taken in the Rue St. Jacques episode, made him realize the terrible danger threatening the Reformation movement in Scotland. This knowledge undoubtedly explains much of his violently antagonistic attitude towards both French and Romanists during the next few years, a fact that some of his modern critics should keep in mind.

The Scotland to which Knox returned was also a country very different from that which he had known before. It was a divided land teetering almost on a knife edge over chaos. On the one hand, the Reformation was apparently gaining strength and support, while on the other, English influence so important to the movement was waning with the withdrawal of the English from their strongholds in the Lowlands and their replacement by French troops and French advisers who sought to dominate the government. The situation was confused and confusing to say the least, but to understand it we must glance back to the period following the Battle of Pinkie Cleugh in 1547.

Although Pinkie had been an overwhelming English victory, it had not brought Scottish acceptance of England's claims that the Treaties of Greenwich, providing for the marriage of Edward VI and Mary, should be implemented. Furthermore, as Somerset faced increasing trouble at home, he found it necessary to pull out his troops, and in so doing left his Scottish allies on the lurch.[2] While a number of them were subsequently executed for treason, others under threat of death and forfeiture by the governor, now strengthened by the arrival of contingents of French troops, returned to their allegiance. Those, however, with strong religious convictions, such as Ormiston, Brunston and New Grange, knowing that they would probably be tried for heresy if they submitted, found it wise to leave for England. For this their lands were seized by the governor and their towers razed to the ground.[3] Then, with the accession of Mary Tudor to the English throne most of them found it wise to return home where they were eventually rehabilitated and their lands restored. A few, however, remained in England, some of them dying in exile, and some returning only after the Reformation had been victorious.[4] By 1552 the "assured lords" of Lothian had ceased to be of any importance.

At the same time, the dominant position of the French in the country had led to a change in the whole political pattern. Mary of Guise, the Queen mother, along with some of the nobles, was seeking to oust the unstable Earl of Arran from the position of governor. A preliminary move in this direction had been made with the granting to him in 1548 of the French duchy of Châtelherault. When it became clear, with the accession of Mary Tudor to the English throne, that he could not look to England for help, further pressure was applied, with the result that in April 1554 he demitted his office and parliament appointed the Queen mother to take his place. The French element now had firm control.[5] Mary proved to be a capable ruler, who was a strong advocate of the fortunes of both the French monarchy and the house of Guise as well as a staunch supporter of the Roman Church. Consequently her policies did not always receive the Scots' whole-hearted approval. Nevertheless, she succeeded in persuading the Scottish nobles that her young daughter, now in France, should marry a French prince, by this means moving Scotland closer to becoming a French province.[6]

Mary's political policies were closely linked to her ecclesiastical plans. An unexpected aid in this was the former governor, now Duc de Châtelherault who, although he had originally shown himself favorable to the Protestant movement, by the time of his removal was once again fully committed to the Roman Catholic Church. In 1551, apparently with his approval, parliament had passed a law against disturbers of Kirks, presumably Protestants. At the same time a provincial synod was convened to reform the church by preparing a catechism for the instruction of the ignorant and by taking steps to improve clerical morals. Although a catechism was produced, the move to amend morals achieved little. The synod was more important for what it said about the condition of the church than for any concrete accomplishments.[7] Mary was determined that the old church would be maintained; despite the council's ineffectiveness, she gave strong support to both ecclesiastical and civil provisions that would protect the church or clergy and restrain Protestant growth.

This close interrelationship of politics and religion, as expressed by the actions of the Queen Regent, had its effect on the Scottish nobles, who at length began to see that the French were taking over the country. Consequently the Protestants were now appearing to many as the patriotic or nationalist party. This point of view naturally assisted the Protestants in their drive for a thorough-going reform in religion. Jealousy of and antipathy to the French, coupled with opposition to the Roman Church, thus worked to frustrate the hopes of Mary of Guise.[8]

Throughout the early fifties Protestantism expanded its influence and gained ever increasing numbers of adherents. Following the pattern already established in France, Protestants began to organize house churches or "privy kirks" in which the Bible was studied and discussed. In some cases, men such as Paul Methven and William Harlaw became ministers of congregations. Although the great nobles, with a few exceptions such as the Earl of Argyll, seem to have been none too enthusiastic over these developments, the lairds of Angus, the Mearns, Fife, Lothian, and the southwest, along with the burgesses of towns such as Dundee, Perth, and Edinburgh gave their hearty support. In this way the new doctrines were spreading underground, to erupt every so often in attacks upon monasteries which the Protestants regarded as the core of resistance to reform.[9]

It was at this stage of Protestant development that Knox had returned to Scotland in 1555. Although he does not reveal in his *History* who was responsible for this move, we do know that Mrs. Bowes had been urging him to come home, presumably to assume his responsibilities as Marjory's husband and perhaps to help them both to leave England.[10] He does not seem to have received any public call from Scotland, but may have been encouraged to come back by Protestant leaders such as Erskine of Dun, the Earl of Argyll, and the Earl of Glencairn. He may also have been anxious to find out what was taking place in Scotland, perhaps with the intention of remaining there if circumstances seemed propitious. From a letter to Mrs. Bowes, written shortly after his arrival, we gather that he was taken quite by surprise at the enthusiasm manifested by those adhering to the Reformed faith. As he explained:

> Gif I had not sene it with my eyis in my awn country I culd not have believit it. . . . But the fervencie heir doith fer exceid all utheris that I have sene; and thairfoir ye sall pacientlie beir, althoucht I spend heir yit sum dayis; for depart I can not, unto sic tyme as God quenche thair thrist a litill.

In an undated letter probably written a little later he tells her that the trumpet has blown the old sound on three successive days in Edinburgh, in private houses which were so crowded that there was no room left. He ends with the jubilant cry that victory will soon be won.[11] Yet much remained to be done before that would be achieved.

After a few days in Edinburgh he set out on a preaching mission around the country through Fife, Angus, the Mearns, Kyle, and Lothian which meant that he covered most of the central area of Scotland as well as the eastern section as far north as Montrose. From his history, it would seem that his headquarters was the house of Sir James Sandilands of Calder who had long been one of the leaders in the movement, but he also spent considerable time with John Erskine and the Protestants of the Mearns at Dun, between Brechin and Montrose, and at Castle Campbell in Dollar, Clackmannanshire, with the old fourth Earl of Argyll. Probably most profitable of all his time in Scotland were the days he spent in Edinburgh. On his arrival, he lodged in the house of James Syme where he carried on private consultations and services with the burgesses. These resulted in the conversion of a considerable number of the Edinburgh population, including probably such important individuals as the merchant James Barron and his wife Elizabeth Adamson.[12]

Towards the end of his visit to Scotland he became somewhat bolder taking over what he refers to as "the great house of the Bishop of Dunkeld," where he preached to large audiences for ten days both morning and afternoon.[13] The location of this building and the reason for the bishop's permitting him to use it have both been mysteries. It may be, however, that the solution lies in the fact that there was a property on the north side of the High Street known as "the Bishop of Dunkeld's tenement" which was in 1555 the property of Thomas Marjoribanks, one of the Protestant merchants. This location would make the building a good place for such services, particularly as they would be held under the sponsorship of influential Protestant burgesses and lairds.[14]

It may have been during this period of his visit that he preached his sermon on Christ's first temptation, which he published when he returned to Geneva. Since we do not have many examples of his sermonizing, it gives us some idea of the type of exposition that he employed. He had four divisions: 1. What the word temptation means and how it is used in Scripture; 2. Who is here tempted and at what time it happened; 3. How and by what means he was tempted; 4. Why he should suffer temptation and what fruit comes of it for us. Having thus carefully analyzed his text he ends with an application of the words: "Man shall not live by bread alone":

> . . . the verie lyfe and felicitie of man consisteth not in abundance of corperall thingis, for the possessioun and having of them maketh na man blissit nor happie; nether sall the lack of thame be the caus of his finall miserie; but the verie lyfe of man consisteth in God, and in his promissis pronunced by his awne mouth, unto the whilk whoso cleaveth and sticketh unfeanidlie, sall leif [live] the lyfe everlasting.[15]

From what he reports, one of the most important problems facing him was that caused by those who although they had made profession of being Protestants, still attended Mass. It would seem that in his sermons he constantly dealt with this matter, pointing out that such participation was idolatry. Moreover, he did not hesitate to rebuke personally those who tried to compromise their Protestantism by taking part in such ceremonies. As a result Erskine of Dun held a supper–meeting with David Forrest, Master of the Mint, Robert Lockhart, probably a burgess of Edinburgh, John Willock, the minister, and William Maitland of Lethington, later secretary to Mary of Guise, to discuss the matter with him. According to Knox, he answered so clearly and effectively all the excuses advanced that Maitland eventually admitted: "I see perfectly, that our shifts will serve nothing before God, seeing that they stand in so small stead before man." [16] This would seem to mark the point at which the Protestants began to realize that they either had to back down or take a firm stand for what they believed to be the Gospel. In bringing them to this decision Knox's visit to Scotland was of the very greatest importance to the reform movement.

The reactions to his preaching varied considerably. The ecclesiastical authorities, recognizing the danger of his preaching against Roman Catholic doctrine, summoned him to appear before them in the Black Friars Church in Edinburgh on May 15, 1556. Knox promptly signified his willingness to do so, but when he arrived in the burgh with Erskine of Dun and other nobles and gentry, the bishops dropped the case. A number of nobles, now hoping to influence Mary of Guise, asked him to write her a letter to persuade her to reform the church. This he did in his most statesmanlike and diplomatic style, but with little effect, for she handed it over to the Archbishop of Glasgow calling it "a pasquil," or a lampoon. His subsequent reply to this action took the form of the publication of the letter with additions, which as we have seen were somewhat less polite.[17] But the immediate consequence seems to have been his holding of services in the "Bishop of Dunkeld's Great House."

During his sojourn in Scotland he also found time for something more personal. He journeyed south across the border to Norham or Berwick where he was united in marriage with Marjory Bowes. When this took place he does not tell us. All we know is that following the wedding, he made arrangements to send Marjory and her mother over to Dieppe where he joined them in July. Thence they travelled to Geneva where on September 18th he, Marjory, Mrs. Bowes, his servant James and his pupil Patrick were all received into the English congregation.[18]

His return to Switzerland has been variously explained by different writers, some of whom have accused him of plain cowardice.[19] If it is cowardice to recognize one's life is threatened and that one can gain nothing by remaining in a dangerous situation, he could be guilty. Certainly he recognized that the Queen Regent—who at this time, in order to gain support for her pro-French policies, was treating the Protestants rather leniently—might suddenly change. If she did he would be the first to go. The other side of the coin was the urgent call he received from the congregation in Geneva to return to take up his duties as their pastor. This would certainly appeal to him, for it would mean peace and quiet for study, for the first time a home of his own, and freedom from the continual conflict endemic in Scotland. It seemed that the Lord was calling him to minister to those who had followed him to Geneva, a summons he could not ignore.[20] His departure, however, did not assuage the anger of the ecclesiastical authorities. Immediately after he left, the bishops met once again, condemned him and burned him in effigy, an action which caused him to write his "Appellation" in which he called upon the nobles for total reform of the church.[21]

Before leaving for Geneva, Knox had made it quite clear, as he did on a number of subsequent occasions, that he would be prepared to return to Scotland when there were more Protestants and the great nobles, *i.e.* the "natural" political leaders, called for him. In the meantime, in "A Letter of Wholesome Counsel," which he published later, he advised them how to organize their "privy kirks." The order of service that he outlined followed in general that already in use in Geneva: confession and invocation of the Holy Spirit; the reading of Scripture from both Old and New Testaments; exposition, discussion, and questions; and closing with thanksgiving and prayers for the magistrates and the church. He added that should they have difficulty in interpreting certain passages of Scripture he would be glad to help them if they would send him their questions.[22]

It is quite clear that the Protestants accepted Knox's advice, developing their privy kirks along the lines that he suggested. What had earlier been somewhat haphazard gatherings, now began to take organized form similar to that of the congregation in Geneva. There has been, however, considerable discussion as to whether these privy kirks used the second Edwardian *Book of Common Prayer*. Some authors simply take it for granted that they did, while others advance arguments to prove their case.[23] The latter point to the use of the term "Common Prayers," to the fact that Kirkcaldy of Grange in

1559 stated to Cecil that the Scots were using the Prayer Book, to individual pro-Reformation cleric's employing the book in their services as a guide, and to the small circulation of the *Geneva Service Book* in a distant congregation, as proof of their thesis.

As one considers the evidence, however, one cannot but take much of this argumentation with a grain of salt. For one thing, the use of the term "Common Prayers," despite a statement to the contrary by Cardinal Gasquet, was not a technical term, but one that seems to have referred generally to public worship. In the Edinburgh edition (1562) of the *Geneva Service Book*, it is pointed out that two of the prayers were used in the French church, one after the Sunday sermon and the other on Wednesday "which is the day of the Commune Prayer," *i.e.* a prayer meeting.[24] Furthermore, there would seem to be little doubt that the Genevan congregation hoped that this book would take the place in England and Scotland of *The Book of Common Prayer* from whose form of service, by virtue of the freedom given to the minister, it differed radically. Although Kirkcaldy spoke of the use of the Prayer Book and some of the clergy may have used it as a guide, the attitude of Knox, Goodman and others to it from 1555 on, gives little basis for the idea that they favored it. To imply that Knox's opposition to it in 1559 was purely a spiteful reaction to Elizabeth's refusal of a passport through England, flies in the face of the evidence of the preceding years in Frankfort and in Geneva.[25] After all, the whole trouble in Frankfort was over this very issue. Finally Knox's suggested form of service in his "Letter of Wholesome Counsel" provided for discussion and questions, so that the service had little resemblance to a present day Anglican service conducted in accordance with the Prayer Book.

In Scotland the ecclesiastical authorities were now becoming worried over the development of Protestant influence and power. From 1555 on one sees, even in the charters granted by the clergy to laymen, evidence of this concern. Repeatedly grants were made on condition that the grantee promised to remain faithful to, or because he had displayed his obedience to, the Roman Church. It is also interesting to note that in these documents usually the rents were increased greatly, one of the reasons given being that the clergyman, abbot or bishop wished to repair and restore the fabric of the church, abbey or cathedral. It would seem that somewhat belatedly the clergy had decided to refurbish the church, at least outwardly.[26]

The growth of the Protestant movement and the adherence to it of some of the leading nobles along with a large number of the lairds, led to increasing boldness on the part of the preachers. From 1556 on, men such as John Douglas, Paul Methven, William Harlaw, and John Willock held services openly in Leith, Dundee, Perth, and Edinburgh. Although we do not have the texts of their sermons, they apparently not only did the work of evangelists and pastors, but also tended to rouse up the people to destroy the expressions of "idolatry" in the churches, sometimes with cataclysmic results.[27] In the light of these developments, and since Knox had promised to return when called by a large body of people, some of the leading nobles, including the Earl of Glencairn, Lord Lorne, son of the Earl of Argyll, Erskine of Dun and Lord James Stewart, Prior of St. Andrews and half-brother of Queen Mary, on March 10, 1557, invited him to assume the spiritual leadership of the movement for reform.[28]

When he did eventually arrive in Dieppe on October 24th, he found letters advising him not to come at the moment. The situation had changed in Scotland for Mary of Guise had convinced the nobles that her daughter should be married to Francis, the Dauphin of France. Indeed, she had even succeeded in having a number of the leading Protestants among whom were signers of Knox's invitation, appointed to go to Paris for the final negotiations and the wedding ceremony on April 24, 1558. As they seem to have been very much in favor of the whole project, they did not want to cause any trouble at the moment by bringing in the trumpetting preacher.[29]

As recounted in the previous chapter, Knox did not approve of this uncertain and compromising attitude, with the result that he wrote his stinging rebuke to the nobles, charging them with shirking their duty and compromising with evil. This letter had an immediate effect, for on December 3rd the earls of Argyll, Glencairn, Morton, Lord Lorne, Erskine of Dun, and many others entered into a covenant or band in which they swore before God and his congregation to forward a true reformation with all their power, by having only true ministers of the Gospel, by defending "the whole Congregation of Christ, and every member thereof, at our whole powers and waring of our lives," and by forsaking the congregation of Satan with its "abomination and idolatry." [30] This covenant they then sought to have others sign in order that all the Protestants might stand together in their demands. Knox's remonstrance had probably accomplished more than if he had been personally present in Scotland.[31]

That this was no empty agreement soon became apparent, for the signatories began to hold meetings to formulate plans for action. According to Knox they sought to have the regular services of worship in the vernacular with lessons from the Old and New Testaments "conform to the order of the Book of Common Prayers," and if the curates were not able to perform this service, then the most qualified layman in the parish should do so. While this may be a reference to the lectionary of the English Prayer Book, it is gratuitous to imply that this meant that the liturgy was used in its entirety, especially when it is obvious that a layman could perform the function of the curate. It was also resolved that the preaching and interpretation of Scripture, phrases used in the Genevan book, should be held in private houses until the Queen Regent granted permission to hold preaching services in public.[32]

The lords then prepared a petition to the Queen Regent embodying both these ideas, along with a demand that the bishops be reformed. This they sent to Mary by the hand of Sir James Sandilands of Calder.[33] The reaction of Mary to the petition was outwardly quite mild, for she promised that she would not object to the preachers so long as they did not conduct their services in Edinburgh or Leith, and did not foment tumult elsewhere. In response to this the Lords of the Congregation stopped John Douglas from preaching in Leith, and he thereupon became chaplain to the Earl of Argyll.[34] The clergy, on the other hand, seemed to have favored a harder approach to heresy, for in April they arrested Walter Myln, an old priest, whom they tried and burned at the stake in St. Andrews, a deed that shocked not only the people of the burgh, but the Protestants generally. "Which thing," as Knox explains, "did so highly offend the hearts of all godly, that immediately after his death began a new fervency among the people . . ."[35] About the same time the Rothesay Herald was sent to Dundee to summon George Lovell, David Ferguson and others to appear in Edinburgh

> for thair wrangis using and wristing of the Scripture and for disputing upown erronius opiniouns and eiting of flesche in Lenterone.[36]

But what happened to them we do not know.

The new fervency resulted in increasing militancy on the part of the Protestants in Dundee, Perth, and other of the east coast burghs, where public preaching now seems to have increased. The Queen Regent, however, felt that with her daughter safely married she could take steps to stop this. In mid-July, therefore, she summoned the Protestant preachers to appear before her to answer for their sermons. But with them came the gentry of the west, led by James Chalmers of Gadgirth, who, after a violent verbal attack upon the clergy, putting on his steel bonnet, dared her and the bishops to take any further anti-Protestant action.[37] It was, however, at the St. Giles Day celebration on September 1st, that Edinburgh witnessed the most dramatic Protestant demonstration. Knox reaches a climax of humor and dramatic writing as he tells how after the Queen Regent had participated in the parade, the Protestants moved in, knocked the image of St. Giles off the frame on which it was carried, and "dadding his head to the calsay" [knocking his head on the road], smashed it.

> The priests and friars fled faster than they did at Pinkie Cleuch. There might have been seen so sudden a fray as seldom been seen amongst that sort of men within this realm; for down goes the crosses, off goes the surplice, round caps corner with crowns. The Grey Friars gaped, the Black Friars blew, the priests panted and fled; and happy was he that first got the house; for such a sudden fray came never amongst the generation of Antichrist within this realm before.[38]

The Protestants had won another skirmish, although the main battle had not yet been joined.

Yet such actions as these do not seem to have roused Mary of Guise to violent counter-measures, for she had other objectives in view. When young Queen Mary had been married to the Dauphin in April, Henry II had demanded that Francis be given the crown of Scotland. This the Scottish envoys had refused as outside their terms of reference, and many believed that the deaths of a number of them in Dieppe on the way home was due to their being poisoned because of this stand. Mary naturally favored the granting of the crown, for it would bring Scotland completely under French control. But it could be made only with the consent of parliament in which the Protestants were now so strong that they had to be cozened into agreeing. Active persecution, therefore, was clearly impolitic. Moreover, she could afford to abide her time. Once the crown matrimonial had been delivered to Francis, French troops could be brought over in numbers sufficient to crush the recalcitrant reformers.

Parliament met in Edinburgh in November 1558, and with Frenchmen holding most of the chief offices in the kingdom, and with Mary being her most diplomatic self, it was not surprising that on the 29th it ratified the sending of the crown matrimonial to Francis, and agreed that all Frenchmen be granted naturalization in Scotland.[39] Mary, having now gained her objective, was ready for the final blow which was greatly facilitated both by the Peace of Cateau-Cambrésis (1558) that brought the Franco-Spanish war to an end, and by the accession of Elizabeth to an isolated and apparently tottering English throne.

Therefore, the Protestants met with no harsh words when they drew up a letter which they presented to parliament and supported with a protest before that body prior to its adjournment. These two statements were quite different from the first petition presented in March to the queen. They represented a situation very different from that presupposed in the earlier document, for whereas the first request had stressed the Protestants desire for freedom of worship and instruction, the two present statements to parliament called for a cessation of persecution, the trial of accused heretics by due process of law, protection from the arbitrary actions sanctioned by the anti-Protestant statutes enacted during the early 1540s, and removal of persecuting ecclesiastical officials from office. The protesters also made it clear that while they were calling for religious reform, they were not seeking political revolution. Although the parliament refused to record the protest in its minutes, Mary said that: "Me will remember what is protested; and me shall put good order after this to all things that now be in controversy." The Protestants were satisfied with this statement of Delphic ambiguity. After all, she agreed at the same time to quash the sentences of forfeiture against the formerly "assured" lairds Cockburn of Ormiston and Crichton of Brunston, so why should they not be happy?[40] According to Knox, they even wrote Calvin praising her for her favorable attitude towards them.

That they had been fooled, however, became apparent once Francis had become co-sovereign with Mary. The Queen Regent then came out into the open as a supporter of the ecclesiastical establishment by placing restrictions on the Protestant preachers and summoning them to appear before her to answer for their activities.

The Earl of Glencairn and Hugh Campbell of Loudon, sheriff of Ayr, acting as representatives of the Protestants, objected strongly to her actions, even threatening rebellion. While this temporarily slowed her down, it did not do so for long. With the assurance that she could now call upon France for armed assistance, she took steps to repress Protestantism in Perth, ordering the sheriff of Dundee to arrest Paul Methven who was preaching there. She also issued proclamations to the various centers of Protestant influence: St. Andrews, Cupar, Dundee, Montrose, and Aberdeen forbidding the interruption of Catholic church services, the striking of priests or the eating of flesh in Lent.[41] Nevertheless, despite all her efforts Protestantism continued to gain adherents. Even those not convinced theologically, were joining Protestant ranks, fearful that Scotland was now becoming nothing more than a French province for the benefit of France and of the family of Guise.

While attempting to contain Protestantism, Mary must have realized that something was seriously wrong with the Scottish church which would have to undertake some self-reform, for she now called for a provincial synod to be held in March 1559. According to Leslie, by this means she hoped to bring about some unity in the country to resist more effectively both England and heresy. The bishops convened at the beginning of March, but the acts of this body reveal only too clearly the clergy's moral and intellectual condition. It was perfectly obvious that the council would be no more successful than that of 1551–2. When some of the nobles appeared demanding radical changes, the purely negative reaction of the bishops indicated that there was no interest in internal reform nor hope of any move towards a Protestant position. The bishops re–stated existing canon law and dogma, but took no effective action for moral reform and refused any compromise with those they considered heretics.[42] Yet even if they had it would have been too late, for the tide was moving strongly against them.

Mary now decided that direct action must be taken. She therefore again summoned the Protestant preachers to appear before her on May 10, 1559 in Stirling. The Protestant answer to this was the gathering of a large body of nobles and gentry in Perth, albeit without armor, to march to Stirling in support of the ministers. Somewhat taken aback by this, Mary persuaded Erskine of Dun, who had come to explain what was happening, to have the Congregation stay in Perth or go home, until she could "take some better order." To this the gathering in Perth agreed, but when the preachers did not appear before her on May 10th they were declared rebels and "at the horn." [43]

On May 2nd, 1559, just a day or so before the outlawing of the preachers, Knox arrived in Scotland.[44]

CHAPTER IX

The Trumpet Sounds in Scotland

IT WAS PERHAPS FORTUNATE that neither Elizabeth nor Cecil cared enough for Knox to allow him to pass through the country, for he might have been persuaded to settle down in one of his old English congregations. As it was, having to go directly to Scotland, he found himself immediately in the center of the conflict that was arising. One contemporary source tells us that on receiving the news that Knox had appeared in Edinburgh, probably on the 3rd or 4th of May, the Provincial Synod that was meeting dissolved, never to reassemble. All the bishops did was pass on the news of his return to the Queen Regent, then in Glasgow, who immediately "put him to the horn." Knox meanwhile had gone himself to Dundee whence, with some of the brethren from that town, he went on to the Protestant forces in Perth, where he at once became, as Sir James Croft reported to Cecil a little later, the center of the movement. Nevertheless, he was at this time "uncertain as yet what God shall further work in this country, except that I see the battell shall be great, for Satan rageth even to the uttermost." [1]

Satan, was not the only one who raged. When word reached the Protestants in Perth that the Queen Regent had outlawed the preachers on May 10th for not appearing before her as ordered, feelings ran high, as many believed that they had been deceived. Consequently after Knox preached a sermon the following day against the idolatry of the Mass tension increased to such an extent that when a priest, following the Protestant service, sought to celebrate the Mass, a riot ensued. It began with the destruction of the images in the church, but soon spread to the nearby monasteries. Knox is very insistent that this whole affair was the result of "the rascail multitude," who attacked and looted houses of the Grey and Black Friars and the Carthusians for the spoil that they could find.[2] While he has received much of the blame for this outburst, it would seem that he had not intended that his words should be taken literally (but as in so many riots in the later 1960s) hooliganism used any excuse as a cover for its own ends.[3] Neither Knox nor the leaders of the Scottish Reformation ever advocated the destruction of churches or monasteries, but rather urged that they should be converted to what they believed were proper uses.

The Queen Regent's reaction to the events in Perth was naturally anything but favorable. Consequently when Erskine of Dun appeared before her in Stirling to ask that the preachers be allowed to debate with the clergy concerning religion, he received a blunt refusal and an abrupt dismissal that was followed by his own outlawry.[4] The Queen Regent then issued a call for the nobles to come in with all their forces to suppress what she declared was obvious rebellion in Perth.[5] The Protestants replied to this by preparing letters, of which Knox was undoubtedly the author, addressed to the Queen Regent, d'Oysel the French commander, the French troops, some of whom were Protestants, and the nobility of Scotland. The general theme was that they were quite prepared to obey the duly constituted authority, if that authority would leave them in peace to practice their own religion. At the same time they warned the Queen Regent and the Roman Catholic nobles that if they continued the persecution, civil war would result. Shortly afterwards a further letter was addressed "To the Generation of Antichrist, the Pestilent Prelates and their shavelings within Scotland," pointing out the dire consequences of their continued attacks.[6] The Protestant actions and violent statements, however, hardly favored a "live and let live" policy.

The effect of these letters was to bring in some 5,000 to 6,000 Protestant supporters from the area surrounding Perth and to stimulate the western lairds, under the Earl of Glencairn, to organize a body of troops to give aid. As Mary saw these forces gathering she despatched Lord James Stewart and the Earl of Argyll, both of whom were Protestants, to find out what was going on, and to persuade "the rebels" to return home. When the latter pointed out to these two emissaries that they were not seeking to overturn the government but only to reform religion, they replied that they would seek to bring about an agreement with the Queen Regent, but that if she refused they would throw in their lots with the group in Perth. The outcome of their negotiations with both sides was a truce which provided for the withdrawal of the forces of the Congregation from Perth and the admission of Queen Regent, who for her part, promised that there would be no French garrison placed in the town and no persecution of the Protestants.[7] But neither side trusted the other, each realizing that this was but a truce until it had established its own lines in preparation for the final battle.

The question arises at this point as to the sincerity of Knox and his supporters. It appears that they were speaking truly when they said they did not purpose a political revolution. Their desire to rid Scotland of the French was hardly in that class. As Knox had stated repeatedly that the nobles represented the nation as a whole, if they sought to control the Regent's government in order to remove the foreign forces, he and those with him would feel that they were quite within their rights. The real problem is their apparently contradictory claim that they sought only toleration for themselves, while at the same time they were actually seeking the reformation of religion on a national scale. Although we cannot always look for consistency in men engaged in what is an ideological struggle, it may well be that Knox would see no conflict here. If the Protestants did but have freedom "to blow the Maister's trumpet," he was quite confident that they would by God's Spirit, soon win over the nation as a whole, with a reformation resulting. That he did not believe that toleration would be granted, however, is quite clear. Consequently he accepted the view that *force majeure* would have to settle the issue.

The Congregation now retired from Perth eastwards towards St. Andrews, but not before they had signed another mutual agreement or band by which they guaranteed that they would stand by each other in all matters relating to the reform of religion.[8] As soon as they had vacated the town the royalist forces entered but in their jubilation manifested in the firing of their hackbuts, they killed a child for which Mary showed no sorrow, a fact, duly noted by the

Protestants. Furthermore, she immediately proceeded to reestablish Roman Catholic services, remove the Protestants from the burgh council, replace Patrick, Lord Ruthven, Provost of the town, with John Charteris of Kinfauns and "oppress" the Protestants. Finally, she placed four ensigns of troops in Perth as a garrison, and when it was protested by some that she had promised that she would not introduce French soldiers, she replied that although they were paid by the French, they were Scots. They may have been Scots mercenaries sent over from France. According to Knox she added further "that she was bound to keep no promise to heretics. . . ." and that "Princes must not so straitly be bound to keep their promises." When all this was known, Lord James Stewart, the Earl of Argyll, Lord Ruthven and various others quietly left town to join their fellow Protestants.[9]

The Queen Regent, having gained control of Perth, now decided that action should be taken to oust the Congregation from their quarters in St. Andrews, and to this end her army marched towards that city. Although the Lords of the Congregation, led by Lord James, had relatively few men available, they decided to make a stand at Cupar Muir where they took up their positions on the evening of June 12th. Yet since word of their predicament had gone out, by noon of the next day forces led by Ormiston, Calder, and other lairds from as far away as Lothian had arrived. As Knox wrote "it appeared as if men had rained from the clouds." The result was another truce in which the Queen Regent promised to remove all Frenchmen from Fife and to appoint a number of nobles to negotiate a firm peace with the Congregation. When she failed to provide her representatives and continued to dominate Perth with her troops, the Congregation called for "the brethren of Fife, Angus, Mearns and Strathearn" to meet at the burgh on June 24th. At the same time Lord James and Argyll wrote Mary demanding that she fulfill the two agreements between her and the Congregation. When again they received no satisfaction the whole body of Protestants moved on Perth arriving there on the evening of June 24th. Since the garrison saw that it was useless to resist such numbers, they surrendered but were allowed to depart the next day.[10]

In all of this what part did Knox play? During the time of the Congregation's mobilization in Perth to defend the preachers

summoned to Stirling, we gather from his history, he was present
and ready to give his confession along with the other's. Furthermore,
we can hardly doubt from the style of the letters of the Congregation, that he was largely responsible for their wording. The
communication to the Queen Regent is very reminiscent of his first
letter to her, and we know that he commissioned Lord James Stewart
and the Earl of Argyll to bear a special message to her when they
returned from Perth to Stirling to negotiate the first truce. Then on
the retreat of the Congregation St. Andrews on June 4th he went
along with them.

Up to this point, apart from his stirring sermon and the probable
authoring of the various public letters in Perth, he had taken no
significant part in the events of the day. Those who had determined
what would happen were the nobles, the lairds and the burgesses
making up the Congregation's armed forces. On his arrival in St.
Andrews, however, he seemed to take on a new dimension. He had
returned to the city in which he had been originally called to the
ministry of the Gospel. Moreover, while a French galley-slave he had
prophesied that he would again proclaim the Gospel in St. Andrews,
and now the opportunity had come. He, therefore, announced that
he would preach on the following Lord's Day. The Friday and
Saturday before he went to Crail and Anstruther in the south of Fife
where he "blew the trumpet" so effectively that the people removed
all traces of the old religion from the church buildings. To this no
one offered any strong resistance, but when he spoke of preaching in
St. Andrews, Archbishop Hamilton threatened that he would have
him "saluted with a dozen culverins, whereof the most part should
light on his nose." At the same time, the leaders of the Congregation
tried to dissuade him from such action as unnecessarily provocative.
Knox, however, notwithstanding the opposition of even his friends
persisted. In the parish church he delivered such an effective sermon
on Christ's cleansing of the temple that the town authorities led by
the provost, Learmonth of Dairsie, "did agree to remove all
monuments of idolatry, which also they did with expedition,
including the images in the Cathedral, which they burned on the site
of Walter Myln's execution." [11] By his stance, he was becoming the
moral and spiritual, if not the political leader of the movement.

From St. Andrews he wrote on June 23rd in quite a jubilant tone

to Mrs. Locke telling her of what had happened. Not only had St.
Andrews been purified, but Lindores Abbey had likewise been
reformed. What was of even greater importance

> the long thirst of my wretched heart is satisfied in abundance, that is
> above my expectatioun for now fortie days and more, hath my God used
> my tongue in my native countrie, to the manifestatioun of his glorie. . . .
> The thirst of the poore people, als weill as of the nobilitie hier, is
> wondrous great which putteth me in comfort that Christ Jesus sall
> triumphe for a space heir, in the North and extreme parts of the earth.[12]

Yet even in his elation over the way events were moving he
obviously felt lonely, for he asked Mrs. Locke to see to it that
Christopher Goodman, Marjory and her mother might come to him
as soon as possible. Although, as Janton points out, he was being
carried along by the passionate piety of the crowd he still had the
need for the intimate companionship of those dear to him.[13] He may
also have desired their presence that they might share in his triumphs.

Yet his feeling of success and achievement tended to be diluted as
he discovered that the "poore people" were not entirely motivated by
a hunger and thirst for righteousness, but frequently for the property
and goods of ecclesiastics, particularly of the monks. With the return
of the Congregation to Perth the indwellers of Dundee decided that
they should "reform" the nearby Abbey of Scone, held *in com-
mendam* by Patrick Hepburn, Bishop of Moray, well-known as an
opponent of the Reformation and a persecutor of the brethren. They
therefore gathered a mob to carry out this project. When the Provost
of Dundee and his brother failed to stop them they sent for Knox, but
he likewise was unsuccessful. Finally a call went out to Argyll and
Lord James who succeeded in saving the bishop's palace and the
church for the moment, while Knox persuaded the crowd to leave the
granary unmolested. Nevertheless, the next day when the crowd
returned looking for loot, the bishop's servants' resistance resulted in
a riot which ended in the demolition of the whole complex of
buildings. According to Knox many were offended at this wanton
destruction, but one old lady standing by said that it was the
punishment of God for the immorality and seduction carried on by
the monks within its walls, "at whose words were many pacified;
affirming with her, that it was God's just judgment."[14]

Knox then goes on to point out that if human efforts could have preserved the place it would not have been destroyed "for men of greatest estimation laboured with all diligence for the safety of it." Here again we see the attitude of the leaders of the Congregation towards ecclesiastical buildings. Despite all that has been written during the past four hundred years and told by various guides to tourists, the fact is that the Congregation did not seek the destruction of the church edifices. In a good many cases those in the south of the country had already been destroyed by the English, others were in a state of disrepair owing to neglect and some, particularly monasteries, now fell victim to mob violence. The Reformers, on the other hand, looked to the time when they would be able to use these buildings for their own church services, so why should they seek to destroy them once they had been "cleansed" of the evidences of idolatry? While they did remove vestments and valuable objects such as crucifixes, reliquaries and monstrances, frequently these were sold and the funds used, especially by burgh councils, for the upkeep of the building or the payment of the ministers.[15]

Once Perth had been retaken, the word in the Congregation was, "On to Edinburgh!" Although Mary sought to block the passage of the Firth of Forth at Stirling, the Earl of Argyll and Lord James succeeded in forestalling her. This obliged her forces to retreat to Edinburgh. There, according to Leslie, she sought to persuade the burgesses to resist the Congregation, but they answered that they did not have the force to do so,

> chiefly when the people are allured with the hope of a prey, of liberty and a new kind of life, which fervor apparently scarce can be slackened by either command or force.[16]

On hearing this significant reply, Mary left for Dunbar, and by the time the Congregation arrived on June 29th "the rascail multitude" had again done its work, stripping the Grey and Black Friars' houses to the bare walls, leaving not even doors or windows.[17]

When the Lords of the Congregation marched into Edinburgh they faced many problems, the most important being the Queen Regent who lay at Dunbar with her French troops. The Lords hoped to force her to send the Frenchmen back to France and to agree to a reformation of religion, but when the people of Leith, doubtless influenced by Logan of Restalrig their feudal superior, and also by their dislike of Edinburgh, surrendered to the French without a blow,

and Lord Erskine, captain of Edinburgh Castle, threatened to turn
his guns on the Congregation if they sought to hold the town against
the French, the Protestants found it expedient to negotiate some sort
of settlement.[18] This they did at Leith Links on July 24th, when "an
appointment" was signed between the representatives of Mary and
the Congregation. The latter had demanded toleration for the
Protestants and their preachers, that Romanism should not be
reestablished in those places where it had been abolished, and that the
Frenchmen should be removed from Scotland. The treaty, however,
in its final form, had other provisions added. It stipulated that the
Congregation was to leave Edinburgh the following day, the minting
irons they had taken from Holyrood Palace were to be returned, all
clergy were to continue to enjoy their revenues until January 10th
next, Edinburgh was to be free to choose its own religion, the queen
or her officials were not to molest the Congregation's ministers, and
all were to be good obedient subjects.[19] The removal of the
Frenchmen was not included, although it may have been agreed to
verbally.

While Mary had done her utmost to break down the unity of the
Congregation, particularly by wooing both Argyll and Lord James,
she had not succeeded. On the morning after the signing of this
agreement, therefore, the Congregation, after proclaiming their own
original four points at the market cross, retired to Stirling. There
they signed another band by which each promised to have no
separate dealings with the Queen Regent, and to notify all the others
if she made any secret approach to any individual.[20]

While the Congregation's operation in Edinburgh may seem to
have been fruitless, this was by no means the case. For one thing a
large number of the burgesses of Edinburgh had now come out on
the side of the Reformation. This they indicated at a meeting in the
Tollbooth on July 7th by publicly calling Knox to become minister
of St. Giles Kirk. From this time on until almost the day of his death
he remained the pastor of this congregation and spiritual leader of the
burgh. Although he undoubtedly had his opponents within the town,
the support given him by the burgesses, indicates that he was
generally popular. At times he might thunder from the pulpit against
the government, but as his usual sermons were directed towards the
spiritual problems of his flock, we can assume that he carried on the
same type of pastoral care and counselling that he had for some years

by means of his letters. The constant attention of the burgh council
to his welfare demonstrates clearly the high regard in which they
held him. Yet the beginning of his ministry was fraught with
difficulty, for when the Congregation retired to Stirling, as a marked
man, they took him with them, leaving the more diplomatic John
Willock in his place until he could return in peace.[21]

Another reason, no doubt, for this action of the Protestant lords
was that he had been assuming a more important place in their
counsels. On his return to Scotland he had immediately pressed the
leaders of the Congregation to look to England for assistance against
Mary and her French troops. After all, England and Scotland had
much in common: Protestantism, similar languages, and geographical
ties. To this end he also wrote Sir William Cecil on June 28th and
Sir Henry Percy on July 1st, his theme being that the Protestants
sought no political revolution, but only religious reform which would
in turn open up the way for settled amity between the two nations.

> My eie hath long looked to a perpetual concord betuix these two Realms,
> the occasion wharof is now present yf God shall move your hartes
> unfeanedlie to speak the saim. . . .

He therefore sought permission to visit northern England in order
that he might preach, and also speak in secret to someone in authority
about what could be done.[22]

To back Knox's suggestion of English support for the Congregation, Sir William Kirkcaldy of Grange also wrote letters to both
Cecil and Percy.[23] While he generally followed the same line of
approach as Knox he was more detailed, stating that the Congregation was only reforming religion by pulling down some recalcitrant
friaries and abbeys, cleansing parish churches and establishing
services according to the second Edwardian Prayer Book.[24]

The English reaction to these representations was very cautious.
Cecil told Percy to assure Kirkcaldy that he desired a perpetual
alliance as had been suggested, and that if a French army came into
Scotland, England would be prepared to assist the Scots to drive them
out. One difficulty, however, was that since both Kirkcaldy and
Knox were merely private individuals he could make no official or
public pronouncement. Furthermore, he could not be sure that the
Lords of the Congregation might not later turn against the English.
After all, his countrymen had had some rather uncertain treatment

before at Scottish hands. To this Kirkcaldy replied that even though
the earls might prove untrustworthy, their supporters and servants
would not, by this statement indicating where he thought the
Reformers' principal strength lay.[25] Although the English had some
doubts about Kirkcaldy's *bona fides* as a Protestant at this time, his
letter was followed on July 19th by others, one to Cecil and one to
Queen Elizabeth, written in Knox's hand and signed by the leaders
of the Congregation. In these the Scottish lords called upon England
for assistance in ousting the French and promised a close alliance if
such aid was forthcoming. They also added that they were not
seeking to overthrow the government, but only to defend their
country against Roman Catholic and French domination.[26]

Yet despite these assurances and a personal letter from Balnaves to
Cecil, all of which were probably carried to England by the Laird of
Ormiston, the English still hesitated. Cecil and the Privy Council
wrote the Lords of the Congregation on July 28th that they could
hardly have dealings with them since they were not an official body.
Should many more join with them, especially such nobles as the Duc
de Châtelherault, the premier noble of the realm, they could then
declare themselves "the Great Council of the Realm," with whom
the English authorities could properly negotiate a treaty. At the same
time, Cecil kept prodding the nobles to take more drastic action
against the Roman Catholics, apparently failing to realize that by the
Appointment of Leith (July 24th) this was simply impossible.[27]

Yet despite his doubts, Cecil had come to the conclusion that he
must have closer and more direct contact with the Protestant lords.
Consequently on July 11th he had written Sir Henry Percy that he,
himself, would meet Knox secretly at his house in Burghley. When
Knox received this news we do not know, but it probably inspired
him to write from Edinburgh on the 20th a letter to Queen Elizabeth
which he sent enclosed with one to Cecil. In his letter to the queen
he assured her that he believed that she had been called by God to
rule over England, but at the same time, he insisted that this was by
God's grace alone and not because of her name or descent, a view
that would cast doubt on her legal right to her throne. That Cecil
passed on this letter is uncertain, but he probably did not.[28] Knox did
not wait to find out, but immediately set about preparing for his
journey. Unfortunately at this point the agreement with the Queen
Regent forced the lords and Knox to retire to Stirling. Only when

established there were they able to complete the necessary plans for Knox's embassy.

The instructions he received were that he was to promise that the lords would not submit to the French, but at the same time he was to ask for military assistance in the form of garrisons in such strengths as Eyemouth and Broughty, and for funds to pay for a garrison in Stirling. In return the lords offered a perpetual alliance in which both countries' liberties, laws, and privileges would be preserved inviolate. The last provision shows that they were no more prepared to become a province of England than they were of France.[29] With these instructions in hand Knox, along with another minister, Robert Hamilton, sailed from Pittenweem and landed on Holy Island on August 1st. As it seemed unwise, however, for him to go on south to Burghley and since Sir Henry Percy, Lord Lieutenant in the North, was absent, he was taken to Berwick where he met with Sir James Croft, Percy's deputy. Unfortunately as Knox was still well known in this area he was recognized much to the annoyance of Croft who blamed the lack of secrecy on Knox's deficiencies as a diplomat. He, however, accomplished his mission by setting forth to Croft the lords' needs, which had become more pressing since their retreat to Stirling. Then after handing over some letters to be delivered to Mrs. Bowes, now back in England, he left on August 3rd for home, giving as the reason for his hasty departure the needs of his congregation. He probably felt completely out of his depth, and desired that someone like Henry Balnaves, who took his place, should carry on the negotiations.[30]

Another, and perhaps the most important reason for Knox's hasty return to Scotland was that while in Berwick he had received a friendly letter from Cecil, regretting that they would not meet, and explaining that Elizabeth could not at this time give open aid to the Congregation in its fight against Mary of Guise, because of a treaty of peace with France. Disappointing though this message was to Knox and demoralizing as it was to the lords, they did not collapse, but promptly began a stream of letters to the English government pressing for help. Simultaneously Knox conducted his own personal campaign by writing Cecil and others calling upon the English for assistance, with the warning that if they did not help the French could well take over. If they did so they would prove "slender friends" to England.[31] That Elizabeth and her advisers realized this only too well is indicated by the fact that on August 8th she authorized Sir Ralph Sadler to spend up to £3,000 for rewards to Scots. Of this Balnaves brought a portion, which Knox with the lords' authority, distributed. Unfortunately, however, when Cockburn of Ormiston was carrying a second installment of £1,000 to the lords at the end of October he was intercepted by the Earl of Bothwell who seized the money. Bothwell then turned it over to Mary, who by this coup not only benefitted financially, but also learned of the secret assistance of the English to the Congregation.[32]

Mary should hardly have been surprised at the English action, since she, herself, had been taking every possible step to divide and defeat the Protestant party. When the Congregation left Edinburgh she had attempted to persuade the authorities there to reinstate the celebration of the Mass, but failed owing to the opposition led by Adam Fullarton, although Leith and Holyrood accepted without remonstrance the former ceremonies.[33] Then Mary began a campaign of propaganda consisting of letters and proclamations on the general theme that the Lords of the Congregation were seeking to overthrow the government. To this claim she could give some plausibility since the lords had called for a meeting of all their supporters at Glasgow on August 21st, which Mary claimed was contrary to the Appointment of Leith. What happened at Glasgow we do not know, but on August 28th Mary issued a long proclamation in which she accused the Congregation of treason and of having broken their agreement with her.[34] To these charges the lords replied with their own proclamation and a series of letters, declaring that by her bringing in of French troops, by her debasing of the coinage, by her oppressing of the people with taxes to support French garrisons, who were now arriving with their wives and children as occupiers of the country, and by her anti-Protestant actions, she had not only contravened the Appointment, but had clearly revealed her plan to subjugate the whole country to the French.[35]

As we read the Congregation's statements we cannot escape the feeling that the writing is that of Knox. So many of the phrases parallel those which we find in his letters and other writings. On the other hand, it is obvious that the stress now is primarily upon getting rid of the French, rather than upon the reformation of religion. In fact, the Congregation's reply to the proclamation at one point makes a differentiation between those who "tender true religion" and those who do not, pointing out that although some may not be interested in the reform of the church they should stand with the congregation for Scotland's sake. Even in their answers to the Queen Regent's specific statements, the only time that reference is made to religion is when the writer defends the preachers against charges of stirring up the people to revolution. The whole tone of the movement was beginning to change from one of religions reform and revival to one of political liberation and national independence. The leaders of the Congregation, no doubt influenced by English advice, were placing their hope in the latent Scottish nationalism.

The latter part of August, all of September and the first part of October were taken up with the issuing of proclamations by both sides, secret negotiations of the lords with England and attempts by Mary to woo members of the Congregation and of the uncommitted to her side. The lords repeatedly accused Mary of seeking to subjugate Scotland to foreigners, the French, proof of which they saw in the fortification of Leith. Mary, on the other hand, insisted that the lords were seeking the overthrow of all lawful government under the pretence of religions reform. She accused the lords of conspiring with the English; and when the young Earl of Arran arrived from France to join the lords and eventually persuaded his father to desert Mary, she charged that the lords sought to deprive her of her lawful authority which they planned to turn over to the head of the house of Hamilton. The lords in turn replied that they would be loyal subjects if she would get rid of the French "throat-cutters" and be guided by a council of natural Scotsmen.[36]

Throughout this period Knox, although suffering from a fever, was constantly active. He reported to Mrs. Locke from St. Andrews on September 2nd that he had, despite his sickness, been preaching all over the country and that congregations were now set up in Edinburgh, St. Andrews, Dundee, Perth, Brechin, Montrose, Stirling and Ayr, while on the borders, in Jedburgh and Kelso also, the Gospel was being proclaimed. He realized only too well that the winning of men to the Protestant side was essential to the Congregation's victory. At the same time, he remained convinced that ultimate success would come only if the English intervened, since the Congregation by itself could not repulse the armed might of France. Consequently he repeatedly appealed to Croft and others in England for more financial aid since the money brought back by Balnaves was almost gone, and the large bribes of French money offered by Mary had begun to weaken the morale of the less committed members of the Congregation.[37] Added to her offers of bribes, Mary now attempted to use a known Protestant, Robert Lockhart, to begin secret negotiations with the Protestant leaders, including Lord James and Knox, himself. All of them refused to respond to her approaches but at the same time assured her of their loyalty if she would remove the Frenchmen from her counsels and from Scotland.[38]

The lords now decided that they must take further action. Having convened in Stirling on October 15, 1559, they resolved to return to Edinburgh in order to put an end to the fortifying of Leith as a French stronghold. The following day they marched into the capital whence they promptly dispatched a demand to Mary that the fortification of Leith stop. When it became quite clear that she had no intention of heeding their protests, the lords with some of the preachers among whom was Knox, met in the Tollbooth to take formal action against her. The question was: should and could she be removed from the regency? Willock as the acting minister in St. Giles pointed out that rulers had a responsibility to their subjects, who, if they were neglected or abused could remove them. Since Mary had obviously failed in her duty, the lords as the true-born councillors of the realm could depose her. Knox agreed completely, but stipulated that her actions should not diminish their loyalty to the queen in France, and if the regent repented she should be restored to her honors and authority. Thereupon, the nobles issued a formal decree in the names of Mary and Francis removing the Queen Regent and appointing a council composed of Châtelherault, three earls, three barons and the Provost of Dundee to govern the country.[39]

The lords' action did not really settle anything. Although they summoned Leith to surrender and even attempted to carry it by force, everything went wrong. Mary's policy of dividing and ruling was having its effect. The unpaid soldiers mutinied. Some of those in the lords' inner councils acted as Mary's spies. When the Dundonian contingent on October 31st attempted a sortie on Leith they were forced to leave their cannon and retreat to Edinburgh, a defeat that was followed a week later by another in the same locality. But probably most disastrous of all was Bothwell's capture of the English

£1,000. Nobles and commons alike began to desert what they felt was a sinking ship. The only thing to do was to retreat once again to Stirling.[40]

Meanwhile in Edinburgh Knox had begun to preach in St. Giles, although apparently Willock remained officially the minister until, with the departure of the Congregation for Stirling, he left for England. While occupying the pulpit of the High Kirk and performing some pastoral duties for his flock, Knox must also have been in constant consultation with the leading lords, for whom he was probably writing letters and proclamations. As he pointed out in a letter of October 23rd to Gregory Railton in England, he had hardly four hours in twenty-four for rest and wrote "with sleaping eis." At the same time, his life was in constant danger. As he explained to Railton he needed a good horse, which he hoped his brother-in-law, George Bowes, would procure for him, "for great watch is laid for my apprehension, and large money promissed till any that sall kyll me." Meanwhile Marjory, who having arrived in Dundee on September 20th with their two sons, must have been a comfort, although in other ways an added care, to the busy man.[41] But when the Congregation once again left Edinburgh for Stirling, the Knox family also had to move.

As long as the fortunes of the Congregation were rising, Knox had been pushed into the background by leaders such as Lord James Stewart, the Earl of Argyll and, with the adherence of the Hamiltons, by the Duc de Châtelherault and the Earl of Arran. But with what was now a breakdown of morale he once again came to the fore. As more than one historian has commented, he never showed up so well as when in the midst of defeat, for he could point to the Congregation's complete dependence on God for victory. This was the theme of his sermon in Stirling on November 8th, when he continued the exposition of Psalm 80 which he had already commenced in Edinburgh. Basing his words on verses 4–8, he declared that the Congregation had been guilty of lamentable lack of faith, particularly since the coming of the Hamiltons, for they had turned from trust in God to trust in man. Moreover, even though the duke, who had been a persecutor of the faithful, had confessed his sin, he had not known the grief and sorrow of their former defeats. Nevertheless, if they all would repent and turn to God.

> I no more doubt that this our dolour, confusion, and fear shall be turned
> into joy, honour and boldness than that I doubt that God gave victory to

the Israelites over the Benjaminites. . . . For as it is the eternal truth of the eternal God, so shall it once prevail, howsoever for a time it be impugned.

The effect was apparently electric, for the lords promptly met and after prayer by Knox, authorized William Maitland of Lethington, who had but recently deserted the Queen Regent for the Congregation, to repair immediately to London to seek English aid.[42]

Some of Knox's biographers believe that this very plain spoken sermon drove a wedge between him and the lords of the Congregation, who appointed Lethington rather than him to go to England.[43] Knox, however, realized that he was not cut out for the diplomatic maneuverings required in dealing with Cecil and Queen Elizabeth.[44] This feeling was reinforced by his failure to gain Croft's support for a scheme, whereby 1,000 English troops would be sent across the border as volunteers to help the Congregation, but would be disowned and declared rebels by the English government. Although this has a very modern ring and was later employed at times by Elizabeth herself, Croft was suitably shocked although he revealed his true reason for rejecting it when he complained to Knox that "ye are so open in your doings as you make men half affrayed to deale with you." [45] To this Knox replied that Croft might well appear morally indignant, but that the English had better do something to help the Congregation, otherwise they would soon have a large French force sitting on their northern border. It was with this same message that Maitland now went to London.[46]

Although Knox had succeeded in raising morale by his sermon, the more material needs of men and money pressed equally hard upon the Lords of the Congregation. For this reason, Balnaves had in September opened negotiations with Croft at Berwick, in the hope of obtaining immediate military and financial assistance.[47] The English, however, by their reluctance to move, played right into the hands of Mary of Guise, who now issued a proclamation saying that she was prepared to receive back into favor all the nobles except Balnaves, Lethington and Ormiston who had misled the duke and the others of the Congregation. As the Protestants were in serious straits financially, many whose motivation was more political than religious, began to waver.[48]

In this difficult situation, Knox wrote two significant letters on

·November 18th. The first he addressed to Cecil to whom he pointed out that many of the Protestant lords were so impoverished as a result of fighting the Guisan forces, that they could do no more. If, therefore, the French should gain control of Scotland, the conquest of England would be next on the agenda. It sounded almost like the despairing cry of a dying man. The other letter, written to Mrs. Locke had a very different tone. He expressed his confident expectation that the Protestant cause would eventually be victorious through the blessing of God who had allowed the Congregation to be humbled for a moment, because they had put their confidence in man. He then urged her to appeal to the faithful in London to help support the Protestant cause in Scotland by contributing money which he felt would be a true demonstration of Christian charity. He concluded with a request that she obtain for him Calvin's commentary on Isaiah, recently republished with a dedication to Queen Elizabeth, along with the new edition of Calvin's *Institutes* for which he would pay her, although, he added, he had little time for his own business.

While these two letters show a strong contrast, there is nothing contradictory in their contents, for Knox as- a staunch Calvinist believed firmly that God controls and rules over all things, but he does so by means of human action. Therefore, he could write as forcefully as possible to Cecil, believing that both he, himself, and the Secretary were but agents of God's sovereign purpose. He could also ask Mrs. Locke to raise money for the cause, although he was confident of ultimate victory. Cecil, recognizing the correctness of Knox's analysis, urged Elizabeth to act. Mrs. Locke, on the other hand, having strong quietist tendencies, replied in December saying that since this was God's battle all Knox should do was pray, and God would give the victory without the need of such mundane things as money, a point of view that Knox certainly did not appreciate.[49]

It must have been some time towards the end of November that Knox received a letter from Calvin. In August he had written him about two practical problems. The first was whether he should baptize bastard sons of idolators and excommunicated persons unless either the parents had repented and submitted or the children were old enough to ask for baptism themselves. The second was whether the monks and priests who did not serve God in the church should receive their yearly stipends from the church. Knox took a negative position on both these matters. Calvin, on the other hand, did not see the answers in black and white terms. He pointed out that as God's covenant with his people is eternal to a thousand generations, the children probably came from faithful progenitors, and if this were the case, they should be baptized on condition that proper and conscientious sponsors promised to see to their adequate training in the faith. As for the *fainéant* clergy, while they had no legal or moral claim to ecclesiastical revenues, they should be treated humanely since many of them had taken their vows in ignorance of the truth and also had no trade or skill by which they could support themselves. Therefore, if they could not earn their livelihood they should be given enough to supply their needs.[50] How far Knox accepted this advice we do not know, but it may have had its effect on the actions taken with regard to the old church a little later.

While Knox was writing letters to England seeking support for the Lords of the Congregation, they were experiencing great trouble. Unable to resist the Queen Regent's forces they now found it necessary to abandon Stirling, the western lords retreating to Glasgow where they would be within easy reach of their own lands, and the others including Arran, Lord James, the Earl of Rothes, and the Master of Lindsay concentrating their activities in Fife, with their headquarters in St. Andrews. Balnaves became secretary of the western group and Knox of the eastern. Both these forces, however, soon found themselves in serious difficulties, for they could only carry on a sort of guerrilla warfare, which though vigorous was not enough to stop the French. As Knox pointed out to Croft at the end of December, 900 additional French troops had arrived and 15 more ensigns were expected. With these, Mary could crush all resistance and capture Stirling and St. Andrews. His prophecy proved only too true, for early in January the French had taken Stirling and were advancing on St. Andrews despite the hit-and-run tactics of Arran, Lord James and Kirkcaldy of Grange. Then within six miles of the city, they suddenly found themselves forced to halt.[51]

Although Mary of Guise, according to Knox, after a French victory at Kinghorn sneered, "Where is now John Knox's God? My God is now stronger than his, yea even in Fife," the arrival of an English squadron of eight ships under Admiral Winter, seemed to indicate that Knox's God was still in control. Dispatched by Elizabeth early in January 1560 as a result of the negotiations of Maitland of Lethington, Winter arrived just in time. As Knox wrote to Mrs. Locke: "We have had a wonderful experience of God's merciful providence." [52] Simultaneously, the Duke of Norfolk had come to Berwick intent upon negotiating with the Lords of the Congregation, but the western lords, led by Châtelherault, who sought to control, asked that the meetings be held in Carlisle. Knox, thereupon, wrote them a strongly worded letter accusing them of ignoring the eastern lords. As a result, representatives of both groups repaired to Berwick where, after further negotiations, a treaty between England and the lords was signed on February 27, 1560. Both sides agreed to assist each other against mutual enemies, but in particular, the English promised to help rid Scotland of the French, while making no attempt to conquer the country themselves. [53]

In fulfillment of this agreement, an English army crossed the border on April 2nd and for the next three months made half-hearted and ineffectual efforts to capture Leith which housed the French troops. The common foot soldiers, both English and Scottish, proved to be completely inefficient and the officers were little better. Nevertheless, hunger took such a toll of the French garrison that by the end of June they were only too glad to know that the government of France had opened negotiations for their evacuation. [54]

Meanwhile Mary of Guise had died. About the time of the arrival of the English expeditionary force, she had retired sick with dropsy to Edinburgh Castle, which Lord Erskine was holding in strict neutrality. From this vantage point, according to Knox, she rejoiced at the defeat of an English attack on Leith calling the naked bodies of the dead which the French hung over the ramparts "the fairest tapestry I ever saw." The only difficulty is, however, that it is extremely doubtful that she could see the Leith fortifications from Edinburgh Castle. In the last days of May she was nearing her end, and since the Protestants in Edinburgh refused her permission to see d'Oysel, the French commander, she consented to meet with Argyll, Glencairn, Marischal, and the Lord James, with whom she made her peace. She then had a private interview with John Willock, who had recently returned from England, and on June 11th she passed away. [55] One cannot help feeling that if she had been less devoted to France and to the family of Guise, she would have made a better ruler of Scotland for she undoubtedly had the ability to do so, a fact that even Knox who disliked her intensely rather grudgingly admits.

In writing of Mary of Guise's death in his *History* Knox, as W. C. Dickinson, the most recent editor of his work comments, "descends to the worst of his innuendos, making a double attack upon Mary Queen of Scots and her mother." [56] To this we must agree, but we should also remember that his comments were probably written early in 1566 when Mary, as a consequence of Riccio's murder seemed to be in a position to dictate her own religious settlement to the country, a possibility that Knox, who had seen religious persecution in France, feared greatly. Furthermore, during the period from January 1560 on, Knox had found himself pushed more and more into the background. As he explained to Railton on January 29th, since he was judged by the leaders as too extreme in his views, he had withdrawn from all public assemblies to private study.[57] The lords and Thomas Randolph, the English representative, losing much of their interest in the religious aspects, had made the struggle primarily a secular movement for the liberation of the Scots from French domination. Consequently Knox no longer had a first hand knowledge of events. He depended instead upon the reports, often highly colored, of others which may explain both his remarks about Mary of Guise, and the obvious confusion in his dating of events at this time. Even the modern press suffers from such troubles occasionally.

On June 16th negotiations commenced between Charles de Rochefoucault, Sieur de Randan, and Jean de Monluc, Bishop of Valence, representing France, and Dr. Nicholas Wotton, Dean of Canterbury and York, and Sir William Cecil representing England. As Knox points out, the drawing up of a satisfactory treaty was "langsum," for neither side trusted the other. At the same time about fifty of the Lords of the Congregation who had signed another "band" at Leith on April 27th submitted to the negotiators certain demands which became annexed to the Treaty of Edinburgh. The general theme of these "concessions," as they are sometimes called, was that all foreign troops should be removed from Scottish soil and that the king and queen should govern through their native born councillors, the nobility of the realm. Added to this, they desired that both the Congregation and Mary of Guise's supporters should agree to an "act of oblivion," whereby everyone was to forgive and forget all unlawful acts committed since March 1558—a rather tall order.

The final treaty signed on July 6th, 1560, provided for a general peace between the three countries, Mary's and Francis' abandonment of the English coat of arms which they had quartered with those of France and Scotland to signify Mary's claim to Elizabeth's throne, the evacuation of all French troops, except 120 at Dunbar, and the destruction of the fortifications of Leith and the new buildings at Dunbar. The question of religion was left in suspense. The English had hoped that the treaty would establish a church order similar to that of England, for they did not like, as Archbishop Parker put it, "such a visitation as Knox has attempted in Scotland," (November 5, 1559). The Scots, on the other hand, led by Knox, were not prepared to adopt the English pattern and the French objected to both. Therefore, the settlement of the religious question was postponed until a delegation of nobles appointed by the Estates had been able to discuss the matter with Mary and Francis.[58]

When the Treaty was signed a great service of thanksgiving was held in St. Giles Kirk, presumably led by Knox who reproduces in his History *verbatim* the prayer he offered at the time. This treaty, along with the "concessions" seems to indicate that Knox's ideas of political government had been wholeheartedly adopted by the leaders of the Congregation. Their insistence that the country should be governed by the crown through the "natural" representatives of the people, fitted right in with the pamphlets he had written to both nobles and "commonalty" in Dieppe in 1557. Furthermore, the French plenipotentiaries' agreement to the calling of parliament which could send a delegation to the monarchs to discuss the matter of religion, accorded well with his view that it was up to the people themselves to take action to reform the church if the rulers would not do so. One is rather hard pressed, therefore, to understand the surprise expressed by some writers at the actions of the Estates when they met on August 1st and took steps to bring about reforms.[59]

During the meeting of the Estates, Knox, having now resumed his position as the minister of St. Giles commenced preaching a series of sermons on the Prophecy of Haggai, who had called upon Israel recently returned from exile, to forget the building of their own houses in order to build the house of God. His views on the necessity of rebuilding the temple in Scotland, caused considerable controversy, for *politiques* such as Maitland of Lethington disliked his emphasis on the need for radical religious reform, which would oblige them "to bear the barrow to build the house of God." Since parliament, therefore, hesitated to take action, Knox and his allies presented a petition to it, asking that a full reformation of the church now be instituted. After much discussion pro and con, Knox, along with five other ministers, was commissioned to draw up a confession of faith. This they did, presenting it within four days to the Lords of the Articles who approved it and transmitted it to the whole parliament. Knox and his colleagues appeared on August 15th to support their statement, but faced little opposition despite the fact that many of the Roman Catholic bishops were present. When the matter came to the vote only one or two opposed enacting the confession into law. On August 17th the confession was adopted and a week later came into effect. At the same time two other acts abolished the celebration of the Mass and papal authority throughout the realm.[60]

The victory that Knox had anticipated by the power of God, although some others attributed it to a more sinister influence, had been achieved. He could be well satisfied for Scotland was now at least officially a Protestant country, a fact for which he could take much of the credit. Furthermore this had been accomplished through the action of the Estates, who, he believed, were the true rulers of the country. Two comments of Scottish historians sum up the matter. W. C. Dickinson remarks that

> It may be true that the Army of the Congregation was dependent upon the support of the Protestant nobility, and upon the adherence of the small barons and burgesses who composed its ranks; but it is equally true that Knox was the leader who stood firm when others faltered, and who could inspire others by the inspiration which he himself derived from his assurance in his cause.

To this James MacKinnon adds:

> But he was ready to lead a religious revolution to the bitter end, under constitutional form if it could be done; if not, with supreme indifference to royal rights or susceptibilities, if needs must.[61]

The trumpet had blown to good effect. It would now be necessary to see that the tune continued in the same key. The great danger, as far as Knox was concerned, was that the religious reforms might be supplanted by aristocratic factionalism and political intrigue.

CHAPTER X

More Than Five Hundred Trumpets

AUGUST 1560 WAS THE turning point in both the Scottish Reformation and in the life of its leading exponent, John Knox. Protestantism had now gained the victory by parliamentary enactment. Scotland had officially become a Protestant country with a Calvinistic church established by law. Yet this did not make Scotland Protestant in fact, nor did it really establish a Scottish Reformed church.[1] The majority in the country still clung to the old faith or were as they had been before, indifferent to the whole matter, seeking only to ascertain where and when the religious change would bring them some economic, social or political advantage. Consequently, the apparent victory of Protestantism led not to religious and political unity but to division between those who were reformers primarily for conscience sake and those who sought mainly for "goods and grandeur." The former seem to have been drawn largely from the "middling sort" of folk, the burgesses and the lesser nobility or lairds, and the latter principally from the upper nobility. And it was the identification of the "middling sort" with Knox and he with them that was to be crucial during the sixties.[2]

That this should be the case hardly seems strange. He had come from the class of small farmers who were in close contact with the local gentry, particularly in Lothian. He had commenced his career as a notary, a teacher and a preacher among them. When he returned

to Scotland in 1559 most of his supporters came from among the
gentry and the burgesses of towns such as Dundee, Perth, Edinburgh, and Irvine. It is, therefore, by no means surprising that when
division appeared within the ranks of the Lords of the Congregation
that Knox, the lairds and the burgesses should be on one side and the
great nobles on the other, a point that is extremely important for our
comprehension of subsequent events.

In order to understand what took place, however, we must first
take a closer look at the Confession of Faith passed by parliament and
also at the proposed organization of the new church as set forth in
The Book of Discipline. The Confession was strongly Calvinistic in
its theology, but contrary to some opinions it was neither purely
theoretical, nor was it scholastic in its tone. Similar to, and
undoubtedly influenced by the confession adopted by the French
Reformed Church in the preceding year, it had a strongly practical
bias. Stressing its total loyalty and obedience to the Bible as the
Word of God, it sought to be a statement of the faith of the Scottish
people as a whole.[3]

Although some have claimed that Knox and his collaborators in
drawing up the Confession were very much influenced by the
Forty-two Articles of the Edwardian Church of England, a close
examination of the document does not bear this out. The reason for
Thomas Randolph's opposition to the hasty production of the
Confession in four days seems to have been that it was not English
enough in its formulation, a fact that may also have persuaded
Maitland of Lethington and some of the others to attempt without
success to modify it.[4] Yet it was by no means purely Scottish. The
principal influence was undoubtedly Genevan, for Calvin's catechism
and espiecially the confession of the Genevan English congregation
clearly provided the foundation. At the same time the French
Confession of 1559 which Knox had probably brought to Scotland
with him had both verbal and theological connections with it. One
can also trace resemblances to other confessional statements such as
those of à Lasco and Bullinger, as well as Valerian Poullain's *Liturgia
Sacra*, particularly the section on the "Marks of the Church." Thus it
is clear that the Scots confession came directly out of the Continental
Reformed milieu.[5]

Yet notwithstanding its undoubted indebtedness to the continental
Reformed churches, the Scots Confession was also Scottish, one

might even say Knoxian. It followed the usual Trinitarian division of the Apostles' Creed, but changed the positions of certain of the statements in other confessions, added some of its own, and elaborated others as the authors felt the need to stress certain topics to meet the Scottish situation. Finally, its view of the civil magistrate expressed is clearly Knoxian, albeit presented in positive rather than negative terms. To this statement, Maitland of Lethington and some of the more "politique" Protestant nobles took exception, as it emphasized too strongly for them the responsibility of the magistrate to God, which might well give the church a toehold in political affairs.[6]

The significance of the Scots Confession was that it set the Scottish Reformed Church in a unique position. Naturally it sought to differentiate its own theology from that of the Church of Rome by stating such doctrines as justifications by faith alone, divine election by grace, and the final authority of the Bible in all matters religious as clearly and exactly as possible, while rejecting the decrees of General Councils, which set forth non-biblical doctrines or imposed humanly devised ceremonies. In so doing the authors of the Confession seem to have been determined to keep out even such things as kneeling in the Communion Service and similar deviations from biblical precept and example. This interpretation is confirmed by the attitude of the Scottish ecclesiastical leaders who when later dealing with other churches, stated frankly that they considered the Scottish church to be the most perfectly reformed church in existence.

While some who opposed the adoption of the Confession insisted that parliament acted *ultra vires* by virtue of the fact that the Treaty of Edinburgh had said that the settlement of religion would be left until negotiations had been completed with Mary in France, it was in fact the most representative parliament held in Scotland between 1488 and 1603. The usual number of earls, lords of parliament, archbishops, bishops and abbots or lay commendators of abbeys attended, but eighty-five lairds and the representatives of twenty-two towns also came. As one looks at the parliamentary records for the preceding century, such attendance of gentry and burgesses was virtually unknown. Now they insisted that they had a right to a say in parliament's decisions by appointing their representatives to the Lords of the Articles and by voting on their recommendations.[7] Although the lords and the prelates at first hesitated, they eventually agreed, for as R. S. Rait has put it, the lairds and townsmen were "representative of a large and insistent section of national opinion." [8] This would seem to explain why parliament accepted the Confession. Burgesses and lairds together overwhelmed all opposition.[9]

As we glance at the personnel of the Reformation Parliament we find that at the apex were the great lords: the Duc de Châtelherault and thirteen earls. Of these, Sutherland and Caithness from the most northerly areas voted against the Confession. Others present also did not approve but were apparently unwilling to say so; of these Cassillis and Huntly were the two most important. Probably too, some did not care, but felt that they could profit from the change. Argyll, Glencairn, and Rothes, on the other hand, were convinced Protestants as they had already demonstrated.[10]

Among the nineteen lords of parliament, much the same situation prevailed. While lords Ruthven, St. John, Maxwell and Lindsay seem to have had strong religious convictions, others such as Lord Erskine apparently supported the religious change for what they could get out of it.[11] According to Knox only Somerville and Borthwick from the lords took their stand against the new Confession.[12]

The representatives of the ecclesiastical estate seem to have participated very little in the discussion. According to Maitland of Lethington all the clergy accepted the Confession except the Archbishop of St. Andrews and the bishops of Dunblane and Dunkeld who abstained at the time of the vote. The Archbishop of Glasgow, however, retired shortly afterwards to France with the departing French troops, while others of the clergy and members of the religious orders continued in their parishes and monasteries to carry on as had been their wont. This state of affairs would face Knox and his colleagues with one of their major problems in the near future.[13]

Yet while we must take note of the earls, lords, bishops, and abbots, the truly important group would seem to have been that made up of the lairds and the burgesses who obviously attended in order to see that the Reformation was made a reality. This group, when their leaders began proceedings by spending all their time discussing the Anglo-Scottish alliance, perhaps in the hope of avoiding the ecclesiastical issue, demanded that immediate action be taken to reform religion. While no doubt partially the result of Knox's sermons which he preached to large crowds every day during the sittings of parliament, their Protestant zeal needed little external stimulus.[14] As one examines the list of lairds and burghs and plots them upon a map, one soon discovers that the great mass of the gentry came from the Lowland area extending south from Aberdeen through Angus and the Mearns, Fife, and Lothian, then west to Lanark, Ayrshire, and Dumfriesshire. Moray and Elgin in the north, and the border areas around Selkirk, Galashiels, and Jedburgh, had a few representatives, but the large majority had their origin in the areas that had been increasingly militantly Protestant since 1540. The twenty-two burghs represented were located in the same areas. Consequently, with eighty-five lairds and the delegates of twenty-two burghs against a total of sixty from all the other groups, the Protestant element had an overwhelming majority which could not be denied. Led by Knox they made certain that a new church would be established.[15]

Yet if Knox and the other Protestants believed that they had legalized the Reformation in Scotland by parliamentary action, such was not the view of Mary and Francis in France. The Treaty of Edinburgh had not provided for any such action. Therefore, although Knox claimed that the most representative parliament in years had met with royal authorization, the monarchs could state that parliament had acted without its authority in dealing with the matter of religion. On the other hand, it could be argued that as the most representative parliament held so far in the century, it had the right to legislate on anything it desired.[16] But whatever its theoretical rights, Mary and Francis would not recognize its action when James Sandilands, Lord St. John, brother of the Laird of Calder, came to Paris to present its legislation for ratification. On November 16th, Francis wrote a curt letter to the Estates to the effect that he and Mary were displeased with their enactments, but because of his love for them he would send over representatives who would assemble a legal parliament in order that they might fulfil their duty properly.[17] This communication must have made some wonder as to the future of Scotland under such a monarch, particularly as he was known to be a man who had no love for Protestant beliefs.[18]

While agreement on the matter of the Confession had been reached within parliament with comparative ease since it involved no economic or social changes, the problem of implementing the Confession by establishing an institutional church soon brought trouble. Two main questions arose in this connection. What form should this new church take? Should it simply be a purified adaptation of the old institution, or should it be built anew from the ground up? Closely related to this was the matter of financial support for the new body. Should it receive the existing ecclesiastical endowments, should it be supported directly by the government, or should it depend upon the free-will offerings of the people? While the old church's organization had grown up over the years by a process of trial and error—the Protestants would say mainly error—the action of parliament required the establishment of a new church all at once, which meant that a complete plan had to be devised immediately.

That Knox had undoubtedly realized the need for such a plan before parliament met would seem clear, but at this point a problem arises. Knox reports that the Great Council of nobles on April 29, 1560 instructed him along with those who later drew up the Confession to prepare "a book of Reformation." While David Laing, W. C. Dickinson, and others have accepted Knox's statement at face value, J. K. Cameron, who has recently published a detailed study of the first *Book of Discipline* (which apparently was "the book of Reformation") indicates that it is probable that two if not three revisions of the book took place before it reached the form in which it has come down to us in Knox's *History*. He seems to feel that probably the committee of which Knox speaks did not prepare the first draft, but acted as a committee of revision in the autumn of 1560 in preparation for the book's submission to the new church's first General Assembly which met in December of that year. As a result of the Assembly's acceptance of the book it may have undergone further revision before or after its submission to the Privy Council in the following January. It is this final form which we have. This hypothesis fits in well with facts and may well explain certain characteristics of the book.[19]

Knox was undoubtedly responsible for the original idea of preparing the book and was probably largely responsible for its contents. Dickinson has characterized this as an example of his "forward mindedness"; the triumph of the Congregation was at that time by no means assured. Wishing to have a plan at hand for the new church's organization which could be implemented immediately when victory had been achieved, Knox and his collaborators, whoever they may have been, submitted the book to the lords by May 30th. At the moment, however, with the English and French troops facing each other, everything was moving toward a military crisis. Consequently no action was taken, except that the book was ordered translated into Latin and sent to various continental reformers for their comments.[20] Although we have no evidence that the reformers ever offered their criticisms, if they did, no doubt these had their influence on the subsequent revisions.

The book in its original form was obviously intended to be both a confession and, to use the French term, a discipline, i.e. a plan of church organization and government. This appears even in the final version of 1561. "The First head, of Doctrine," however, was relatively short, affirming the final authority of Scripture and rejecting the prescription of laws, councils or constitutions not derived from it. The second head dealt at more length with the administration of the sacraments and the third with the abolition of idolatry. The fourth head then took up the question of ministers and their election, moving into the area of organization. It would seem from the short space allotted to doctrine and sacraments, that either the authors felt that they already had a clear enough idea of the true nature of Christian belief, or as is more likely they recognized that they would later have to draw up a complete statement, which they did on the instruction of parliament the following August.

The key to the proposed constitution of the church was the parish minister, who had to be properly called by the congregation and inducted into his office, after he had been duly examined by learned ministers appointed for this purpose. No laying on of hands was to take place since no spiritual gifts were conferred in ordination or induction. The ceremony simply recognized the gifts that the candidate already possessed and set him aside for their official use. The statement that the government should insist that men who had such gifts should enter the ministry fully confirms this view of ordination. At the same time, owing to the scarcity of qualified men, there were only twelve in 1560, others might be appointed as readers who would not have the right either to preach or administer the sacraments, but could conduct services of worship and in certain cases might be licensed as exhorters. Some readers might aspire to be ministers, but they would not be ordained until they had undergone further training and testing.

In order to organize and extend the church, the authors of the book felt that "for this time" some ten or twelve "godly and learned" men should be chosen to act as diocesan superintendents. These men were to be ministers who would each have a central place of residence, but who would also be responsible to oversee the extension work of the church throughout their areas. They were to be diligent preachers and active in setting up new congregations. They could not on their own authority appoint men as ministers of charges, although if a congregation failed to call a man within a reasonable time the superintendent and his council, made up of ministers from other congregations, could present a candidate to the people who should either accept him or propose someone else. Although at the beginning the government was to appoint the superintendents, the usual procedure would be election for a term of three years. The superintendent was always to be subject to the scrutiny and criticism of his fellow ministers and generally of the laymen of the province over which he presided. One is reminded in these provisions of the authority given to "superintendents of missions" in Presbyterian churches established in the British colonies during the nineteenth century. The principal reason for their existence in both cases was the scarcity of men available to administer to the religious needs of the people.

With the provision thus having been made for the true preaching of the Word and the proper administration of the sacraments, two of the three marks of the church as set forth in Poullain's *Liturgia* and in the Genevan *Form of Prayers* had been assured. The third was that of discipline to which the seventh head was devoted. Strict rules were laid down, concluding with the statement which led to considerable conflict later, that all estates "as well the rulers as they that rule; yea and the Preachers themselves, as well as the poorest within the Church" must be subject to ecclesiastical discipline in matters of faith and morals. At the same time, considerable emphasis was laid upon the necessity that the whole congregation through its representatives, the elders and deacons elected each year, was to participate in any disciplinary action.

From the earliest days of the Reformation, education held a prime place in the interests of the Protestant leaders. The old church both in Scotland and on the Continent had failed to educate the average layman although it had produced some very able and subtle scholars in its universities.[21] Consequently it is not surprising that when the Genevan *Form of Prayers* was drawn up in 1556 it emphasized the need for colleges and schools to prepare the youth for public service in church and state and to train them in godly living. This contention was reinforced three years later when Calvin's Genevan Academy was opened for the purpose of giving advanced Protestant education.[22] It is not surprising, therefore, that Knox and his collaborators in drawing up their Book of Reformation planned a system of universal, free education to be financed out of the church lands. They proposed the erection of parish schools and high schools for all, followed by attendance, if qualified, at one of the three established universities. Such a system would provide Scotland with the best educated population in western Europe.[23]

Another matter of deep concern to Knox had always been poverty. Repeatedly he had insisted that the members of the church were responsible for the care of those who were in need. In some of his earlier writings he had advised that at the Communion of the Lord's Supper, a special collection should be taken on their behalf. The Book of Reformation, therefore, also recommended that the poor should be relieved of paying teinds (tithes) and that the deacons should collect from those who could pay to provide for a quarterly distribution to those in need. Knox and his fellow authors refused to regard poverty as solely the result of laziness and sin; they believed that the needy were frequently not responsible for their condition.

To finance these plans the book proposed that all lands held by the Roman Catholic Church should be turned over to the Reformed church for its use. It has been estimated that the total annual revenue of the church in Scotland coming from more than fifty percent of the country's real estate as well as offerings and various dues, amounted to about £300,000 (Scot.). This would indeed be a large amount of money to be devoted to religious and social services. In view of the fact that the royal revenues at the same time amounted to only £17,000 (Scot.) it is easy to see why the government could not countenance such a proposal.[24] The reaction, therefore, of the civil authorities was bound to be negative. Furthermore, some might well have questioned the right of the Reformed church to property originally given, as Knox would insist, for "superstitious purposes."

That the *Book of Discipline* did not spring fully grown from the heads of its authors would seem obvious. As in the case of the

Confession it is clear that the Genevan examples of both Calvin and the English *Form of Prayers* were influential. Valerian Poullain's ecclesiastical organization in Frankfort also had its place in the background, as did the 1557 and 1559 disciplines of the French churches, the form of organization devised by à Lasco for the refugee churches in London and the Danish ecclesiastical structure as designed by Bugenhagen.[25] Since both John Willock and John Spottiswoode as well as Knox had experience of continental practices, these were undoubtedly taken into consideration in the revision of the book in the autumn of 1560.

Professor Cameron has pointed out that while much of the original draft largely prepared by Knox was probably preserved in the final version, he has been able to show that there were three major interpolations inserted by the revisers. The first was that concerning superintendents, which in the present writer's opinion probably reflected the views of John Willock and perhaps Spottiswoode. The second was that dealing with schools probably composed by Knox, and the third with universities, probably the work of John Winram and John Douglas, both of whom had spent most of their lives teaching at St. Andrews.[26] Thus the book presented to the General Assembly and to the Privy Council was rather different from that originally drawn up.

While the sections on education are quite clear, there has been considerable discussion concerning the provision of superintendents. Some recent writers have adopted the position that these officials were really bishops, albeit "godly bishops" in the same class as the bishops in Elizabeth's church, or at least after the pattern established in Denmark. Yet it would seem that they are drawing too many inferences from the material available. It is important to note, first of all, that superintendents were apparently not mentioned in the original draft. The supervision of the churches of an area or region was to rest in the hands of the most truly reformed church of the area, usually that in the most important town, which would follow the usual economic practice whereby the royal burgh controlled the trade of the surrounding area. It would seem that superintendents were only brought into the picture when revision began in the autumn of 1560, when perhaps Willock and Spottiswoode were added to the number working on the book. We can well imagine that Knox might have been very dubious of such an innovation after his experiences in England and Frankfort-am-Main. In the light of the scarcity of trained men for the ministry in Scotland, however, the reformers could hardly have done anything else. On the other hand, the comment that this arrangement was for the time being, and the implication that appointment as Willock, Superintendent of Glasgow, understood, was for a limited time only, as well as the fact that the superintendents were subject to the criticism and discipline of their provinces and that the first order of business of every General Assembly was an examination of the superintendents' activities, all indicate that the office was very different from that of a bishop. Furthermore, since the superintendent received no other form of ordination than that of a minister, and the Assembly of 1566 specifically rejected the idea of a clerical hierarchy, it seems clear that he was purely an administrative officer. Then too, that Christopher Goodman, a violent anti-Episcopalian was high in the councils of the Scottish church when the discipline was prepared, and that Randolph had to report that the Scottish ecclesiastical leaders were strongly opposed to conforming to the Church of England, lend further support to the view that superintendents were never intended to be bishops in the usual sense. Even Erskine of Dun, superintendent of Angus and Mearns, whom some cite as a typical superintendent-bishop, does not seem to have believed that a superintendent was anything more than a minister fulfilling an administrative function. Writing in 1571 concerning the "Kirk of God," he lays great stress upon the minister, mentions a bishop along with a minister once in passing, and never refers to a superintendent. The evidence does not seem to point to a plan for an Episcopal church, no matter what some of the nobility might have desired.[27]

In spite of their disagreement with the English church order, however, Knox and his allies had no intention of becoming the enemies of England. They even went so far as to say that they were prepared to discuss matters ecclesiastical with any learned men from south of the border. Furthermore, both in public and private, they advocated and prayed for close amity, although apparently not union, between the two countries.[28] In this they were supported by the merchants, who immediately after peace was established, began to apply for safe-conducts to trade in England or to pass through on their way to trade in France. Sometimes they ran afoul of some over zealous English officials or privateers and sometimes Scottish privateers seized English ships, but usually the problem was settled without too much difficulty. The Scottish government at this point to show their friendship even abolished all privateers' *letters of marque*.[29] Travellers to the Continent also, because of the changed relations between the two countries could now avoid the dangerous North Sea route, while the lairds of Lothian and the borders slept more secularly in their beds than they had done since the early 1540s.[30] The culmination of all this new attitude came soon after the Reformation parliament when a Scottish deputation went south to make sure that the English would support the Protestants against any French attempt to restore Romanism, and to persuade Elizabeth that she should marry the young Earl of Arran.[31]

Although Knox for religious, political, and sentimental reasons strongly favored this pro-English attitude, he did not determine policy. Once the parliament had adopted the Confession of Faith in August of 1560, he had turned to what he considered his primary duty, the preaching of the Gospel and the work of a pastor in a congregation. As he stated in his preface to a sermon published in 1565,

> . . . considering my selfe rather cald of my God to instruct the ignorant, comfort the sorowfull, confirm the weake, and rebuke the proud, by tong and livelye voyce in these most corrupt dayes, than to compose bokes for the age to come, seeing that so much is written (and that by men of most singular condition), and yet so little well observed; I decreed to containe my selfe within the bondes of that vocation, whereunto I found myself especially called.[32]

Consequently he now settled down to the work of a minister, but particularly to that of the preacher in Edinburgh's High Kirk.[33] He was at last doing what he wanted to.

Yet despite his expressed feeling that he should not bother with the writing of books, his well-known facility with the pen which had already produced enough material to fill four modern quarto volumes, brought a demand for more literary endeavors. Thomas Randolph, probably on the advice of Cecil in England and perhaps some of the Scottish leaders, now urged him to write a history of the whole Reformation movement in Scotland. He had produced as a propaganda pamphlet an account of what had happened in Scotland betwen 1558 and November 1559, but owing to the change in the situation with the arrival of the English early in 1560 it had not been published. Randolph and others, however, felt that it would be good to have the story continued. Knox apparently agreed, but insisted that he needed more information and source material than was available in Scotland. He believed not only that further research was necessary to dig out all the facts, but that what he had already written needed considerable revision. This was a task on which he was to labor for the rest of his life.[34] He wrote his history as a prophet, sometimes slipping up in details, but wherever he could using original sources, many of which he reproduced. Andrew Lang regards the *History* as a piece of dishonest and biased special pleading, largely because Knox had heard neither of Auguste Comte nor of Leopold von Ranke and their ideas of "objective" history.[35] It is true that his own personal prejudices and convictions do shine through constantly, but it is still a work that no one interested in this area can afford to neglect. As W. C. Dickinson has commented, it is his monument, for in it he puts flesh and blood on the whole Reformation movement.

Other matters, much more demanding than the writing of a history, were, however, pressing in on him. The problems of the condition of the new church, its organization and its operation were still unsettled. Presumably, although one can find no evidence of it, *The Book of Discipline*, translated into Latin, had been sent to the continental reformers for their criticisms, but as yet nothing had been done in Scotland to set up a proper church organization. In the principal burghs: Edinburgh, Dundee, St. Andrews, Glasgow, and Perth the civic authorities had taken action to obtain ministers and to commence public services, but throughout the country areas little was being done. As superintendents had not yet been appointed and many of the nobles were seizing church lands or pocketing the revenues, acts which left the congregations practically destitute of funds, Knox had good reason to be distressed over the state of the church.

But distress of a more personal nature came to him in the month of December 1560 when Marjory died leaving him two sons aged two and three years. Knox gives us no information concerning her death so we do not know the cause. We do know, however, that he felt the loss keenly, for this appears in many ways. Even in his will, written some years later, with its reference to his "darrest spouse" of "blessit memorie," we can see that Marjory's passing struck him a severe blow. And Calvin's comments to him in a letter of consolation written the following April, indicate how much Knox had depended upon her in all his work. Goodman also reported what a blow it had been to Knox.[36]

Marjory's, however, was not the only death in December that was to affect Knox. On the 5th, Francis II of France, husband of Queen Mary, died of an infection in the ear. Knox, whose lines of communication to both the Reformed churches and the court of France seem to have been very direct, received word before anyone else of this event, which he promptly reported to the duke and Lord James. When his news was confirmed by word from England, a convention of the nobles was called for January 15th, at which Knox hoped *The Book of Discipline* would be accepted and the church established on a firm basis, now that this enemy of reform was out of the way.[37]

One of the means of establishing the church would be the creation of a General Assembly of ministers, elders, and other laymen. Some have raised doubts about such a gathering, claiming that it did not fit into the pattern of the *Book of Discipline*. This, however, hardly seems to be the case.[38] True, the *Book of Discipline* makes no provision for a General Assembly, but the framers of the scheme may have thought that parliament would act as the governing body for both church and state. The first assembly met primarily for the purpose of making representations to parliament, so to begin with it may not have been regarded as a permanent body. Nevertheless, it had good precedent for viewing itself as the chief court of the church. For one thing there was the example of the French Reformed church which had held its first national synod in Paris in May of 1559. But Scotland also had its tradition of ecclesiastical assemblies. As early as 1225 a provincial council had been established and we must remember that it had met as recently as the spring of 1559 to discuss reforms. Furthermore, the Lords of the Congregation had formed a kind of assembly in 1558, and a considerable number of those at the earlier meeting attended that convened on December 20, 1560.

This Assembly, which was held in Edinburgh, consisted of six ministers and thirty-six laymen, presumably elder-commissioners from the various established congregations.[39] It is important to note that all the laymen were either burgesses or lairds, none of the nobility being present. Although not large this body proceeded to initiate action on various matters. The most important steps were those regarding the ordination of more ministers and the appointment of readers. Altogether forty-four men were nominated for these positions.[40] The Assembly then drew up a petition to parliament asking for strict enforcement of the laws against those clergy still celebrating the Mass, and naming those whom it knew to be offenders.[41] It also decided to hold future Assemblies twice a year. At the next meeting in the following June all commissioners would bring complete statements of the income and revenues of the church nearest to them, the names of the tacksmen holding church lands and what duties they paid for their tacks. The church was preparing to take over the income of the old church. The Assembly then adjourned to reconvene on January 15th when the nobles would be meeting.[42] The leaders of the church recognized that a supreme ecclesiastical council was of great importance if they were to consolidate the reform.

The convention of nobles, which was not a true parliament since it had not been authorized by the queen, met with the intention of settling a number of matters which had remained unresolved while Francis II was alive. Some felt that Protestantism was now quite secure since the French king, who was also king of Scots, was out of the way. Knox and others, however, realized that this was not the case. As Randolph pointed out to Cecil, Knox in the pulpit and Maitland of Lethington in the convention's debates constantly stressed that nothing was really settled.[43] That this was so was indicated by a major debate in the convention between the advocates of the new religious structure, probably led by Knox himself, Alexander Anderson, sub-prior of Aberdeen, and John Leslie, later Bishop of Ross. Although the maintainers of the old faith according to Knox were defeated, their very presence indicated that the Protestant victory of 1560 was by no means total.[44] In the light of this situation it was more important than ever that a properly organized church should be set up to carry on the work of reformation by implementing the recommendations of *The Book of Discipline.*

For six days the convention debated whether it should agree to the plan presented by Knox and his colleagues. Although some, among whom were the leading nobles such as Châtelherault, Arran, Argyll, Glencairn, and Lord James, as well as many lords and lairds, had already signified their support of it, a considerable number were opposed. The earls of Crawford and Cassillis, Lord Somerville and especially Lord Erskine, later Earl of Mar, clearly feared that they would lose much of the land they had seized. They termed the recommendations "devout imaginations," but Knox pointed out concerning Erskine:

> if the poor, the schools and the ministry had their own, his kitchen would lack two parts, and more, of that which he now unjustly possesses.[45]

Knox reports further that a good many nobles and lairds on January 27, 1561 signed a statement accepting *The Book of Discipline* with the proviso that those who held benefices should continue to hold them for life, while paying the ministers' salaries out of the revenues. But the book was in fact never adopted officially. Randolph reported that it was accepted by common consent, but added that he did not think that it would work because the Reformation had not taken deep enough root.[46]

Randolph's analysis of the situation was quite correct. Although many nobles gave lip-support to the book, the financial provisions were simply impossible to implement. Professor Donaldson has pointed this out quite clearly in his work on the *Thirds of Benefices*. With over half the country's real estate in the church's hands, although much of the revenues went into the nobility's pockets, it was not only impossible but also would have been unfair to turn all the property over to the new church.[47] Others have maintained that, equally influential in its rejection was the fear in certain quarters of "a Calvinistic inquisition. . . . with an obtrusive sanctity," the establishment of a theocracy and similar unpopular institutions.[48] However, knowing how skilfully the Scottish nobles had circumvented ecclesiastical laws and regulations in the past, we can hardly take this interpretation seriously. The basic reason for the rejection of *The Book of Discipline* would seem to have been that its provisions, if carried out, would bring about a virtual social revolution. In the first place, in the individual congregations both ministers and elders, usually chosen from the burgesses and lairds, would gain new power and influence, which could ultimately lead to the serious limitation of the nobles' prestige and authority. This, coupled with the possible loss of revenues now coming from church lands, made the book completely unacceptable to the aristocracy and their backers such as

Maitland of Lethington.[49] Furthermore, if it were adopted, Roman Catholicism could never return, the realization of which roused the opposition of the adherents of the old system.

As might be expected, Knox was very upset by the nobles' refusal to adopt *The Book of Discipline*, but its proposed financial provisions finally wrecked his whole plan. This rejection of the book, on the other hand, worked ultimately for the benefit of the church, in that it gave the church freedom from close governmental control, a point on which Knox constantly insisted, and made it a more democractic, effective and even stronger body.[50] The necessity of holding a semi-annual General Assembly now became firmly established. By no means deterred as a result of the nobles' refusal to act, Knox and his *confrères* went ahead anyway to set up a permanent supreme body and to organize the church in accordance with *The Book of Discipline*. The preachers, he tells us,

> exhorted us that we should constantly proceed to reform all abuses, and to plant the ministry of the Church, as by God's word we might justify it, and then commit the success of all to our God in whose power the disposition of the kingdom stands.[51]

The only other matter dealt with by the convention was the appointment of Lord James Stewart to go to France to explain everything to the queen. He was warned at the same time that he should beware of her guile and that he should insist that the Mass would not be permitted under any circumstances in Scotland. His reply to this was that if she wanted to have it in her own apartments who could stop her.[52]

Just before Lord James' departure the first concrete steps were taken toward the setting up of the organization of the church. Indeed, he may have delayed his voyage to France in order to be able to report that the new ecclesiastical regime was in operation. On March 9th, the election of superintendents was held. Knox preached the sermon and propounded the induction questions to the candidates and people. The ministers and elders present then gave the new superintendents the right hand of fellowship and Knox inducted each into his office by prayer. Nowhere is there any idea of a special ordination for the superintendent. In fact the heading of the prepared form of investiture refers to the superintendent's election as serving "also in election of all other ministers." Five men had been nominated for superintendencies at the Reformation parliament: John Spottiswoode for Lothian, John Winram for Fife, John Willock for Glasgow, Erskine of Dun for Angus and the Mearns, and John Carswell for Argyll. But not until the church had vainly waited for six months for government confirmation and appointment were they finally inducted into their offices in order that they might carry out their duties.[53]

One naturally asks why Knox was not made a superintendent. Randolph provides the answer in a report of March 5th to Cecil in which he states that Knox had refused this position, since he felt that being minister of the High Kirk of Edinburgh was a great enough honor, and presumably an onerous enough burden, if God would but give him strength.[54] In this Knox showed his usual understanding. He realized that in the capital city, close to court and parliament, he would be in a much better position to influence by his preaching the country as a whole, than if he were travelling around his diocese as a superintendent with only occasional residence in Edinburgh. Furthermore, he was undoubtedly convinced that he was called not to administer church affairs, but to preach the Gospel.

While Knox was seeking to have the Reformed church established within the country, he was also endeavoring to keep in touch with his allies outside of Scotland. Knowing Mary's French background and the influence of her uncle, the Cardinal of Lorraine, he was afraid that she might well prove to be a very dangerous person if she returned to Scotland. Shortly after the election of the superintendents and about the time of departure of Lord James for France, therefore, he approached Randolph with a request that he might have a conference with some of the ministers in Berwick. At the same time in certain articles that he had given to Lord James, to be left in London on the latter's journey to France, he had sought to mitigate the rigor of his attack upon "the monstrous regiment of women," claiming that in it he was referring principally to the situation that prevailed in 1557, and to the persecuting activities of Mary Tudor.[55] Likewise he also sought to patch up a misunderstanding that he had had with Calvin somewhat earlier over the question of baptism. Yet while he seemed to be accomplishing something in these areas, he was less successful at home, for the Protestant nobles were beginning to suffer from divisions within their own ranks.[56] They had not been unanimous on the subject of *The Book of Discipline* and other influences were now having their impact, resulting in what Calvin called "intestine" conflict.

One of the major problems that faced the Protestants was that the Roman Catholic forces, apparently looking to Mary's return, were beginning to, as Knox said, raise their heads. Moreover, they were hopeful that John Leslie, whom they had sent to Mary in France, would succeed in persuading her to ignore Lord James, and return to Scotland via Aberdeen where she would be greeted by the Earl of Huntly at the head of 20,000 loyal Roman Catholics.[57] With the assurance that the queen would be on their side, they were also preparing to seize Edinburgh, in readiness for the meeting of Parliament on May 20th. When this was known a considerable number of Protestant lairds and burgesses gathered in the Edinburgh Tollbooth where they drew up a petition to the Lords of the Privy Council. On May 28th it was adopted by the General Assembly, which then sent it by the hands of four lairds and two burgesses to the Privy Council for consideration by parliament.[58]

The petition was summed up in the words of the covering letter as requesting

> that God's Evangel may be publicly within this realm preached; the true Ministers thereof reasonably sustained; Idolatry suppressed, and the committers thereof punished, according to the laws of God and man.

The lords, now supported by the Lord James who on his return had delivered a letter from Mary calling for quietness and peace in the country, promptly enacted an ordinance embodying all the items in the petition. Again, however, the financial provisions which called for all those receiving teinds to provide for the support of the ministers and also for the setting aside of six acres of land in each parish for a glebe, were the most difficult to enforce. Yet this action of the Council as well as their dismissal of the French ambassador who had come to persuade them to break their alliance with England and to reestablish Roman Catholicism, indicated their desire to maintain Protestantism as by law established.[59] This to Knox's way of thinking was the time at which Satan received a "second fall."

While Knox had been seeking to strengthen and extend the church throughout the country, he had also been working hard ministering to the people of Edinburgh. Not only did he preach frequently, both on week days and on the Sabbath, but he also became involved in the problems of the burgh itself. In June of 1560 the burgh council had enacted a law against harlots and whoremongers who were to be carted publicly through the city for the first offense, branded for the second and executed for the third. In November it enforced this law against John Sanderson, deacon of the Fleshers' Gild who, separated from his lawful wife, had been living with another woman. The members of his gild, however, having attacked the officers and cart upon which he was being carried, freed him. Thereupon a number of the leaders of the riot were arrested and warded in the castle. When with the backing of the other crafts, the burgh authorities then proceeded to try the offenders, Knox was asked by a number of craft deacons to intervene on the Fleshers' behalf which he did, apparently with good effect. Thus the conflict was settled for the moment, the various crafts promising on November 28th before God and under the influence of the Gospel, to abide by the laws and statutes of the burgh authorities.[60]

The peace, however, did not endure for long. From ancient times the Scots had been accustomed to celebrate such festivities as the Queen of the May, Robin Hood, and Little John, the Abbot of Unreason, and similar peculiar characters, all of which had become excuses for drunkenness, brawling, and riot. For this reason, in 1555 parliament, on the recommendation of Mary of Guise, had enacted a law banning all such activities under pain of stiff penalties. Because craft journeymen and apprentices, however, still enjoyed these times of jollification and rowdiness, they sought to continue them. In Edinburgh on May 12, 1561, therefore, they convened fully armed to carry on as of old. Despite the orders to disperse by the council, the revellers continued on their way until some of them were seized and imprisoned in the Tollbooth, one of their number eventually being condemned to death. The outcome was another riot on July 21st in which the officers of the crafts took no part, but also refused, contrary to their oath of November 28th, to assist the magistrates. Shots were fired, the Tollbooth broken open, and the prisoners released. Again Knox was called upon to plead the craftsmen's cause, but he refused since he felt that they were merely using him to cover "their impiety." Although they threatened him, he maintained his position. Eventually the captain of the castle intervened to bring about a truce which guaranteed that the authorities would not prosecute the rioters. Although this brought peace and saved the necks of some of the craftsmen, action was later taken against a number of them both for causing a disturbance and for refusing to obey or assist the magistrates. Knox also seems to have moved to discipline them, for he reports that the ecclesiastical authorities excommunicated them until they satisfied the magistrates and submitted to the church.[61]

The riot did not arise from the fact that the magistrates, as some have implied, had under Protestant influence suddenly banned the May Day celebrations. This had already been done by a Roman Catholic parliament earlier.[62] Knox seems to have felt, however, that the Roman Catholics were behind these troubles, although this may have been partially his own prejudice. On the other hand, the insistence of some both then and later that the craftsmen were still pro-Roman Catholic may give credence to his views. The primary reason would seem to be, however, the class conflict which characterized the internal relations of the burgh. The abolition of the "deacons of gild" in 1555 by parliament at the suit of the burgh council, and their subsequent restoration by the executive action of Mary of Guise, indicates that friction was common between the craftsmen and the controlling merchant group. Knox's account of the riots reveals that this was one of the principal causes of the trouble. Yet up to this point the craftsmen appear to have gone along with Knox. Their appeals to him in their difficulties indicate that he was held in esteem by most of the Edinburgh folk. Nevertheless, the question that now must have worried him and his principal supporters, was whether Mary on her return would attempt to follow her mother's policy of stirring up the gilds against the strongly Protestant upper classes in the town. If she did they could see plenty of trouble ahead.

That this was no hypothetical matter soon became apparent, for Lord James brought back word that the widowed queen was planning to return to live in her kingdom. This meant danger for the Protestant cause. Many of the nobles at the time and many writers since, have tended to think that Mary planned to act as an independent ruler who would go her own way without reference to her uncles or to France.[63] As Knox knew only too well, however, from a very tender age she had been trained up in the French court under the tutelage of the Guises. This meant that she had imbibed both absolutist and Roman Catholic points of view which were in direct contradiction to everything for which Scotland now officially stood.

In June, Throckmorton, the English ambassador in Paris, had had an interview with Mary in which he had tried to persuade her to sign the treaty of alliance with England and also to become a Protestant. She, however, had put him off with the claim that she had to discuss further the matter of the alliance with her advisers in Scotland, and that with regard to religion since she was the queen, her subjects should follow her as their lawful ruler.[64] Randolph who apparently knew of this conversation, reported that the Protestants feared her return would mean the beginning of persecution but that Knox was determined to remain "and others will not leave him till God have taken his life and theirs together." Queen Elizabeth should therefore, he explained, give some encouragement to Knox, by indicating that she did not take Mary's strictures on him too seriously and should also hint that she would not support Mary if she took anti-Protestant action. Knox, he added, constantly prays for amity between the two kingdoms.[65]

Mary's return was not a cause of uncertainty and fear for the Scottish Protestants alone. Elizabeth also had her grave misgivings, for Mary had refused to sign the Treaty of Edinburgh which obligated her to surrender her claim to the English throne. Elizabeth had heard from Maitland of Lethington, however, that the Protestant element would certainly prefer an alliance with England to one with France.[66] To make sure of this, early in July she sent a message to the Privy Council expressing the hope that they would stand by the Treaty of Edinburgh and their promised alliance, even if Mary did not. Their reply dated July 16th stated unequivocally that as far as they were concerned they planned to maintain their friendship with England. The only difficulty was that Mary heeded her French councillors more than she did those in Scotland. The Council also explained that although they had not been able to assemble the estates to reply to her communication, they had called in others to advise them; and among these Knox would appear to have had a place.[67]

Elizabeth was coming around to the position many of the Scottish Protestants expressed much earlier through Knox, that if Roman Catholic and French influence gained the ascendency in Scotland, it would not be long before England also would face the threat of a

French-Roman Catholic take-over. To drive home this point, on August 8th Knox addressed a personal letter to Elizabeth in which he informed her that Mary was planning to have some learned persons refute his *First Blast,* a move for which she would undoubtedly ask Elizabeth's and her council's support. He warned Elizabeth that in so doing Mary was aiming more at her than she was at him, for she hoped to supplant her on the English throne. He added that he had no desire to see Elizabeth removed, but hoped that God would bless her in her reign.[68]

On Tuesday morning, August 19, 1561, Mary landed in Leith. Although she had sought a safe-conduct from Elizabeth to protect her in case she were forced to land in England, she does not seem to have planned to use it. She left Calais on August 14th with a considerable convoy of French vessels, perhaps fearing that the English might seek to waylay her. But as the latter paid no attention to her, she sailed safely into Leith with but two galleys which brought also her attendants and three uncles, along with a number of other French nobles, who were no doubt to act as her advisers.[69] Yet despite the presence of these relatives and friends she returned to Scotland with a heavy heart. As Hubert Languet reported from Paris

> The miserable young woman is said to have wept both night and day. And no wonder since she was being deported from such delights to a horrid and rough island, and to a people unappreciative of her and dissenting from her in religion.[70]

Knox and many Scottish Protestants, on the other hand, saw the tremendous downpour of rain in which she arrived as heaven's indication of "what comfort was brought into this country with her, to wit, sorrow, dolour, darkness and all impiety." [71]

A new factor had now entered into the problem of the establishment of the Reformed church in Scotland. While admirers and defenders of Mary have sought to paint Knox as an egotist who could not stand to see Mary occupy the center of the stage, or as a bully who could do no better than make a poor young thing cry, the fact would seem to be that Mary's arrival with the Guise contingent indicated what treatment the Protestants might well expect.[72] Furthermore, Mary's personal attractiveness to the aristocrats, some of whom may have hoped to become her second husband, persuaded many of them that Protestantism had nothing to fear. They therefore fell over each other in seeking to win her favor.[73] The result was almost immediate division between the nobles on one hand and the lairds and burgesses on the other. When Mary laid plans to have Mass said in the private royal chapel on her first Sunday in Scotland, the lairds of Fife led by the Master of Lindsay took such strong exception, that only the presence of Lord James himself at the door of the chapel, prevented them from breaking up the service. Meanwhile, in St. Giles Kirk, Knox, in Randolph's words, "thundered out of the pulpit," against the Mass. "He rules the roost and of him all men stand in fear—would God you knew how much!" [74]

At this point we must attempt to put things in some perspective. Knox has been attacked by various writers for his intolerance, his violence, his inconsiderateness in dealing with Mary. It is well to note, however, that Knox's blasts against Roman Catholicism were no more violent than those of Luther or of the English Reformers such as Tyndale and Bale, or of Huguenots such as Du Plessis Mornay. Violence in expression was also not confined to Protestants, for one only has to read the writings of continental Roman Catholic polemicists such as Cochlaeus and Eck, or of Scots such as Archibald Hamilton, to appreciate their powers of vituperation. But Roman Catholics had gone much farther than name calling, for they had burned at the stake those who had maintained "heretical doctrines." And Knox could not only think back to George Wishart's execution but he, himself, may also have witnessed more recently the horrible deaths of some of the French martyrs. Therefore when Mary landed in Scotland with her three Guise uncles, Knox and his supporters had good grounds for fearing that if the French should gain control, the same treatment would be meted out to them as had been to their Protestant brethren in France.

Some have insisted that Mary was quite prepared to tolerate Protestantism if only Knox and his followers would tolerate her private use of her own religion. Yet it would seem that she was but playing a waiting game, which Knox well understood, for Protestantism conflicted not only with her religion, but also with her French concept of absolute royal authority. He had seen what had happened in England as a consequence of the permission of Mary Tudor's private Mass. He also knew what had happened in France, and he was taking no chances. Therefore, when on August 25th the Council, made up largely of Protestants, agreed to her proposal that an edict should be issued forbidding any change in religion at the moment, Knox spoke out against it, since it permitted private Mass for the queen and her French servants.[75] Although Randolph felt that Knox was extreme in his stand, two days after the publication of the edict he asked to be relieved of his responsibilities, since he could not cope with the deceit of Mary and her uncles.[76] As P. Hume Brown has put it

> Even in the point of worldly wisdom, events were to prove that Knox had seen deeper into the possibilities of things than the politicians themselves.[77]

He, therefore, continued to blow the alarm to warn the Protestants of the danger of compromise with the queen.[78]

This soon brought him face to face with Mary. He had not gone to court to pay his respects, nor had she attended his services. Yet their ignoring of each other could not go on forever, for from her reception by the townspeople of Edinburgh it was obvious that they stood behind Knox in objecting to the Mass as much as he did. Consequently, because of his sermons against the Mass he was soon summoned to appear before her. The resulting dialogue on September 4th was long and is reported by Knox, himself, and in part confirmed by Randolph. From what Knox tells us, he stated his position clearly, denying any attempt to raise a rebellion against her, but insisting that since his position was the truly biblical one over against that of Rome, she should accept it. Also he asserted that the people could resist with force a persecuting monarch, thus following the teaching of men such as John Major. He ended this discussion by wishing her well in her reign, but expressed the judgment afterwards that "if there be not in her a proud mind, a crafty wit, and an indurate heart against God and his truth my judgment faileth me." Her reaction to the meeting was to shed tears of frustration, for trained in the absolutist court of France, she was not used to opposition against which she was unable to take immediate and summary action.[79]

Yet while Knox clearly felt that he had won the argument with Mary, he realized that it was but an empty achievement. Not only had she reestablished the Mass in principle, but many of his erstwhile supporters and friends, particularly among the nobles, insisted that she had every right to do so, as long as it was said only in private. But as she toured the country she had Mass celebrated wherever she went, thus encouraging the Roman Catholics to remain faithful. In writing to Mrs. Locke on October 2nd, Knox said that he wished he could die, since there was no hope of stopping this "unless we would arme the hands of the people in whome abideth yitt some sparkes of God's feare." [80] To Cecil who had advised him to deal with Mary more tactfully, he replied five days later that Lord James and Lethington were losing credit with the more convinced Protestants because of their compromising, and that he now wished that he, himself, had spoken out more directly earlier. Not the vehemence of the preachers, but the faint heartedness of the nobles, he believed, would soon destroy the Reformation.[81] Then on October 24th he wrote Calvin asking him if the report circulated by Mary that Calvin had said she should be free to have Mass said in private, were true.[82] He did not fear losing the center of the stage, as some would have it, but he did fear the destruction of the whole work of reform.[83] As he said in his letter to Calvin: "I never felt before how weighty and difficult a matter it is to contend against hypocrisy under the disguise of piety." His only hope on earth was in the people, the gentry and burgesses, who remained loyal to the Reformed religion.

Yet despite his pessimism and depression over the way matters were going, Randolph could write to Cecil on September 24th

I assure you the voyce of one man is hable in one hower to put more lyf in us than 500 trumpettes contynually blustering our eares.[84]

And the effect of his trumpetting appeared in many ways. When the priests of the Chapel Royal, in Mary's absence would have said Mass the Earl of Argyll and Lord James stopped them by a physical attack. At the same time other nobles such as Arran, Glencairn, Ruthven, Boyd, and Ochiltree showed their colors by attending the induction of John Willock as superintendent of the Glasgow diocese. The burgesses of Dundee and Edinburgh likewise manifested their support of the Reformation; for when the queen visited Dundee they presented her with a gold heart full of gold, but then put on a pageant condemning "the errors of the world," which so angered her that she had to go to her lodgings.[85] About the same time the Edinburgh burgh council was enforcing laws against "whoremongers, adulterers and idolators," the latter including priests, for which action she peremptorily removed the provost and baillies from office.[86] Knox clearly still had considerable support in his stand against the revival of the Mass.

The Roman Catholic element, however, led by Mary and the Archbishop of St. Andrews were, in contravention of the statutes of 1560, re-establishing the Mass wherever possible while others such as William Balfour were openly attacking Protestant beliefs and worship despite Mary's proclamation that matters religious were to remain as established for the time being.[87] Naturally, Knox spoke out against this revival of the abolished practices, and although he seems to have had general support from the burgesses of Edinburgh and many of the lairds, the courtiers were opposed to him. Randolph while agreeing with his sentiments, felt that he was too harsh with the queen as he prayed publicly "that God will torne her obstinate harte against God and his trothe." With Randolph, Maitland was in complete agreement, for they both believed that by more gentle means Mary might be won over to Protestantism.[88] Knox and others, however, disagreed insisting, after a public Mass held on All Saints Day, that Mary should not be allowed to continue such practices. The argument waxed hot and heavy in the house of James McGill, the Clerk Register, where the Lord James, the Earl of Morton, Maitland, Bellenden of Auchnoull, the Justice Clerk, and McGill maintained the queen's right, while Knox and a number of ministers took the opposite side, "adding, 'That her liberty should be their thraldom ere it was long.' " [89]

With the meeting of the General Assembly of the church in December this difference of view point came out into the open. The courtiers refused to attend but insisted that nothing should be done without their advice. When representatives of the Assembly went to Holyrood to reason with them, they replied that the ministers had been holding secret sessions with the lairds. When this was denied, Maitland of Lethington and some of the others questioned any right of the church to hold its Assembly without the specific approval of the queen. To this Knox replied that she knew of their assemblies, adding: "take from us the freedom of Assemblies, and take from us the Evangel." [90] After some further argument, it was agreed that the queen might send her observers to the Assembly if she suspected that anything subversive was taking place. From all this it became clear that the lairds and the burgesses were supporting the ministers against the nobles who favored Mary.

The two most important matters with which the Assembly had to deal were the problem of lawlessness and the question of the adoption of *The Book of Discipline* which would ensure the financial support and establishment of the church. With regard to the first everything was brought to a head when the Earl of Bothwell, the Marquis d' Elboeuf, uncle of the queen, and Lord John Stewart of Coldingham raided the home of Cuthbert Ramsay in search of his daughter-in-law, Alison Craik reputedly Arran's mistress. A minor riot resulted, which caused great scandal. The General Assembly petitioned the queen to see that the law be enforced immediately against those responsible; but she took no action. Knox points out that such exploits in France were taken for granted, so what could they expect of a queen who had been raised there? We may see from this statement why he placed no trust in Mary.[91]

More important than the nobles' lawlessness was the question of the financial support of the church, for it involved the church's continued existence. Although the original plan sought to have all the old church's assets turned over to the support of the Protestant ministers, education and the poor, this had not taken place. Instead many of the clergy and religious orders had hurriedly granted lands in feu-farm to various tenants, who had frequently gone to Rome at considerable expense to obtain papal confirmation. Since such a drain of funds was contrary to various statutes against "barratry," as it was called, the Privy Council in September of 1561 issued a number of edicts forbidding this practice.[92] Furthermore, in cases of churchmen with Protestant tenants, or of Protestant lords such as the Earl of Arran who had been commissioned by the Privy Council to intromit with ecclesiastical revenues, the Protestants were gradually being pushed out and the control of the land and revenues reestablished by the clerics.[93] Although many Protestant landowners, on the other hand, had taken over the ecclesiastical revenues coming from their properties, most did not think of using them to pay the stipends of the ministers, but put them into their own pockets.

The only solution envisaged by the General Assembly was to put the provisions of *The Book of Discipline* into effect. But when this was proposed opposition immediately arose in court circles with

Maitland of Lethington leading the van. He and others claimed that
they did not know what was in the book, and some even denied ever
seeing it. Knox replied to this by pointing out that after it had been
considered carefully it had been signed earlier in the year by many
now objecting to it.

When it became quite obvious that Mary and her councillors
would do nothing to alleviate the poverty of the ministers, the
"barons," to use Knox's term, presented to the Council certain
articles asking for the suppression of the Mass and the proper support
of the ministers. They affirmed that they would withhold all church
revenues from the Roman Catholic clerics unless some satisfactory
solution to the problem was found.[94] This was the lairds' way of
solving the church's problem. In the face of this threat the Roman
Catholic clergy then offered to give one quarter of their revenues to
the queen for her use. The Protestants, on the other hand, demanded
that all ecclesiastical properties should go to the queen for distribution. The ultimate decision was that the current incumbents should
enjoy the income of two-thirds, while one-third would go to the
queen for her own use and the support of the Protestant church.
Also, the queen was to receive all rentals, annuals and other revenues
from chaplaincies, friaries, and prebendaries within the free burghs,
which were to be applied to hospitals, schools, and other godly uses.
The ecclesiastical buildings of the burghs were also to be employed
for the same purposes. In this way the ecclesiastics and their
supporters kept two-thirds of their property while surrendering a
third, perhaps only temporarily, to the queen. Knox was not misled
by this apparent generosity for he commented "I see two parts freely
given to the Devil, and the third must be divided betwix God and the
Devil. . . . ere it be long the Devil shall have three parts of the third,
and judge you then what God's portion shall be." [95]

Knox was not the only one who was dissatisfied with this
settlement. As Randolph informed Cecil, many of the nobles such as
the Duc de Châtelherault, Lord Erskine, and others stood to lose
heavily. In fact Randolph estimated that many of the Hamiltons
would be beggared since most of their wealth consisted in revenues
from ecclesiastical lands.[96] The clergy also were not happy and many
failed to submit their accounts to the government officials as required
by the edict of the Privy Council. The queen therefore had to issue

stringent orders for the rentals to be presented, while at the same
time she forbade the holders of ecclesiastical lands to attempt to
increase rents or collect back rents still due.[97]

The very fact that the whole arrangement was generally unpopular would seem to indicate that it was at least a reasonable
compromise. The clergy by their gift had not admitted the existence
of a Reformed church, since the money went to the crown.
Furthermore, the Thirds were no heavier a tax than they had been
forced to pay for the establishment of the Court of Session under
James V.[98] For the Protestants, on the other hand, the fact that the
Thirds were to provide for the support of the ministers, the poor and
education was an official recognition of the establishment of
Protestantism within the country. The queen would also have reason
to be satisfied for it meant that she received a considerable
augmentation to her paltry annual revenues of £17,000 (Scots). The
real difficulty, as Knox foresaw from the beginning, would be the
question of the division of the Thirds. If the plans of the church as
expressed in *The Book of Discipline* were carried out the whole of the
Thirds would be taken up in ministers' stipends, poor relief and
education. This, however, the queen could not allow nor did she wish
to do so. Consequently the compromise, as in the case of most
compromises, laid the ground for further conflicts between church
and civil government.[99]

Yet despite Knox's misgivings concerning the future, the last
eighteen months had seen a radical change take place in Scotland.
The Reformation parliament had met, had abolished Romanism in
Scotland, and had accepted a Reformed confession of faith for the
country. Now at long last the government had made some financial
provision, albeit not enough in his eyes, for the Reformed Church
thus giving it *de facto* establishment. In all of this Knox had been the
dominant figure, for it was largely through his drive and leadership
that these accomplishments had been effected. Furthermore, he had
succeeded, largely in the teeth of the nobles' opposition, because of
the support he had received from the lairds and the burgesses of the
principal burghs. Both these latter groups had overwhelmingly
favored the Confession of Faith in parliament, while the lairds had
been largely responsible for the compromise reached over the
financing of the church. In the burghs the civil authorities were also

taking over ecclesiastical lands to use them for "godly purposes."
Among the "middle classes," therefore, Knox's constant "blowing of
the Master's trumpet" had had its effects in bringing into existence a
Reformed church despite aristocratic lukewarmness and opposition.
The rest of his life would be devoted to maintaining, extending and
defending the work established.

CHAPTER XI

The Second Blast

KNOX NEVER GOT AROUND to writing his *Second Blast of the Trumpet*, which perhaps was just as well. But faced with the problems of the Scottish Reformed Church caused by the actions of the compromising nobles and above all of Queen Mary during the period 1562–67, we might say that he blew one constant and long second blast.[1] For what he had said in the *First Blast* seemed to receive repeated confirmation throughout these troublous years. Yet because of the constant turmoil it is not always easy to follow his activities or those of the others who played a part in the unfolding drama.

Concerning his own personal situation and life during this period we know relatively little. Marjory having died in December of 1560, he was left with two young boys to rear. This, with all his involvement in public affairs and constant travelling, must have presented him with a serious problem. It is no wonder, therefore, that in August he requested Cecil's permission for Mrs. Bowes to come to Edinburgh to take charge of the family, a difficult task for a woman of her age.[2] Indeed, it may be partially because of this problem that Knox in 1563 took unto himself a second wife, this time a Scot, Margaret Stewart, daughter of Andrew, Lord Ochiltree, one of Knox's staunchest supporters. This marriage caused both merriment and concern, for the seventeen-year-old bride was connected by blood with both the Duc de Châtelherault and Queen Mary.

Although then as later, some criticized the fifty year old Knox for taking a wife who was so young, such a match was not uncommon in those days. Mary, on the other hand, was furious that he was now related to her by marriage—a fact, if he knew of it, which must have given him some grim amusement.[3] Margaret bore him three daughters.

Although minister of the High Kirk, Knox was also frequently called upon to perform duties for the General Assembly in distant parts of the country. For this reason in 1562 he was given a colleague in the person of John Craig, minister of the Canongate, a man more diplomatic than Knox, but still strong, who seconded Knox's efforts to establish the Reformation firmly in Edinburgh. As a reader, John Cairns, had already been appointed, St. Giles had a staff of three for most of this period. The financial provision made for these men by the burgh council, while at times spasmodic, nevertheless shows that they were regarded with respect and affection.[4]

Support by the burgh council, however, came in forms other than money. For one thing they would not permit the ministers to be slandered in any way, as shown by various cases in the burgh records of people hailed before the burgh court for speaking disrespectfully of them. At the same time the authorities sought to follow the admonitions of the preachers to remove all whoremongers, fornicators, and papists from the town. These attempts, however, particularly when directed against such notable clerical fornicators as Friar John Black, one of Mary's chaplains, brought them into a head-on collision with their sovereign. Yet despite her rebukes and annulments of the Council's actions, they continued in their efforts to cleanse the burgh morally.[5]

On the national scene the state of affairs was not nearly so favorable to Knox and his supporters. Mary had returned with the intention of restoring Roman Catholicism. Numerous apologists for her have tried to deny this, but the evidence derived from her own letters and actions makes it abundantly clear that this was one of her principal aims at least until she became infatuated with Bothwell. Moreover, as a young, beautiful, unmarried queen she had a good hope of accomplishing her design.[6] While some of the nobles had joined the movement for ecclesiastical reform from religious conviction, a considerable number were in it for what they could get out of it. If turning back to Roman Catholicism at Mary's behest would improve their fortunes, they would be quite likely to follow this path. Therefore, although Knox could count on the support of the lairds and burgesses, the nobles were an uncertain quantity, something he understood only too well.

Two of the most unpredictable in the mind of Knox were Lord James Stewart and Maitland of Lethington. The latest biographer of Lord James, in attempting to explain his actions, points out that while he was anxious to maintain Protestantism, he also hoped to gain the succession to the English throne for Mary. This he thought would persuade her to be favorable to him and to the Protestant party which he and Maitland led. Even if Knox had known of this plan, which he probably did not, he would not have approved. Since he had seen at close range the treatment meted out to Protestants by the Guises, he had few doubts that Mary would like to do the same in Scotland. Consequently in February when he performed the marriage of Lord James, now the Earl of Mar, to Agnes Keith, daughter of the Earl Marischal, he warned him solemnly against proving false to the Protestant cause. That evening, during the wedding festivities Mary appeared to give the lie to Knox's fears by knighting a number of the leading Protestant lairds: Wishart of Pittarrow, Learmonth of Dairsie, Murray of Balvaird, Kirkcaldy of Grange and others.[7] But time eventually showed that Knox had more foresight than most.

At this point, in 1561, Knox became involved in another problem. As a result of the Earl of Bothwell's seizure of the £1,000 which Cockburn of Ormiston was carrying from Berwick to the Lords of the Congregation, the Earl of Arran had ridden to Bothwell's house at Crichton from which he had carried off all Bothwell's private papers. The result was a feud of long standing which led to skirmishes on the High Street of Edinburgh, stopped only by the timely arrival of Lord James and the Earl of Huntly, sent by the queen. Bothwell also attacked Cockburn of Ormiston who had an alliance with Arran and with Lord James. Knox eventually succeeded in reconciling the warring factions, at least outwardly, but the real reason for the feud's ending was that Arran at this point became temporarily insane and was confined.[8] Yet this feud was not atypical of many others being carried on by the nobility. Such conflicts did not help to bring about rational decisions or sane solutions to problems.

Events now took a new turn. A rumor arose that the Cardinal of Lorraine, Mary's uncle, had advised her to become an Anglican.

Naturally the English envoy, Randolph, was delighted at this idea.
He wrote to Cecil pointing out, however, that many did not believe
the report, while Knox and his supporters strongly opposed, "preache
that yt is little better than when it was at the warst." Knox, he said
the preceding Sunday in his sermon, had given "the Crosse and
Candle such a wype, that as wyse and lerned as hym selfe wyshed
hym to have hylde his peace." Yet he had redeemed himself at the
close of the service by offering "a vehement and pressing prayer" for
the continuance of amity between the two countries. Clearly, Knox
and the zealous of the brethren, for all their desire for Anglo-Scottish
friendship, did not want to see a replica of the Church of England set
up in Scotland. Yet they did favor a meeting of the two queens in the
hope that Elizabeth would influence Mary. Although Mary also
favored it as a means of securing her succession to the English crown,
the foregathering never took place, disappointing both the queen and
her Protestant subjects.[9]

Meanwhile the leaders of the church had decided that whether *The
Book of Discipline* was accepted by the nobles or not, they would
proceed to organize according to its plan. They clearly believed that
this was their right in the sight of God if not in the eyes of *politiques*
such as Maitland of Lethington.[10] The General Assembly, which met
on June 30, 1562, therefore, spent much time considering the
problems arising from this decision and the means of solving them.

The most pressing matter, as it was to be for some years, was that
of the ministers' stipends. In some cases the thirds of benefices were
so small that they did not meet the needs of the ministry, the poor
and education. At the same time, the queen was using most of the
income from them for her own purposes. A further difficulty arose
from the fact that the people in the past had not been trained to give
voluntarily for such objectives.[11] Even the most devout still relied
upon the revenues derived from ecclesiastical endowments to meet
the financial needs of the church, poor relief, and the schools. A new
outlook and different approach to such matters was necessary. The
Assembly, however, not realizing the need for such a basic change,
felt that the only thing to do was to make further requests for
subventions to the queen and her council.

Finances, however, by no means formed the sole subject of interest
and debate. The problem of morality was also tackled as the fathers
and brethren believed that the government should take strong action

to punish fornicators and whoremongers. But the most important matter in their eyes was the stopping of the celebration of the Mass, even for the queen. The Earl of Mar (Lord James), Maitland of Lethington and others, however, so watered down the petition presented by the Assembly to the Privy Council, that it meant little or nothing.[12] Because of this Mary agreed to it without objection for it really inhibited her in no way. She protested that while she would never constrain any man's conscience, she wished also to be free to follow her own beliefs. With such apparently reasonable thinking the nobles agreed, thus taking what proved to be another step in the division between the church and the aristocracy.[13]

The same Assembly also commissioned Knox to go with the superintendent of Lothian, John Spottiswoode, to the west country, Ayrshire and Galloway, to reform abuses.[14] On this trip Knox took the opportunity to debate with Quintin Kennedy, Abbot of Crossraguel, concerning the Mass. Kennedy, having both published a tract against the reformers and debated with John Willock, after some delay in arrangements met Knox at Maybole. His principal argument in this confrontation was that Melchizedek, who supplied bread and wine for Abraham's retainers, as a type of Christ had by this act performed a sacrifice which proved that Christ actually offered up himself in the Mass. Although Knox obviously found this angle of approach somewhat difficult to understand, his published version of the debate shows that he maintained his Reformed position in the argument.[15] About the same time he was attacked by Ninian Winzet, expelled master of the Linlithgow School, who declared that Knox did not have a lawful vocation to the ministry since he performed no miracles. Although Knox replied from the pulpit of St. Giles, he probably considered Winzet's argument irrelevant for to him ordination was but public recognition of the gifts already bestowed by God upon an individual.[16] Consequently his call at St. Andrews satisfied all the requirements.

Much more important in the eyes of Knox than these theological debates was the threat of French intervention on behalf of Roman Catholicism. News had reached Scotland of the massacre of a Huguenot congregation at Vassy by the Duc de Guise, Mary's uncle, and of the capture of Rouen by royal forces who killed some 800 English and Scottish Protestant troops. Would the next step be the dispatch of an expeditionary force to Scotland perhaps on the pretext of maintaining order? [17] When Mary, therefore, along with Lord James, now Earl of Moray, was in the north to repress the rebellious Earl of Huntly, Scotland's premier Roman Catholic noble, Knox was only too willing to exert his influence to maintain peace in the Lowlands. He even went so far as to write the Duc de Châtelherault urging him not to support his son-in-law, George Gordon, second son of Huntly, and to be wary of following the advice of his brother, Archbishop Hamilton. For the moment but for different reasons Knox and the queen saw eye to eye.[18]

During October word reached Scotland that the French Protestants were everywhere being overcome by the Roman Catholic forces. This naturally gave great satisfaction to Mary, and when some time later she held a ball in Holyrood, dancing to the wee small hours, Knox believed she did this in celebration of the Romanists' victory. He therefore from the pulpit attacked the frivolity and vanity of princes, not because Mary was enjoying herself as some would aver, but because he believed that she did so out of pleasure at the oppression of God's people. Moreover, he and many others of his day, including even Archbishop Hamilton, an undeniable expert on the subject, believed that such carrying on led to sexual immorality. In his history he later blamed dancing for the questionable relationships of Mary with Châtelard the French poet who was executed hastily in February 1563 under peculiar circumstances on a charge of trying to rape the Queen.[19]

When Mary heard of his criticisms she promptly summoned Knox to Holyrood, where, surrounded by some of her court including Moray, Morton, and Lethington, and the guards who had reported his statements, she accused him of speaking irreverently of her, of stirring up the people against her and of exceeding the bounds of his text. Thereupon he proceeded to outline to her his sermon in which he had made no direct reference to her. Apparently realizing she had no ground for complaint, she then spoke more kindly to him saying that if she did anything of which he did not approve he should come to her privately. Knowing that this would inhibit his freedom to preach, he pointed out that he was called to the public ministry not to wait at princes' doors to whisper in their ears. If she wished to hear his views on any matter she could do so by attending the services in St. Giles. At this point he was dismissed. As he retired from the royal presence some were surprised at his lack of fear, but his reply was "I have looked in the faces of many angry men, and yet have not been afraid above measure." [20] Mary had again failed to silence the one whom she regarded as the chief obstacle to her plans to re-establish Romanism in Scotland.

A few days later on December 25, 1562, the General Assembly convened in Edinburgh to take up once again the various problems of the church. Of these, Knox was concerned primarily with three important matters. One was the care of the poor, on whose behalf he was authorized to prepare and present a petition to the Queen. Another was the securing of better living conditions for the ministers by having the manses and glebes of their churches turned over to them. To assist in this the superintendents were instructed to notify a government committee appointed to "modify" the ministers salaries of the names of all incumbents in the churches. Finally and most important of all, the Assembly agreed that for the services of the sacraments, marriages and burials, *The Book of Geneva* was to be used, communion being celebrated four times a year in urban and twice a year in rural parishes. Although in *The Book of Discipline* the Genevan liturgy had been taken for granted, it now officially became *The Book of Common Order*. The limitation of its authority to the three special services mentioned indicates that it was not regarded as a prayer book, since the ordinary services were to be conducted according to the discretion of the individual minister and his session. [21] In this the Scottish ministers enjoyed far more freedom than their English counterparts. [22]

Yet while the General Assembly was taking steps to set up the Reformed worship on a firm basis, the Roman Catholic element, led by Archbishop Hamilton and probably with the connivance of Mary, was seeking to re-establish the Mass. At Easter 1563 Hamilton and a number of others celebrated Mass in Ayrshire, for which they were arrested by a number of the Protestant gentry as breaking the statute of 1560. Mary, very much angered, summoned Knox to Lochleven where she was hunting to put pressure on him to stop the Ayrshire gentry from such actions. Rather than seeking religious peace at the expense of zealous Catholics, as stated by Antonia Fraser, she seems to have desired the freeing of Hamilton and others from the consequences of breaking the law. Knox, in his account, tells us that he replied to her demands that if rulers did not enforce the law, the subjects could.

> And therefore it shall be profitable to your Majesty to consider what is the thing your Grace's subjects look to receive of your Majesty, and what it is that ye ought to do unto them by mutual contract. They are bound to you and that not but in God. Ye are bound to keep laws unto them. Ye crave of them service: they crave of you protection and defence against wicked doers. Now, Madam, if ye shall deny your duty unto them . . . think ye to receive full obedience of them? I fear Madam, ye shall not.

Here Knox was stating the covenant idea of the mutual responsibility of ruler and subject a principle later expounded by some of the French Calvinist political writers, but a doctrine disliked by Mary. Nevertheless the next morning she talked to him again, warning him against Alexander Gordon, bishop-elect of Galloway who was seeking to become superintendent, and asking his help in reconciling the Earl of Argyll and his wife who was her half-sister. Although Knox attempted to do her bidding with regard to this marital problem he succeeded only in offending and alienating the earl.[23]

As parliament was to convene soon after Hamilton's attempt to revive the Mass, awkward questions might be asked if Mary did nothing to enforce the anti-Roman Catholic laws. Consequently she brought to trial the archbishop and his forty-seven supporters whom, when they were found guilty, she imprisoned during the meeting of parliament. Shortly after its conclusion, however, most of the prisoners, including the archbishop, were released. Knox felt that the whole procedure was nothing more than a trick to prevent any parliamentary investigation into her favoring of Roman Catholics.[24]

That Mary would find it advisable to head off criticism is clear, for both the Secret Council and parliament were extremely suspicious of the actions of many of the clergy. From the statutes enacted at this time it appears that various ecclesiastics had been giving church manses and glebes out in long feus with the result that the ministers serving the congregations were deprived of their use. Furthermore, they had been neglecting the church buildings which were falling into disrepair; they were forcing "kindly tenants" (tenants-at-will) off their lands in favor of men who would take long leases; and the authorities of St. Andrews University had been wasting its endowments.[25] The Council and parliament, therefore, took steps to stop these abuses, although Knox and the General Assembly still did not feel that the civil authorities had done all they could to suppress Romanism and support the church financially.

Even more important than the threatened revival of Romanism by the clergy was Knox's uncovering, through his friends in London, of Maitland's negotiations there for the marriage of Mary with Don Carlos of Spain. Knox knew that such a marriage would mean the doom of Scottish, and probably also of English, Protestantism. Moreover, once Britain returned to Catholicism, the hopes for Protestantism on the Continent would become extremely dim. He therefore took the opportunity in a sermon during the meeting of parliament to remind the members that they would be held responsible by God for the well-being of the church. He then warned them that if Mary married a Roman Catholic, Protestantism would be destroyed in Scotland. This they must prevent.[26] Maitland returning shortly afterwards (June 24th) was furious at Knox, for he thought that he had carried on his negotiations in complete secrecy. Moray also took exception to Knox's words, for he apparently believed that a Spanish marriage would not hurt Protestantism's fortunes. Since the queen would have to ask the nobles' permission to marry they could make the establishment of Protestantism one of the conditions of their approval. Knox, who did not believe that any agreement would be kept, by his bold speaking put his finger on the weakness in this reasoning. As a result Maitland now became Knox's open opponent and for the next eighteen months Moray and Knox did not speak to each other.[27] The rift between the minister of St. Giles and the aristocratic court party was almost complete.

The queen was even more annoyed than her courtiers. Consequently Knox received his fourth summons to her presence for another royal rebuke. As on the three former occasions, the queen, not he, sought the interview. Furthermore, despite what some said at the time and others have said since, he did not try to bully and browbeat her. On the contrary, in the absolutist tradition of France, she sought to bully him, but without much effect. Apparently from sheer vexation and frustration, she broke into tears at the beginning of the interview when she demanded by what right he had anything to say about her marriage. Who did he think he was? When Knox attempted to point out that he was only fulfilling his duty as a preacher, she interrupted him again with a demand that he defend his right to speak of her marriage. Who did he think he was in the commonwealth? To this he replied in words that have become famous:

A subject born within the same, Madam. And albeit I neither be Earl,
Lord nor Baron within it yet has God made me (how abject that ever I be
in your eyes), a profitable member within the same: Yea, Madam, to me
it appertains no less to forewarn of such things as may hurt it, if I forsee
it, than it does to any of the Nobility; for both my vocation and
conscience crave plainness of me. And therefore, Madam, to yourself I
say that which I speak in public place: Whensoever that the Nobility of
this Realm shall consent that ye be subject to an unfaithful husband, they
do as much as in them lieth to renounce Christ, to banish his truth from
them, to betray the freedom of this Realm, and perchance shall in the end
do small comfort to yourself.

He then went on to say that he did not enjoy seeing her or anyone
else, even his sons cry, but that he had to state his mind as a minister
of the Gospel. Such a stance certainly did not endear him to the
Queen nor to her courtiers. Yet no action was taken to punish him
since no legal justification could be found.[28] Such an opportunity,
however, would soon arise.

In the meantime, another General Assembly met in Edinburgh.
To this body Knox brought a report on the case of adultery of Paul
Methven, minister of Jedburgh, who had been one of the earliest
leaders in the Reformation movement. Knox and his commission,
following proper legal procedure, had carefully examined the
evidence with the result that Methven had been found guilty and
removed from the ministry. This must have been a difficult action for
Knox to take against one of his earliest colleagues, but not only did he
believe that Methven should be disciplined, he also realized that if
nothing were done, the Papists would be able to say that the new
church was no better than the old. The Assembly confirmed the
commission's verdict, but declared its willingness to take Methven
back if he would acknowledge his sin before the whole church,
particularly "in the face of" his former congregations of Dundee and
Jedburgh. As he could not do this he retired to England to end his
days.[29]

The same Assembly also commissioned Knox to spend some time
preaching in the north of Scotland since for lack of ministers "the
preaching of the word was precious in those places." Most important
of all, the court also instructed him to draw up a form of
excommunication to be used in judicial actions by the church. This
document, which he produced and which was adopted by the church

some years later, shows the strict views that he and his fellow ministers and elders held with regard to church discipline. In particular, sins against the church and against society were to be confessed and atoned for publicly.[30] This may seem in our own day overly rigorous but we must remember that Knox and his colleagues were dealing with a country whose population had known, and still knew, much lawlessness and immorality not only among the laity, especially the aristocracy, but even among the clergy who were supposed to give an example of Christian living.[31]

While carrying out his various duties for the church after the adjournment of the General Assembly, Knox began to feel ever more certain that Mary, with the tacit connivance of courtiers such as Moray and Maitland, was working hard to restore Roman Catholicism.[32] He was finally convinced of this by events that now took place. While the courtiers had agreed that Mary should be allowed to hold Mass privately, no one had ever sanctioned the restoration of the Mass where the queen was not present. Yet during Mary's absence from Edinburgh in 1563 members of her court arranged for Mass in the chapel at Holyrood. Word of this came to the ears of some of the Edinburgh burgesses who, armed with pistols and led by Andrew Armstrong, George Rynd and Patrick Cranston invaded Holyrood and broke up the service. Infuriated at this treatment of her servants, Mary had the three ringleaders summoned to trial for their action. Knox, who ever since the Easter Mass in Ayrshire had been growing increasingly uneasy about Mary's actions, on the advice of some of the Protestants in Edinburgh now promptly sent out a letter to "the Brethren" informing them of what had happened and advising them to come to Edinburgh to protect the accused from an unfair trial.[33]

This action, which Antonia Fraser somewhat petulantly terms "a flagrant insult to the authorities and to the queen," immediately brought him into conflict not only with Mary, but also with Moray, Maitland, and others at the court. Knox, however, knew something which the Earl of Bothwell proved shortly afterwards when accused of murdering Darnley: that the courts in Scotland were not always on the side of justice. Moray, Maxwell of Terreglies, and others turned on him with the demand that he should confess that he had done wrong and apologize to the queen. This he refused.[34] As a result he was summoned before the Privy Council where Mary and Maitland felt that they would humiliate him completely. But they were disappointed, for Knox, supported by a large group of Protestants, insisted that he had acted on earlier instructions from the General Assembly. He then went on to warn the lords that the Roman Catholics were preparing to overthrow the Reformation by force. At the same time he explained to Mary once again that he did not rejoice when he saw her cry as she had at their last interview, but that unless she obtained better councillors than she had, presumably referring to Maitland, she would soon be in serious trouble. From what we can gather from the records and Knox's account, it was not the gathering of the Protestant forces that brought about his acquittal, but the fact that he clearly had not committed treason. Mary, who at the beginning of the trial boasted that she would make him cry as he had made her cry, was very angry at the Council's decision to exonerate him but could do little about it.[35]

Knox, who had based his defence on the fact that his action had been merely that of a faithful watchman, now appealed to the General Assembly with the request that they certify that he had been commissioned some years earlier to keep an eye on matters ecclesiastical and political, in order that he might warn "the Brethren" of any attempt to overthrow the Reformed church. To this demand the General Assembly not only gave its unanimous assent, but also instructed him to carry on the good work, a point ignored by some of his critics.[36]

Yet this victory by no means persuaded Knox that he could now relax his vigilance. For he heard that the Archbishop of Glasgow and the Abbot of Dunfermline, who had been attending the Council of Trent, were returning home with its decrees. They would be followed by Bothwell who would have authority to impose whatever the church council demanded. "And then shall Knox and his preaching be pulled by the ears," said the Róman Catholics at the court. To the reformer, this posed another threat to Scottish Protestantism.[37]

In this situation the gravest danger was the uncertain loyalty of many of the Protestants. Knox could depend upon the lairds and the burgesses, but the lords who should give the leadership, with a few exceptions such as the Earl of Glencairn and Lord Ruthven, could not be relied upon to stand firm. That a cleavage had developed between Knox along with his supporters of "the middling sort," and the court party made up of the upper nobility led by Maitland of

Lethington, Moray, and Argyll became increasingly apparent after his trial before the Privy Council, but it came out into the open at the meeting of the General Assembly in June 1564.

When the Assembly gathered on June 25th the Protestant lords, presumably at the instigation of Maitland, refused to meet with the church's representatives, insisting that they should hold a separate conference with the superintendents and ten ministers. From Knox's account of this subsequent meeting we learn that he quickly became involved in an argument with Maitland over the basic question of the necessity of subjects' obeying their princes and never rebelling. Maitland insisted that because Mary had permitted the Kirk to have liberty of worship, that the ministers were wrong in attempting to rouse the people to force her to abandon the Mass. Knox, arguing from the Old Testament, pointed out that God punished a nation which imitated an idolatrous prince. He therefore insisted upon two points. The first was that ministers had the right to speak out against idolatry, even of the ruler. The second was that while a prince's office was sacrosanct, his person was not. Therefore, if he failed to maintain justice and equity the people could resist without breaking God's ordinance. When Maitland quoted Luther, Musculus, Calvin, and others to support the requirement of absolute obedience, Knox replied that they either spoke in a situation in which they had no power to resist the ruler or they were refuting arguments of Anabaptists who rejected all civil government. Unfaithful rulers could therefore be removed by the people if they had the power to do so. In this position he was supported by John Craig, his colleague in St. Giles, and by most, although not all, of the other ministers.[38]

The implications of this debate were far-reaching. On the one hand, it brought out very clearly Knox's view, and presumably that of his supporters, on the rights of the subject in relation to the ruler. He set forth a theory of sovereignty that was contrary to the views of the continental reformers, but was taken up by the Monarchomachs in France after the Massacre of St. Bartholomew's Eve. On the other hand, the debate brought into sharp focus the division between the leaders of the Kirk and the courtiers, who, according to Knox, held the "precise" ministers "as monsters." Yet because some Protestant lords still hoped to win Mary over to the Protestant position, or at least to effect a compromise, they did not withdraw themselves completely from the Assembly. For when later a commission of that body made up entirely of lairds and burgesses prepared a strongly worded petition for presentation to the queen, Moray, Argyll, Glencairn, and Maitland intervened as they had done earlier to take over the responsibility of presenting the document themselves. They then so toned down the articles that the queen accepted them without committing herself to anything.[39] Although the Assembly replied to her expressed approval with a message of loyal devotion, Knox and those with him were not deceived, and were to be proven right in the end.

As far as Knox personally was concerned this debate also marked a turning point in his career. The Earl of Moray and the other nobles seem at this juncture to have broken all their ties with him. Consequently, from 1564 on, the possibility of his influencing political events on behalf of the reformed religion largely disappeared. Furthermore, as he saw what he regarded as a declension of many from the Reformed Kirk he became increasingly discouraged. Owing to the inability of the lairds and the burgesses who supported him to do anything effective in the circumstances, because Mary had to all appearances won over the lords who were the natural leaders, the danger of his earlier achievements in 1560 being nullified completely came closer. The Reformation could be wrecked. It is therefore, no wonder that from this time on he frequently expressed the wish to die.[40]

Yet the situation, at least on the surface, did not appear quite so gloomy. Knox and Craig were appointed by the Assembly as a commission of two to study the powers of church courts and to report to the December meeting. At the same time he was sent to the north on a preaching mission, while Craig went to the south of the country.[41] Then in October the Privy Council took action to ensure the collection of the Thirds of Benefices in order that both the queen and the preachers should receive what was due to them. This action was followed by stringent decrees against the saying of the Mass, against the use of churches and churchyards for fairs and against notorious fornicators. Thus it seemed that the Protestant cause was advancing rather than retreating. Yet a cloud the size of a man's hand was appearing.[42] At the parliament of December 1564, the Roman Catholic Lennox's forfeiture was reduced, his lands being restored, and the Archbishop of St. Andrews and the Bishops of Dunkeld and Moray resumed their seats in the Parliament, despite their refusal to be "joined to the religion." Coming events were casting their shadow before.[43]

Nevertheless, the year 1564 ended calmly. The General Assembly of December ordered the investigation of some of the men who had been provided to churches by superintendents but who had proven to be useless pastors. Knox was appointed to visit the congregations in Fife, Strathearn, Gowrie, and Menteith with the authority to try the incumbents and remove those who were unsuitable. At the same time the Assembly prepared the usual petition to the Privy Council with requests for the total abolition of the Mass, the proper payment of ministers and similar matters.[44] It seemed as though the situation had become stabilized.

The next year, as foreseen by Knox, was very different. Polarization and conflict between the Protestant and Roman Catholic elements became radical and violent. The parliament which had restored Lennox's lands had also reduced the forfeitures of Grange, Ormiston, Melville, and other Protestant lairds who had been involved in reputedly treasonable activities much earlier. This action was probably taken in order to facilitate the rehabilitation of the Roman Catholic Lennox, but it led to conflict particularly between the restored lairds and those who had long held their forfeited lands. Indeed, it even led to a fight between Douglas of Longniddry and Lord Seton, ending in the death of Douglas.[45] Yet these events were but indications of the underground movement that was going on as the Roman Catholics, trusting in Mary's support, sought to restore their church. Knox's fear of the continuation of the Mass was only too well-founded.

The rise to favor at court of the Earl of Lennox who had returned to Scotland in September 1564 now presaged a radical change in royal policy and in the alignment of parties within the country. After deserting the French cause in Scotland in 1543, Lennox had fled to England where he had married Margaret Douglas, the niece of Henry VIII and daughter of the Earl of Angus and Margaret, the widow of James IV of Scotland. Therefore his son, Henry, Lord Darnley, born of this marriage, could claim to be, next to Mary Queen of Scots, heir to the English throne by right of descent. In February 1565, Lennox was followed to Scotland by Darnley a tall well-favored young man.[46] It would appear that his coming at this particular time was partially an English ploy in the hope of preventing Mary from marrying a continental prince, but it may also have been partially the result of Mary's deciding that she might marry him, both to strengthen her hand in Scotland and also her claim to the English throne. Once Mary had made up her mind to take this step there was an immediate change in her general attitude. She became less diplomatic and more determined and headstrong in her actions, refusing to follow the advice of Moray and Maitland who had hitherto been her chief mentors.[47]

Although at first some seemed to think that Darnley was a Protestant, he soon indicated the error of such a view. This raised many doubts in the minds of the Protestant burgesses and lairds, and even of the nobles at court. Consequently they began to hold private consultations on the matter of the queen's marriage. Mary, however, ordered them to deal directly with her, which they did, declaring that in return for their consent to her marriage she would have to give an iron-clad guarantee of the establishment of Protestantism.[48] While she was prepared to make many general promises, they could obtain nothing specific from her. Furthermore, without their consent she created Darnley Knight of Torbolton, Lord Ardmanoch, and Earl of Ross. Yet she still needed the support of lairds, burgesses and lords since, as Randolph pointed out to Cecil, she required between £3,000 and £4,000 beyond her current annual revenues to do as she pleased in Scotland, particularly if she were to become strong enough to overthrow Protestantism and break the link with England.[49]

In the midst of the growing tension over the probable marriage of Mary and Darnley, the General Assembly met at the end of June. Knox reported to it on his tour of inspection in Fife and contiguous areas. But the most important items on the agenda were the state of the church and the moral condition of society. A petition was again drawn up calling for the suppression of the Mass, the proper payment of the ministers, the protection of the poor from exploitation and similar points. James Barron of Edinburgh and a number of the leading lairds then carried the message to the queen with the request that she give her answer to John Knox.[50] Mary, however, in the euphoria of her love affair was in no mood to make serious concessions to the Kirk's representatives.

Yet she was by no means ignorant of the growing opposition to her marriage. Elizabeth, who had allowed Darnley to go to Scotland, now summoned him to return to England. She did not really want him to marry Mary. Simultaneously Moray and Maitland were becoming worried, for they had begun to realize that this marriage might lead to the suppression of Protestantism and political realignment with France. While this meant little in principle to Maitland, it meant much to Moray who was still a staunch Protestant.[51] Knox, who had realized before most other people the dangers involved in this marriage, was already rallying his forces. Since April he had been consulting with the uncertain Hamiltons about the matter since if Darnley became king, Châtelherault would lose his place as next in line to the throne. But for his principal support he counted on the leading burgesses in the east coast ports, particularly Edinburgh, and on many of the lairds throughout the country. By July 6th Moray and the other Protestant nobles had also come to the conclusion that force of arms alone would stop Mary's marriage. They, therefore, called for a meeting at Glasgow on the 15th.[52]

To counter these moves Mary proceeded to issue proclamations, one on the 12th and another on the 15th stating that she had no intention of changing the religious settlement in Scotland. Yet despite these assurances and present-day claims that "Mary had *au fond* an unhypocritical and undissembling nature," the truth is that she had already shown her hand.[53] She had been increasingly holding public Roman Catholic services; she had persuaded the pope to appoint a new Bishop of Dunblane; she had been inordinately angry at the "egging" of a priest pilloried in Edinburgh for breaking the law against saying Mass; and she had constantly added Roman Catholic members to her council. At the same time she was in secret correspondence with Philip II of Spain and the pope, discussing means and ways of overthrowing Scottish Protestantism.[54] The evidence indicates quite clearly that she was carrying on a double game, despite all her proclamations of tolerance. The Protestants' difficulty, on the other hand, was that their leaders, apart from Knox, had only just come to realize this, or at least to admit it.

Mary and Darnley were married on July 29th according to Roman Catholic rites, and almost immediately afterwards set out on a strange honeymoon: in pursuit of Moray, Argyll and others who had risen in revolt against the royal pair. Unfortunately for Moray, in attempting to lead the moderates, he had lost the confidence of the more zealous, radical or "precise" element who followed Knox and who could have provided him with forces. While not trusting Mary, the average

Protestant believed Moray's counter-proclamations and statements even less. The result was that Mary and Darnley gained the support or neutrality of most of the Protestant lairds and burgesses as well as of the Roman Catholic nobility. Then Elizabeth suddenly withdrew her promise of assistance to Moray, which forced the rebels to give up and retreat to England.[55] So ended the Chase-about Raid.

Knox was not involved in this rising. He probably did not believe that Moray would really put up a fight. Nevertheless, he had strongly opposed the marriage as the beginning of the overthrow of Protestantism in Scotland. Therefore, in a sermon on Isaiah 26:13–21 before Darnley in St. Giles on August 19th, he spoke of all political authority as being derived from God and warned his hearers against those who would persecute the faithful church. Although he made no direct reference to the king and queen, the former was so angry that he complained to the Privy Council. Knox was then summoned to appear before them but there was no evidence to convict him of sedition. Nevertheless, he was ordered to refrain from preaching as long as the royal couple were in the burgh. To this command Knox replied by publishing his sermon, as a proof that he was guiltless of *lèse-majesté*.[56] At this point the Edinburgh Burgh Council, so far always quite subservient to Mary, could no longer contain themselves. She had flagrantly interfered with their rights in the past without too much opposition, but this was going too far. Therefore, they passed the following resolution:

> that thai will no manner of way consent or grant that his mouth be closit, or he dischargeit of preaching the trew word, and theirfoir willit him at his pleasour, as God should move his heart, to proceid forwart in the trew doctrine as he has bene of befoir, whilk doctrine thai wald approve and abide at to their lifis end.

Mary, infuriated by this obstreperous behavior, thereupon ordered the replacement of the provost, Douglas of Kilspindie by Simon Preston of Craigmiller. Douglas resigned, but the council passed a resolution saying that as they had no cause for complaint against him they would prefer that he remain to the end of his term.[57] Mary further angered the burgesses by demanding a loan to help finance her activities. When it was not forthcoming she imprisoned some of the merchants until they provided her with the money. When they did, she gave as security for the loan the feudal superiority of Leith, but prevented them from taking control of the port so long as she remained on the throne.[58] She thus alienated the Edinburgh merchants on more than religious grounds.

With Moray out of the way Mary now decided she could go ahead with her plans. According to information sent from Scotland to the English government she not only continued to have Mass celebrated openly, but also promoted various public Roman Catholic functions contrary to her promises to the lords before her marriage. At the same time she continued to add more Roman Catholics both clergy and laity to her council.[59] As Knox had pointed out in his controversial sermon of August 19th, trouble was not very far off for the Protestants.

Against this background the General Assembly met on December 25, 1565. One of the first items of business was the consideration of the reply which the queen had made to the June Assembly's petition. She had stated that she was not convinced of the error of the Mass, and, what was more, if she left the Roman Catholic Church she would lose the friendship and support of all great rulers. On the other hand, she would press no one else to act against his conscience. With regard to the financial establishment of the church she insisted that only parliament could take the necessary action. Finally, she did not feel that she should defraud herself by releasing the thirds of benefices from her own hands for the church's support. It was quite clear from these statements that the Assembly by its earlier expression of loyalty had gained nothing. Randolph even went so far as to prophesy that the next parliament would give liberty to the celebration of the Mass.[60] The situation was not good.

The Assembly's answer to Mary's rejection of their petition was threefold. The first move was to have John Row, minister of Perth, prepare a reply in which he lamented that she had refused to forsake the Mass, since alliance with Christ was more important than alliance with European kings. He then explained that the Assembly did not wish to take from her her proper revenues, but only that qualified men be made ministers and that for their support alone, the teinds should be employed.[61] Knox was then brought into the action, being commissioned to write a letter of comfort to the ministers, readers and exhorters, urging them to continue in their calling despite the economic difficulties under which they were working. Finally, he and Craig were commissioned to draw up an order of service for a fast day in which petitions should be made to God for help. In this last document the fear and disquiet of the Protestant leaders over the direction in which events were moving comes out clearly.[62] They recognized that Mary's plans were working only too well.

We should note in passing that Knox has been roundly criticized by some authors for receiving a relatively good stipend while the ministers in the country parishes were experiencing real poverty. The Edinburgh Burgh Council first paid him £200 per annum along with a house. Later when Mary turned over the properties of religious foundations within burghs to the local authorities who were to employ them for "godly uses," they doubled this amount. At the same time, they also agreed that landward churches whose revenues had provided part of St. Giles' income, should be released from this obligation, presumably to enable them to pay for their own ministers. As the remaining income, however, which came from annual rents on Edinburgh property, teinds, and other sources, did not meet the needs of the burgh authorities for supporting the poor, operating the schools and paying the two ministers and the reader, it had to be augmented by free-will offerings or by taxes on the townspeople.[63] It is a little difficult to imagine that the council would have agreed to some of this money going to other parishes, particularly as their own minister was frequently required to travel around the country on the church's work, without any extra funds being furnished by the General Assembly for his expenses. Knox constantly strove to have the incomes of all the ministers increased, but it is a little difficult to see how a cut in his income would have helped anyone else.

At the time of the Assembly, and perhaps even after its adjournment, Mary seems to have been somewhat hesitant as to her course of action. By early January, 1565–6, however, she was asserting her authority by insisting that the holders of castles such as Tantallon and St. Andrews should give guarantees that they would hand them over to her on demand. Then on January 27th a letter arrived from her uncle, the Cardinal of Lorraine, telling her of the formation of a Catholic League and urging her to join. To this exhortation she gave heed, encouraged doubtless by her new secretary, the Italian David Riccio who had recently come to Scotland in the entourage of the Savoy ambassador. She even wrote the pope saying that in Scotland the time to strike had arrived.[64]

One means of accomplishing the desired end of restoring Roman

Catholicism would be an act of parliament by which a sentence of forfeiture would be passed against the now exiled Moray and his collaborators in the Chase-about Raid. To effect this, parliament was called to meet on March 12th, the Lords of the Articles being chosen the week before, principally from the ranks of the Roman Catholic nobles and ecclesiastics. This executive body then proceeded to restore Huntly and Sutherland, earlier forfeited for treason. The next week parliament would meet to complete action against the Protestant rebels. Despite the Kirk's fast days held on March 2–3 and 9–10 to pray that God would soften the heart of the queen to Moray and his allies, it looked as though nothing could stop the irrevocable banishment of these Protestant leaders.[65] In the light of these actions the frequent claim by modern supporters of Mary that she never intended to overthrow Protestantism seems ridiculous. As D. H. Fleming points out "she had returned to her own country not to strengthen Protestantism but to re-establish the Papacy." [66]

Yet the ease with which Mary was overcoming the Protestant opposition was only apparent. Having had some experience of aristocratic intrigue in France as well as in Scotland, she should have known that a feudal nobility did not submit so tamely. Most of the Protestants seem to have believed that her efforts to restore Roman Catholicism were due to the machinations of the Italian, Riccio, whom many regarded as a papal emissary. Added to this, rumors were circulating concerning Mary's personal relations with him, although this is hard to believe, since he seems to have been partially deformed. More important, however, was the fact that the nobles and Darnley were both opposed to him: the nobles because they felt that Riccio was usurping their functions as advisers, and Darnley, because he, in his own befuddled way, believed that Riccio was both cuckolding him as well as preventing him from obtaining the "crown matrimonial." [67]

For these reasons, mistaken though they may have been, some of the Protestant nobles and lairds felt that Riccio must be removed permanently. In this they had the backing of the exiles who were waiting on the borders. The plan was to seize Riccio and hang him after some sort of trial, but what did happen is well known. Seized in Mary's inner cabinet in Holyrood he was dragged into the next room, where despite his and her entreaties, he was stabbed to death, Darnley's dagger being left in his back for good measure. Those involved in the actual deed included, besides Darnley, Lord Ruthven, the Earl of Morton, Cockburn of Ormiston, Crichton of Brunston, and a number of other lairds.[68] The conspirators obviously also had allies within Edinburgh itself, for Friar Black who had been notorious for his immoral ways and had been attacked earlier, was, at the same time, killed in his bed in Holyrood by some of the townspeople.[69]

Considerable controversy has been raised over the question of Knox's complicity in this murder. One undated and unsigned document states that he was involved, but D. H. Fleming seems to have discredited its statements, although occasionally the charge is still levelled against him. The fact that no accusation was ever laid on this score in his own lifetime and that, although he felt it wise to leave town the day after the murder, he did not accompany the perpetrators, would seem to indicate that he was not involved. He undoubtedly approved of the action as he felt that it had removed a very dangerous enemy of God's people, who was preparing the way for persecution. His reaction was probably the same as that which he had had to the murder of Cardinal Beaton, a reaction shared by most Protestants at the time, and which Roman Catholics also displayed on the assassination of leaders such as Admiral Coligny, William of Orange, and Henry IV of France. The condemnatory comments of such present-day writers as Jasper Ridley, therefore, seem a little beside the point.[70]

Mary immediately began to lay plans for revenge against Riccio's murderers. She persuaded Darnley to desert his collaborators, received Moray, Argyll, and the other rebels of the Chase–about Raid back into favor and proceeded to prosecute the guilty. Of all those involved in the murder, however, only a very few, and they of lesser importance, were executed. Her exertions nevertheless paid off in the departure of the principals in the affair for England where they received Elizabeth's protection.[71] Up to this point Mary had won the battle, but she now had Moray and Argyll back in Scotland which meant that the situation had once again altered radically.

Meanwhile what of Knox? He was somewhere in the west country, probably staying with Campbell of Kinzeancleuch and working on his history of the Reformation in Scotland. He did not even return for the meeting of the General Assembly in June which drew up another ineffectual petition to the queen.[72] He seems to have been very depressed over the whole state of affairs in Scotland. This may explain why in his history, which he was writing at the time, he indulged in so much virulent invective against Queen Mary. Feeling powerless to arrest what appeared to be the inevitable overthrow of Protestantism, his frustration could not but result in a violent reaction against the one he regarded as the author of the trouble, as well as in a feeling that he himself should withdraw from public affairs. Like Elijah on Mount Horeb (1 Kings 19:13ff) he felt very much alone.

Meantime, Mary's active pursuit of Riccio's murderers had come to a halt because she was expecting the birth of her child. On April 5th the Privy Council requested her to stay in Edinburgh until the baby was born. This took place on June 19, 1566, and shortly afterwards the young prince was baptized according to Roman Catholic rites.[73] By this time, Mary had come to the conclusion that the prime culprit in Riccio's murder was her husband, King Henry, which probably explains why she granted remissions to many of the others involved such as Ormiston, Crichton, Calder, Cunningham-head, and why the Earl of Moray was once again restored to power.[74] She was obviously preparing for action on other fronts.

Although Moray used this opportunity to help the church by providing more adequate stipends for the Protestant ministers and to achieve various other aims, it looks as though Mary was using him as a stalking horse in her campaign to restore Roman Catholicism. On August 27th Grindal, Bishop of London, wrote Bullinger in Zurich that Mary was doing everything possible to overthrow the Gospel. She was even holding six or seven Masses a day in Holyrood. He also declared that she had exiled Knox from Edinburgh.[75] While his statements may not be entirely accurate, evidence does exist to show that she was doing much to support the Roman Catholic cause, even to the breaking of the laws of parliament.

The General Assembly of December 1566 saw this conflict come into the open. On the one hand, the queen made further grants for the support of the ministers, no doubt with the advice of Moray and perhaps also because of the threat of Knox's hosts, the gentry of Kyle, to withhold their payments of thirds and teinds.[76] At the same time, however, she also re-established the Archbishop of St. Andrews' consistorial court which would take over authority from a lay court appointed some years earlier. While the Assembly received the royal bounty gratefully, it did not feel that it should remain silent on what was obviously an attempt to restore legal powers to the titular head of the Roman Catholic Church in Scotland. Knox, now back in Edinburgh, was instructed to frame a protest against this action. This he did. Simultaneously, he sent a strong letter to the Protestant nobility and towns warning them that the possible consequences of this re-establishment of St. Andrews' authority might well be rigorous persecution.[77] Mary, for her part, continued on her course without deviating for she had other plans in view.

At the same Assembly Knox, who had been deeply involved both in his congregational activities and in the work of the whole church for over seven years, asked permission to go to England on business and to visit his sons. He was probably tired, as well as emotionally drained and, believing that he could see great danger ahead for the church, he may have felt that he would like to leave Scotland for a time in order to regain his strength for the coming struggle. He may also have felt that since something even more violent than the murder of Riccio might occur, he would prefer to be away when it took place. The Assembly not only acceded to his request but also gave him a letter to the bishops of England, urging them not to force ministers who objected to wearing the Church of England vestments, which were "the dregges of the Romish beast," to do so.[78] Knox did not sign this letter for he probably realized that his advocacy of a cause would hardly endear it to such people as Elizabeth or Archbishop Parker of Canterbury. He need not have worried, however, for the Anglican authorities paid no attention to these representations. Knox, no doubt, spent the next six months in the north of England in the company of his sons and the members of his former congregations.

One other point that might be made about this Assembly of December 1566 was that it approved the Second Helvetic Confession which specifically condemned "the superiority of ministers above ministers." This clearly indicates how the Kirk regarded its own superintendents. At the same time, however, it also rejected the Confession's permission of the celebration of various "holy days" such as Christmas, saints days and the like, insisting that only one day, the Lord's Day, should be kept.[79]

Although Maurice Lee feels that Mary had allowed Moray to take up once again the reigns of power in order that he might protect her against the possibility of her falling in love with Bothwell, this seems hardly likely. She had apparently already decided that she wished to be rid of Darnley for whom she had developed a hatred, not only because of his part in Riccio's murder, but also because of his arrogance and complete undependability, characteristics that had also alienated most of the nobles. Consequently when some of them suggested that she should seek a divorce or that they might take other means to get rid of him she seems to have raised no objections. Moray later stated that at this time no unlawful action had been contemplated.[80]

Mary, however, was now infatuated with the young, vigorous, handsome and totally unscrupulous Earl of Bothwell, who, desirous of becoming king by marrying the queen, had no qualms of conscience about removing Darnley by any means. The result was the blowing up of the house at Kirk o' Field and the strangling of the king. When the smoke had cleared the question was: who had done this? Popular opinion and rumor blamed the Earl of Bothwell who was tried, but under circumstances that could only lead to his acquittal, for he overawed the court both with his armed forces and the support of the queen. Furthermore, if he had been found guilty he might well have revealed facts that many others, including Mary, were reluctant to have had made public.[81]

Matters now came to a head very quickly. Moray, who was by no means convinced of the innocence of either Bothwell or Mary in this affair, seeing himself being displaced at court by Bothwell, decided to go abroad for a time. With Moray out of the way, Mary virtually turned the government of the country over to her lover. At the same time she was taking further steps toward the re-establishment of Roman Catholicism. While reiterating guarantees of the proclamation of 1561 which said no changes of religion were to be made, she was giving special exemptions to Roman Catholics to hold Mass and was also bringing more Roman Catholic ecclesiastics into her council.[82] Despite Knox's continual warnings to the Protestants, even this policy might not have disrupted her plans had she not been guilty of folly in other ways. The action, which finally brought her house of cards tumbling down was her marriage to Bothwell, who forcibly carried her off to Dunbar Castle, and married her according to Protestant rites, following his divorce from his first wife by the Archbishop of St. Andrews re-established Consistory Court. Since neither Roman Catholics nor Protestants could stomach this type of action, indignation ran high. Although Mary gathered forces at

Carberry Hill, after she had bidden a fond farewell to Bothwell, who fled to the north, she surrendered to the opposition. They promptly imprisoned her in Lochleven Castle, forcing her to sign an instrument of abdication in favor of her young son James and to confer the regency on the absent Earl of Moray (July 24, 1567).[83]

While these events were taking place in Scotland, Knox was still in England returning home only in time for the June meeting of the General Assembly. When he did arrive back, however, he immediately raised his voice against Mary demanding that she suffer the death penalty. In this he was strongly supported, not only by the ministers, but also by the rank and file of the Protestant population, especially the citizens of Edinburgh.[84] Some have accused him of being hypocritical in this stance because the anti-Mary group of lords in their proclamation justifying their treatment of Mary spoke of the late King Henry in somewhat glowing terms. But there is no evidence that he was responsible for their statements. He has also been called cruel and anti-feminist not only because of his attitude to Mary but also because of the comments concerning women that he made about this time in the margins of his copy of *The Annals of Bavaria*. We must remember though, that to him Mary had always been the spear-head of French Roman Catholic efforts to bring Scotland back to subservience to both Rome and France. Ever since Mary's return he had been calling for the suppression of the Mass, and if necessary for her suppression also. Her most recent actions, he believed, only proved how right he had been, a view with which many of his fellow countrymen agreed. To imply as Jasper Ridley does that his attitude was a combination of spite and a recent conversion to an acceptance of his own propaganda of the *First Blast* is hard to credit. Knox, believing in Mary's personal responsibility, insisted that she should reap what she had sown.[85]

The General Assembly met as usual at the end of June, but postponed further action until more lords and burgesses could come. The result was a large gathering on July 20th. Some of the nobles one of whom was the Earl of Argyll refused to attend on the grounds that many had come in arms, of which he did not approve. Yet most of the Protestant leaders were represented.[86] The Assembly at this time proceeded to draw up a series of articles which it hoped the parliament would ratify in order finally to establish the church.[87] At the same time the future of Mary came under consideration, and according to Throckmorton, the Assembly agreed unanimously that Mary should be executed. Some have asked why, for although others were guilty of both murder and adultery, the two crimes of which she was accused, they had not been so treated. The position adopted was that as queen she should give a special example of rectitude, but in this she had failed completely. Moreover, in Protestant eyes death was the proper penalty for both murder and adultery. If the government had not enforced it up to this time, so much the worse. But it could and should do so now.[88]

Under the Earl of Moray, the regent, parliament met at the beginning of December, and like that of 1560 it was one of the most fully attended in years. The lairds, and especially the burgesses of the towns, turned out in full strength.[89] They were prepared to deal drastically with Bothwell, and were determined to see that the Reformed church was properly established. First Bothwell was condemned for the murder of the king.[90] Then the acts concerning the church, which Mary had never ratified, were once again brought forward and passed with the approval of the regent. Statutes were also enacted that would guarantee the continued financial support of the ministry. When the parliament concluded, the Reformed Kirk was at last established by law within the land.[91]

In all of this Knox had played an important part right to the end. He had been one of the dominant figures in the Assembly's July "Convention"; had preached the sermon at James VI's coronation on July 31st, and was present, albeit unofficially, when parliament took action to give the church legal establishment.[92] He, therefore, could now relax and give thanks, for his work was accomplished. From this vantage point, he felt that he could look forward to the advance and growth of the church without fears and doubts. Unfortunately, however, the future held as much conflict and as many problems as the past eight years. Nevertheless, his blowing of "his master's trumpet," had accomplished much in that time and he still had the support of the lairds and the burgesses who had consistently backed him until victory had been achieved.

CHAPTER XII

The New Notes

THE ESTABLISHMENT OF Protestantism in Scotland under the regency of the Earl of Moray brought a radical change in the whole position of the Reformed church as well as in that of Knox, himself. Established both legally and financially the Reformed church had achieved a position which guaranteed it a security that it had not known before. It was now the only recognized church of the country. This meant also a new role for Knox. No longer having to fight for the church's very existence he could turn to other activities more in keeping with his office.

Free from the necessity of continual confrontation with the government such as he had experienced under the rule of Mary, Knox could devote his time and energy to matters closer to his heart.[1] He could concentrate on the extension of the church into those areas of the country that so far had not been reached. At the same time, he recognized the need to strengthen and deepen the church's own spiritual life and vitality. This involved the consolidation and establishment of both doctrine and discipline, that the people might possess the knowledge and manifest the conduct required of those who were good soldiers of Christ. All this would require sounding the trumpet but in somewhat different tones.

Yet despite these grounds for optimism Knox would still have his battles. Even after James VI's accession to the throne and Mary's flight a year later to England, he never felt quite sure that she might not return to undo all the good work so far accomplished. He therefore threw his whole weight behind the Regent Moray and the king's party. The Protestant political ascendancy had to be maintained if Protestantism in Scotland was to survive. So convinced of this was he that he prepared to give his unswerving support, even after Moray's assassination in 1570, to those who would keep James on the throne. At the same time he was struggling to hold the Protestants together, no mean task, for once victory seemed to have arrived, they tended in typical Scottish fashion to break up into conflicting groups. He, on the other hand, realized that if Protestantism was to be truly established Protestant unity was essential. These elements in his thinking explain much of his conduct from the accession of James VI down to the day of his own death.

Yet in attempting to deal with these problems he encountered numerous difficulties. For one thing, many of those who were accessories to Darnley's murder, including not only some of the magnates, but also quite a number of his adherents among the Protestant lairds of Lothian became Mary's backers once she had arrived in England. They seemed to forget all her recent actions and from a sense of loyalty, pity, dislike of the Regent, or perhaps all three, felt that she should be brought back to reign. Then later after Moray's murder by the Hamiltons, the queen gained further adherents as a result of a conflict within the King's party over who should head the government. The resulting uncertainty and widespread lawlessness was often fostered by the queen's party, who hoped thereby to persuade the Scots to demand her return.[2]

To all the efforts on Mary's behalf Knox reacted with his usual vigor and directness. He was not surprised at the actions of the Hamiltons, nor of individuals such as Maitland of Lethington whom he regarded as very slippery, but he was extremely disturbed by the defection of some of those who had been his most loyal supporters in the earlier days of the crusade for reform. It hurt him that these men would be willing to sell out the Reformation for some political advantage, or that they would be so blind as to think that a restored Mary would be any more willing to tolerate the Gospel than she had been before her abdication. Furthermore, his failure to have the church enforce discipline on such "turn-coats," as he believed them to be, bred a feeling of frustration and bitterness that showed itself frequently during the last five years of his life.

Despite his disappointment in some of his erstwhile followers, however, he still had loyal supporters in many quarters. Not only did he and the Regent Moray renew their former familiarity, but he also enjoyed the confidence and backing of the nobles and lairds of the south–west as well as the adherence of many of the east coast gentry and the favor of the people of Edinburgh. Concerning the burgh, Throckmorton reported to Cecil in 1566 that the women "be moost furious and impudent against the queen, and yet the men be mad enoughe." It was little wonder, therefore, that when Knox from the pulpit of St. Giles called for Mary's punishment that he received the approval of his congregation. Likewise, the ministers who attended the General Assembly in August 1567 whole-heartedly endorsed this "severe" stance which the English ambassador deprecated.[3] Consequently, it is not fair that some later writers should single out Knox for castigation because of his unbending attitude. Not only did he speak for a considerable proportion of the Protestants, but he also knew what would happen if Mary returned.[4]

His fear of the possible revival of Franco-Roman Catholic control of Scotland never left him. For this reason, he could not refrain from expressing political opinions, although he could also write to John Wood, the secretary of Moray, in February of 1568: "I live as a man alreadie deid from all affairs civill, and thereof I praise my God," and that God had been pleased "to make me not a lord-like Bishop, but a painful preacher of his blessed evangell." Not only did he constantly demand Mary's punishment, but he also urged Wood, who was accompanying Moray to England in 1568, to remind the English rulers of what had happened to the Huguenots in France, and to point out that the same fate would befall England if the French ever obtained control of Scotland. In this he was repeating the warnings which he had given to Cecil at the crucial moment in 1560. At the same time he constantly prayed in public for the continued amity of the two countries. Thus while he insisted that no longer would he participate in the politics of the day he could not help speaking his mind on the critical problem of the Franco-Roman Catholic threat.[5]

Within the church itself the great need at this time was for the extension of its work. John Willock, in the spring of 1568, reported to Cecil that the spiritual condition of the people in Scotland was very poor.[6] This the General Assembly meeting both in December of 1567 and in July of the following year recognized clearly. Because part of the problem was lack of funds for the support of the ministers, Knox and his colleague Craig were appointed to negotiate with the Council on the Assembly's behalf. Even more important for the church's spiritual development, the December Assembly delegated Knox to assist the superintendent of Lothian, John Spottiswoode, in his visitation and examination of the churches of that diocese. When he had completed these duties he was then to visit the churches of Carrick, Kyle, and Cunningham in the southwest to regulate matters there. These activities occupied him all spring, most of his time being spent in Lothian where he found some irregularities over which he and the superintendent disagreed. When the Assembly met in July they renewed his commission to the southwest which he apparently had not had the opportunity to fulfill. At the same Assembly his form of excommunication was revised by a committee, in order that it might be put into use. The Assembly was determined to take effective action to make the church truly "Reformed," an objective with which Knox heartily agreed.[7]

The desire of the Assembly for complete reform also showed itself in other decisions. For example there was the case of Thomas Bassandine, the Edinburgh printer, who had published a book entitled *The Fall of the Roman Kirk* in which the author had called the king the supreme head of the primitive church. To this the Assembly took great exception, since only Jesus Christ is head of the church. Furthermore, in *The Gude and Godlie Ballattis* (1567) he had also published "a bawdy ballad" entitled "Welcum Fourtoun." As neither of these publications accorded with Reformed belief or practice, the Assembly insisted that the magistrate must license all books he would print, and if they dealt with religion the Kirk also should approve. The same attitude showed itself in another way when during the Assembly Sir William Knollys, the English ambassador, sought to discover if the Scots were prepared to move in the direction of conforming to the Anglican pattern. He came to the conclusion that this would hardly be possible, even though Mary seemed to be inclined to the Anglican form of worship, for the towns were quite wedded to the system now established.[8]

Meanwhile, the political situation had changed suddenly for the worse. On May 2, 1565, with the connivance of George Douglas, brother of William Douglas of Lochleven, her custodian, Mary escaped from her prison and fled to the Hamiltons who mobilized their forces to restore her to her throne. As one looks over the list of those who rallied to Mary's cause, it quickly becomes clear that quite a number of those Lothian lairds who had originally supported Knox—Langton, Barnbougal, Preston, and others—had joined Mary's supporters. Such action must have been a great disappointment to Knox and others who believed that the return of Mary to power would mean a renewed struggle if the now legally established Reformed church were to continue to exist.[9]

Despite the large number of magnates and higher ecclesiastics who supported Mary, the Regent Moray, when he found that he could not persuade them to renounce their support of her, took action which led to her defeat at Langside (May 1568) and flight across the border into England. He then had the Privy Council put all Mary's supporters to the horn. In August various Hamiltons were declared forfeited for their actions, all others of Mary's adherents being required to come in and submit by the 24th or suffer the same consequences. *The Diurnal of Remarkable Occurrents* makes special mention of the fact that "All the Lairdis of Lothian fand cautioun, and come in, as said is."[10] From this it would appear that the unexpected defection of the Lothian lairds, hitherto known for their Protestantism, had been occasion for comment on the part of their contemporaries. Their desertion along with that of other lairds may have been the cause of the Privy Council decreeing on August 16th that all lords, earls, barons, gentlemen, and yeomen must come to the Kirk on Sunday under penalty of a fine for absence. Obviously the "first love" of many was waxing cold.

This became ever clearer as time passed. When Moray called a parliament to meet in August, the earls of Argyll and Huntly raised forces against it on behalf of the absent queen. Yet as long as Moray was in the country, despite the adhesion of Crawford and the Hamiltons to their cause, they did little more than some raiding and burning. But when the regent found it necessary to go to England in the autumn to defend the deposition of Mary they took advantage of his departure to stir up trouble.[11] Only Moray's somewhat hasty return prevented the outbreak of a civil war.

The problems caused by Mary's flight into England, on the other hand, affected not only the Regent Moray, but also Elizabeth. If the English government handed Mary back to the Scots, one of two things would happen. Either Scotland would be plunged into civil war or Mary would be tried for adultery and murder, and perhaps executed. In Elizabeth's mind both possibilities were unthinkable. On the other hand, what right had she to keep her cousin imprisoned in England? Then too, as Lee has pointed out, the situation was further complicated by Mary's rather superior attitude toward Elizabeth and the stupidity of the Duke of Norfolk. The outcome after long negotiations in England was that Moray returned home with the assurance that Mary at least for the time being would not be released. To Knox and his supporters this must have come as welcome news.

Yet although absent from her realm Mary constantly sought to maintain her influence within the country. When Moray called a parliament to meet in February 1569 she authorized Châtelherault, Huntly, Argyll, and others, despite her abdication, to hold a rival gathering to govern the country. This open attempt to foment civil war, however, failed for her supporters could achieve little, since Moray, aided by money from Elizabeth, was able to raise sufficient troops to force the Marian nobles, in April, to submit. Furthermore, since he had the backing of the leading burghs and many of the gentry, his own resources in money and men were somewhat greater than those of the opposition. Yet all the time he sought to avoid open conflict, choosing rather negotiation, a policy which eventually resulted in the submission of most of those rebelling against his and the king's authority. Peace seemed ready to return to Scotland when a band of loyalty to the king was signed on April 15th by the leaders of the queen's party.[12]

Throughout all this excitement, Knox had been concentrating upon his work as the parish minister of Edinburgh and as a servant of the whole church. Although we have no detailed account of his activities, we do know that on Dec. 25, 1568 he opened the General Assembly with prayer, and six months later at the next Assembly he was appointed along with Spottiswoode, Craig, and David Lindsay to revise the acts of the assemblies held thus far in order that they might be printed. The same committee was also given the responsibility of revising and publishing the form of excommunication and the order for the inauguration of superintendents and ministers.[13] He may also have been involved in the action taken by the Privy Council to make the faculty of the University of Aberdeen conform to the new religious pattern, but of this we cannot be sure.[14] The only other matter in which we find him involved is in the negotiations of the General Assembly with the Convention of nobles and burgesses at Perth on July 25th. Yet in this gathering he was simply one among many who brought about a more or less satisfactory arrangement for the payment and housing of the ministers.[15] The leadership in such matters was passing from his hands.

That Knox recognized the change in his position *vis à vis* the government appears in a letter that he wrote on August 19, 1569 to an anonymous friend in England. He says that he had not written before, since he felt that there was no point in so doing as he had nothing to say. (This might explain why his correspondence with Mrs. Locke had also ended.) He then continues: "Hath not thy eldest and stoutest acquaintance buried thee in present oblivion; and are not thou in that estate by age, that nature itself calleth thee from the pleasure of things temporall?" If this comment reflects his own situation it would point to the fact that many of his supporters had left him, and that he was beginning to feel the onslaught of old age. He also expressed the desire to be out of the world before troubles revived, but hoped that the recipient of his letter would outlast them by many days. Yet the old fire and fears are still there, for he says that he hears that the English are becoming more foolish than the Scots since they are thinking of marrying Mary to the man (the Duke of Norfolk) to whom "I wish better luck." [16] Although no longer at the center of things he could still see what might lie ahead.

It was at this point that he, along with Moray and his adherents, came into conflict with Maitland of Lethington. The latter had accompanied Moray in 1568 to England when he had dealt with Elizabeth about the return of Mary to Scotland. But although ostensibly part of Moray's entourage, he had constantly worked in secret to accomplish his own purposes, which some believe were primarily that of uniting the English and Scottish successions, and which may at the same time have been aimed at securing power for himself. But whatever his motivation, as a strong advocate of the idea of the union of England and Scotland under Mary or James, he sought to persuade Elizabeth to name the Scottish queen or her son as her successor on the English throne. When Elizabeth refused, his next move was to seek to have Mary returned to the throne of

Scotland. The principal obstacles to this plan were Knox and Moray. Knox's reasons were quite patent: if Mary were to return it should be to judgment, not to rule. Moray, not only agreed with Knox, but having discovered some of Maitland's double-dealing in England, never again trusted him, and indeed took a strong dislike to him. Consequently, when after their return home Maitland was charged (August, 1569) with complicity in the murder of Darnley, the regent promptly had him arrested and lodged in Edinburgh in the house of David Forrester.[17]

Kirkcaldy of Grange now took a hand in the game to the anger of the king's party. Hitherto he had been one of Moray's principal supporters, so trusted that he had received the command of the strategic Edinburgh Castle. At this point, however, he suddenly acted in an unexpected manner, for on the ground that he believed that Maitland had been wrongfully accused he forcibly removed him from Forrester's house and carried him up to the castle without Moray's permission, although he later claimed that the regent had eventually agreed with his action. This change in Maitland's position gave him the opportunity he sought and he made the most of it. As he explained in a letter to Mary in September, while some of the ministers would agree to her return, Knox remained inflexible in his opposition. He believed, however, that he could win over both Kirkcaldy and the latter's son-in-law, Ker of Ferniehurst, to support his design for Mary's re–assumption of power, a feat he had accomplished by January, 1570. At the same time, in order to "reconcile all the nobles of Scotland," he proposed a grandiose plan whereby they would all join in a league of friendship against "the papists" in both countries, confirmed by oaths and writings. To this the regent would also adhere, he hoped, by the persuasions of the ministers. Even Knox thought this a good idea, and with Argyll submitted it to Moray. The latter, however, doubtful of Maitland's sincerity, said he would have to consult the nobles.[18]

While these events were transpiring, rebellion had broken out in northern England under the leadership of the Earls of Northumberland and Westmoreland who hoped, with the cooperation of the Earl of Norfolk, to overturn the English government, re-establish Roman Catholicism and place Mary on the English throne. Naturally the queen's party, encouraged by the promised help and assistance of both the papacy and Spain, heartily endorsed their plan. Elizabeth and her councillors, however, moved too fast. The rebellion was crushed and the earls fled across the border, Westmoreland finding refuge with Buccleuch and Ferniehurst, while Northumberland threw himself into Harlaw whence he was surrendered by Hector Armstrong to the regent who shut him up in Lochleven Castle. Moray then wrote to Elizabeth proposing that Mary should be handed over to the Scots for permanent imprisonment. In support of this plan he pointed out that Elizabeth had the power to stop the trouble in her kingdom but if she did not use it, the situation would go from bad to worse, for he saw Mary as the focus of all the conflict in both realms. In this he was echoing the words of Knox who had written Cecil some weeks earlier telling him that he should forget himself and strike at the root of the trouble i.e. Mary before the broken branches begin to bud. This communication he signed "John Knox, with his one foote in the grave." [19]

In the midst of all this intrigue and maneuvering, disaster suddenly struck the king's party. On more than one occasion since he had assumed the regency, attempts had been made on Moray's life, but they had always been frustrated. Now, however, a more determined effort was made, this time with the assistance and connivance of a considerable number of the magnates, including the archbishop of St. Andrews and Maitland. It is also important to note that a number of Moray's former Protestant supporters such as Ker of Fernehurst and Cockburn of Langton were likewise involved. Knox who had apparently recieved word of the plot, even to the fact that it would be carried out in Linlithgow, warned him. Moray, however, ignored all advice and on his way back from the siege of Dumbarton, held by the Hamiltons, passed through Linlithgow where on January 27, 1570 he was shot from a window in Archbishop Hamilton's house by Hamilton of Bothwellhaugh.[20] The shock of this deed for a short time seemed to bring most of the Scottish nobles together in opposition to the Hamiltons, and had anyone come forward at this point to give leadership, the country might have achieved some kind of unity, but this was not to be. Scotland was soon again to be divided by an irresponsible aristocracy.

Yet while many so sorrowed over the death of "the good Lord James" that Knox could bring three thousand to tears as he preached the funeral sermon on the text: "Blessed are the dead who die in the Lord", others obviously were quite happy with what had taken place.

Almost immediately after the murder, and presumably before the funeral, an anonymous letter was circulated in Edinburgh purporting to be the account of a conversation of Lord Lindsay, the Laird of Pittarrow, John Wood, James McGill the Tutor of Petcur, and John Knox, overheard as they advised Moray to remove James and some of the nobles, in order to take the crown himself. This letter came into the hands of Alison Sandilands, wife of Cockburn of Ormiston, who passed it on to Knox. On the Sunday after the regent's assassination, according to Archbishop Spottiswood, when Knox entered the pulpit he found a piece of paper there which contained the words: "Take up the man whom you accounted another God, and consider the end whereto his ambition hath brought him." Deeply grieved over the death of the regent, Knox was stunned by this note, but preached without any sign of emotion, until in his concluding words he lashed out at the anonymous author of the note and commented that where he would die there would be none to lament him.[21] Knox's reply to the anonymous letter given him by Lady Ormiston came from the pulpit the following Sunday, this time in the form of a blunt denial of its truth and an assertion that it was the work of the devil. Whatever their ultimate origin, the perpetrator of both these tricks of propaganda was Thomas Maitland, brother of Maitland of Lethington, who later died in Italy on the way to Rome, thus to many minds, fulfilling Knox's prophecy.[22]

Knox's reaction to all of this we can well imagine. He had no doubt that since the exiled queen was behind both Darnley's and Moray's murders, the biggest mistake Moray had made was in not executing her when he had the opportunity; she would stop at nothing until she had returned to overthrow the preaching of the Gospel and establish French control. The closing words of the prayer with which Knox ended his family worship at this time show his feelings:

> Oppone they power, O Lord, to the pride of that cruell murtherer of her owne husband: confound her faction and their subtile enterprises, of what condition and so ever they be: and let them and the world know, that thou art a God that can deprehend the wise in their owne wisdom, and the proud in the imagination of their wicked hearts, to their everlasting confusion. Lord, reteane us that call upon thee in thy true feare: lett us grow in the same. Give thou strength to us to fight our battell; yea, Lord, to fight it lawfully, and to end our lives in the sanctification of thy holie name.[23]

Yet while he concluded on something of a courageous note, he was obviously close to despair, for Bannatyne records in his memoirs a statement obviously written by Knox just after Moray's burial:

> And so I end; randering my trubled and sorrowful spirit in the hands of the eternall God; earnestlie thrusting at his good plesour, to be fred fra the caires of this miserabill lyfe, and to rest with Christ Jesus, my only hope and lyfe.
>
> John Knox

> Lord save and blis the small flock within this realme! Amen.
> The 15 of February, 1569 [-70]

> All debtis knawin to me ar payet, death only excepted, which I defy; ffor the sting of it is destroyed by Jesus Christ, who is my life now and ever!

> So long as I live, lat me live, Lord to thy glorie.[24]

The death of Moray had brought him to the position where he felt that his own imminent decease was now his only comfort. But death would not come and he had to carry on.

To carry on, however, was not easy since the nobles were divided among themselves as to who should replace the Earl of Moray. Maitland who had purged himself of complicity in the murders of Darnley and the regent, although many still had their suspicions, was now bending every effort to bring about Mary's return to rule. The gentry, on the other hand, who did not favor her, were anxious to punish the Hamiltons and to prevent any "infidel," which presumably would include Mary, from holding office within the realm. As a result of this division, Maitland succeeded in having all action on the matter postponed until parliament met early in March, at which time a long debate took place as to whether or not a new regent could be appointed without Mary's consent. While this discussion was in progress word arrived that the Earl of Lennox, the young king's grandfather, was on his way back to Scotland. This threw everything into confusion since many felt that he should have the regency. To the annoyance of the queen's adherents, therefore, a decision was again postponed until Lennox's arrival.[25]

During the meeting of parliament the General Assembly of the church had likewise been in session. In this gathering Knox took an active part as a member of what would now be called the "Business Committee" responsible for the agenda of business. He was also one of those appointed to keep in touch with the assembled lords, and formed part of a judicial committee to try complaints brought before the Assembly. As one looks over the proceedings of this Assembly one gains the impression that the church was becoming better organized and more business-like in its conduct of its affairs partially because the commissioners were more experienced and partially because of the provisions that the late regent had made for the church's establishment.[26] Yet happy though Knox may have been about the obvious improvement in the ecclesiastical situation, he was seeking increasingly to withdraw from public life, for as he stated to Sir William Douglas of Lochleven, he had bidden good night to all worldly matters.[27]

We may perhaps sympathize with him in his desire to exit from the world for it was in very great confusion. With only a small child at the head of the government, the rival aristocratic factions disputing over the regency were once again prepared to throw the country into the cauldron of civil war. Furthermore, Kirkcaldy of Grange, captain of Edinburgh Castle, now released Châtelherault and Huntly who had been in his keeping. These men promptly proceeded to raise the country against the king's party which was led, albeit uncertainly, by James Douglas, fourth Earl of Morton, whose main supporters were the Protestant gentry and townspeople. To fend off Mary's adherents, Morton appealed to Elizabeth, who after much hesitation dispatched an army which, although it provided some support, also so ravaged the country that it actually strengthened Mary's party[28]

With Elizabeth playing her usual double game, the Protestants supporting James VI had found themselves in a difficult position for, not knowing what she would do next, they could take no decisive action. Then too the queen's party were appointing lieutenants, issuing proclamations and generally acting as though they formed the lawfully constituted government, while James's adherents were the rebels. All this, however, had produced little effect on the English. It was only the publication of the papal bull deposing and excommunicating Elizabeth (February 25, 1570) that finally brought action, for she then had despatched Lennox in the wake of the army to Scotland.[29]

Although Lennox was himself a Roman Catholic he clearly had the support of the Protestant element in the country, particularly the burgesses and many of the gentry. That a considerable amount of printed propaganda in favor of the queen had been issued subsequent to Moray's death seems to have had relatively little effect upon them.[30] When the convention met in July to elect the new regent, therefore, the representatives of thirteen burghs were present to vote for Lennox.[31] With them were six earls, nine lords, eleven bishops and abbots and thirty-four lairds. Similarly the General Assembly which gathered just before convention came out strongly for the king and against the queen, calling upon all ministers to pray publicly for him and demanding that all earls and barons be obliged to attend church services and to defend the Protestant cause.[32]

Yet despite the apparent support that Lennox received, his was an unenviable situation. For one thing, even before he had been elected, his office had been shorn of much of its power, by being brought under the control of the King's Council. He was required to maintain the Protestant religion and implement all the acts of parliament relating to it. But what was perhaps even more disturbing, Huntly and others of the queen's party refusing to accept him were already raising an army to overthrow his government.[33] Furthermore, Kirkcaldy, now completely devoted to the queen, was ready to hold Edinburgh Castle against all efforts of the regent. When Lennox, on the other hand, in September attempted to rally his forces by ordering all the lairds of Lothian, Fife and Angus to come in and submit to the king's authority, few appeared.[34] Civil war once again was brewing.

In the midst of all this conflict, Knox found his situation extremely difficult. Although he had determined to withdraw completely from political affairs, he simply could not, for with his sense of his prophetic calling and his position in Edinburgh he felt that he had to refer to current affairs from the pulpit. For example, the obvious sinfulness of the lives of leaders of both parties came under his scrutiny and criticism, which did not increase his popularity with either group. Furthermore, he was unpopular with the craftsmen of the town whom he had refused to support on certain occasions when they were waging a battle with the burgh council over the holding of May Day and Abbot of Misrule celebrations. Yet this was not the whole story. Craig's attack from the pulpit of St. Giles Kirk on the regent's forces who had spoiled the poor tenants of the Hamiltons on Bothwell Muir, indicated that while the preachers were attempting to gain fair and righteous treatment for all, by so doing they alienated

some of the regent's supporters.[35] These and other incidents indicate
how difficult it was to know where anyone stood in the conflict.[36]

At this time Knox also came into direct conflict with Kirkcaldy
and the queen's supporters holding the castle. So far he had refrained
from speaking out against the Castilians mainly because Kirkcaldy of
Grange, who had been his old ally and "comrade in arms," had
caused little trouble to the town. Now, however, an event, which at
first did not seem to be out of the way, brought a confrontation
between the two former friends. Kirkcaldy had ordered six of his
men to administer a beating to a certain Henry Seaton who had
earlier taken part in the beating of John Kirkcaldy, Grange's
nephew. The soldiers had gone too far in their attack and had killed
the man, whereupon one of the perpetrators of the deed was arrested
and imprisoned in the Edinburgh Tollbooth. Kirkcaldy, who seems
to have become very autocratic, insisted that nothing should be done
to one of his men who was simply obeying his orders, and with the
aid of some of the craftsmen he effected his rescue by breaking down
the door of the Tollbooth. Naturally such action caused a stir in
Edinburgh, nor did Knox miss the opportunity to point out to his
congregation the next Sunday that this act had not been committed
by a "throat-cutter" who knew not the truth, but by one who had
made a clear profession of Christianity. "For within these few yeiris
men wald have luiked for uther fruitis of that man than now buddis
furth."

Kirkcaldy's response to this attack was almost instantaneous. That
very afternoon he had a "ticket" passed to Craig who was preaching,
stating that Knox had called him a throat-cutter and murderer, but
that he had never given orders that Seaton should be killed. As Craig
refused to read the communication without the permission of the
church, Kirkcaldy then laid formal charges against Knox before the
Session of St. Giles. His accusation was that Knox had slandered him
by calling him a murderer and throat-cutter, and by saying that he
was a person who always sought bloodshed. The letter was turned
over to Knox who the next Sunday replied by pointing out that he
had never said what Kirkcaldy charged, but that he had only
bemoaned the falling of such a star from heaven. The following
Thursday, he presented to the session a written reply in which he
also contended that Kirkcaldy's statement that he should first have
been admonished in private was wrong since from the earliest days of

the Christian church, it had been the custom to make public declaration on such notorious enormities "as I suppose your Wisdomes does well enough remember and understand." To these statements Kirkcaldy replied by saying that he was willing to accept Knox's version of what he said. However, Knox, unwilling to let the matter rest, walking with a stick because of a stroke he had suffered the preceding month, appeared before the Session and asked that the Superintendent of Lothian go to Kirkcaldy in order to make him see the error of his ways. Although this was done, the superintendent never reported the result of his conversations with the captain of the castle.

All now seemed tranquil once again, but such was not the case. On January 10, 1571 Knox preached a sermon on repentance using as his text Elijah's rebuke of Ahab's approval of the murder of Naboth. This apparently came very close to home for it enraged Kirkcaldy once more. Following this, on the last Sunday of the month when Kirkcaldy, accompanied by some of those involved in the Seaton incident, made one of his infrequent visits to the church to meet the widow of the regent Moray, Knox again dealt with the subject of repentance, which Kirkcaldy took as a personal attack although there is no evidence that Knox knew that he would be at the service. It may be that Kirkcaldy's conscience was bothering him, but at any rate the outcome could not be anything but a final and complete estrangement between the two men.[37]

This incident, however, was not just a private quarrel between Knox and Kirkcaldy for it had far-reaching consequences. The first reaction to the dispute from outside Edinburgh came in a letter dated January 3rd to Kirkcaldy from "the Brethren of the West," who had heard that he was planning to injure Knox, whom they declared "God has made both the first planter, and also the chief waterer of his Kirk amonges us." They warned him that they would be very disappointed in him if he did anything to the preacher, for Knox was as dear to them as their own lives. Those subscribing were Glencairn, Ochiltree, Knox's father-in-law, Cunninghamhead, Bar, Bargany, and various other Kennedies.[38]

More important than this letter was one written by Cecil on January 10 in reply to an anonymous missive purportedly sent by Kirkcaldy seeking Cecil's support for Mary. Cecil stated that he was convinced that Kirkcaldy had not only engineered the break-in to the

Tollbooth but that along with his man had also released a woman implicated in Moray's death. He said that he did not wish to think ill of the laird since he was in government service and also a professor of the Gospel, but he was evidently rather shocked. Ten days later John Leslie, Bishop of Ross, who was negotiating with Elizabeth for Mary's return, reported to Kirkcaldy that Elizabeth was convinced that he was plotting the murder of Lennox as confessed by some of his soldiers, a possibility that received support from his raid on the Tollbooth to rescue his retainer. To this Kirkcaldy wrote a forceful reply, insisting that his man had been wrongfully imprisoned and that in the rescue his men made sure that no other prisoners escaped. He claimed that he had offered satisfaction to the council, who had refused it, and that he was prepared to stand trial before the church for any slander he made against his brethren.[39] Whether these protestations satisfied the English is doubtful, but the burgesses of Edinburgh seemed still to have been uncertain of his plans as late as February, 1571, for on the 2nd they asked him what would happen if the queen's lords came to the town. To this question he replied that he would assist the town authorities if they would but keep the king's law and be good neighbors to him.[40] Thus the question of Kirkcaldy's intentions toward the crown, the town and Knox was laid to rest for the moment.

Knox, however, was not allowed to continue in peace. A foretaste of what was about to happen came in the rumor that circulated in Edinburgh early in March just before the opening of the General Assembly to the effect that Kirkcaldy would take action against Knox before the church's highest court. To everybody's surprise no charge was laid. Knox, along with the superintendents of Angus and Fife and some other ministers, was appointed to draw up the points concerning the jurisdiction of the church and later he was named one of a committee to consider questions brought before the Assembly.[41] On the third day of the gathering, however, action began. An anonymous accusation against Knox was placed in the Assembly, but that body refused to consider an unsigned document, although Knox, himself, stated that he was quite prepared to answer the charges. The following morning an enlarged version of the bill of indictments was found nailed to the door of the Assembly hall. The principal charge was that when Knox should have prayed for the queen he railed against her and said that she was a reprobate for whom there was no hope. In this way he not only slandered Mary, but also divided the nation and the Kirk. The document ended with a threat that if the Assembly did not restrain him in his preaching the composers of the document would take more violent action.[42]

Some of the brethren, desirous of peace, advised him to forget the whole matter, since no one had come forward to substantiate the charges. It had never been his custom, however, to forget matters of this type, and on this occasion he may well have been correct, since his silence might well have implied guilt. Consequently, he insisted that if the Assembly forbade him to preach he would say nothing, but if he were allowed to occupy the pulpit the next Sunday he would state his position, which he did. After his sermon he took up the accusations point by point, insisting that he had never said that Mary was reprobate, but that pride and repentance could not dwell together in the same heart, and declaring that he had no responsibility to pray for Mary as queen for he had never acknowledged her as such, nor was she now ruler of the country. According to the *Diurnal* at his reply "the maist pairt of the peopill grudgit." After this a third handbill was distributed throughout the town saying that if the present Assembly allowed him to continue his attacks on Mary full charges would be presented at the next Assembly. Since Knox was too weak to attend all the sessions, Richard Bannatyne, his servant, without his knowledge, took a copy of this document to the Assembly asking its members to make a public statement that they agreed with Knox's doctrine, but much to Bannatyne's chagrin, they refused. If Knox heard of this decision he too must have been disturbed that even his fellow ministers would not give him their support.[43]

After the adjournment of the Assembly some of "the brethren" attempted to persuade Knox to say nothing more, but as he had the bit in his teeth he was determined to explain his stance. The next day, which was Sunday he went over all the charges again and presented his answers. This, however, did not settle the matter for within a few days another bill was circulated accusing Knox of sedition, schism and heresy. The ground of this accusation was that in his *First Blast* he had attacked the idea of a woman bearing rule, but now he was calling upon Queen Elizabeth to use force against his own country. This was both treason and schism, and either erroneous doctrine or obstinacy against the truth. To these accusations Knox, as was his custom, replied after the sermon the next Sunday, pointing out that his anonymous accusers had not proven his doctrine wrong according to the Scriptures. Furthermore, the Old Testament showed that even if one worked with a monarch, one did not necessarily have to approve of everything he did. He concluded on this note:

> But one thing, in the end, I may not pretermit, that is to give him a lie in his throat that either dare or will say, that ever I sought support against my native country. What I have been to my country albeit this unthankful age will not know, yet the ages to come will be compelled to bear witness to the truth.[44]

Nevertheless, in spite of his brave words and his insistence upon replying to his anonymous detractors, it was clear that he was fighting a losing battle at the moment. The constantly reiterated charges which probably came from the pen of Maitland of Lethington, or of his brother Thomas, were having their effect. Added to all this Lennox was personally not popular and the church's strict discipline was equally disliked, causing the enthusiasm of many of those who had been his most devoted followers in 1560 to wane. Not only many of the Protestant magnates, such as Argyll and Rothes, but also a goodly number of the local gentry such as Crichton of Brunston, Mowbray of Barnbougal, and perhaps Lawdor of Haltoun continued to favor the queen. A considerable number of the craftsmen of the burgh were apparently also on Kirkcaldy's side as they had shown at the time of his raid on the Tollbooth. The situation had changed radically in ten years, a fact that Knox and the other leaders of the Kirk had to recognize.

Yet he also had his supporters who remained loyal to him through thick and thin. James Barron the merchant, the Sandilands of Calder, the Cockburns of Ormiston and others continued to give him their adherence as did a good many of the ordinary indwellers of Edinburgh and Leith. As events progressed, however, they had their work cut out to make sure that despite his bodily weakness, he had the freedom to preach, and that he was protected from any physical attack by the members of the castle's garrison.

That their fears were not groundless became apparent during the month of April 1571. On the 2nd the king's men captured Dumbarton Castle and with it John Hamilton, Archbishop of St.

Andrews, whom they carried off to Stirling. There he was quickly tried on charges of complicity in the murder of Darnley and Moray, which in the latter case he confessed, and was hanged. Elizabeth made no protest concerning this action, one of the reasons being that recently Cecil had discovered that Mary was involved in a plot of an Italian adventurer to murder her and some of her council. Kirkcaldy and the Hamiltons, on the other hand, were very incensed at Lennox's execution of the cleric. To unite their forces, the queen's lords, led by Huntly, Lethington, and the Hamiltons, came to Edinburgh where they were received into the castle. Then to make sure that he would be able to defend the castle against an attack by the king's forces, Kirkcaldy seized and fortified Holyrood and St. Giles Kirk, demolishing part of the latter and planting cannon in the steeple, as Strozzi had done when attacking St. Andrews in 1548.[45] The queen's party was now in control of the whole city.

This put Knox in a very difficult and dangerous position, for he insisted that he must continue his preaching. Yet in so doing he constantly spoke and prayed for the regent and the king, while at the same time condemning the queen and her party. Furthermore, after the arrival of Claude Hamilton, the Duke of Châtelherault's son, on April 20th he made a formal protest against Kirkcaldy's reception of the Hamiltons into the castle, because of their connection with the assassination of Moray. His supporters were so afraid of what the Hamiltons might do to him because of this that they set up a special guard at his home to protect him from any attack. That such precautions were necessary was demonstrated by an attempt on his life shortly afterwards, when someone fired a bullet into his dining room through the back of the chair in which he usually sat. But as at that time he was sitting at the side of the table, he escaped injury.[46]

Word had now reached the Castilians that Elizabeth was not favorable to their cause, but was supporting the regent. This news made Kirkcaldy all the more determined to assure his continued possession of the castle. To this end he issued a proclamation defending his holding of the castle against Lennox. While some of the burgesses may have approved of his action, many did not, displaying their opposition by holding secret meetings which they attended fully armed. For a time it looked as though open warfare would result. To protect himself, therefore, Kirkcaldy decided that the adherents of the king should be flushed out; and to achieve this on

April 20th he ordered all those who were for the regent to leave town within six hours.[47] It may well be that it was at this point that a number of the clergy, including Knox, along with some of the king's party went to the castle to see if they could effect a reconciliation. Lethington, however, made it only too clear that the sole condition of peace was the queen's return. To Knox this could spell nothing but disaster, for Mary's rule would mean French and Roman Catholic domination. When Knox pointed out to Lethington that Lethington, himself, had supported the setting up of James as king, Lethington replied that this had been only a temporary shift. To this Knox replied that Lethington was far too full of shifts. Since the parliament that had accepted James was a legal body, he was lawfully king. Although the conference seems to have been conducted with a certain amount of banter between the two groups, when Knox and his colleagues said good-bye to Kirkcaldy, Maitland and the others, it was a final parting.[48] As he came down from the castle Knox must have felt a great sadness that those who once had been his closest allies were now on the other side supporting a party that he believed had not only been responsible for Moray's murder, but which if it had its way would be instrumental in destroying his life's work.

The question then arose as to what Knox should do. After the arrival of the Hamiltons, his friends had called upon Kirkcaldy to see that no ill befell him, but the captain of the castle had replied that although neither he nor the Hamiltons would harm him, there were so many rascals in town that they could not guarantee his safety. He therefore offered to have Captain Melville, one of his officers and a Protestant, act as Knox's guard, a suggestion Bannatyne drily comments, that looked as though "he wold give the wolf the wedder [sheep] to keep." When the laird of Elphinstone warned Melville that God would hold him and his friends responsible for any injury done to Knox, the captain stated that he could not be blamed for anything the rabble might do. Knox would be safe only if he entered the castle or left town.[49]

We cannot doubt that Kirkcaldy, both because of their association of old and because of what Knox's martyrdom would do to the queen's cause, wished to have the minister of St. Giles out of harm's way. Furthermore, Knox's colleague Craig and some of the other ministers who sought to maintain a position of neutrality between the two factions also wished to have him leave town, as they felt that he stirred up too much controversy. Kirkcaldy said that Knox's protection was the duty of the burgh council, but this body said that they could do nothing in face of the number of rowdy Hamiltons now crowding the town. In view of all this a number of the burgesses who supported Knox approached him and pointed out that if he continued his preaching in St. Giles they would have to guard him, which might well lead to bloodshed. Therefore, for their sakes if not for his own, they advised him to leave. Only after great heart-searching and much against his will did he finally decide to accede to their request.[50]

On May 8th while the town swarmed with Hamiltons and Kirkcaldy's men worked at erecting fortifications at the gates and making loop-holes in the walls of St. Giles Kirk, Knox set out for Leith where he took a boat across the Forth to Abbotshall, now part of Kirkcaldy. There he stayed for two days in order to participate in the Communion of the Lord's Supper, after which he left for St. Andrews where he was to spend more than a year in exile from his congregation.[51]

His wife and their three daughters did not accompany him, but remained behind under the care of his colleague Craig and the burgh council. They may, however, have joined him later when he was settled in the abbey next to St. Leonard's College.

What his thoughts were as he travelled the road across the moorlands of Fife to St. Andrews, we can only imagine. No doubt his mind went back to the other times that he had followed the same route, usually in high expectation of what lay ahead whether as a student, as a tutor with his charges or as a leader in the Protestant forces going once again to preach in the church where he had first been called to the ministry. This time, however, he must have been heavy of heart. Most of his friends had deserted him, while those whom he might have expected to support him strongly, such as his colleague Craig, wished to play a neutral part in the nation's conflicts. Virtually alone, he was once again in exile on his way to a none too favorable town where Romanism still lurked, and all, he believed, because he had sought faithfully to "blaw his maister's trumpet."

CHAPTER XIII

The Last Call

ON MAY 7, 1571 KNOX, now in his 59th year, arrived in St. Andrews where he stayed until August of the following year. For the first few weeks he seems to have done little or nothing except rest. By July, however, he was in the pulpit of the parish church preaching a series of sermons on the book of Daniel. As long as he was alive, he would continue to preach, for since that was the work to which God had called him he would fulfil his duties to the best of his ability.

As usual his sermons brought strong reactions in his hearers. He had on more than one occasion both in letters and in conversations stated that he had bidden farewell to this world's affairs, but try as he would he could not separate himself entirely from the political events of the day. He may have been "out of the world" but he was certainly not free of it. When preaching he would begin quietly exegeting the passage with which he was dealing, but after half an hour of this he would turn to the application of his exposition. Then the fire began to burn, and as James Melville records, he became "sa active and vigorus, that he was lyk to ding the pulpit in blads and flie out of it. . . . he maid me sa to grew [quake] and tremble, that I could not hald pen to wryt." [1] His principal targets were the Hamiltons, all of whom he held responsible for the murder of Moray, the Castilians who were supporting Mary, and Mary herself. According to Melville he made a number of prophecies foretelling the evil ends to which all of these parties would come. As Melville, however, was writing considerably later than Bannatyne who makes no mention of the prophecies, this may have been part of the popular mythology that grew up around Knox after his death.

His excoriations of the Hamiltons and the others were not, however, mythological, for they brought him into conflict with many of the academics and clergy in the city. While St. Leonard's College had always supported the Reformation the two other colleges, St. Salvator's and St. Mary's, were strongly inclined to the queen's party and some of the faculty and students even to Roman Catholicism. John Rutherford, Provost of St. Salvator's, was particularly noted for his support of the queen. Most important of all, Robert Hamilton who had succeeded Christopher Goodman as minister of St. Andrews was very incensed at Knox's statements in his sermons concerning the Hamiltons. He said in private that Knox was as much a murderer as the Hamiltons for he had agreed to the assassination of Darnley. When Knox heard this he immediately called upon him to prove his charges. Hamilton, however, denied that he had ever said any such thing and there the matter ended. But there is little doubt that Knox caused a cleavage in public opinion in St. Andrews.[2]

No sooner was he well enough to preach than he was also back at his letter writing. On July 17th he penned a letter to the "brethren of the Church of Edinburgh" warning them against those who would lead them astray, and exhorting them to mutual charity and love. He lamented that he could not come to them adding that he was scarcely in a fit state of health to write even a few lines. Two weeks later he sent off another communication, this time to the General Assembly at Stirling, warning them as his last admonition to make sure that they were faithful to the flock by securing only proper men for the ministry and by making certain that the church was not robbed of its patrimony.[3] Calderwood states that after this letter was read to the Assembly that body expressed its complete agreement with it. Then to guarantee that the exhortation would be implemented, it immediately issued instructions for anyone who had a complaint against a superintendent to present it forthwith to the Assembly, and that those who had published libels against Knox in the preceding March should, as he had requested, prove their charges.[4]

In spite of the strength of his spirit, Knox was not well physically. James Melville reports that when a student at St. Leonard's he used

to see Knox walking to the church leaning on a staff and on the arm
of his servant Richard Bannatyne, obviously very weak. He used on
occasion also to enter St. Leonard's yard, where he had crossed verbal
swords with Friar Arbuckle some twenty or more years earlier.
There he would sit in the sun while the students gathered around to
receive his blessing and to hear his advice on the way in which they
should conduct themselves as Christians, particularly as ministers of
the Gospel. One sees here a different and softer side of Knox's
character of which we often lose sight. He apparently did not feel
welcome in the other colleges, for we have no references to his
visiting their precincts.[5]

Meanwhile the situation in Edinburgh had gone from bad to
worse. Kirkcaldy had taken complete charge of the town, had seized
some of the burgesses whom he imprisoned in the castle and had
gone so far as to forbid the holding of a parliament within the
Tollbooth.[6] Furthermore, and far worse in Knox's eyes, John Craig,
his colleague, who was now the sole minister of St. Giles, was
endeavouring to maintain a neutral stance in spite of the evil deeds
and rebellion of the Castilians. Craig apparently felt that a gentler
approach to Mary's party, and particularly to Kirkcaldy, might lead
to peace. Knox, however, along with many others could see this only
as treachery.[7]

Despite Kirkcaldy's threats against Lennox's parliament the regent
convened one in the Canongate in mid-May, but it was short-lived.
The castle's guns made it impossible to carry on, so the meeting was
prorogued to meet in Stirling on August 3rd. To counter-act this, the
Marians held a parliament in Edinburgh on the 12th and 13th of June
at which time they declared that since Mary had been forced to
abdicate, her demission of the crown was not legal.[8] Thus the two
parties made it perfectly clear that neither would give in to the other.
Meanwhile, both England and France were seeking to bring about a
cessation of hostilities, but without success. The Castilians continued
to force uncooperative burgesses to leave town taking over their
goods and houses; and the king's party sought by every possible
means to capture the castle. A condition of stalemate had been
reached by the end of July with neither party able to force the other
to come to terms.[9]

Toward the end of August, however, the position of the king's
party was clearly improving. Although Lennox's forces failed to gain

Edinburgh, outside the burgh the nobles were once again beginning
to swing over to his side. In a list of the lords and earls sent to
England on August 26th, most of the names mentioned are noted as
supporters of the king. Furthermore, it contains the names of a
number of the leaders of the queen's party, such as Argyll who had
submitted, as well as those who had been neutral, such as Mar.[10] As
the *Diurnal of Remarkable Occurrents* remarks, "the greedie and
insatiable appetite of benefices wes the maist cause thairof," but
nevertheless the nobles were gradually moving over to Lennox's
support.[11] What was happening in the ranks of the aristocracy was
also taking place among the burgesses of Edinburgh, for Maitland on
September 5th reported to Mary that the merchants who had been
lending the Castilians money, probably under duress, were no longer
willing to do so, since their credit was no longer good. He then adds:
"The yielding of Argyle, Cassilis, Eglinton and L. to the other party
makes the merchants despair that our case shall prosper, seeing the
few that stick to your cause." [12]

Because of this desperate situation, the Castilians decided that they
had to bring an end to the stranglehold which Lennox's forces had on
the castle. The Laird of Ormiston in Teviotdale, not Knox's
supporter, but the man who had largely engineered the murder of
Darnley and who was supporting Kirkcaldy, had already made one
sortie to St. Andrews where he had captured the French ambassador,
M. de Verac. It was now decided by Kirkcaldy that an attack should
be made on Stirling in the hope of taking Lennox. The raid was
successful in that the Castilians' forces led by the Earl of Huntly,
Lord Claude Hamilton, and others seized Stirling, but in the ensuing
fight not only did they lose a considerable number of men, Lennox
was also shot and killed.[13] This was more a disaster for the Castilians
than for the king's party. Not only did it show the Castilians to be
clearly traitors to the king, but it also opened the way for the Earl of
Mar, formerly Lord Erskine, to become regent with James Douglas,
fourth Earl of Morton, as the power behind the throne.[14] While Mar
was a compromiser, Morton, totally unscrupulous, was not a man
with whom one could trifle. He immediately laid plans for the
capture of the castle calling on the English for aid and ordering all the
remaining inhabitants of Edinburgh to leave the town on pain of
being declared rebels. In this way he sought to seal off the castle in
preparation for an all-out attack.[15]

The change in regents meant more than a political move, for Mar, and particularly Morton, also had plans to deal with the church. At the parliament of Stirling early in August, the first steps had been taken toward the restoration of episcopacy to the Kirk, when the title of bishop had been revived and the holders of that office allowed to take their old places as members of the first estate. This move would seem to have been largely the work of Morton who saw a way of dipping his grasping hand further into the church's coffers. Then on November 5th, the Privy Council issued orders for all the collectors of thirds and the superintendents who had not been remitting the money as they should to appear before them on the 12th in Leith to give account of their collections. Erskine of Dun, Superintendent of Angus and Mearns, thereupon wrote a letter protesting this action since both the revival of the episcopacy which threatened to displace the superintendents and the attempt to control the collections of monies for the church were unwarranted interference by the civil power. As Calderwood points out in his history, Erskine seems to have equated bishops and superintendents in his communication, although he objected strongly to bishops being appointed by the state without examination by the church. His protest was effective to the extent that Mar withdrew the letter to the collectors, but did not rescind the creation of parliamentary bishops, for Morton sought to use them for his and the other nobles financial advantage.[16]

Because of parliament's action the superintendents, ministers and commissioners from the towns and landward churches met in Leith in January 1572 to discuss the whole matter of bishops, in order to devise a policy which they could follow in dealing with the Privy Council. While asserting its authority to be that of a General Assembly the convention turned over the matter of bishops to a commission, headed by Erskine of Dun, which soon came to an agreement with the government. While the commission sought to guarantee the ministers' stipends, it granted that bishops and archbishops should be restored, although they were not to have more power than superintendents, and it also agreed that much of the church's revenues should remain in the hands of laymen. This compromise having been reached by January 16th, a move was made immediately to appoint a new Archbishop of St. Andrews. On February 8th an election was held at which John Douglas, Rector of St. Andrews, after he had given proof of his ministry, was chosen archbishop. His appointment was really made on the nomination of Morton with whom he had already come to an arrangement that gave the earl part of the archiepiscopal revenues.[17]

Bannatyne and Calderwood both record that there was no little opposition to the revival of the office of archbishop. Patrick Constan preached a sermon in which he attacked the whole proceeding and others went so far as to register their dissent in spite of the Earl of Morton's presence. On Sunday, February 10th, Knox preached at the inauguration of the archbishop, but having, according to Calderwood, pronounced a "curse" on both the giver and receiver of the benefice, refused to take part in the ceremony of induction. When John Rutherford, Provost of St. Salvator's College, said that Knox opposed Douglas's appointment because he wished to have the archbishopric himself, Knox replied from the pulpit the next Sunday that he had been offered a much larger bishopric, but had turned it down, obviously referring to Northumberland's offer of Rochester in 1552. He then expressed, according to Bannatyne, his dislike of the whole proceeding and his opposition to "Sic ordour as was then uset," as being in direct conflict with the organization established by the *Book of Discipline* which many of the nobles now favoring bishops had signed.[18]

Biographers of Knox have disagreed violently on the question of whether he opposed or accepted bishops. The older writers have usually accepted Bannatyne's and Calderwood's statements that he was anti-episcopal, while many of the more recent writers have adopted the attitude that he was quite prepared to favour an episcopally governed church—but with certain modifications. A letter which he wrote to the General Assembly in August of 1572 refers to bishops and apparently accepts them, which seems to contradict Bannatyne.[19] Yet it is also quite possible that he recognized that since the appointment of bishops had been agreed to by many he could do little to change the situation, but hoped that proper bishops would be appointed. We must remember two other facts also in this connection. First of all he was a sick man with ebbing physical strength. This would make him diffident about offering violent opposition. Secondly, with his usual realism he could see that with Mary's supporters still holding Edinburgh Castle coupled with the constant threat that she might return, he should not divide the Protestant forces. Added to this, knowing Morton, he probably decided that he would accomplish nothing by his opposition. His attitude towards bishops at this point hardly proves anything for either side, although Bannatyne's and Melville's reports of his aversion to episcopacy seem to agree more fully with his earlier views.[20]

On March 6th, the twenty-fourth General Assembly convened in St. Andrews in St. Leonard's College. The authorities may have chosen this location because of the situation in Edinburgh, but they may also have made this decision because of the presence of Knox, for they had some very important and serious matters with which to deal. The first problem which faced them was that of the position of the superintendents now that bishops had been reinstated. The issue came to a head when John Winram, Superintendent of Fife, after being severely criticized for his dictatorial actions resigned on the grounds that the archbishop should take over. The Assembly, however, ordained that the superintendent's authority should continue to be exercised alongside the Archbishop of St. Andrews' jurisdiction, only he should concur with the archbishop in arrangements for his visitations. The same instructions were given to the superintendent of Angus and Mearns. At this time also, a committee made up of a number of ministers, including both the archbishop and Knox, was appointed to meet in Knox's house to discuss matters that had been agreed upon by some commissioners and the Privy Council, to see if they were according to God's Word. It was probably at this time that Knox began to regret that such a burden had been laid upon the back of the archbishop who was too old to carry it, but he would not say so because of his love for one who had been among the earliest preachers of the Gospel in Scotland.[21] While all these events were transpiring a letter arrived from Theodore Beza congratulating Knox on ridding the Scottish church of bishops, but also warning him against allowing their reintroduction, since they had been the cause of all the trouble before. Beza may have been aware of the struggle that was going on in the church and hoped to strengthen the hands of those fighting for a non-episcopal ecclesiastical structure.[22] His message, however, arrived too late to have any effect.

Meanwhile what was happening in Edinburgh? The days of the queen's garrison of the castle were numbered. Yet the regent was by no means in an entirely favorable situation, for from the judgments passed at this time by the Privy Council against the queen's supporters, it would appear that quite a number of the Lothian gentry, formerly Knox's principal allies, still favored her side. Likewise a considerable number of Edinburgh burgesses, with Thomas M'Calzeane at their head, were also charged with being traitors to the king.[23] Those burgesses loyal to the king now left their homes, although the Castilians promised not to molest them if they paid them protection money. The regent and his advisers, however, declared this to be treason which could not but result in their punishment if they paid. The resulting confusion led a good many to move to Leith. On July 2, 1572 these men entered into a covenant among themselves, acknowledging the judgment of God against them, lamenting their loss of houses, goods, trade and the ministry of the Gospel through the expulsion of their ministers, but agreeing to stand fast against the Castilians and to defend each other in case of need.[24] To counter the actions of Kirkcaldy and his men the regent and his council then sought to establish a blockade of the city both by forcing all the inhabitants to leave and by cutting off all supplies. As this tactic, however, was unsuccessful, the only recourse was the reduction of the castle by direct assault.[25]

With all these developments Knox seems to have been kept informed and to have made his views of them known. In May (1572) he wrote to Sir James Douglas of Drumlanrig expressing the opinion that compromise with the Castilians could only lead to disaster. Then in July in a letter to Wishart of Pittarrow he lamented that neither side had any particular interest in the Gospel, for while the Castilians were undoubtedly murderers, the only interest that the regent's forces had in the church was what they could take from it. He felt that the king's party was worse than the papists who through ignorance kept the truth from the people, for the former did the same, not through lack of knowledge, but to line their own pockets.[26]

By July, he was becoming physically weaker. Writing to Douglas in May he had referred to himself as "half deid," while in his letter to Wishart he said that he left his bed only once a week, and in another to Goodman in England, he commented that he was so weak that he could not possibly travel to see him. Yet in spite of, or perhaps because of his feeling of approaching death he was straining to complete the writing of his history down to 1564, and perhaps beyond. In December of 1571 he had Alexander Hay searching for documents that he required, particularly his letters to Lennox. But although the list of documents that Hay reported he had collected were useful, Book IV never passed the 1564 date.[27] The so-called Book V David Buchanan probably wrote in the next century, perhaps with the help of some of Knox's notes and the documents discovered by Hay.[28]

While writing the *History*, Knox was also preparing an answer to a letter of a Jesuit, James Tyrie, who some years earlier had sent a plea to his brother, a Protestant, to return to the Church of Rome. The brother had sent the letter to Knox for reply, but as he had never had the time to answer it he was now at the end of his life working hard at dealing with Tyrie's arguments. The principal point of the Jesuit's letter was that the Church of Rome by virtue of its succession and its unity showed itself to be the true church. To this Knox replied, denying the validity of the proofs of such a claim by pointing out the moral and doctrinal errors of Romanism. He then added a copy of the letter that he had sent to Mrs. Bowes from Dieppe, July 20, 1554, explaining that he had written it to comfort her and published it now that it might in the present circumstances comfort others. He also explains, however, perhaps because some had again raised the matter of his relations with Mrs. Bowes, "before that he [God] put an end to my wretched life, I could not cease but declare to the worlde what was the caus of our great familiaritie and long acquentance; which was nether fleshe nor bloode, but a troubled conscience upon her part . . ." He then adds to his introduction an explanation of how he felt this letter would help those with the same doubts and fears. He closes by bidding the world good-night, "for as the worlde is wearie of me, so am I of it." [29]

Yet his bidding of the world good-night was not final. He still felt that he had a duty to warn Scotland against those who had not only broken both the laws of God and man, but were also endangering the work of reform. At the end of his introduction to his letter to Mrs. Bowes he penned a prayer that the Lord would either convert or confound those who were holding Edinburgh Castle against the king's forces. Although his prayer was not answered literally at the moment, on July 31st, under pressure from both England and France the two sides agreed to a truce for two months.[30]

The immediate effect in Edinburgh of the cessation of hostilities was the return of most of the inhabitants to their homes. The members of the congregation of the High Kirk also began to think of the necessity of recalling Knox, for they had lost confidence in Craig who had, in their eyes, compromised with the Castilians. Therefore on August 4th they dispatched Nicholas Uddart and John Johnston to St. Andrews to call upon Knox to return to his flock. To this summons Knox replied that he was prepared to accede to their request, but only on condition that he would not be inhibited in any way from speaking out against Kirkcaldy, Maitland, and their cohorts who were "traitors and murderers." When the delegation assured him that they would in no way restrict his freedom in the pulpit, he agreed to move back.[31]

His insistence upon his freedom to speak as he pleased in the pulpit was probably the result of a conflict which he had had the preceding month in St. Andrews with the Hamiltons. A certain Archibald Hamilton had refused to attend Knox's sermons because he called all Hamiltons murderers for supporting Hamilton of Bothwellhaugh, the assassin of the Regent Moray. When Archibald gave this as his reason for his absence from divine worship Archbishop Douglas, the Bishop of Caithness, the Superintendent of Fife and others from the university had him appear before them in an attempt to persuade both to modify their stands. Knox, however, refused to change anything, insisting that neither the pulpit in St. Andrews, nor any other should be subject to the control of the "schools," but only to God and to the General Assembly of the church. He gave as his reason "that universities, orderis well establishit, and men raised up to defend the Kirke of God, have opprest it." Hamilton, on the other hand, contended that Knox had no right to deal with matters and doctrines which he was not prepared to defend in the universities, since these institutions were set up to maintain sane doctrine and prevent schism. With this view Knox did not agree, as it would lead to the bondage of the preacher.[32] Thus they parted.

Knox, ever since his own day, has been strongly criticized for the severity and violence of his attacks upon those who did not agree with him. Even some who have favored much that he said and did have been inclined to become apologetic when considering his vigorous condemnations of Queen Mary, the Hamiltons, Kirkcaldy of Grange and others. We must, however, always keep in mind the situation in which he found himself: in a country ruled by a factious and violent nobility, and by a queen trained by some of the most adept practitioners of court intrigue and backed by the might of France; in a newly reformed church which had neither universal popular support within the country nor an adequate financial provision for its maintenance, and which might be overturned at any moment by a "palace revolution"; and in a society in which sweet reasonableness could accomplish little or nothing, since only strong words and violent acts were ever heard above the clash of interests and of arms. Perhaps equally important, he saw the danger of the Reformation becoming merely a political movement, resulting in the subversion of what he believed to be the Gospel. Ever conscious of his calling to blow his master's trumpet, he recognized that soft words would achieve little in the Scotland of his day. His statement from his deathbed to the office-bearers of his congregation seems to put the whole matter in perspective, particularly for our own age in which violent words and deeds have once again become common currency:

> I know that many have complained much and loudly, and do still complain of my too great severity; but God knows that my mind was always free from hatred to the persons of those against whom I denounced the heavy judgments of God. In the mean time, I cannot deny but that I felt the greatest abhorrence of the sin in which they indulged; still, however, keeping this as one thing in view, that if it were possible I might gain them to the Lord. But a certain reverential fear of my God who called me, and was pleased of his grace to make me a steward of divine mysteries, to whom I knew I must render an account, when I shall appear before his tribunal, of the manner in which I have discharged the embassy which he hath committed to me—had such a powerful effect as to make me utter so intrepidly whatever the Lord put into my mouth, without any respect of persons. Therefore, I profess before God and his holy angels, that I never made gain of the sacred word of God, that I never studied to please men, never indulged my own private passions or those of others, but faithfully distributed the talent intrusted to my care for the edification of the church over which I did watch. . . .[33]

The Massacre of St. Bartholomew's Eve (1572) lent even greater plausibility to his opposition to Mary and her party. Had not the whole terrible affair been largely organized and carried out by her relatives? And if she returned to rule in Scotland might she not attempt, with the aid of the Castilians, the Hamiltons and the whole body of Roman Catholic nobles and churchmen, to imitate her

French cousins? To many Protestants his attacks upon Mary and her supporters made much sense, for they now had clear proof before their eyes of what the French Roman Catholic forces would do once they gained the upper hand.

Knox's fear of the dangers threatening the church appears in his letter written to the General Assembly meeting early in August in Perth. Before he received the request from Edinburgh for his return, he dispatched his communication to Perth warning against allowing the universities to control the pulpit, insisting instead that the church should keep control of the universities. At the same time he urged the Assembly to make sure that the established position of the church be guaranteed, not only formally, but also by ensuring that proper bishops be appointed, that the patrons and civil authorities not be allowed either to take over church revenues or provide unsuitable incumbents to churches or other ecclesiastical offices, and that the laws against "massmongers and excommunicate be enforced." He closed by propounding certain questions concerning both bishops, superintendents and lay abbots which needed clarification. To this communication the Assembly returned a most favorable answer, for he was still very much the leader. At the same time, they authorized the superintendent and some ministers, with the advice of Knox and the session of St. Giles Kirk, to choose a qualified minister to assist him in his work when he returned to his flock.[34]

On August 23rd he and his family arrived in Leith and after a few days went on to Edinburgh where they were lodged in the house of a goldsmith, Mossman (the present "John Knox's House"). Despite his ill health he immediately attempted to carry on his preaching as before, but his voice was so weak that he could be heard by only a few who were close to the pulpit. Yet despite this difficulty, when word arrived early in September of the Massacre of St. Bartholomew's Eve in France on August 24th, he spoke with such vehemence that the French ambassador complained to the Privy Council of his attacks on the French king. They replied that they could do nothing, since they could not stop the preachers from attacking even them from the pulpit.[35]

In view of Knox's physical weakness the necessity of choosing a successor now became pressing. But since the congregation obviously would not accept John Craig, Knox and his advisers had to look elsewhere, with the result that their choice fell on John Lawson of

Aberdeen to whom Knox wrote on September 7th inviting him to come to Edinburgh to preach before the congregation. Since he was approaching his end and wished to consult with him on heavenly things, he urged him to hasten lest he should come too late. To this plea Lawson responded by leaving immediately for Edinburgh where, after preaching a number of times before the congregation, he was called to be their minister.

This did not mean, however, that Knox ceased his preaching. Although he could no longer be heard in St. Giles, which is none too easy a building in which to speak even for a man with a strong voice, he wished to continue his "blawing of his maister's trumpet." Arrangements were therefore made for him to hold services in the Tollbooth for those who wished to continue to enjoy his ministry.[36] As long as he could, he would fulfil his calling as a "painful preacher of the evangell." But in spite of his desire to continue to preach he was daily growing weaker.[37]

November 9, 1572 saw Knox's last public act. After preaching in the Tollbooth he went to St. Giles where he participated in Lawson's induction, by delivering the sermon. In this he pointed out the mutual duties of minister and congregation, and closed with a fervent prayer for divine blessing on both minister and congregation.[38]

Two days later he was afflicted with a violent cough which further weakened him. Yet he was not suffered to depart in peace, for on the following Thursday, Maitland of Lethington sent down from the castle a letter in which he accused Knox of making false statements about him and demanding that he be disciplined. To this the Kirk session replied by insisting that Maitland must give the bearer a commission to act as his representative. This was obviously a delaying tactic for they realized that Knox was in no physical condition to reply to the charges.[39] Yet he still had the sense of his calling for on Friday, November 14th, he arose from his bed in the belief that it was Sunday, in order that he might preach in the church. He also seems to have retained his sense of realism, for the next day when two men came to visit him about noon he sat down to dinner with them and "caused peirce ane hoggeid of wine which was in the seller, and willed the said Archibald [Stewart] send for the same so long as it lasted, for he wald never tarie untill it was drunken."[40]

Throughout the following week many others came to see him.

The officebearers of St. Giles appeared at his bedside on Monday, at which time he made a full reply to Maitland's accusations. At the same time he asked David Lindsay, minister of Leith to go to Kirkcaldy in the castle to try to persuade him to change his ways, by warning him that if he did not repent he would come to certain disaster. On another occasion a pious gentle-lady who came to see him praised him for all that he had done. To her flattery he replied, "Tongue! Tongue! ladie; fleche of itself is over proud, and neidis no meanis to esteame the self." The nobles also flocked in to bid their last farewells. The end was drawing very near. Nevertheless according to Richard Bannatyne, his servant, his mind was continually on the state of the church in Scotland for which he was much in prayer. On Monday the 24th he took a turn for the worse, asking his wife about noon to read to him the fifteenth chapter of 1 Corinthians. Then five hours later he asked her to "Go reid whair I cast my first ancre!" which was John 17. From this time on he sank rapidly until after evening prayers, about eleven o'clock, he quietly passed away.[41]

On Wednesday he was buried in the graveyard of St. Giles Kirk, being conveyed to his last resting place by the newly elected regent, the Earl of Morton the successor of Mar who had recently died, some suspected with Morton's help, and by the lords and commons. Melville reports that as they closed the grave the regent declared "Here lies one who never feared any flesh." This epitaph coming from the mouth of such a one as the ruthless and cynical earl, spoke volumes concerning Knox.[42]

In his will Knox showed assets of some £1500 (Scots) of which over half was money owing to him. Margaret, his wife, and his three daughters Martha, Margaret and Elizabeth he named as his executors. To his sons by Marjory Bowes he left £500 along with some silver plate and £30 worth of his books. To his nephew Paul Knox, his brother William's son, he left £100 to help him with his education; to his wife and three daughters he left everything else.

Both Knox's sons entered Cambridge after his death and subsequently took orders in the Church of England. But as they died at a relatively early age, Nathaniel when about 23 years and Eleazer at 33, neither having married, the male line came to an end. Margaret, still a young woman, survived her husband for some forty years, within two years of his death becoming the wife of Andrew Ker of Fawdonside, one of those involved in the murder of Riccio. The daughter Martha married at the age of eighteen Alexander Fairlie of Braid, Margaret married Zachary Pont, the son of Robert Pont, one of Knox's fellow ministers, and Elizabeth married John Welsh, one of the most determined upholders of Presbyterianism against James VI.[43]

Although James Melville reports various prophecies that Knox was reputed to have made concerning Kirkcaldy and the Castilians, we have no other evidence on the subject. Bannatyne never mentions such prophecies, as he undoubtedly would have, if Knox had made them. Rather, they seem to have been part of the tradition that grew up shortly after his death. As for Knox, himself, his only claim was that he had been a faithful interpreter of the Word of God. As he stated in his will:

> I protest that God be my mouth, be I never so abject, has schawin to yow his trewth, in all simplicitie. Nane I haif corrupted; nane I haif defraudit; merchandies haif I not maid; to Godis glorie I write of the glorious evangell of Jesus Christ, bot according to the measure of the grace granted unto me, I haif dividit the sermont of trewth in juist pairtis; beatin doun the pryde of the proud, in all that did delcair thair rebellioun againis God, according as God in his law gevis to that testimonie; and raising up the consciences trublit with the knawledge of thair awin synnis, be the declaring of Jesus Christ, the strenth of his death, and the michtie operatioune of his resurrectioune, in the hartis of the faithfull. Of this, I say, I haif ane testimony this day in my conscience, befoir God; how that evir the warld rage.[44]

In these words he sums up what it meant for him to be "the trumpeter of God."

CHAPTER XIV

John Knox After Four Hundred Years

JOHN KNOX DIED JUST a little over four hundred years ago. The realization of this should cause us to ask two questions: How important was he in his own day? Does he have any significance today? To answer them, we must attempt to look back over his life to see what his impact was on his contemporaries, and through them, on those who have followed afterwards.

We have seen in the preceding pages that opinions concerning Knox varied greatly during his lifetime, as they have done ever since. There were, and still are, those who could see in him no fault whatsoever. From his servant Richard Bannatyne down to the present day we find numerous members of the "John Knox Fan Club." On the other side of the fence were his opponents: Roman Catholics, *politiques,* and those who wanted only peace and quiet. They too have their descendants at the present time. Usually, however, the attitudes of both protagonists and antagonists in the sixteenth and in the twentieth centuries have been determined by whether they agreed with his basic principles or rejected them.

Between these two extremes we have two other groups. One is completely indifferent to Knox, feeling that he was and is of little importance in the history of Scotland and of the Reformation movement as a whole. They only tend to become annoyed with him when someone writes his biography. The other group is made up of those who see him as a man who sought to accomplish a certain purpose, and who attained considerable success, yet who at the same time had all the weaknesses, failings and foibles of every man, but who has had an influence on history down to the present day.

The author has sought to place himself in the last named company, attempting to be objective in his estimates and understanding of the man without either praising or condemning him from the distance of four centuries. He has endeavored to explain the rationale of Knox's conduct, although some may feel that the stress has been laid too much upon his intellectual and not enough on his emotional reactions. But the truth is that we do not know very much about his emotional life, apart from some outbursts against Queen Mary, the Guises, and the Hamiltons. We see a little of his emotional side in his letters to Mrs. Bowes and to some of his other consultants, as well as in his letters to Mary of Guise, the Scottish nobility, and the Scottish commonalty, but even in these cases, the intellectual aspect plays the major part. Consequently it is to this that the most attention has been paid, in the hope of making him somewhat more comprehensible as a man to the twentieth century.

How far was he right in his judgments? Could he have followed any other path and still have reached his goal? These are questions for speculation. We may, however, estimate his actual importance in history by seeing exactly what he did accomplish in his life-time and the effects which he has had on subsequent generations.

Chronologically, the first place in which Knox had any considerable impact and effect was not Scotland, but England. That his ministry in Berwick and Newcastle was influential in the border country is indicated by the attacks made on him by some followers of the old religion. More important, however, was his impact on the Reformation as it was developing in London under the aegis of the Edwardian government. Largely responsible for the "Black Rubric" of the second Prayer Book, he laid the foundation for later objections to the Anglican liturgy. Furthermore, his attacks upon Mary Tudor from Dieppe undoubtedly stirred up anti-Roman Catholic sentiment and opposition to the dominance of Spanish influence. Yet all of this was relatively ephemeral. As he, himself, admitted even those whom he had instructed so diligently in the north of England, when the crisis came, failed to stand by their early professions of faith.

Knox's lasting effect on England came from his dealings with the

English religious refugees on the Continent. Although he had no desire to become pastor of the English congregation at Frankfort, when he did so, he took a firm but conciliatory line with the Anglican minority. He would not use the Prayer Book in the services and spoke out strongly against some of the practices of the English church during the reign of Edward VI. In this stance he placed himself on the side of the "non-conformist" majority in Frankfort headed by such men as William Whittingham, Anthony Gilby and Christopher Goodman. After his forced departure from Frankfort and return to Geneva he became the leader of what was to be the first Puritan congregation. Although others who came from Frankfort to form the congregation already held views in conflict with those of the English refugee "establishment" in Strasbourg, Knox seems to have brought them into focus and expressed them in his writings in such a way that he became a kind of symbol of resistance to Anglicanism. At the same time, he did not favor their plans to separate from the Church of England on their return after Elizabeth's accession in 1559. He has been accused of letting down those who followed him when he did not favor their breaking with the church later in the 1560s. His policy always had been, however, that reforms should be sought with all the influence and persuasion possible, but separation from Christian brethren should take place only in the last extremity. This was his advice to his congregation in Berwick with regard to the second Edwardian *Book of Common Prayer* and a principle to which he still adhered in the 1560s even though he did not approve of the English ecclesiastical policy under the Elizabethan regime. He did not sanction the rigid attitude which became characteristic of the separatist Puritans.

England, however, was not Knox's only sphere of action. He had close relationships with the French Huguenots, probably from the time of his service as a galley slave. That he was apparently quite fluent in French appears from the fact that he preached in French in Dieppe and even on his death-bed had some of Calvin's sermons in French read to him. It is not strange, therefore, that he seems to have exercised considerable influence, particularly in persuading the Protestant leaders in Dieppe to expand their efforts to make their message known to the people of the town. Moreover, as a result of his own work as a co-pastor in the congregation a number of the local gentry became Protestant, and in many other ways he seems to have left his mark upon this Protestant community. Indeed later, when they were faced with persecution he urged them to take up arms to defend themselves, if necessary to the extent of staging a rebellion. When speaking of Protestant-Catholic relations he was much more drastic and absolute than when he gave advice to Puritans in the Church of England. But then, as he saw it, the cases were different.

Apart from his direct contacts with the Huguenots in Dieppe and also La Rochelle, we do not have much evidence on which to go. As we have mentioned earlier, however, he may have made contact with the *Eglises Réformées* in Poitou, at Poitiers and Châtelherault, and may even have taken part in the preparation of their confession of faith. He may also have exercised some influence on the political thinking of the Huguenot writers who produced a number of works on political theory after the Massacre of St. Bartholomew's Eve. We know that some at least of these authors had read Knox's *First Blast* and probably some of his other political writings. Although they at first seemed to disagree with him, eventually when they themselves had experienced severe persecution they came around to his position on the right of rebellion. Even a cursory content analysis of their works seems to indicate a relationship between them and Knox's writings. While these conclusions may seem somewhat speculative, they have behind them facts which makes their probability rather strong.

Knox's greatest impact, however, was undoubtedly upon Scotland which was the center of his interest. This is of course natural since he was a Scot and spent his most active years in the Reformation on his native heath. We must note too that his influence was not merely on a few unrelated matters, nor in a few separate instances, but was what one might call "organic" in that it affected the whole Reformation in Scotland, both in its formulation and in its continuance ever since.

From what has been said in this study, however, it would seem clear that Knox was by no means the originator of the Scottish Reformation. For that matter, none of the Protestant reformers held that position within their own spheres, for they all worked against the background of a movement of protest and religious reform which had already developed spontaneously at "grass roots" level. Like Luther, Calvin and Zwingli, Knox was able to capitalize on what had already begun, bring it into focus and organize it, at least partially, for victory. Moreover, he was the one person as "God's trumpeter" who seemed capable of maintaining and strengthening the morale of the forces which were seeking to make the Reformation successful. He was above all else the one who, when the clouds seemed darkest and the outlook most threatening, was able to keep his faith and stimulate those threatened with defeat to action and achievement. Randolph was quite right when he said that he could do more than five hundred trumpets continually blustering in their ears. We can surely say that he was the key figure in the Scottish Reformation, however important were others such as Moray, Balnaves, and the rest.

In specific matters we also see Knox's hand. The Scots Confession undoubtedly reflected his point of view, although others such as John Winram and John Willock undoubtedly also played their part in its composition. Knox, however, as the one who had the closest contact with the Reformed churches abroad and who may well have brought with him copies of the French documents of 1559, as well as various materials from Geneva, certainly must have wielded a decisive influence in drawing up the document. The same can be said of the *Book of Discipline*. Again he was the leading man on the committee which prepared it, and although others exercised their influences he seems to have been the person that gave it its focus and its direction. He had garnered ideas from Poullain, Calvin, à Lasco, the Huguenots, and others, all of which he pulled together to form a system of organization and government which would enable the church not only to manifest its "marks," but also through its care of the poor and control of education to exert a powerful influence upon society as a whole.

That his was the position of leadership in the movement was recognized by his contemporaries. Archbishop Parker, for instance, expressed the hope that England would not experience the "same visitation" that Knox had inflicted on Scotland. Another English witness to Knox's position of dominance, Sir Thomas Randolph, the English ambassador, stated that Knox ruled the roost. Closer to home we find the "Brethren of the West" who included the Earl of Glencairn, Lord Ochiltree, and Cunningham of Cunninghamhead, in 1571 telling Kirkcaldy of Grange not to harm Knox "in whose protection and lyfe (to our judgment) standis the prosperitie and incres of Godis Kirk and religione." [1] Even the Earl of Morton who differed from Knox in a great many ways, according to Calderwood, could say at Knox's funeral:

> Here lyeth a man who, in his life, never feared the face of man, who hath often been threatened with dag and dager, but yitt hath ended his days in peace and honour. For he had God's providence watching over him in a special maner, when his verie life was sought.[2]

His contemporaries on the Continent held the same view of the Scottish reformer, for Beza writing to Knox shortly before the latter's death refers to him as the helmsman of the Reformation in Scotland, the one who had been able to bring about the restoration of the Scottish church.[3] But it was not only his Protestant friends and foes who acknowledged his dominant position, for the Roman Catholics by their attacks upon him in their pamphlets and tracts bore witness that he was the leader and the framer of the movement of Protestant reform. To his contemporaries he was undoubtedly the man who had brought the religious revolution in Scotland to its successful conclusion.

Knox's influence, however, did not cease with his death or that of his contemporaries. In his own land he laid the groundwork for Andrew Melville's establishment of a truly presbyterian church. Some historians have endeavored to show that Melville sought to establish a church in conflict with Knox's ideas. It is true that the first *Book of Discipline* did not establish a fully articulated presbyterial system, but that would have been difficult considering the state of Scottish Protestantism in the spring of 1560. Nevertheless, the Genevan and French examples, the establishment of the "weekly exercises" and the superintendents' councils all pointed in the direction of a presbyterial organization, with the result that Melville's moves were by no means untoward as far as Knox's views were concerned.[4] Beyond Melville, Knox's influence shows in the development of the "covenanting" tradition of the seventeenth century, for the Presbyterians adopted his concept of the "covenanted nation" in their resistance to Stewart attempts to Anglicanize both Scottish church and state. His spirit of resistance to state interference in the church and insistence upon the rights of congregations continued on into the eighteenth century, resulting in various withdrawals from the Established Kirk which culminated in the Disruption of 1843.

Like John Brown of Harper's Ferry fame, Knox's soul has kept "marching on."

His influence, however, has extended beyond the wall of the church. For one thing his concept of the responsibility of the church for the care of the poor was maintained down into the nineteenth century, reaching its fullest expression in the work of Thomas Chalmers in his St. John's Parish, Glasgow. Likewise his emphasis upon the importance of education as stated in the *Book of Discipline*, became a basic characteristic of the Scot both at home and abroad, as we can see, for instance, from the fact that most of the universities established in Canada in the nineteenth century had Scots as their founders. Added to all this, Knox brought into focus the Scottish concept of the right of the people to resist the government. To be sure this tendency had already shown itself repeatedly in Scottish history, but Knox seems to have given it a philosophical or theoretical basis which has become part and parcel of the Scottish pattern of thought.

One could perhaps refer to other Scottish characteristics which might be traced to Knox's influence. For instance so many of the themes of Scottish romanticism of the eighteenth and early nineteenth centuries have their parallels and perhaps their origins in Knox's writings. As an example, one could compare Knox's statement to Mary when she demanded by what right he spoke of her marriage to a Spaniard, with Rabbie Burns' "A Man's a Man for a' that." Even Scottish Roman Catholics, who naturally have little love for the reformer, have been affected by some of the influence which he has wielded. Thus for good or for ill, according to our points of view, Knox has done much to set the tone for Scotland and the Scot since the sixteenth century.

One confirming piece of evidence for this thesis is the continuing characteristics of Scots who have migrated to other parts of the globe. Even before the Reformation the Scots, because of economic and political conditions, had tended to be somewhat migratory, but with the opening up of the New World and the Far East from the sixteenth century on, this tendency became much more pronounced. With the migrants went the patterns of thought and action which they had developed at home; and in many cases even after three or four generations, the same characteristics and tendencies are still very noticeable.

Prior to 1707 and the union of the parliaments, the migrants could be classed roughly in three groups: soldiers, merchants, and scholars. But whether they went to Holland, to France, to Sweden, to Russia, or to Poland one finds that they all gained the same reputation, not always complimentary, for their Scottish characteristics which included among other things the desire to establish a Reformed church for their own use. At one time there were some twenty Scottish Reformed churches in Holland built for the use of the Scottish mercenary troops and merchants in the country. The only one left today is the English Reformed Church in Amsterdam founded originally in 1606 by Lord Rae's regiment of MacKays.

After 1707 the same tendencies are observable only much more clearly. As the Scots settled throughout the Empire, in North America (the Carolinas, the Shenandoah Valley, Nova Scotia, Lower and Upper Canada), Africa and the Antipodes, the fact that many were the heirs of Knox and the Reformation showed itself in various ways, not the least obvious being the erection of numerous Presbyterian churches bearing the name of Knox. Although Roman Catholic Scots did not display some of the typical Protestant characteristics, it is interesting to note that they tended to be on better terms with their Protestant "brither Scots" than they ever had been at home and to develop the same approaches particularly their independence, their stress upon diligence, frugality and education, and their habit of being "agin' the government."

Thus while it is a long way back to John Knox, as one looks at the Scottish influence in many parts of the world today, he must admit "that he being dead yet speaketh." Furthermore, that many are writing about him and his ideas, whether they like them or not, indicates that his trumpet notes still sound down the glens of time.

Principal Abbreviations
Used in the Notes

ALCPA   *Acts of the Lords of the Council in Public Affairs*

ALHT   *Accounts of the Lord High Treasurer of Scotland*

ANF   *Archives Nationales de France*

APC   *Acts of the Privy Council of England*

APS   *Acts of the Parliament of Scotland*

BOEC   *Book of the Old Edinburgh Club*

BUK   *Book of the Universal Kirk or Acts and Proceedings of the General Assembly of the Church of Scotland*

CSP, Dom.   *Calendar of State Papers, Domestic*

CSP, For.–Ed VI   *Calendar of State Papers, Foreign, Edward VI*

CSP–Scot   *Calendar of State Papers, Scottish*

CSP–Sp   *Calendar of State Papers, Spanish*

EHR   *English Historical Review*

History   John Knox's *History of the Reformation in Scotland*, W.C. Dickinson, ed.

L & P Hen. VIII   *Letters and Papers Foreign and Domestic of the reign of Henry VIII*

PRO   *Public Record Office* (London)

RMS   *Registrum Magni Sigilli*

RPC   *Register of the Privy Council of Scotland*

RSS *Registrum Secreti Sigilli*

SHR *Scottish Historical Review*

SRO *Scottish Record Office*

Works *The Works of John Knox,* D. Laing, ed.

NOTES

CHAPTER I

1. F. Mauro, *Le XVIᵉ Siècle Européen: Aspects Economiques*, (Paris, 1966), pp. 319ff.

2. J.U. Nef, "Industrial Europe at the Time of the Reformation," *Journal of Political Economy*, XLIX (1941), 6.

3. Mauro, *op. cit.*, pp. 99f, 143, 158, 212, 257; B.H. Slichter van Bath, *The Agrarian History of Western Europe*, A.D. 500–1850, O. Ordish, tr., (London, 1963), pp. 78ff, 196f.

4. *Ibid.*, pp. 128ff; Nef, *op. cit.*, pp. 200f; Mauro, *op. cit.*, pp. 161ff.

5. *Ibid.*, pp. 166ff; Nef, *op. cit.*, pp. 20, 218ff; B. Moeller, *Villes d'Empire et Réformation*, (Geneva, 1966), pp. 18ff.

6. Mauro, *op. cit.*, pp. 199ff; Nef, *op. cit.*, pp. 192ff; A.F. Pollard, *Factors in Modern History*, (Boston, 1960), 3rd. ed., chap. IV; J.H. Hexter, *Reappraisals in History*, (New York, 1961), pp. 26ff; H. Lapeyre, *Les Monarchies Européennes du XVIᵉ Siècle* (Paris, 1967), part III.

7. J.D. Mackie, *The Earlier Tudors*, (Oxford, 1952), *passim*; G. Donaldson, "Foundations of Anglo-Scottish Union," in *Elizabethan Government and Society*, S.T. Bindoff et al., edd., (London, 1961), pp. 282f.

8. P. Janelle, *The Catholic Reformation*, (Milwaukee, Wis., 1963), chap. I; Moeller, *op. cit.*, pp. 25ff.

9. G.V. Jourdan, *The Movement Towards Catholic Reform in the Early XVI Century*, (London, 1914), pp. 99ff; H. Hauser, *La Naissance du Protestantisme*, (Paris, 1962), pp. 6ff.

10. J. Rilliet, *Zwingle*, (Paris, 1959), pp. 93ff; J.T. McNeill, *The History and Character of Calvinism*, (New York, 1954), parts I and II.

11. *Ibid.*, pp. 237ff; A.A. van Schelven, *Het Calvinisme Gedurende Zijn Bloeitijd*, (Amsterdam, 1943), II, 10ff.

12. K. Holl, *The Cultural Significance of the Reformation*, (New York, 1959), pp. 45ff; *Cultuurgeschiedenis van het Christendom*, J. Waterink *et al*, edd., (Amsterdam, 1950), III, 288ff.

13. I.F. Grant, *Social and Economic Development of Scotland Before 1603*, (Edinburgh, 1930), pp. 159ff; S.G.E. Lythe, *The Economy of Scotland in its European Setting 1550–1625*, (Edinburgh, 1960), pp. 24ff.

14. *Ibid.*, pp. 116ff; Grant, *op. cit.*, pp. 327ff; M.P. Rooseboom, *The Scottish Staple in the Netherlands*, (Hague, 1910), pp. 27ff.

15. Grant, *op. cit.*, pp. 186ff, 559f; P.H. Brown, *Scotland in the time of Queen Mary*, (London, 1904), pp. 184ff.

16. *Exchequer Rolls of Scotland*, G.P. McNeill, ed. (Edinburgh, 1885), XV, lxvff; (1898) XVIII, lxii; (1897) XVII, xlff; W.S. Reid, *Skipper from Leith*, (Philadelphia, 1964), pp. 125ff; *Accounts of the Collectors of The Thirds of Benefices 1561–1572*, G. Donaldson, ed., (Edinburgh, 1949), p. xv.

17. G.R. Elton, *England under the Tudors*, (London, 1959), pp. 88ff, 150ff; W.K. Jordan, *Edward VI: The Young King*, (Cambridge, USA, 1968), pp. 241ff.

18. *Thirds*, pp. xivf; D. Mahoney, "The Scottish Hierarchy 1513–1625," *Essays on the Scottish Reformation*, D. McRoberts, ed., (Glasgow, 1962), p. 42.

19. *Ibid.*, pp. 67ff; W.S. Reid, "Clerical Taxation: The Scottish alternative to dissolution of the Monasteries, 1530–1560," *Catholic Historical Review*, XXXV (1948), 129ff; *Letters and Papers of Henry VIII*, Gairdner, *et al*, edd., (London, 1898), XVI, no. 964.

20. *Ibid.*, nos. 719, 990, 1178, 1288, 1378, 1130, 1138, 1143.

21. W.L. Mathieson, *Politics and Religion*, (Glasgow, 1902), I, 27; D.H. Fleming, *The Reformation in Scotland*, (London, 1910), pp. 106ff.

22. P.F. Tytler, *The History of Scotland*, (Edinburgh, 1864), II, 315.

23. Mahoney, *op.cit.*, pp. 55, 60

24. *Ibid.*, pp. 39, 57; Fleming, *op.cit.*, pp. 39ff.

25. The popular poetry of the day gives one of the best indications of the general view of clerical morality. cf. *Ibid.*, pp. 171ff; *Poems of William Dunbar*, J. Small, ed., (Edinburgh, 1881), II, 79; *Poems of Sir D. Lindsay*, D. Laing, ed., (Edinburgh, 1871), I, 101, 131ff.

26. D. MacKay, "Parish Life in Scotland, 1500–1600." *Essays*, McRoberts, pp. 93ff; Brown, *op.cit*, pp. 163f; P. Janton, *Concept et Sentiment de l'Eglise chez John Knox*, (Paris, 1972), pp. 19ff.

27. *Journal d'un Bourgeois de Paris, (1513–1536)*, V.L. Bourrilly, ed., (Paris, 1910), pp. 363f.

28. J. Knox. *History of the Reformation in Scotland*, W.C. Dickinson, ed., (Edinburgh, 1944), I, 25.

29. *Ibid.*, p. 26; *The Acts and Monuments of John Foxe*, J. Pratt, ed., (London, 4th ed.), V, 606ff.

30. J. Spottiswoode, *History of the Church of Scotland*, (Edinburgh, 1847), I, 138.

31. *Ancient Criminal Trials of Scotland*, R. Pitcairn, ed., (Edinburgh, 1833), I, 210f.

32. *Acts of the Parliament of Scotland*, (Edinburgh, 1814), II, 370f.

33. Mahoney, *op.cit.*, p. 70; Knox, *History*, I, 34; J. Herkless & R.K. Hannay, *The Archbishops of St. Andrews*, (Edinburgh, 1913), IV, 55f.

34. *History*, I, 30; George Buchanan, *History of Scotland*, (Glasgow, 1799), II, 165ff, *Hamilton Papers*, J. Bain, ed., (Edinburgh, 1890), I, 99; R.K. Hannay, "Letters of the Papal Legate in Scotland, 1543," *Scottish Historical Review*, XI (1914), pp. 1ff. The reports of Cardinal Farnese on the situation in Scotland indicate the concern of the curia at this time. He pointed out that many Scots were going to England because of their heretical views and neither the king nor Beaton could provide any remedy. (Roman Transcripts, Public Record Office, London, 31/9/65. Cf. *L&P Henry VIII*, XVIII:1 (1901), no. 31).

35. Knox, *History*, I, 33f; G. Donaldson, *Scotland, James V to James VII*, (Edinburgh, 1961) pp. 26, 60ff offers an able estimate of James V's character which does not differ radically from Knox's view. Cf. Burns, *op.cit.*, pp. 5ff.

36. Knox, *op.cit.*, I, 42.

37. *Ibid.*, I, 46; Donaldson, *op.cit.*, pp. 67ff.

38. APS II, 415, Knox, *op.cit.*, I, 43ff.

39. *L&P Hen.*, XVIII: 1, nos. 364, 572; Roman Transcripts, PRO, 31/9/66, pp. 111, 113.

40. *History*, I, 47ff; Donaldson, *op.cit.*, p. 68.

41. Hannay, *op.cit.*, pp. 1ff.

42. Roman Transcripts, PRO, 31/9/66, p. 139; Mahoney, *op.cit.*, p. 71.

43. *History*, I., 48; *L&P Hen.*, XVIII: 2, no. 299.

44. *APS* II, 448.

45. *History*, I, 53; *L&P Hen.*, XVIII: 2, nos. 425, 454, 471; G. Buchanan, *History of Scotland*, J. Aikman, ed., (Glasgow, 1827).

CHAPTER II

1. H. Cowan, "When was John Knox Born?" *Records of the Scottish Church History Society*, I (1926), 221ff; "Notes and Comments," SHR, I (1904), 467.

2. J. Miller, *The Lamp of Lothian*, (Haddington, 1844), pp. 373ff; *History*, I, 71, n. 8.

3. J.H. Burns, "The Political Background of the Reformation 1513–

1625," *Essays*, McRoberts; John Major, *A History of Greater Britain*, A. Constable, ed., (Edinburgh, 1892), pp. 217ff.

4. H. Bonar, "John Knox and Ranfurly," *SHR*, V (1908), 370f; T. Thomson, "Where was Knox Born?" *Proceedings of the Society of Antiquaries of Scotland*, (Edinburgh, 1862), III, 67.

5. *Works*, I, 393.

6. Major, *op.cit.*, pp. xxxif.

7. Cowan, *op.cit.*, p. 220.

8. *History*, I, 15ff.

9. *Ibid.*

10. J. Durkan, "The Cultural Background in Sixteenth Century Scotland," *Essays*, McRoberts, p. 278.

11. *History*, I, 12, n. Knox's editor, W.C. Dickinson, believes he went to Marburg.

12. Durkan, *op.cit.*, p. 280.

13. *Ibid.*, pp. 279, 287.

14. *Ibid.*, pp. 279, 310.

15. *Ibid.*, pp. 280ff.

16. D. MacKay, "Parish Life in Scotland 1500–1600," McRoberts, *Essays*, 1964, pp. 93ff. For the discussion of Knox's ordination cf. *Innes Review*, VI (1955), 42ff, 99ff.

17. *Works*, VI, xixff; Thomson, *op.cit.*, p. 67.

18. *Extracts from the Council Register of the Burgh of Aberdeen*, J. Stuart, ed., (Aberdeen, 1844), p. 110; W.Thom, *History of Aberdeen*, (Aberdeen, 1811), I, 166.

19. *Ext. from Co. Regs.*, pp. xxix, 110, 189f.

20. Index to the Burgh Records of Perth 1500–1699, SRO, pp. 26ff.

21. *Ibid.*, pp. 58ff.; *History*, I, 52f; S. Cowan, *The Ancient Capital of Scotland*, (London, 1904) I, 316ff.

22. *History*, I, 55. It is interesting to note that about the same time all the ornaments of the Lady Altar in the parish church were turned over to Thomas Ramsay, apparently for safe-keeping in case of an attack by the Protestants on this symbol of idolatry. (Index to Perth Recs. pp. 68f.)

23. D. Calderwood, *The History of the Kirk of Scotland*, T. Thomson, ed., (Edinburgh, 1842), I, 145ff; Brother Kenneth, "The Popular Literature of the Scottish Reformation," *Essays*, McRoberts, pp. 173ff; R.Wedderburn, *The Gude and Godlie Ballatis*, A.F. Mitchell, ed., (Edinburgh, 1897), pp. xixff.

24. Calderwood, *op.cit.*, I, 175; *Two Missions of Jacques de la Brosse*, W.C. Dickinson, ed., (Edinburgh, 1942), p. 37n.

25. *History*, I, 24f; Calderwood, *op.cit.*, I, 474.

26. *History*, I, 43.

27. M.H. Merriman, "The Assured Scots," SHR, XLVII (1968), 22f.

28. *Missions of de la Brosse*, p. 23; W.M. Bryce, "The Black Friars of Edinburgh," BOEC, (Edinburgh, 1910), III, 57.

29. G. Koenigsberger, "The Organization of Revolutionary Parties in France and the Netherlands in the sixteenth century," *Journal of Modern History*, XXVII (1955), 341n.

30. W.S. Reid, "The Lollards in Pre-Reformation Scotland," *Church History*, XI (1942), 14ff; *History*, I, 8, 62, 121.

31. *Ibid.*, I, 121ff; *The Scots Peerage*, J.B. Paul, ed., (Edinburgh, 1904–1914), I, 339.

32. Thom, *op.cit.*, I, 183; Inventory of Gordon Castle Writs, (Typescript), SRO I, 2; II, 175, 177.

33. *History*, I, 55; C. Rogers, *Three Scottish Reformers*, London: 1874, pp. 16ff.

34. *History*, I, 24, 46, 54, 74; *A Diurnal of Remarkable Occurrents in Scotland*, (Edinburgh, 1833) p. 31; Index to Perth Recs., p. 71.

35. Rogers, *op.cit.*, p. 16; L.A. Barbé, *Kirkcaldy of Grange*, (Edinburgh, 1897), pp. 19f.

36. Merriman, *op.cit.*, has a rather full discussion of the "assured lords," but does not seem to realize quite fully how closely they were bound to each other. Cf. Burns, *op.cit.*, pp. 10ff.

37. *Scots Peerage*, II, 280.

38. *Registrum Magni Sigilli*, J.B. Paul & J.M. Thomson, edd., (Edinburgh, 1883), III, nos. 2215, 2517, 3055.

39. *History*, I, 69, 82.

40. Calderwood, *op.cit.*, I, 155f, 160.

41. *Ordnance Gazetteer of Scotland*, F.H. Broome, ed., (London, 1903, new edition), I, 80.

42. *Works*, VI, 643; Janton, *Concept et Sentiment*, pp. 25ff.

43. *Hamilton Papers*, I,541; *Diurnal*, p. 33. Cardinal Grimani stated that: ". . . . the Kingdom is so divided and in such confusion that if God does not stretch forth his hand, and inspire these lords to unite together, manifest ruin both public and private, lies before it." "Letts. of Pap. Leg.," SHR, XI, 15.

44. *L&P, Hen. VIII*, J.S. Brewer, *et al*, edd. (London, 1902), XVIII:2, no.351.

45. *Ibid.*, XIX:1, nos. 314, 518; *Diurnal*, pp. 31ff; Calderwood, *op.cit.*, I, 176ff.

46. *History*, I, 57.

47. Cf. J. Ridley, *John Knox*, (New York, 1968), pp. 36ff; Lord Eustace Percy, *John Knox*, (Richmond, Va.) pp. 28ff; "Letts. of Pap. Leg.," SHR, XI, 19.

48. *Ibid.*, p. 21; *Diurnal*, p. 29.

49. *Works*, I, 534f; VI, 667ff; Foxe, *op.cit.*, V, 625ff; Durkan, *op.cit.*, pp. 300, 325.

50. *Hamilton Papers*, I, 344, 351; *L&P Hen. VIII*, XIX:1, no. 350.

51. Foxe, *op.cit.*, V, 626; *Works*, I, 60, 537.

52. *RMS* III, no. 3065; Argyll Transcripts, Inverary Castle, IV, 129; *Reliquiae Antiquae Scotiae*, (Edinburgh, 1848), p. 150.

53. *Register of the Privy Council*, J.H. Burton, ed., (Edinburgh, 1877), I, pp. 5, 14, 15, 19, 22.

54. I.F. Grant, *op.cit.*, pp. 338f.

55. *History*, I, 72ff; *Works*, I, 485; *RPC*, I, 20.

56. *History*, I, 71n, 79.

CHAPTER III

1. C. Bourgeaud, "Le 'Vrai Portrait' de John Knox", *Bulletin de la Société de l'Histoire du Protestantisme français*, LXXXIV (1935), 11ff.

2. *The Presbyterian Tradition*, (London, 1933), p. 256; cf. G. MacGregor, *The Thundering Scot*, (Philadelphia, 1957), p. 20.

3. *History*, I, 72ff, cf. Knox's comment on Mary of Guise's acceptance of a crown when she became regent: "as seemly a sight . . . as to put a saddle on the back of an unruly coo." (p. 116). cf. *Works*, VI, 640.

4. R.L. Stevenson, *Memories and Portraits*, (London,n.d.) p. 29.

5. P. Janton, *John Knox, l'homme et l'oeuvre*, (Paris, 1967), pp. 62ff.

6. *Ancient Criminal Trials*, I:2, *333.

7. *History*, I, 75ff; *Works*, I, 183.

8. Buchanan, *History*, II, 359.

9. *History*, I, 75.

10. Buchanan, *op.cit.*, II, 359.

11. *History*, I, 52, 75ff.

12. Buchanan, *op.cit.*, II, 360; Spottiswoode, *History*, I, 166.

13. *History*, I:77ff. Knox's account is largely substantiated by the account of James Lyndsay written on the following day. (cf. *L&P Hen. VIII*, XXI:1, no. 948).

14. *History*, I, 79; *Works*, III, 396f.

15. L.A. Barbé, *Kirkcaldy of Grange*, (Edinburgh, 1897), pp. 21, 23, 28; C. Rogers, *Three Scottish Reformers*, (London, 1874), p. 16; *Works*, I, 182n; Spottiswoode, *op.cit.*, II, 167.

16. *APS*, II, 470; *RPC*, I, 28f; *Anc. Crim. Trials*, I:2, *335.

17. Barbé, *op.cit.*, p. 33; *Peerage*, IV, 279; *RSS*, III, 1541.

18. Merriman, "The Assured Scots," 27f; *Spalding Club Miscellany*, John Stuart, ed., (Aberdeen, 1849), IV, 48–52.

19. *APS*, II, 471; *Scottish Correspondence of Mary of Lorraine*, A.I. Dunlop, (Edinburgh, 1927), nos. CXVII, CXXI.

20. *Anc. Crim. Trials*, I, *333; *Registrum Secreti Sigilli Regum Scotorum*, J. Beveridge, ed., (Edinburgh, 1952), IV, 2582.

21. *APS*, II, 466ff.

22. *Scott. Corr. Mary*, CXXI; *Acts of the Lords of the Council in Public Affairs*, R.K. Hannay, ed., (Edinburgh, 1932), pp. 545, 550, 555, 562.

23. *APS*, II, 467, 477; *RPC*, I, 31ff.

24. *RSS*, IV, 1865, 1872, 2345, 2355, 2386.

25. *APS*, II, 472, 476.

26. *Ibid.*, II, 471, 479. The Bishop of Dunkeld and Abbot of Paisley, half-brother of the Earl Arran, succeeded Beaton (1549) in St. Andrews.

27. *Diurnal*, p. 43; *RPC*, I, 38; R. Lindsay of Pitscottie, *The Historie and Cronicles of Scotland*, A.J.G. MacKay, ed., (Edinburgh), 190 II, 85f.

28. *APS*, II, 472.

29. *History*, I, 80; *RSS*, III, 2644.

30. *Diurnal*, p. 43; *Works*, III, 409f; Rogers, *op.cit.*, pp. 18f.

31. *History*, I, 81.

32. *Ibid.*; P.F. Tytler, *History of Scotland*, (Edinburgh, 1864), IV, 51.

33. *History*, I, 93ff; Pitscottie, *op.cit.*, II, 86ff.

34. *RSS*, III, 1857, 1865, 2345, 2386.

35. *History*, I, 81.

36. *Ibid.*, I, 82.

37. *Ibid.*

38. Janton, *op.cit.*, p. 66.

39. P. Schaff, *History of the Christian Church*, (New York, 1916), VI:552.

40. T. Dempster, *Historia Ecclesiastica*, (Edinburgh, 1829), I, 182; *Works*, I, 185, n.3.

41. Rogers, *op.cit.*, p. 19; *CSP-Scot.*, 1, 2.

42. *Scott. Corres. Mary*, CXXXI, CXXXIII; *CSP-Scot*, 1, 6.

43. Cf. Janton, *op.cit.*, pp. 68ff; Ridley, *Knox*, pp. 55; *History*, I, 81ff.

44. *Ibid.*, I, 87.

45. *Ibid.*, I, 93, note 2; Ridley, *op.cit.*, p. 59.

46. Percy, *op. cit.*, p. 56; *History*, II, 266ff.

47. CSP, Scot., I, 22; *Works*, I, 537ff; VI, 622f.

48. *History*, I, 95.

49. *Ibid.*, I, 94.

50. *CSP-Scot.*, I, 4.

51. ". . . . they would rather have a boll of wheat than all the pope's remissions." *Ibid.*

52. *History*, I, 94.

53. Lang, *op.cit.*, p. 27; *CSP-Scot.*, I.

54. *History*, I, 955f; cf. Lang, *op.cit.*, 29f; *Diurnal*, p. 44.

CHAPTER IV

1. *Diurnal*, p. 44.

2. *History*, I, 96.

3. Melville, Sir James, *Memoirs of his own Life, 1549–93*, (Edinburgh, 1837), pp. 25f; cf. W.S. Reid, "The Lion Rampant in Sixteenth Century France," *Scottish Colloquium Proceedings*, (Guelph,Ont.,1970) III, 1ff.

4. *History*, I, 97; Barbé, *Kirkcaldy*, p. 41.

5. *Ibid.; History*, I, 107; E. Dupont, "Les Prisonniers de Mont St. Michel," *Scottish Historical Review*, III, (1903), 506.

6. Cf. *infra*. p. 61.

7. *History*, I, 97; M. Mollat, *La Commerce Normande à la Fin du Moyen Age*, (Paris, 1952), p. 78.

8. *Ville de Nantes, Inventaire Sommaire des Archives Communales*, R. Blanchard, ed., (Nantes, 1888), I, 242, 267.

9. *History*, I, 109.

10. *Ibid.*, I, 108; A. Jal, *Archeologie Navale*, (Paris, 1840), I, 297ff.

11. *Ibid.*, pp. 303ff; "Galley," *Encyclopaedia Britannica*, 11th ed.

12. *History*, I, 108, 182.

13. *Ibid.*, I, 108.

14. *Ibid.*, I, 107.

15. J. Pannier, "Les residences successives des étudiants écossais à Paris," *Association Franco-Ecossais Bulletin*, (1929), p. 33.

16. *History*, I, 108; *Works*, III, 4, 8, 431ff.

17. Lang, *Knox and the Ref.*, pp. 29f; Reid, *op.cit.*, p. 9; F. Michel, *Les Écossais en France et les Français en Écosse*, (London, 1862), I, 530ff.

18. Paris Transcripts, London: PRO, 31/3/18, fo. 124 vo. f.

19. *Works*, III, 8ff.

20. J. MacKinnon, *A History of Modern Liberty*, (London, 1906), II, 400.

21. *Works*, III, 15.

22. *Ibid.*, III, 13ff.

23. Cf. *Institutes of the Christian Religion*, J.T. McNeill, ed., F.L. Battles, tr., (Philadelphia, 1959), bk. 3, chaps., 11–16 in which the material from the different editions is indicated. Also V.E. D'Assonville, *John Knox and the Institutes of Calvin*, (Durban, 1968), especially chap. I.

24. *History*, I, 92.

25. *Ibid.*, I, 107.

26. *Ibid.*, I, 106; *CSP-Scot.*, I, nos. 26, 88, 94.

27. *History*, I, 98ff; *CSP-Scot.*, I, nos. 31, 34; J. Leslie, *Historie of Scotland*, E.G. Cody and W. Murison, ed., (Edinburgh, 1895), II, 298f.

28. *History*, I, 101f; Leslie, *op.cit.*, II, 302.

29. *CSP-Scot.*, I, 34, 41ff.

30. *History*, I, 101.

31. *CSP-Scot.*, I, 34, 37ff.

32. *Ibid.*, I, 33.

33. *Ibid.*, I, 35, 50.

34. Merriman, "The Assured Scots," 27ff; *Spalding Club Miscellany*, IV, 48–52.

35. *CSP-Scot.*, I, 14, 17f., 22, 25, 27, 39, 41.

36. *Ibid.*, I, 27.

37. *Ibid.*, I, 38. Merriman with reason attributes their steadfastness in their purpose to their religious convictions, while others submitted merely from pressure of circumstances.

38. *Ibid.*, I, 22, 28, 31, 40, 42; Paris Trans. fos. 13, 70, 118.

39. *CSP-Scot.*, I, 119; Merriman, *op.cit.*, pp. 28ff; W. Forbes-Leith, *The Scots Men-at-Arms and Life-Guards in France*, (Edinburgh, 1882), I, 96.

40. *History*, I, 103f; *CSP-Scot.*, I, 263; *Nantes:Invent.*, I, 26.

41. *History*, I, 105; Forbes-Leith, *op.cit.*, I, 97f.

42. Merriman, *op.cit.*, p. 31; *CSP-Scot.*, I, 118, 151.

43. Rothes Chartulary, SRO, no. 15; *CSP-Scot.*, I, 136f., 146; *Scot. Corres. Mary*, nos. CLXX, CLXXIX.

44. *CSP-Scot.*, I, 118f, 133, 151.

45. Paris Trans. 31/3/17, fo. 39; 31/3/18, fo. 124f; 31/3/19, fos. 88, 150, 157, 162.

46. *Works*, III, 31f; *CSP-Spanish*, IX, 347.

47. *History*, I, 109f.

48. *Ibid.*, I, 110.

49. *Ibid.*; *Works*, III, 31; Barbé, *op.cit.*, pp. 46ff.

50. *History*, I, 111; *CSP-For. Ed.VI*, nos. 221, 224.

CHAPTER V

1. A.F. Pollard, *England under Protector Somerset*, (London, 1900), p. 137; *The Chronicle and Political Papers of Edward VI*, W.K. Jordan, ed., (Ithaca, N.Y.), p. 38.

2. H.C. Porter, *Reformation and Reaction in Tudor Cambridge*, (Cambridge, 1958), pp. 58f; M.M. Knappen, *Tudor Puritanism*, (Chicago, 1939), pp. 2ff.

3. *Ibid.*, pp. 33ff; A.G. Dickens, *The English Reformation*, (London, 1956), pp. 170ff.

4. Knappen, *op.cit.*, pp. 54ff; Foxe, *Martyrs*, VI, 636; C.H. Smyth, *Cranmer and the Reformation under Edward VI*, (Cambridge, 1926), pp. 88ff.

5. The most recent account of Edward VI's reign is that of W.K. Jordan,

Edward VI: The Young King, (Cambridge, Mass., 1968) and *Edward VI: The Threshold of Power*, (Cambridge, Mass., 1970).

6. N. Pocock, "The Conditions of Morals and Religious Belief in the Reign of Edward VI," *The English Historical Review*, X, (1895), 418; Pollard, *op.cit.*, pp. 92ff, 157ff; C. Read, *Mr. Secretary Cecil and Queen Elizabeth*, (London, 1955), p. 38; Dickens, *op.cit.*, pp. 203f; Knappen, *op.cit.*, pp. 79f; J. Hooper, "A Declaration, of Christ, and his office" (1547), *Early Writings* (Cambridge, 1843).

7. Cf. Jordan, *Young King*, passim; Pollard, *op.cit.*, pp. 14, 15.

8. *Op. cit.*, p. 42.

9. D. Neal, *History of the Puritans*, (New York, 1858), I, 47f; Jordan, *op. cit.*, pp. 308ff; Knappen, *op. cit.*, pp. 54ff.

10. J. Strype, *The Life of Sir John Cheke*, (London, 1821), p. 7; Read, *op.cit.*, pp. 27f; Smyth, *op.cit.*, pp. 82f, 88f; Knappen, *op.cit.*, pp. 61ff. Edward VI's tutors, Thomas Smith, John Cheke, Roger Ascham and Anthony Cooke, were all members of the "establishment" group.

11. *Ibid.*, pp. 64ff, 79ff; Read, *op. cit.*, pp. 34, 42ff; Pollard, *op.cit.*, pp. 102ff.

12. Dickens, *op.cit.*, p. 194; Neal, *op.cit.*, p. 49.

13. J.A. Froude, *The Reign of Edward VI*, (London, 1909), pp. 68ff; Jordan, *op.cit.*, pp. 402ff.

14. *Ibid.*, pp. 416ff; S.T. Bindoff, *Tudor England*, (Harmondsworth, 1950), pp. 128ff; Foxe, *op.cit.*, VI, 296.

15. Hooper, *op.cit.*, pp. 363, 387 ff; H. Latimer, *Works*, G.E. Corrie, ed., (Cambridge, 1844), 2 vols; Bindoff, *op.cit.*, pp. 130ff; Pollard, *op.cit.*, pp. 127ff, 215ff.

16. *CSP, Dom. Edward VI*, I, 22.

17. Jordan, *op.cit.*, pp. 263ff.

18. *Ibid.*, pp. 283ff; G. Dickinson, "Instructions to the French Ambassador, 30 March 1550," SHR, XXVI, (1947), 156.

19. M.H. Merriman, "The Assured Scots," p. 32; *Negotiations de la France dans le Levant*, E. Charriere, ed., (Paris, 1850), II, 121; cf. Roman Transcripts (Mss), Public Record Office, London, 31/9/67, p. 19.

20. *Works*, III, 79; *CSP, Dom., Ed. VI*, I, 5.

21. P. Lorimer, *John Knox and the Church of England*, (London, 1875), pp. 17f.

22. Jordan, *op.cit.*, pp. 130f.

23. Merriman, *op.cit.*, pp. 32ff; APC, III, 92, 103, 106.

24. *Works*, III, 351ff, 364.

25. *Ibid.*, III, 201, 350, 352.

26. *Ibid.*, III, 168; Lorimer, *op.cit.*, p. 53, 67.

27. *Works*, III, 205, 368.

28. *Ibid.*, III, 258ff.

29. *Ibid.*, V, 480f.

30. Lorimer, *op.cit.*, pp. 21, 69ff.

31. *Ibid.*, pp. 290ff.

32. *Works*, III, 73; Lorimer, *op.cit.*, p. 295.

33. *Works*, III, 165ff.

34. *Ibid.*, III, 364; Lorimer, *op.cit.*, p. 53.

35. "Vindication that the Mass is Idolatry," *Works*, III, 33ff.

36. *Ibid.*, III, 167, 205; V, 479f; *CSP-Dom., Ed. VI*, I, 33; *Original Letters Relative to the English Reformation*, H. Robinson, ed., (Cambridge, 1846), no. XL.

37. *Works*, III, 205, 122.

38. *Ibid.*, III, 373.

39. Cf. Knox's "Exposition on Psalm 6," and also his letter to Mrs. Bowes, *ibid.*, III, 124ff, 373.

40. *Ibid.*, III, 333f.

41. *Ibid.*, III, 142, 348ff, 360ff, 386ff.

42. *Ibid.*, III, 333, 364; VI, 513ff.

43. *Ibid.*, III, 386.

44. *Ibid.*, III, 368.

45. Lorimer, *op.cit.*, p. 43.

46. H. Trevor-Roper, "John Knox," *The Listener*, 80 (1968), 745ff, is a good example of this type of interpretation.

47. *Works*, III, 355. Although dated 1553 in the ms., 1551 would seem to be the correct year. cf. Ridley, *John Knox*, p. 540.

48. *Works*, III, 348, 387, 394; Lorimer, *op.cit.*, p. 164n.

49. *Ibid.*, p. 23; *Works*, III, 83ff.

50. *Ibid.*, III, 103.

51. Lorimer, *op.cit.*, pp. 44ff, 65ff.

52. *Works*, III, 167, 277f.

53. *Ibid.*, III, 79, 372; Lorimer, *op.cit.*, pp. 79ff; *Chronicle of Edward VI*, p. 101.

54. Lorimer, *op.cit.*, pp. 86f, 149.

55. *Works*, III, 395.

56. Jordan, *Ed. VI; Threshold*, pp. 265ff; Hooper, *op.cit.*, pp. 21ff, 27ff, 82f; J. Strype, *Ecclesiastical Memorials*, (London, 1822), II, 399f, 531ff; Smyth, *op.cit.*, pp. 100, 194; *Orig. Letts.*, nos. LX, CXXII.

57. Knappen, *op.cit.*, p. 74; *Calendar of State Papers, Foreign, Edward VI*, W.B. Turnbull, (London, 1863), I, 19; *Orig. Letts.*, nos. IX, XI, XII; Strype, *op.cit.*, II, 123.

58. C. Hopf, *Martin Bucer and the English Reformation*, (Oxford, 1946), pp. 12ff; Pollard, *op.cit.*, p. 92; Dickens, *op.cit.*, pp. 200f; J. Calvin, *Lettres Anglais*, A.M. Schmidt, ed., (Paris, 1959), *passim*.

59. Smyth, *op.cit.*, pp. 132f, 172f; Hopf, *op.cit.*, p. 125; *Orig. Letts.*, nos. XXX, CXXI, CCLIII; M. Bucer, *De Regno Christi*, W. Pauck, ed. (Philadelphia, 1969), bk. II. For a fuller discussion of these divisions see W.S. Reid, "The Divisions of the Marian Exiles," *Canadian Journal of History*, III: 2, (1968), 1ff.

60. *Orig. Letts.* nos. IX, XII, XIV, XV.

61. *Ibid.*, no. CXXI.

62. Smyth, *op.cit.*, pp. 190ff; 222ff; C. Martin, *Les Protestants Anglais Refugiés à Genève au temps de Calvin, 1555–60*, (Geneva, 1915), pp. 7ff, 11f; Neal, *op.cit.*, I, 55; *Chron. of Ed. VI*, p. 37; *CSP, Dom., Ed. VI*, 28.

63. Strype, *op.cit.*, II, 378f; Strype, *Memorials of Archbishop Cranmer*, (Oxford, 1840), I, 348ff; Dickens, *op.cit.*, p. 239; Knappen, *op.cit.*, pp. 90ff; Smyth, *op.cit.*, pp. 199ff; Calvin, *op.cit.*, pp. 109, 177; *APC*, IV, 160.

64. *Ibid.*, III, 31; *Orig. Letts.*, no. XXXVIII; Hooper, *op.cit.*, p. 433; Knappen, *op.cit.*, pp. 81ff; Neal, *op.cit.*, I, 51ff.

65. *Orig. Letts.*, nos. XIII; XCIX, *APC*, III, 136, 191; Strype, *Eccl'l Memorials*, II, 351ff; Foxe, *Martyrs*, IV, 642; J. Ridley, *Cranmer*, pp. 309ff; Porter, *op.cit.*, p. 64; Hopf, *op.cit.*, pp. 133f.

66. Read, *op.cit.*, pp. 52, 84; Smyth, *op.cit.*, pp. 203–218.

67. *Ibid.*, p. 9; Dickens, *op.cit.*, pp. 221f; Jordan, *op.cit.*, chap. XV; *Orig. Letts.*, XXXIII.

68. Bindoff, *op.cit.*, pp. 135ff; P.F. Tytler, *England under the Reigns of Edward VI and Mary* (London, 1839), I, 364; H. Trevor-Roper, *Historical Essays*, (London, 1957), pp. 86ff.

69. Strype, *Eccl'l Mems.* II, 535ff; Jordan, *Edward VI: Threshold*, chap. IV.

70. *CSP, Dom., Ed. VI*, I, 35; Read, *op.cit.*, pp. 46, 56ff, 76; Constant, *op.cit.*, pp. 435ff.

71. *Orig. Letts.*, nos. CXCII, XXXIX, CCVIII; *CSP-Dom., Ed. VI*, I, 37.

72. *Orig. Letts.*, no. CCVIII.

73. *CSP-Dom. Ed. VI*, I, 39; *Orig. Letts.*, no. CXCIX.

74. *Ibid.*, no. XXXIX.

75. *APC*, IV, 61, 63, 253; Smyth, *op.cit.*, 274ff; Constant, *op.cit.*, pp. 443ff.

76. J.A. Froude, *Edward VI*, p. 290; N. Ridley, *Works*, H. Christmas, ed. (Cambridge, 1841), p. 59.

77. Jordan, *op.cit.*, pp. 346ff; *APC*, III, 392.

78. *Orig. Letts.*, no. LX; *Chron. of Ed. VI*, pp. 159f; Hopf, *op.cit.*, pp. 99ff; Bucer, *op.cit.*, bk. II; Lorimer, *op.cit.*, p. 14.

79. *Ibid.*, pp. 263ff.

80. Strype, *Ecc'l Mems.*, III, 20; Smyth, *op.cit.*, pp. 232ff; N. Pocock, *op.cit.*, p. 20.

81. *Works*, V, 479f.

82. Smyth, *op.cit.*, p. 224, 260f; Knappen, *op.cit.*, pp. 96f; Strype, *op.cit.*, III, 32ff; Hopf, *op.cit.*, pp. 61ff.

83. *Orig. Letts.*, no. CCLXXIII; Lorimer, *op.cit.*, pp. 98ff.

84. *Ibid.*, pp. 104f; *CSP-Dom.*, Ed. VI, I, 45; *APC*, IV, 138.

85. *Ibid.*, IV, 148; Lorimer, *op.cit.*, pp. 108ff, 267ff.

86. *APC*, IV, 154; Lorimer, *op.cit.*, pp. 126ff; *The Two Liturgies of Edward VI*, J. Ketley, ed., (Cambridge, 1845), 283, 536.

87. Lorimer, *op.cit.*, pp. 156ff, 254ff, 263; C. Wriothesley, *A Chronicle of England*, W.D. Hamilton, ed., (London, 1877), II, 78f.

88. *CSP-Dom.*, Ed. VI, I, 46; Lorimer, *op.cit.*, pp. 76f, 149f; *Works*, III, 81f.

89. *Ibid.*, III, 83; *CSP-Dom.* Ed. VI, I, 48.

90. *Ibid.;* Lorimer, *op.cit.*, p. 151ff; *Works*, III, 122.

91. Dickens, *op.cit.*, pp. 251f.; Smyth, *op.cit.*, pp. 259ff; N. Pocock, "The Restoration Settlement of the English Church," *EHR*, I, (1886), 680.

92. *Works*, III, 167, 220; Lorimer, *op.cit.*, pp. 146ff.

93. *APC*, IV, 154, 190.

94. *Works*, III, 83*f, 297; Lorimer, *op.cit.*, p. 162.

95. *Works*, III, 357.

96. *Ibid.*

97. *Ibid.*, III, 84*

98. *APC*, IV, 212.

99. *Works*, III, 355, 360.

100. *Ibid.*, III, 355ff, 368.

101. *Ibid.*, III, 369, 379.

102. J. Calvin, *Opera qui supersunt Omnia*, C. Baum *et al.*, edd., (Brunswick, 1878), XVIII, 434f.

103. *"Godly Letter to the Faithful in London,"* etc., *Works*, III, 175ff; Ridley, *Works*, p. 59.

104. *Works*, III, 167; Strype, *op.cit.*, III, 69ff; Lorimer, *op.cit.*, 81ff.

105. *Ibid.*, III, 176.

106. *Ibid.*, III, 86* ff; Calderwood, *Hist. of the Kirk*, I, 280f.

107. Strype, *op.cit.*, III, 70; *APC*, IV, 283.

108. *Works*, III, 122.

109. Lorimer, *op.cit.*, p. 170; Ridley, *Cranmer*, pp. 340f; Jordan, *op.cit.*, p. 359.

110. *Ibid.*, pp. 510ff.

111. *Works*, III, 337f.

112. *APC*, IV, 324, 328, 335, 337, 420, 427.

113. *Works*, III, 380f.

114. *Ibid.*, III, 111, 157; Lorimer, *op.cit.*, p. 186.

115. *Works*, III, 374f.
116. *Ibid.*, III, 376f.
117. *Ibid.*, III, 369ff.
118. *Ibid.*, III, 132.
119. *Ibid.*, III, 133.

CHAPTER VI

1. P. Boissonade, "Le Mouvement Commercial entre la France et les Îles Britannique en le 16ème Siècle," *Révue Historique*, 134 (1920), 214ff.

2. C. Desmarquets, *Histoire Chronologique pour servir à l'histoire de Dieppe*, (Paris, 1785), I, 137; H. Hauser, "Le Capitalisme en France au XVIe Siècle," *Révue des Cours et Conférences*, Paris, (1922), p. 133; Trésor des Chartes, A.N.F., Ser. J.J. 262, nos. 352, 508; A. Boudier, *A Travers les Siècles*, (Dieppe, 1950), p. 9.

3. *The Gude and Godlie Ballattis*, pp. xviff; Calderwood, *History*, I, 141ff.

4. S. Hardy, *Histoire de l'Église Protestante de Dieppe*, (Paris, 1897), p. 35.

5. M.C. Guibert, *Mémoires pour servir à l'Histoire de la ville de Dieppe*, (Dieppe, 1878), I, 41; F. Michel, *Les Écossais en France et les Francais en Écosse*, (London, 1862), I, 472.

6. Desmarquets, *op.cit.*, I, 137ff.; Guibert, *op.cit.*, I, 102ff.; *La Naissance et progrès de l'Hérésie de la ville de Dieppe, 1557-1609*, E. Lesens, ed., (Rouen, 1877), 3f.

7. Knox, *Works*, III, 133.

8. *Ibid.*, III, 159, 215, 235.

9. Calvin, *Opera*, XV, 38, no. 1909.

10. *Works*, III, 154.

11. *Ibid.*, III, 159ff.

12. *Ibid.*, III, 205.

13. *Ibid.*, III, 210.

14. *Ibid.*, III, 83ff; Lorimer, *Knox and the Church of England*, p. 23.

15. *Works*, III, 235, 370.

16. *Ibid.*, III, 120, 154.

17. *Ibid.*, III, 203.

18. *Ibid.*, III, 154f.

19. J. Bonneret, "Esquisse de la vie des routes au XVIe siècle," *Révue des Questions Historiques*, CXV (1931), 33f., 88.

20. Calvin, *op.cit.*, XV, 38, no. 1909; *Works*, III, 235.

21. *Ibid.*, III, 220ff.

22. Calvin, *op.cit.*, XV, 125, No. 1947.

23. *Works*, III, 220f.; *Orig. Letts.* no. CCCLII; Brown, *Knox*, I, 156.

24. F. Isaac, "Egidius van der Erve and English Printed Books," *The Library*, ser. 4, XII (1931–2), 336ff.

25. *Works*, III, 235.

26. Read, *Mr. Secretary Cecil*, pp. 104ff.

27. Neal, *Hist. of Puritanism*, I, 66.

28. *Works*, III, 233.

29. *Ibid.*

30. *Ibid.*, III, 259ff.

31. *Ibid.*, III, 266ff.

32. *Ibid.*, III, 280ff.

33. *Ibid.*, III, 295.

34. *Ibid.*, III, 296.

35. *Ibid.*, III, 298ff.

36. C. Martin, *Les Protestants Anglais*, pp. 163ff.; *Works*, III, 307ff.

37. *Ibid.*, III, 184.

38. *Ibid.*, III, 540; cf. 103f, 194.

39. W.S. Reid, "The Ecumenicalism of John Calvin," *Westminster Theological Journal*, XI (1948), 38ff; Lorimer, *op.cit.*, p. 259; Donaldson, *Scot. Ref.*, pp. 76ff.

40. *Works*, III, 235, 269; cf., Ridley, *Knox*, p. 188.

41. *Orig. Letts.*, nos. LXXVII, LXXX.

42. *APC*, IV, 328, 335.

43. Knappen, *Tudor Puritanism*, pp. 106ff; Dickens, *Eng. Ref.*, p. 283.

44. C.H. Garrett, *The Marian Exiles*, (Cambridge, 1938) pp. 2ff, 46ff.

45. W.M. Southgate, "The Marian Exiles and the influence of John Calvin," *History*, XXVII (1942), 148.

46. Read, *op.cit.*, pp. 103ff, 112.

47. Cf. Reid, "Divs. of Marian Exiles," *Can. Jour. Hist.*, III (1968), 1ff.

48. *Orig. Letts.*, nos. CCXL, CCCLIII, CCCLVI; H.J. Cowell, "Sixteenth Century English-speaking Refugee Congregations in Strasbourg, Basle, Aarau, Wesel, Emden," *Proceedings of the Huguenot Society of London*, XV (1933–37), 643f.

49. G.T. Peck, "Sir John Hales and the Puritans during the Marian Exile," *Church History*, X, (1941), 163.

50. Dickens, *op.cit.*, p. 283; Cowell, *op.cit.*, 617; Garrett, *op.cit.*, p. 27.

51. Southgate, *op.cit.*, pp. 149ff; *Orig. Letts.*, no. LXXII; Garrett, *op.cit.*, p. 27.

52. *Ibid.*, p. 18; Porter, *Reformation and Reaction*, p. 74.

53. "English Refugees in Germany and Switzerland," *Proceedings of the Huguenot Society of London*, IV (1891–3), 90; C.A. Rahlenbeck, "Quelques notes sur les 'reformers' flamands et wallons du 16e siècle refugiés en Angleterre," *Ibid.*, IV, 24.

54. G.B. Beeman, "The Early History of the Strangers' Church, 1550–1561," *Ibid.*, XV (1933–7), 274; *APC-Eng.*, IV, 341.

55. J. Strype, *Mems. of Cranmer*, I, 580; K. Bauer, *Die Beziehungen Calvins zur Frankfurt-am-Main*, Leipzig, 1920, pp. 7ff; Knappen, *op.cit.*, p. 118.

56. C.H. Smyth, *Cranmer and Reformation*, p. 225; Martin, *op.cit.*, pp. 22f.

57. V. Poullain, *Liturgia Sacra 1551–5*, A.C. Honders, ed., (Leiden, 1970), pp. 45ff; *Works*, IV, 144.

58. *Ibid.*, IV, 144ff; *Calvin's Tracts*, W. Beveridge, ed., (Edinburgh, 1849), II, 95ff; *Johannis Calvini Opera Selecta*, P. Barth, D. Scheuner, edd., (Munich, 1952), II, 1ff.

59. *Lit. Sac.*, p. 13; W.D. Maxwell, *The Liturgical Portions of the Genevan Service Book*, (Philadelphia, 1931), p. 33.

60. Neal, *op.cit.*, I, 66; *A Brief Discourse of the Troubles Begon at Frankfort, 1554*, J. Petheram, ed., (London, 1846), p. vif. A number of different editions of this work have been issued, although most commonly used is Laing's shortened edition in Knox, *Works*, IV, 1–51. The identity of the author is unclear. Thomas M'Crie argued for Whittingham, while more recent thinking has turned to Thomas Wood. (cf. Petheram's edit., pp. v f; *Reformation and Revolution*, D. Shaw, ed. Edinburgh, 1967, pp. 17ff.)

61. J. Collier, *The Ecclesiastical History of Great Britain*, (London, new ed., 1852), VI, 145.

62. *Brief Discourse*, Petheram, p. vii; *Works*, IV, 11.

63. Garrett, *op.cit.*, pp. 61f, 327ff, 335, 343; Martin, *op.cit.*, p. 49ff.

64. *Works*, IV, 11; Knappen, *op.cit.*, p. 119.

65. Pocock, "Conditions of Morals . . . ," pp. 418, 429; Brown, *op.cit.*, I, 167; Knappen, *op.cit.*, p. 121.

66. *Ibid.*, p. 49.

67. *Works*, IV, 13ff.

68. *Ibid.*, IV, 19f.

69. *Ibid.*, IV, 12ff; Knappen, *op.cit.*, pp. 122ff.

70. *Works*, V, 479.

71. *Ibid.*, IV, 21ff; Knappen, *op.cit.*, pp. 122; Brown, *op.cit.*, I, 174ff.

72. Garrett, *op.cit.*, p. 134f.

73. *Orig. Letts.*, no. LX.

74. *Works*, IV, 32f, 43f.

75. *Ibid.*, IV, 46.

76. *Ibid.*, IV, 39, 47.

77. *Ibid.*, IV, 40, 46.

78. *Ibid.*, IV, 53ff.

79. *Ibid.*, IV, 50ff; Knappen, *op.cit.*, p. 132; Garrett, *op.cit.*, p. 219.

80. *Orig. Letts.*, no. LXIV; Dickens, *op.cit.*, p. 292.

81. *Ibid.*, p. 292; G. Donaldson, *The Making of the Scottish Prayer Book of 1637*, (Edinburgh, 1954), pp. 3f.

82. Brown, *op.cit.*, I, 172; Southgate, "Marian Exiles" p. 148; P. Collinson, *The Elizabethan Puritan Movement*, (Berkeley, 1967), p. 72; cf. also Ridley, *op.cit.*, and Janton, *op.cit.*

83. *Orig. Letts.*, no. CCCLXIII.

CHAPTER VII

1. *Histoire de Genève*, (Genève: Société d'Archaeologie et Histoire de Genève), pp. 246f; W. Monter, *Calvin's Geneva*, (New York: 1967), chap. III; R. W. Collins, *Calvin and the Libertines of Geneva*, F. D. Blackley, ed., (Toronto, 1968), pp. 182f.

2. *Original Letters*, no. LXXII.

3. Percy, *John Knox*, pp. 169f.

4. Cf. review of M. Berengo, *Nobili e Mercanti nella Lucca del Cinquecento*, (Torino, 1965), in *Bibliotheque d'Humanisme et Renaissance*, Geneva, 31 (1969), 420f.

5. *Hist. de Genève*, I, 319ff.

6. *Ibid.*

7. L. Wencelius, *L'Esthétique de Calvin*, (Paris), pp. 250ff; W. S. Reid, "The Battle Hymns of the Lord: Calvinist Psalmody of the Sixteenth Century," *Sixteenth Century Essays and Studies*, II (1971), 39ff; G. Reese, *Music in the Renaissance*, (New York, 1959), p. 358.

8. Martin, *Protestants Anglais*, p. 65; Monter, *op.cit.*, p. 65.

9. *Works*, IV, 352ff.

10. *Ibid.*, IV, 240.

11. A. Ruchat, *Histoire de la Réformation de la Suisse*, (Nyon, 1856), IV, 493ff; Knappen, *Tudor Puritanism*, p. 148; *Orig. Letts.*, no. LXXVII; *Works*, IV, 50.

12. Garrett, *Marian Exiles*, p. 295; Porter, *Reformation and Reaction*, p. 86; Knappen, *op.cit.*, p. 142.

13. *Works*, IV, 146; Régistre du Conseil de Genève (ms), Archives Municipales de Genève, XLIX, fo. 102; L, fo.17vo.

14. Brown, *John Knox*, I, 203; Knappen, *op.cit.*, p. 142; Martin, *op.cit.*, p. 65.

15. *Ibid.*, pp. 41f, 47, 331ff.; Garrett, *op.cit.*, *passim*.

16. Dickens, *English Ref.*, pp. 288f; *Works*, IV, 147f.; Martin, *op.cit.*, p. 40.

17. *Works*, IV, 172f.

18. *Ibid.*, IV, 157ff; Martin, *op.cit.*, p. 86.

19. *Works*, IV, 178ff, 186.

20. *Ibid.*, IV, 186.

21. *Ibid.*, IV, 191ff.

22. W. McMillan, *The Worship of the Scottish Reformed Church, 1550–1638*, (London, 1931), pp. 56ff; W. D. Maxwell, *John Knox's Genevan Service Book, 1556*, (Edinburgh, 1931), pp. 33f; Donaldson, *Making of Scot. Prayer Book*, p. 15.

23. MacMillan, *op. cit.*, pp. 57f., seems to have misread or misinterpreted Calvin, for the latter was advocating some form of service that would prevent a minister or a congregation from adding unscriptural elements to the communion service. (See his letter to Somerset, Oct. 22, 1548, *Lettres de Jean Calvin*, J. Bonnet, ed., Paris, 1854, I, 261). Furthermore Calvin's own order of service allowed great freedom to the minister who was conducting the service. The attempt, therefore, to prove that Calvin favored a required set form of prayers has no support. (John Calvin, *Tracts*, H. Beveridge, ed., Edinburgh, 1849, II, 100ff; Calvin, *Opera Selecta*, II, 18ff).

24. J. MacRae, "The Scottish Reformers and Public Worship," *Records of the Scottish Church History Society*, (Edinburgh, 1929), III, pp. 23f; *Works*, IV, 30.

25. *Ibid.*, IV, 179ff; Poullain, *Liturgia Sacra*, pp. 55f.

26. Lorimer, *Knox and the Church of England*, pp. 290f; *Works*, III, 73ff.

27. *Ibid.*, III, 102ff, 196; V, 479f.

28. *Ibid.*, IV, 192ff; VI, 85.

29. *Ibid.*, IV, 167, 169ff.

30. *Ibid.*, IV, 174ff.

31. *Ibid.*, IV, 173, 203f, cf. 119f, 126f; Martin, *op. cit.*, pp. 98ff.

32. R. G. Usher, *The Presbyterian Movement in the Reign of Queen Elizabeth*, (London, 1905), Camden Society, Ser. 3, VIII, ix.

33. Donaldson, *Scot. Prayer Book*, p. 6.

34. *Works*, IV, 157ff; Martin, *op. cit.*, pp. 267ff; H. Trevor-Roper, *Historical Essays*, pp. 100ff.

35. *Works*, IV, 147, 237, 239; Martin, *op. cit.*, p. 332.

36. *Ibid.*, pp. 45ff.

37. *Works*, IV, 239.

38. Calvin, *Opera*, XVIII, 434ff; *Works*, V, 3; VI, 124f; Martin, *op. cit.*, p. 63.

39. *Works*, IV, 85ff, 138.

40. *Ibid.*, IV, 219, 222.

41. *Ibid.*, IV, 241f.

42. *Ibid.*, IV, 225ff.

43. *Ibid.*, IV, 230.

44. *Ibid.*, IV, 240, 244.

45. R. L. Stevenson, "John Knox and his relations to women," *Familiar Studies of Men and Books*, (London, 1963), pp. 299ff.

46. P. Collinson, "The Role of Women in the English Reformation

illustrated by the Life and Friendships of Mrs. Anne Locke," *Studies in Church History*, (1956), II,261ff.

47. Stevenson, *op. cit.*, pp. 306f; Janton, *John Knox*, p. 51; Trevor-Roper, "John Knox," pp. 739f.

48. Collinson, *op. cit.*, pp. 258ff.

49. *History*, I, 132.

50. Martin, *op. cit.*, p. 336.

51. *History*, I, 133.

52. *Ibid.*, I, 133ff; *Works*, IV, 248f.

53. *Ibid.*, IV, 261ff.

54. *Ibid.*, IV, 276ff.

55. *Ibid.*, IV, 287ff; J. Pannier, *Les Origines de la Confession de Foi et la Discipline des Églises de France*, (Paris, 1936), p. 83.

56. Brown, *op. cit.*, I, 238f; J. W. Allen, *A History of Political Thought in the Sixteenth Century*, (London, 1951), p. 109.

57. E. Trocmé and M. Delafosse, *La commerce rochelais de la fin du XVᵉ siècle*, (Paris, 1952), pp. 85, 197; Ms.Bruneau,I, 520ff, (Archives Municipale de La Rochelle).

58. [T. Bèze] *Histoire Ecclesiastique des Eglises Reformées au Royaume de France*, P. Vesson, ed. (Toulouse, 1882), I, 77ff; Ms. Bruneau, I, 520, 526; J. Row, *Historie of the Kirk of Scotland* (Edinburgh, 1842), p. 10.

59. Bèze, *op. cit.*, I, 34, 56f; J. Delumeau, *Naissance et Affirmation de la Réforme*, (Paris, 1968), pp. 143ff, 261, 342ff; E. Léonard, *Le Protestant Français*, (Paris, 1955), p. 15.

60. Châtelherault itself had a Protestant congregation that suffered considerable persecution during the fifties and sixties, the Earl of Arran actually having to flee the country. *Archives Historique de Poitou*, (Poitiers, 1896), XVII, 31ff; Bèze, *op. cit.*, I, 97; A. Lièvre, *Histoire des Protestants et des Eglises Protestants de Poitou*, Paris, 1856, I, 62, 68; J.Rondeau, *Les Calvinistes Châtelleraudais*, (Châtellerault, 1907), pp. 6ff; Bèze, *op. cit.* pp. 40, 109; Pannier, *op. cit.*, p. 99; *Documents Protestants du XVIᵉ Siècle*, E. Arnaud, ed., (Paris, 1872), pp. 81ff.

61. Genève: Régistre du Conseil, LIV, fo.217.

62. *Works*, IV, 356.

63. *Ibid.*, IV, 389.

64. *Ibid.*, IV, 416.

65. *Ibid.*, IV, 420.

66. *Ibid.*, IV, 357ff; Martin, *op. cit.*, pp. 195ff; Ridley, *op. cit.*, p. 281.

67. *Works*, IV, 424ff.

68. *Ibid.*, IV, 523ff.

69. *Ibid.*, IV, 539f.

70. *Ibid.*, V, 510ff.

71. Martin, *op. cit.*, pp. 156f; Major, *History of Greater Britain*, pp. 158ff, 161; Allen, *op.cit.*, p. 107.

72. *Works*, III, 190ff, 217f.

73. Knappen, *op. cit.*, p. 145; Martin, *op. cit.*, p. 177; P. Meissner, *England in Zeitalter von Humanismus, Renaissance und Reformation*, (Heidelberg, 1952), pp. 359f.

74. *Op. cit.*, p. 107.

75. *Works*, IV, 249.

76. Neal, *The Puritans*, I, 83.

77. *Works*, V, 7ff.

78. *Ibid.*, V, 16; Reg.du Conseil, LV, fo.144.

79. Martin, *op. cit.*, pp. 244ff.

80. *Ibid.*, pp. 256ff; Knappen, *op. cit.*, pp. 164ff.

81. Warr, *Presbyterian Tradition*, pp. 271f.

82. G. & J. Daval, *Histoire de la Réforme à Dieppe*, E. Lesens, ed., (Rouen, 1878), I., 9ff; *Naissance et Progrès de L'Hérésie de la Ville de Dieppe, 1557–1609*, E. Lesens, ed., (Rouen, 1877), p. 15.

83. Bèze, *op. cit.*, I, 109; Pannier, *op. cit.*, p. 85.

84. *Works*, VI, 15f.

CHAPTER VIII

1. *Works*, VI, 86f.

2. Merriman, "The Assured Lords," *SHR*, XLVII,26ff.

3. *Ibid.*, pp. 21ff; RPC., I, 82; APS, II, 480;

4. Merriman, *op.cit.*, pp. 33ff; *APC*, new ser. V, 166, 177, 205; APS, II, 590.

5. *Ibid.*, II, 600ff; Leslie, *Hist. of Scot.*, II, 354; *Scott. Corresp. of Mary of Lorr.*, pp. 336f; Archives Départmentales de Vienne, E², 166; *History*, I, 104, 116f.

6. *Ibid.*, I, 103.

7. APS, II, 485; *The Statutes of the Scottish Church*, D. Patrick, ed., (Edinburgh, 1907), pp. 135ff; *The Catechism of John Hamilton, 1552*, T.G. Law, ed., (Oxford, 1884), pp. 171ff, 230ff.

8. *History*, I, xxix; C.L. Warr, *Presbyterian Tradition*, p. 262.

9. "A Historie of the Estates of Scotland 1559–1660," *Miscellany of the Woodrow Society*, D. Laing, ed., (Edinburgh, 1844), I, 53f; *RSS*, IV, no. 2580; *Historie*, I, 124f.

10. *Works*, III, 217.

11. *Ibid.*, III, 218.

12. *History*, I, 118ff.

13. *Ibid.*, I, 122 and note; H.F. Kerr, "Cardinal Beaton's Palace: Blackfriars' Wynd," *B.O.E.C.*, XXIV, (1942), 240.

14. Edinburgh Burgh Archives, ms. bundle 264, nos. 8224–7.

15. *Works*, IV, 95ff.

16. *Ibid.*, IV, 71; *History*, I, 120.

17. *Ibid.*, I, 122f; cf. also *supra*, p. 148.

18. *History*, I, 123; Warr, *op.cit.*, p. 264.

19. *History*, I, 123; cf. Ridley, *Knox*, pp. 235ff.

20. Martin, *Protestants Anglais*, p. 332.

21. *History*, I, 124; cf. *supra*, p. 149; *Works*, IV, 467ff.

22. *Ibid.*, IV, 29ff; 247.

23. For the main arguments in favor of the *Book of Common Prayer* see MacMillan, *Worship of the Scot. Ref. Church, 1558–1638*, W. McMillan, "The Anglican Book of Common Prayer in the Church of Scotland," *Records of the Scottish Chruch History Society*, IV (1932), 138ff; D. Davidson, "Influence of English Printers on the Scottish Reformation," *Ibid.*, I, (1926), 86ff; Donaldson, *Making of the Scot. Prayer Book of 1637*; Donaldson, *Scot. Ref.*, pp. 83ff.

24. *Works*, IV, 186.

25. *Ibid.*, VI, 11.

26. Cf. Calendar of Charters and other Documents, SRO VIII, nos. 1669, 1692, 1703, 1721, 1736, 1741, 1744, 1766, 1788; *Calendar of the Laing Charters*, J. Anderson, ed., (Edinburgh, 1899), nos. 648, 666, 668ff.

27. *History*, I. 125.

28. *Ibid.*, I, 132; *Works*, IV, 257ff.

29. Fleming, *Mary Queen of Scots*, pp. 22ff; A. Fraser, *Mary Queen of Scots*, (New York, 1969), pp. 55ff; Buchanan, *History*, II, 228ff.

30. *Works*, IV, 257ff; *History*, I, 136ff.

31. Buchanan, *op.cit.*, II, 232f.

32. *History*, I, 132ff.

33. *Ibid.*, I, *The Calendar of State Papers, Foreign, Elizabeth*, without any authority dates the petition as November 20, 1558. Not only does this seem a very long time after December 3, 1557, but so many conflicts between Protestant and Catholic arose during the interval we can hardly credit the mild tone of the wording if this were the correct date. Added to this, Knox states that a certain Walter Myln was burned at the stake *after* the presentation of the petition and we know that his execution took place in April 1558. Consequently it would seem more logical on all grounds to date the petition in March. If that is done everything else falls into place. W.C. Dickinson points out that the dating of the *CSP* is unsupported by evidence, but then proceeds to use it as though correct. Cf. Buchanan, *op. cit.*, II, 232ff.

34. *History*, I, 125, 238, 152.

35. *Ibid.*, I, 153.

36. ALIIT, X, 369.

37. *History*, I, 126.

38. *Ibid.*, I, 128.

39. *Ibid.; APS*, II, 505f; *Parliamentary Records of Scotland*, (1804) I, 732.

40. *History*, I, 154ff; *APS*, II, 520ff; Janton, *Knox.*, p. 150; with regard to the earlier statutes cf. *supra*, p. 157.

41. *History*, I, 158ff; X, lxxxiii, 416; Buchanan, *op.cit.*, II, 235.

42. Leslie, *Historie*, II, 397ff; *Stats. of Scot. Church*, pp. 149ff.

43. *History*, I, 160f; Pitcairn, *Ancient Crim. Trials*, I, 406f; cf. A. Lang's discussion of Knox's accusations of perfidy against Mary of Guise over this matter. Knox maintains that she acted dishonestly in condemning the preachers when they did not appear, a charge that Lang on other evidence seems to deny. It may well have been, however, that Erskine of Dun in reporting his negotiations with Mary misrepresented what she had said to him. *John Knox and Ref.* pp. 275ff.

44. *History*, I, 161; *Works*, VI, 15ff.

CHAPTER IX

1. *Ibid.*, VI, 21, 28f; "Hist. of Estate of Scot," I, 56; Lang, *Knox and Ref.*, pp. 277f.

2. *CSP, Scot.*, I, 212; *History*, I, 161.

3. Warr., *op.cit.*, p. 274; Ridley, *op.cit.*, pp. 330f.

4. *CSP, Scot.*, I, 212.

5. Drummond Writs, Box 2, Bundle XII, SRO; *History*, I, 163.

6. *Ibid.*, I, 164ff.

7. *Ibid.*, I, 176.

8. *Ibid.*, I, 178.

9. *Ibid.*, I, 180.

10. *Ibid.*, I, 184ff.

11. *Ibid.*, I, 181f; D.H. Fleming, *Guide to St. Andrews*, (St. Andrews, 1947), pp. 17f; do. *Ref. in Scotland*, pp. 361ff.

12. *Works*, VI, 23f.

13. Janton, *op.cit.*, p. 158.

14. *History*, I, 189ff.

15. Ridley, *op.cit.*, pp. 330f; J. Jamieson, *Bell the Cat, or who Destroyed the Scottish Abbeys?* (Stirling, 1902), *passim*.

16. Leslie, *History*, II, 405f.

17. *History*, I, 191f.

18. *Ibid.*, I, 200f.

19. *Ibid.*, I, 202f. For the problems related to the "Appointment" cf. Lang, *op.cit.* pp. 142ff.

20. *Ibid.*, I, 203f.

21. *Ibid.*, I, 211; "Hist. of Estate of Scot.," pp. 65f; cf. W.S. Reid, "The Coming of the Reformation to Edinburgh," *Church History*, 42 (1973), 27ff.

22. *Works*, VI, 31, 35; *CSP-Scot.*, I, 218, 220, 223ff.

23. *APC*, n.ser., VI, 408, 425.

24. *CSP-Scot.*, I, 219ff; cf. *supra*, pp. 161f.

25. *Works*, VI, 38f; *CSP-Scot.*, I, 226.

26. *Ibid.*, I, 226, 230, 233; *Works*, VI, 40f.

27. *Ibid.*, pp. 51ff; *CSP-Scot.*, I, 228, 231, 234.

28. *Works*, VI, 45ff.

29. *Ibid.*, VI, 56f.

30. *History*, I, 294f; *CSP-Scot.*, I, 239; *Works*, VI, 60f.

31. *Ibid.*, VI, 62ff.

32. *History*, I, 258f, 298; *CSP-Scot.* I, 259.

33. *History*, I, 211ff; *Extracts from the Records of the Burgh of Edinburgh*, (Edinburgh, 1875), III, 46ff.

34. *History*, I, 215ff.

35. *Ibid.*, I, 219ff.

36. *Ibid.*, I, 226ff.

37. *Works*, VI, 77f, 79f.

38. *History*, I, 244ff.

39. *Ibid.*, I, 249ff; "Hist. of Estate of Scot.," XX, 69. Cf. Knox: "Appellation to the Nobility of Scotland," p. 496, where he sets forth his position on this matter; *CSP-Scot.*, I, 254.

40. *History*, I, 257ff.

41. *Works*, VI, 83, 88f.

42. *Ibid.*, I, 265ff.; "Hist. of Estate of Scot.," p. 72; G. Buchanan, *Opera Omnia*, T. Ruddiman, ed. (Leyden, 1725), I, 579.

43. Ridley, *Knox.*, p. 360; Brown, *Knox.*, II, 62.

44. *Works*, VI, 94.

45. *Ibid.*, VI, 89ff.

46. *Ibid.*, I, 92ff.

47. *History*, I, 232, 236.

48. *CSP-Scot.*, I, 265, 267

49. *Works*, VI, 98ff, 103.

50. *Ibid.*, 75f, 94ff.

51. *Ibid.*, VI, 105ff; *History*, I, 277ff.

52. *Ibid.*, I, 281; *Works*, VI, 108; *Two Missions of Jacques de la Brosse*, G. Dickinson, ed. (Edinburgh, 1942), pp. 60f.

53. *History*, I, 302ff.

54. *Ibid.*, I, 312ff; *CSP-Scot.*, I, 398ff.

55. *Ibid.*, I, 422; *History*, I, 322.

56. *Ibid.*,I, 322, n. 5.

57. *Works*, VI, 105.

58. *History*, I, 314ff; *Diurnal*, p. 59; *CSP-Scot.*, I, 444ff; *CSP-Dom.*, I, 142; MacKinnon, *Modern Liberty*, II, 422.

59. J. MacKinnon, *The Constitutional History of Scotland*, (London, 1924), p. 285.

60. *History*, I, 322ff; *Works*, VI, 114ff.

61. *History*, I, xlviii; MacKinnon, *Constit. Hist.*, p. 285.

CHAPTER X

1. Cf. *Thirds of Benefices*, Introduction.

2. Antonia Fraser points out that the peers and lords were not much interested in either religious or moral reform. "The laurels for purity of spirit and intensity of theological vision seem to belong mainly to a lower social class than theirs." *Mary Queen of Scots*, pp. 148, 175. Cf. also H.G. Koenigsberger, "The Organisation of Revolutionary Parties in France and the Netherlands in the 16th Century," *Journal of Modern History*, XXVII (1955), 337; G. Donaldson, "The Parish Clergy and the Reformation," *Essays*, McRoberts, ed., 136.

3. *APS* II, p. 526.

4. Donaldson, *Scot Ref.*, pp. 177f; *Works*, VI, 120f; cf. Southgate, "The Marian Exiles" pp. 151f.

5. *History*, II, 257ff; *Calvin Opera Selecta*, II, 297ff; V. Poullain, *op.cit.*, pp. 171ff, 207; D. Shaw, "John Willock," *Ref. and Rev'n*, p. 59.

6. Cf. Article XXIV.

7. *C.S.P., Scot.*, I, 455, 458, 463; *APS*, II, 525ff; *Diurnal*, pp. 61f; *History*, I, 334ff.

8. *Ibid.*, II, 81; R.S. Rait, *The Parliaments of Scotland*, (Glasgow, 1924), p. 48; MacKinnon, *Modern Liberty*, II, 274f, 424f; Janton, *Knox*, pp. 171f.

9. *History*, I, 338f.

10. There is a difference between Knox's and Randolph's accounts of how the earls and lords voted. Cf. Dickinson's note 2, *History*, I, 339.

11. *Ibid.*, I, 344; *Thirds*, p. xviii.

12. *History*, I, 338.

13. *CSP-Scot.*, I, 459f; *Works*, VI, 114; Janton, *op.cit.*, p. 172.

14. *Ibid.*, p. 171; *CSP-Scot.*, I, 461.

15. Rait, *op.cit.*, p. 48f; MacKinnon, *op.cit.*, p. 274; *Thirds*, lxf.

16. MacKinnon, *op.cit.*, pp. 424f; *History*, II, 81.

17. *Ibid.*, I, 342; *Papiers d'État Relatifs à l'Histoire d'Écosse*, A. Teulet, ed., (Paris, 1854), I, pp. 638f.

18. Fraser, *op.cit.*, p. 104f; *History*, I, 351.

19. *The First Book of Discipline*, J.K. Cameron, ed., (Edinburgh, 1972), pp. 8ff. Individual references to the sections of the book will not be made.

20. *History*, I, 1, lxviii; II, 280, 323; *Works*, VI, 119.

21. J. Edgar, *The History of Early Scottish Education*, (Edinburgh, 1893), pp. 220ff.

22. *Works*, IV, 177; W.S. Reid, "The Founding of the Genevan Academy," *West. Theol. J.*, XVIII (1955), 1ff; G.M. Trevelyan, *A Shortened History of England*, (London, 1942), p. 342.

23. Edgar, *op.cit.*, pp. 261f; A. Morgan, *The Rise and Progress of Scottish Education*, Edinburgh, 1927, pp. 50f.

24. *Thirds*, p. xv.

25. Calvin, *op.cit.*, II, 325ff; Poullain, *op.cit.*, pp. 220ff; *Works*, IV, 174ff; Bèze, *Hist. Eccles.*, I, 105ff; *Documents Protestants*, pp. 5ff; D. Shaw, "John Willock," *Reformation and Revolution*, pp. 60ff.

26. *Bk. of Discipline*, pp. 20, 26, 38, 43f, 49ff, 122ff; Warr, *Presbyterian Tradit.*, pp. 286ff; Donaldson, *op.cit.*, chap. V, and "The Example of Denmark in the Scottish Reformation", *SHR*, XXVII (1948), pp. 57ff.

27. *History*, II, 272ff; W.S. Reid, "John Knox's Attitude to the English Reformation," *West. Theol. J.*, XXVI (1963), 1ff; *CSP-Scot.*, I, 257, no. 554; *Works*, VI, 118f; *Miscellany of the Spalding Club*, IV, pp. 92ff; Shaw, "John Willock," *Ref. and Rev'n*, p. 61.

28. *Ibid.*, VI, 136, 146, 554.

29. *CSP-Scot.* I, 216ff *passim*, *RPC*, I, 166.

30. *CSP-Scot.*, I, 468, 560.

31. *Ibid.*, I, 506, no. 948; *History*, I, 347f. Languet, however, writing from Paris pointed out that the Scottish nobles were still taking pensions from France. (H. Languet, *Epistolae Secretae*, I.P. Ludovico, ed., (Halle, 1589) p. 67.)

32. *Works*, VI, 229.

33. *Ibid.*, VI, 119.

34. Cf. Dickinson's interesting comments in *History*, I, lxxxviiiff; M. Lee, Jr., "John Knox and his *History*," *SHR*, XLV (1966), 45ff, *Works*, VI, 121.

35. Lang, *Knox and the Ref.*, pp. 128ff.

36. *History*, I, 351; *Works*, VI, lvif, 125.

37. *History*, I, 351.

38. Donaldson, *Scot. Ref.*, p. 148.

39. *Acts and Proceedings of the General Assembly of the Kirk of Scotland, 1560–77*, known as the *Book of the Universal Kirk* [BUK] (Edinburgh, 1837), p. 3. Calderwood, *Hist. of Kirk*, II, 44f; Row, *Hist. of the Kirk*, p. 13f.

40. Calderwood, *op.cit.*, II, 44f; BUK., I, 3ff.

41. *Ibid.*, I, 6.

42. *Ibid.*, I, 7; Calderwood, *op.cit.*, II, 47. A tacksman was a tenant who held a large farm or quantity of land and rented all or part of it to sub-tenants. A tack is the rent paid by a tenant.

43. Brown, *op.cit.*, II, 105ff; *CSP-Scot*, I, 512.

44. *History*, I, 352f; Brown, *op.cit.*, II, 98f.

45. *History*, I, 344f; *Diurnal*, pp. 63, 281f.

46. *CSP-Scot*, I, 509ff.

47. *Thirds*, viiff; *History*, I, lif.

48. MacKinnon, *op.cit.*, II, 429; Warr, *op.cit.*, pp. 297ff; Allen, *Hist. Pol. Tho't*, p. 115.

49. Janton, *op.cit.*, p. 172.

50. Rait, *op.cit.*, p. 50; *Diurnal*, p. 63.

51. *History*, I, 347.

52. *Ibid.*, I, 354f.

53. *Ibid.*, I, 334; II, 273ff.

54. *CSP-Scot*, I, 523.

55. *Works*, VI, 122.

56. *Ibid.*, VI, 123f.

57. Leslie, *Hist. of Scot.*, II, 452ff.

58. *History*, I, 359ff; *BUK*, I, 8ff.

59. *History*, I, 361ff.

60. *Ibid.*, I, 355f, 357; *Edin. Recs.*, III, 65, 89ff.

61. *History*, I, 357f; *Ancient Laws and Customs of the Burghs of Scotland*, (Edinburgh, 1910), II, 81; *Ancient Criminal Trials*, I: 2, 409*f; *Diurnal*, p. 65f.

62. Fraser, *op.cit.*, p. 187.

63. *Ibid.*, p. 112.

64. *History*, I, 365ff; *CSP. Elizabeth-Foreign*, IV, no. 265.

65. Teulet, *Papiers*, I, 3f; *CSP-Scot.*, I, 542.

66. *Ibid.*, I, 516.

67. *History*, I, 365ff.

68. *Works*, VI, 126.

69. Fraser, *op.cit.*, pp. 128ff; *History*, II, 7; cf. Fleming, *Mary*, pp. 42ff.

70. Languet, *op.cit.*, p. 127.

71. *Diurnal*, p. 66; *History*, II, 7.

72. Cf. W.L. Mathieson, *Politics and Religion*, (Glasgow, 1902), I, chap. III; Lang, *op.cit.*, pp. 194ff; Fraser, *op.cit.*, pp. 153ff.

73. *History*, II, 8f.

74. *Ibid.*; *CSP-Scot.*, I, 547; Janton, *op.cit.*, pp. 175f.

75. *History*, II, 9f; *RPC*, I, 157f; Fraser, *op.cit.*, pp. 153f, 157.

76. *CSP-Scot.*, I, 1038; *Works*, VI, 129.

77. *Op.cit.*, II, 156ff.

78. Janton, *op.cit.*, p. 179.

79. *Ibid.*, 181f; MacKinnon, *op.cit.*, II, 440f; Watt, *Knox in Controversy,* pp. 102ff; *History*, II, 13ff; *CSP-Scot.*, I, 551.

80. *Works*, VI, 129f.

81. *Ibid.*, VI, 131f.

82. *Ibid.*, VI, 133f; Teulet, *Papiers*, I, 12ff.

83. Janton, *op.cit.*, pp. 190ff; Fraser, *op.cit.*, p. 154.

84. *CSP-Scot.*, I, 551.

85. *Ibid.*, I, 553.

86. *Works*, VI, 131.

87. *Anc. Crim. Trials*, I: 2, 426*ff.

88. *CSP-Scot.*, I, 564f, *Works*, VI, 136.

89. *History*, II, 23f.

90. *Ibid.*, II, 26.

91. *Ibid.*, II, 33.

92. *RPC*, I, 162, 192. A number of such grants appear in *Calendar of Charters*, VIII, IX.

93. *History*, II, 27f.

94. *Ibid.*, II, 28.

95. *Ibid.*, II, 24; *RPC*, I, 192ff, 201f; *Diurnal*, p. 70; *Thirds*, p. xff; *CSP-Scot.*, I, 582.

96. *Works*, VI, 137.

97. *RPC*, I, 199ff.

98. W.S. Reid, "Clerical Taxation: the Scottish Alternative to dissolution of the monasteries, 1530–1560," *Catholic Historical Review*, XXXV (1948), pp. 139ff; *Thirds*, p. xif; R.K. Hannay, "The Church Lands at the Reformation," *SHR*, XVI (1919), 52ff.

99. *Thirds*, p. xxi.

CHAPTER XI

1. *History*, II, 3ff.

2. *Works*, VI, 141.

3. Ridley, *Knox*, pp. 433ff; *CSP-Scot.*, I, 680, no. 1163.

4. *BUK*, I, 17; Law, *Collected Essays*, P. H. Brown, ed. (Edinburgh, 1904), pp. 279ff; *Edin. Rec.*, III, 131.

5. *Ibid.*, III, 131ff, 152, 162, 173; *Works*, VI, 147f.

6. Ridley, *op.cit.*, pp. 405ff; Michel, *Les Écossais en France* . . . , II, 50; *Selections from Unpublished Mss. Illustrative of the Reign of Queen Mary,* (Glasgow, 1837), pp. 101f; *Works*, VI, 526f; *Papal Negotiations with Mary Queen of Scots*, J.H. Pollen, ed., (Edinburgh, 1901), pp. 162ff, 171f.

7. *Diurnal*, p. 70.

8. Ridley, *op.cit.*, pp. 401ff; R.K. Hannay, "The Earl of Arran and Queen Mary," *SHR*, XVIII (1921), pp. 258ff; *RPC*, I, 452.

9. *Works*, VI, 137ff; *CSP-Scot*, I, 603.

10. *BUK*, I, 15ff.

11. *Ibid.*, I, 16f; *Thirds*, xvf, xxi.

12. *BUK*, I, 18, 20ff; *History*, II, 49; Janton, *Knox*, 177f; *RPC*, I, 208.

13. *History*, II, 52.

14. *CSP-Scot.*, I, 649; *Works*, VI, 143f.

15. *Ibid.*, VI, 139, 144, 150ff; H. Watt, *Knox in Controversy*, pp. 57ff. Cf. Quintin Kennedy, "Ane Compendious Tractive," (1558), *Miscellany of the Woodrow Society*, D.Laing, ed., (Edinburgh, 1844), I, 89ff.

16. *Pap. Negots.*, p. 198; N. Winzet, *Certain Tractates*, J.K. Hewison, ed. (Edinburgh, 1888), I, 15; Leslie, *Historie*, II, 464; Watt, *op.cit.*, pp. 31ff; Ridley, *op.cit.*, p. 408.

17. *Works*, VI, pp. 146f;

18. *History*, II, 55ff; *Works*, VI, 145f; *RPC*, I, 218ff; *Diurnal*, pp. 73f; Fleming, *Mary, Queen of Scots*, pp. 78ff.

19. *CSP-Scot.*, I, 657; *Catechism of Hamilton*, pp. 90ff; Ridley, *op.cit.*, pp. 418f; Fraser, *Mary*, pp. 182, 186, 204; *History*, II, 68f.

20. *Ibid.*, II, 44ff; *Works*, VI, 140f; Ridley, *op.cit.*, p. 421; Brown, *Knox*, II, 195ff; Janton, *Knox*, pp. 183f.

21. *BUK*, I, 25ff; Donaldson, *Thirds*, p. xxii.

22. Attempts have been made to prove that the Genevan *Form of Prayers* which became the *Book of Common Order* was much the same as the *Book of Common Prayer* of the Church of England, as it was quite acceptable to the Scottish reformers, including Knox. (Donaldson, *Scott. Ref.*, pp. 179ff; *Making of the Scot Prayer Book of 1637, passim*; MacMillan, *Worship of Scot. Ref. Church, passim*.) But the dissimilarity of the two books, and the fact that Knox and the other Scottish ministers criticized the *Book of Common Prayer* so vigorously, would seem to discredit any such thesis. (Reid, "Knox's Attitude to the Eng. Ref.," 1ff; *Works*, VI, 11, 12ff, 30, 85f, 119, 123, 519; *CSP-Scot.*, I, 471f.)

23. *History*, II, 70ff; Ridley, *op.cit.*, pp. 422f; Watt, *op.cit.*, p. 91; Fraser, *op.cit.*, p. 214.

24. *Diurnal*, p. 75; Pitcairn, *Ancient Criminal Trials*, I:2, *427; *CSP-Scot.*, II, 9.

25. *APS*, II, 539ff; *RPC*, I, 217, 246.

26. *History*, II, 79ff; Ridley, *op.cit.*, p. 425.

27. *History*, II, 84ff, 105; Fleming, *Mary*, pp. 84ff.

28. *Ibid.*, p. 91; *History*, II, 98; Watt, *op.cit.*, pp. 94f.

29. *History*, II, 66f; *BUK*, I, 29ff.

30. *Ibid.*, I, 37.

31. Fleming, *Scot. Ref.*, pp. 39ff.

32. *Works*, VI, 528, 530; *CSP-Scot.*, II, 25.

33. *RPC*, I, 266f; *History*, II, 87ff; *CSP-Scot.*, II, 26; *Anc. Crim. Trials, op.cit.*, pp. 434*f.

34. *History*, II, 90; Fraser, *op.cit.*, p. 216; Ridley, *op.cit.*, p. 429.

35. *History*, II, 91ff.

36. *BUK*, I, 38.

37. *CSP-Scot.*, II, 61.

38. *History*, II, 108ff; Brown, *op.cit.*, II, 202; Ridley, *op.cit.*, p. 437. Knox has been accused of perfidy at this conference because he did not reveal that he had written privately to Calvin after Maitland had refused to do so officially. He may not have said anything about his writing because he does not seem to have received an answer. (Works, VI: 687f).

39. *BUK*, I, 47f; *History*, II, lvii, lxiv; Brown, *op.cit.*, II, 168ff.

40. Janton, *op.cit.*, pp. 188f; Lang, *Knox and the Ref.*, pp. 170, 246.

41. *BUK*, I, 50ff.

42. *RPC*, I, 287f, 296; *CSP-Scot.*, II, 88, 100.

43. *Diurnal*, pp. 78f; *CSP-Scot.*, II, 100.

44. *BUK*, I, 52ff.

45. *CSP-Scot.*, II, 88, 100, 113, 126, 136, 140.

46. *RPC*, I, 17, note B; Fraser, *op.cit.*, pp. 220ff.

47. *CSP-Scot.*, II, 118f; Fraser, *op.cit.*, 221.

48. *CSP-Scot.*, II, 136f, 141; *History*, II, 144ff.

49. *Diurnal*, p. 79; *CSP-Scot.*, II, 153, 154, 158f, 164, 171.

50. *BUK*, I, 54, 57ff., 60, 64ff; *CSP-Scot.*, II, 178.

51. Lee, *Moray*, pp. 113f.

52. *Ibid.*, pp. 132ff; Fraser, *op.cit.*, p. 229; *CSP-Scot.*, II, 175, 189; *RPC*, I, 342.

53. These are Fraser's words, *op.cit.*, p. 238.

54. *RPC*, I, 304, 338ff, 342f; *RMS*, IV, no. 1611; *CSP-Scot.*, II, 140, 144ff; Fleming, *Mary*, pp. 122ff; Lee, *op.cit.*, pp. 149f.

55. *Ibid.*, pp. 134f; Fleming, *op.cit.* pp. 104ff; *Diurnal*, p. 79; *CSP-Scot.*, II, 200, 205, 218; *RPC*, I, 362ff.

56. *Diurnal*, p. 81; Ridley, *op.cit.*, p. 441; *Works*, VI, 221ff.

57. *Edin. Recs.*, III, 200ff.

58. *Ibid.*, III, 213, 227, 233.

59. *CSP-Scot.*, II, 209ff, 218f; *RPC.*, I, 389.

60. *BUK*, I, 65, 67; *CSP-Scot.*, II, 185, 247; *RPC*, I, 412.

61. *BUK.*, I, 68ff.

62. *Ibid.*, 73, 76ff.

63. *RPC.*, I, 416f; Lee, *op.cit.*, 158; W.S. Reid, "The Coming of the Reformation to Edinburgh," *Church History*, 42 (1973), 33.

64. *Diurnal*, p. 89; "Inventory of Gordon Castle Writs," I; *RPC*, I, 416f,

Memoirs of Sir James Melville of Halhill, A.F. Steuart, ed., (London, 1929), pp. 105, 113; Fleming, *op.cit.*, pp. 122ff, 376ff; *Papal Negots.*, p. 208.

65. *Diurnal*, p. 88.

66. *Op.cit.*, p. 123.

67. Lee, *op.cit.*, pp. 160ff; Ridley, *op.cit.*, 447f; *Diurnal*, pp. 92ff.

68. *CSP-Scot.*, II, 270; RPC, I, 437; *Diurnal*, p. 94; Spottiswood, *Hist.* II, 38; *History*, II, 203.

69. *RSS*, V:2, no. 3149; *Diurnal*, pp. 96f; *CSP-Scot.*, II, 274f.

70. *CSP-Scot.*, II, 270, Fleming, *op.cit.*, pp. 395ff; Ridley, *op.cit.*, p. 448f. It may of course have been that Knox had been told that the nobles were planning to try Riccio, but there is no clear evidence upon which Ridley can base his claim that Knox no longer had any qualms about murder.

71. *CSP-Scot.*, II, 269, 274; *Diurnal*, pp. 96ff.

72. *Ibid.*, p. 94; *CSP-Scot.*, II, 291.

73. RPC, I, 445; *CSP-Scot.*, II, 290f.

74. Calendar of Charters, SRO, IX, no. 3066; Torphichen Writs, SRO, p. 44.

75. Lee, *op.cit.*, p. 177; *Works*, VI, 543; *Edin. Recs.*, III, 215; *RPC*, I, 569.

76. *BUK*, I, 82; *RPC*, I, 471–507, *passim; History*, II, 194.

77. *Ibid.*, II, 194f; *BUK*, I, 88f; *CSP-Scot.*, II, 309.

78. *BUK*, I, 84ff.

79. *Ibid.*, I, 90; *Works*, VI, 544f; "The Second Helvetic Confession," XVIII:5, 16, *The Creeds of Christendom*, P. Schaff, ed., (New York, 1882), III, 279, 283.

80. Lee, *op.cit.*, pp. 180f; Fleming, *op.cit.*, pp. 135ff, 141.

81. *CSP-Scot.*, II, 320f; Lee, *op.cit.*, pp. 189ff; Fleming, *op.cit.*, 152ff; 172f.

82. *CSP-Scot.*, II, 321; *RPC*, I, 509, 512f.

83. *CSP-Scot.*, II, 326; *Diurnal*, p. 111; *RPC*, I, 521ff, 533, 539f.

84. *BUK*, I, 115f; *CSP-Scot.*, II, 326ff., 355; *Diurnal*, p. 107; *RPC*, I, 526.

85. C.P. Finlayson, "A Volume Associated with John Knox," *SHR*, XXXVIII (1959), 170ff; Ridley, *op.cit.*, pp. 467ff.

86. *BUK*, I, 93, 101ff.

87. *RPC*, I, 534f; *BUK*, I, 104ff.

88. *CSP-Scot.*, II, 355f; Ridley, *op.cit.*, pp. 396ff, 434ff.

89. Rait, *Parl'ts of Scotland*, pp. 51f; *RPC*, I, 596.

90. *APC*, III, 5.

91. *Ibid.*, III, 11ff, 24; *RPC*, I, 573ff.

92. *CPS-Scot.*, II, 369f.

CHAPTER XII

1. Watt, *Knox in Controversy*, pp. 3, 98ff.

2. *Diurnal*, pp. 125ff., 132, 136; *CSP-Scot.*, II, 269, 403.

3. *Ibid.,* II, 351, 359; *Works,* VI, pp. 551ff.

4. Ridley, *Knox,* pp. 466, 468, 470f, 483ff.

5. *Works,* VI, 558ff.; *CSP-Scot.,* II, 359, 502.

6. *Ibid.,* II, 412, 421, 453.

7. *BUK,* I, 113, 123, 130f.

8. *Ibid.,* I, 125; *CSP-Scot.,* II, 403.

9. *RPC,* I, 628f; *APS,* II, 479.

10. *Diurnal,* p. 136.

11. *Ibid.,* p. 134; *CSP-Scot.,* II, 485, 497, 516.

12. *Ibid.,* II, 626, 630, 632, 646ff; *RPC,* I, 644, 665f.; *Diurnal,* pp. 159f; Lee, *Moray,* pp. 256f.

13. *BUK,* I, 132, 155.

14. *RPC,* I, 675.

15. *Ibid.,* II, 3ff.; *CSP-Scot.,* II, 663f; Calderwood, *History,* II, 490ff.

16. *Works,* VI, 565ff.

17. Lee, *op.cit.,* pp. 265ff; E. Russell, *Maitland of Lethington,* (London, 1912), pp. 392ff.

18. *Ibid.,* pp. 402f; *Diurnal,* p. 149; *CSP-Scot.,* II, 691; III, 19, 28.

19. *Ibid.,* III, 53ff; *Works,* VI, 568f.

20. R. Bannatyne, *Memoires of Transactions in Scotland, 1569–1573,* (Edinburgh, 1836), pp. 1f.

21. Spottiswoode, *History,* II, 121f.

22. Bannatyne, *op.cit.,* pp. 5ff; Calderwood, *op.cit.,* II, 515ff.

23. *Works,* VI, 568ff.

24. Bannatyne, *op.cit.,* p. 16.

25. *Ibid.,* pp. 15f, 20.

26. Calderwood, *op.cit.,* II, 529ff; *BUK,* I, 157ff.

27. *Works,* VI, 574.

28. *Diurnal,* pp. 167ff; Calderwood, *op.cit.,* II, 553; *CSP-Scot.,* III, 143.

29. Calderwood, *op.cit.,* II, 565f; *CSP-Scot.,* III, 266.

30. *Ibid.,* III, 114, 158ff.

31. *Ibid.,* III, 267.

32. *Ibid.,* III, 251, 257.

33. *Ibid.,* III, 265, 268, 275, 277.

34. *Diurnal,* pp. 187f; *CSP-Scot.,* III, 319. For the various suggestions as to why Kirkcaldy changed sides cf. Russell, *op.cit.,* p. 420f; Barbé, *Kirkcaldy,* pp. 108ff; *Mems of Melville,* pp. 198ff.

35. *CSP-Scot.,* III, 325; *Diurnal,* p. 194.

36. *Ibid.,* p. 196.

37. This account is based upon the report of Bannatyne in his memoirs, although there are documents of various kinds that support his statements, *Memoires,* pp. 70ff; *Works,* VI, 575ff.

38. *Ibid.,* VI, 585.

39. *CSP-Scot.*, III, 462, 471ff.

40. *Edinburgh Recs.*, III, 282.

41. *BUK*, I, 185, 191.

42. Bannatyne, *op.cit.*, pp. 90ff.

43. *Ibid.*, p. 94; *Diurnal*, 201.

44. Bannatyne, *op.cit.*, pp. 100ff.

45. Calderwood, *op.cit.*, III, 54ff; *Diurnal*, pp. 208ff.; *CSP-Scot.* III, 544.

46. Bannatyne, *op.cit.*, pp. 109ff.; Calderwood, *op.cit.*, III, 242.

47. *Diurnal*, pp. 209f; Calderwood, *op.cit.*, III, 71.

48. Bannatyne, *op.cit.*, pp. 125ff.

49. *Ibid.*, pp. 111f.

50. *Ibid.*, pp. 113f.; Calderwood, *op.cit.*, III, 73.

51. Bannatyne, *op.cit.*, p. 114.

CHAPTER XIII

1. *The Diary of Mr. James Melville, 1556–1601* (Edinburgh, 1829), pp. 21, 26.

2. Bannatyne, *Memoires*, pp. 255ff.

3. *Works*, VI, 602, 604f.

4. Calderwood, *Historie*, III, 134f.

5. Melville, *Diary*, p. 21.

6. *RPC*, XIV, 99; *CSP-Scot.*, III, 573.

7. Law, *op.cit.*, "John Craig," p. 293.

8. *CSP-Scot.*, III, 532ff, 604f, 620; *RPC*, XIV, 96f.

9. *CSP-Scot.*, III, 610, 632, 664.

10. *Ibid.*, III, 667.

11. *Diurnal*, p. 238.

12. *CSP-Scot.*, III, 683.

13. *Ibid.*, III, 672, 679.

14. *RPC*, II, 78; *APS*, III, 65.

15. *RCP*, II, 85f; *CSP-Scot.*, III, 707, 956.

16. Calderwood, *op. cit.*, III, 156ff; *RPC*, II, 90f.

17. Calderwood, *op. cit.*, III, 168ff; Bannatyne, *op. cit.*, p. 223.

18. *Ibid.*, p. 256; Calderwood, *op. cit.*, III, 206ff; *Works*, VI, 625.

19. T. M'Crie, *The Life of John Knox*, (Edinburgh, 1839), pp. 328ff; Brown, *John Knox*, II, 270; Donaldson, *op. cit.*, p. 170; R. S. Louden, *The True Face of the Kirk*, (London, 1963), pp. 12ff.

20. Cf. Reid, "Knox's Attitude to the Eng. Ref.," pp. 1ff.

21. Calderwood, *op. cit.*, III, 208ff.; Bannatyne, *op. cit.*, pp. 227ff; *BUK*, I, 238ff.

22. *Works*, III, 613ff.

23. *CSP-Scot.*, IV, 135; Bannatyne, *op. cit.*, pp. 220ff.

24. *Ibid.*, pp. 247ff; *RPC*, II, 101, 121f.

25. *Ibid.*, II, 125, 131f, 140ff, 187.

26. *Works*, VI, 616ff.

27. *Ibid.*, VI, 606ff; 608ff.

28. *History*, I, xciiif.

29. *Works*, VI, 481ff.

30. *Works*, VI, 514; *CSP-Scot.*, IV, 381, 399.

31. Bannatyne, *op. cit.*, pp. 253f.

32. *Ibid.*, pp. 264f; *Works*, VI, 631.

33. *Ibid.*, VI, 654f.

34. Bannatyne, *op. cit.*, pp. 250ff; *BUK*, I, 245, 247.

35. Bannatyne, *op. cit.*, pp. 265ff; Lang, *Knox and the Reformation*, p. 269; Melville, *Diary*, p. 26.

36. *Works*, VI, 632f; Bannatyne, *op. cit.*, p. 264.

37. *Works*, VI, 633.

38. *Ibid.*, VI, 634; Bannatyne, *op. cit.*, 281.

39. Bannatyne, *op. cit.*, pp. 282ff; *Works*, VI, 635f.

40. *Ibid.*, VI, 637; Bannatyne, *op. cit.*, pp. 283.

41. *Ibid.*, pp. 285; *Works*, VI, 638ff.

42. Calderwood, *op. cit.*, III, 242.

43. *Works*, VI, lxiiiff.

44. *Ibid.*, VI, lv; Melville, *op. cit.*, 26ff; Bannatyne, *op. cit.*, p. 370.

CHAPTER XIV

1. *Works*, VI, 584f.

2. Calderwood, *op.cit.*, III, 242.

3. *Works*, VI, 613.

4. "The Erskine of Dun Papers," *Spalding Club Miscellany*, IV, 71f, 99ff; Anonymous, *Memoir of Erskine of Dun*, (London, 1855), pp. 24f.

BIBLIOGRAPHY

Primary Sources

MANUSCRIPT MATERIAL

Argyll Transcripts, Inverary Castle.

Ms. Bruneau, Bibliothèque Municipale de La Rochelle.

Calendar of Charters and other Documents, VIII, IX, Scottish Record Office, Edinburgh.

Collection of Charters, Edinburgh City Archives.

Crawford and Balcarres, Scottish Muniments, John Rylands Library, Manchester, England.

Genève, Régistre du Conseil, LIV, L. Archives Municipales.

Gordon Castle. Inventory of Muniments, Scottish Record Office, Edinburgh.

Paris Transcripts, Public Record Office, London.

Perth, Index of the Burgh Records of (1500–1699), Scottish Record Office, Edinburgh.

Rothes Cartulary, Scottish Record Office, Edinburgh.

Roman Transcripts, Public Record Office, London.

Torphichen Writs, Scottish Record Office, Edinburgh.

Trésor des Chartes, Ser. J.J., Archives Nationales de France, Paris.

Vienne, Archives Departmentales de, E.², Poitiers, France.

PRINTED MATERIAL

Accounts of the Collectors of the Thirds of Benefices 1561–1572, G. Donaldson, ed., (Edinburgh, Scot. Hist. Soc., 1949).

Accounts of the Lord High Treasurer, J.B. Paul, ed., (Edinburgh, 1913), XI.

Acts and Proceedings of the General Assembly of the Kirk of Scotland, 1560–77, known as *The Buik of the Universal Kirk*, (Edinburgh, Bannatyne Club, 1837), I, II.

Acts of the Lords of the Council in Public Affairs, R.K. Hannay, ed., (Edinburgh, 1932).

Acts of the Parliament of Scotland, (Edinburgh, 1814), I, II, III.

Acts of the Privy Council of England, J.R. Dasent, ed. (London, 1890–1907) I–III.

Ancient Criminal Trials, R. Pitcairn, ed., (Edinburgh, Bannatyne Club, 1833). 3 vols.

Ancient Laws and Customs of the Burghs of Scotland, (Edinburgh, Scottish Burgh Rec. Soc. 1910).

Archives Historique de Poitou, (Poitiers, 1896) Vol XVII.

M. Bucer, *De Regno Christi*, W. Pauck, ed., (Philadelphia, 1969).

Calendar of the State Papers, Domestic, Edward VI, Mary, Elizabeth, R. Lemon, and M.A.E. Green, edd., (London, 1856), I.

Calendar of State Papers, Foreign, Edward VI, W.B. Turnbull, ed., (London, 1861).

Calendar of State Papers-Scottish, J. Bain, ed., (Edinburgh, 1898–1905), I–IV.

Calendar of State Papers-Spanish, M.A.S. Hume, and R. Tyler, edd., (London, 1912) IX.

Calendar of the Laing Charters, J. Anderson, ed., (Edinburgh, 1899).

J. Calvin, *Calvin's Tracts*, W. Beveridge, ed., (Edinburgh, 1849), II.

J. Calvin, *Institutes of the Christian Religion*, J.T. McNeill, ed., F.L. Battles, tr., (Philadelphia, 1959), 2 vols.

J. Calvin, *Lettres Anglais*, A.M. Schmidt, ed., (Paris, 1959).

J. Calvin, *Johannis Calvini Opera Selecta*, P. Barth, and D. Scheuner, edd., (Munich, 1952), I, II.

J. Calvin, *Opera Omnia*, C. Baum *et al.,* edd., (Brunswick 1878), XV, XVIII.

Documents Protestants inédits du XVIᵉ Siècle, E. Arnaud, ed., (Paris 1872).

The Chronicle and Political Papers of Edward VI, W.K. Jordan, ed., (Ithaca, N.Y., 1966).

William Dunbar, *Poems of William Dunbar*, J. Small, ed., (Edinburgh, Scot. Text Soc. 1881), 3 vols.

Extracts from the Council Register of the Burgh of Aberdeen, J. Stuart, ed., (Aberdeen, Spalding Club, 1844).

"Erskine of Dun Papers," *Miscellany of the Spalding Club*, J. Stuart, ed., (Aberdeen, 1849) IV.

Extracts from the Record of the Burgh of Edinburgh, J.D. Marwick, ed., (Edinburgh, Scot. Burgh Rec. Soc., 1875), II, III.

Hamilton Papers, J. Bain, ed., (Edinburgh, 1890), II.

J. Hamilton, *The Catechism of John Hamilton, 1552*, T.G. Law, ed., (Oxford, 1884).

J. Hooper, *Early Writings*, (Cambridge, Parker Society, 1843).

Q. Kennedy, "Ane Compendius Tractive", (1558), *Miscellany of the Wodrow Society*, D. Laing, ed., (Edinburgh, 1844) I.

John Knox, *Works*, David Laing, ed., (Edinburgh, Wodrow Society, 1864) 6 vols.

H. Languet, *Epistolae Secretae,* I. P. Ludovico, ed., (Halle, 1699).

H. Latimer, *Works*, G.E. Corrie, ed., (Cambridge, Parker Soc., 1844), 2 vols.

Letters and Papers, Foreign and Domestic, of the reign of Henry VIII, J. Gairdner, *et al.*, edd., (London, 1898) 21 vols.

Sir David Lindsay, Poetical Works of, D. Laing, ed., (Edinburgh, Scot. Text. Soc., 1871), 2 vols.

Nantes, Ville de, Inventaire Sommaire des Archives Communales, R. Blanchard, ed., (Nantes, 1888).

Negotiations de la France dans le Levant, E. Charrière, ed., (Paris, 1850).

Original Letters Relative to the English Reformation, H. Robinson, ed., (Cambridge, Parker Soc., 1846–7), 2 vols.

Papal Negotiations with Queen Mary of Scots, J.H. Pollen, ed., (Edinburgh, Scot. Hist. Soc., 1901).

Papiers d'État Relatifs à l'Histoire d'Écosse, A. Teulet, ed. (Paris, Bannatyne Club, 1854), I.

Parliamentary Records of Scotland, I (1804).

V. Poullain, *Liturgia Sacra 1551–5,* A.C. Honders, ed., (Leiden, 1970).

Register of the Privy Council of Scotland, J.H. Burton, ed. (Edinburgh, 1877), vols. I, II.

Registrum Magnum Sigilli, J.B. Paul and J.M. Thomson, edd. (Edinburgh, 1883), I, II.

Registrum Secreti Sigilli Regum Scotorum, J. Beveridge, ed. (Edinburgh, 1952), 6 vols.

Reliquiae Antiquae Scotiae, (Edinburgh, 1848).

N. Ridley, *Works,* H. Christmas, ed., (Cambridge, Parker Soc., 1841).

Scottish Correspondence of Mary of Lorraine, A.I. Dunlop, ed., (Edinburgh, Scot. Hist. Soc., 1927).

Selections from Unpublished Manuscripts Illustrative of the Reign of Queen Mary, J. Stevenson, ed., (Glasgow, Maitland Club, 1837).

The Statutes of the Scottish Church, D. Patrick, ed., (Edinburgh, Scot. Hist. Soc., 1907).

The Two Liturgies of Edward VI, J. Ketley, ed., (Cambridge, Parker Soc. 1845).

R. Wedderburn, *The Gude and Godlie Ballatis,* A.F. Mitchell, ed., (Edinburgh, Scot. Text Soc., 1897).

N. Winzet, *Certain Tractates,* J.K. Hewison, ed., (Edinburgh, Scot. Text Soc., 1881), I.

CONTEMPORARY ACCOUNTS

R. Bannatyne, *Memoires of Transactions in Scotland, 1569–1573,* (Edinburgh, Bannatyne Club, 1836).

[T. Bèze,] *Historie Ecclésiastique des Églises Réformées au Royaume de France,* (Toulouse, 1882), 2 vols.

A Brief Discourse of the Troubles Begon at Frankfurt, 1554, J. Petheram, ed., (London, 1846).

J. de la Brosse, *Two Missions of Jacques de la Brosse,* W.C. Dickinson, ed., (Edinburgh, Scot. Hist. Soc., 1942).

G. Buchanan, *History of Scotland,* J. Aikman, tr. (Glasgow, 1827), II.

G. Buchanan, *Opera Omnia,* T. Ruddiman, ed., (Leyden, 1725), I.

D. Calderwood, *The History of the Kirk of Scotland*, T. Thomson, ed., (Edinburgh, Wodrow Soc., 1842) III, IV.

T. Dempster, *Historia Ecclesiastica, Gentis Scotorum*, D. Irving, ed., (Edinburgh, Bannatyne Club, 1829) 2 vols.

G. and J. Daval, *Histoire de la Réforme à Dieppe*, E. Lesens, ed., (Rouen, 1878).

A Diurnal of Remarkable Occurants in Scotland, (Edinburgh, Bannantyne Club, 1833).

J. Foxe, *Acts and Monuments of the Martyrs*, J. Pratt, ed., (London, 4th ed., n.d.), 8 vols.

"A Historie of the Estates of Scotland 1559–1660," *Miscellany of the Wodrow Society*, D. Laing, ed., (Edinburgh, 1844), I.

Journal d' un Bourgeois de Paris, (1513–1536), V.L. Bourrilly, ed., (Paris, 1910).

J. Knox, *History of the Reformation in Scotland*, W. C. Dickinson, ed., (Edinburgh, 1949), 2 vols.

J. Leslie, *Historie of Scotland*, E.G. Cody and W. Murison, edd., (Edinburgh, Scot. Text Soc. 1895), II.

R. Lindsay of Pitscottie, *The Historie and Chroniclis of Scotland*, A.J.G. MacKay, ed., (Edinburgh, Scot. Text Soc., 1899, 1911), 3 vols.

J. Major, *History of Greater Britain*, A. Constable, ed., (Edinburgh, Scot. Hist. Soc. 1892).

J. Melville, *The Diary of Mr. James Melville, 1556–1601*, (Edinburgh, Bannatyne Club 1829).

Sir James Melville of Halhill, *Memories of His Own Life, 1549—93*, (Edinburgh, Bannatyne Club 1837).

La Naissance et progrès de l'Hérésie de la ville de Dieppe, 1557–1609, E. Lesens ed., (Rouen, 1877).

J. Row, *Historie of the Kirk of Scotland 1558–1637*, (Edinburgh, Wodrow Soc. 1842).

J. Spottiswoode, *History of the Church of Scotland*, (Edinburgh, Bannatyne Club, 1850), 3 vols.

C. Wriothesley, *A Chronicle of England*, W.D. Hamilton, ed., (London, Camden Society, 1877), new ser. XX, XXI.

Secondary Sources

BOOKS

J. W. Allen, *A History of Political Thought in the Sixteenth Century*, (London, 1951).

L.A. Barbé, *Kirkcaldy of Grange*, (Edinburgh, 1897).

K. Bauer, *Die Beziehungen Calvins zur Frankfurt-am-Main*, (Leipzig, 1920).

W. Bell, *A Dictionary and Digest of the Law of Scotland*, (Edinburgh, 1838).

S.T. Bindoff, *Tudor England*, (Harmondsworth, 1950).

A. Boudier, *À Travers les Siècles*, (Dieppe, 1950).

P.H. Brown, *John Knox*, (London, 1895) 2 vols.

P.H. Brown, *Scotland in the time of Queen Mary*, (London, 1904).

J. Collier, *The Ecclesiastical History of Great Britain*, (London, new ed., 1852), VI.

R.W. Collins, *Calvin and the Libertines of Geneva*, F.D. Blackley, ed., (Toronto, 1968).

P. Collinson, *The Elizabethan Puritan Movement*, (Berkeley, Cal., 1967).

S. Cowan, *The Ancient Capital of Scotland*, (London, 1904).

Cultuurgeschiedenis van het Christendom, J. Watterink *et al.*, edd., (Amsterdam, 1950), III.

J. Delumeau, *Naissance et Affirmation de la Réforme*, (Paris, 1968).

C. Desmarquets, *Histoire Chronologique pour servir à l'histoire de Dieppe*, (Paris, 1785)

A.G. Dickens, *The English Reformation*, (London, 1956).

G. Donaldson, *The Making of the Scottish Prayer Book of 1637*, (Edinburgh, 1954).

G. Donaldson, *Scotland, James V to James VII*, (Edinburgh, 1961).

G. Donaldson, *The Scottish Reformation*, (Cambridge 1960).

J. Edgar, *The History of Early Scottish Education*, (Edinburgh, 1893).

G.R. Elton, *England under the Tudors*, (London, 1959).

Memoir of Erskine of Dun [Anonymous], (London, 1855).

D.H. Fleming, *Guide to St. Andrews*, (St. Andrews, 1947).

D.H. Fleming, *Mary Queen of Scots, from her birth to her flight into England*, (London, 2nd ed., 1898).

D.H. Fleming, *The Reformation in Scotland*, (London, 1910).

W. Forbes-Leith, *The Scots Men-at-Arms and the Life-Guards in France*, (Edinburgh 1882), 2 vols.

A. Fraser, *Mary Queen of Scots*, (New York, 1969).

J.A. Froude, *The Reign of Edward VI*, (London, 1909).

C.H. Garrett, *The Marian Exiles*, (Cambridge, 1938).

I.F. Grant, *Social and Economic Development of Scotland Before 1603*, (Edinburgh, 1930).

M.C. Guibert, *Mémoires pour servir à l'Histoire de la ville de Dieppe*, (Dieppe, 1878).

S. Hardy, *Histoire de l'Église Protestante de Dieppe*, (Paris, 1897).

J. Herkless & R.K. Hannay, *The Archbishops of St. Andrews*, (Edinburgh, 1913) 5 vols.

H. Hauser, *La Naissance du Protestantisme*, (Paris, 1962).

J.H. Hexter, *Reappraisals in History* (New York, 1961).

K. Holl, *The Cultural Significance of the Reformation*, (New York, 1959).

C. Hopf, *Martin Bucer and the English Reformation*, (Oxford 1946).

A. Jal, *Archéologie Navale*, (Paris, 1840).

J. Jamieson, *Bell the Cat, or who Destroyed the Scottish Abbeys?*, (Stirling, 1902).

P. Janelle, *The Catholic Reformation*, (Milwaukee, Wis., 1963).

P. Janton, *Concept and Sentiment de l'Église chez John Knox*, (Paris, 1972).

P. Janton, *John Knox, l'homme et l'oeuvre*, (Paris, 1967).

W.K. Jordan, *Edward VI: The Young King*, (Cambridge, Mass., 1968).

W.K. Jordan, *Edward VI: The Threshold of Power*, (Cambridge, 1970).

G.V. Jourdan, *The Movement toward Catholic Reform in the Early XVI Century*, (London, 1914).

M.M. Knappen, *Tudor Puritanism*, (Chicago, 1939).

A. Lang, *John Knox and the Reformation*, (London, 1905).

H. Lapeyre, *Les Monarchies Européennes du XVIᵉ Siècle*, (Paris, 1967).

T.G. Law, *Collected Essays*, P.H. Brown, ed., (Edinburgh, 1904).

M. Lee, *James Stewart, Earl of Moray*, (New York, 1953).

E. Léonard, *Le Protestantisme Français*, (Paris, 1955), I.

A. Lièvre, *Histoire des protestants et des églises protestantes de Poitou*, (Paris, 1856) I.

P. Lorimer, *John Knox and the Church of England*, (London, 1875).

R.S. Louden, *The True Face of the Kirk*, (London, 1963).

S.G.E. Lythe, *The Economy of Scotland in its European Setting 1550–1625*, (Edinburgh, 1960).

G. MacGregor, *The Thundering Scot*, (Philadelphia, n.d.).

J.D. Mackie, *The Earlier Tudors*, (Oxford, 1952).

J. MacKinnon, *The Constitutional History of Scotland*, (London, 1924).

J. MacKinnon, *A History of Modern Liberty*, (London, 1906) II.

W. MacMillan, *The Worship of the Scottish Reformed Church, 1558–1638*, (London, 1931).

T. M'Crie, *The Life of John Knox*, (Edinburgh, 1839).

J.T. McNeill, *The History and Character of Calvinism*, (New York, 1954).

C. Martin, *Les protestants anglais réfugiés à Genève au temps de Calvin, 1555–1560*, (Genève, 1915).

W.L. Mathieson, *Politics and Religion*, (Glasgow, 1902), I.

F. Mauro, *Le XVIᵉ Siècle Européen: Aspects economiques*, (Paris, 1966).

W.D. Maxwell, *John Knox's Genevan Service Book, 1556*, (Edinburgh, 1931).

W.D. Maxwell, *The Liturgical Portions of the Genevan Service Book*, (Philadelphia, 1931).

P. Meissner, *England in Zeitalter von Humanismus, Renaissance und Reformation*, (Heidelberg, 1952).

F. Michel, *Les Écossais en France et les Français en Écosse*, (London, 1862), 2 vols.

J. Miller, *The Lamp of Lothian*, (Haddington, 1844).

B. Moeller, *Villes d'Empire et Reformation*, (Geneva, 1966).

M. Mollat, *La commerce normande à la fin du Moyen Age*, (Paris, 1952).

W. Monter, *Calvin's Geneva*, (New York, 1967).

A. Morgan, *The Rise and Progress of Scottish Education*, (Edinburgh, 1927).

D. Neal, *History of the Puritans*, (New York, 1858), I.

Ordnance Gazetteer of Scotland, F.H. Broome, ed., (London, Blackwood, 1903, new edition), 4 vols.

J. Pannier, *Les origines de la confession de foi et le discipline des églises de France*, (Paris, 1936).

Lord Eustace Percy, *John Knox*, (Richmond, Va., n.d.)

A.F. Pollard, *England under Protector Somerset*, (London, 1900).

A.F. Pollard, *Factors in Modern History*, (Boston, 3rd. ed., 1960).

H.C. Porter, *Reformation and Reaction in Tudor Cambridge*, (Cambridge, 1958).

R.S. Rait, *The Parliaments of Scotland*, (Glasgow, 1924).

C. Read, *Mr. Secretary Cecil and Queen Elizabeth*, (London, 1955).

G. Reese, *Music in the Renaissance*, (New York, 1959).

W.S. Reid, *Skipper from Leith*, (Philadelphia, 1964).

J. Ridley, *John Knox*, (New York, 1968).

J. Ridley, *Thomas Cranmer*, (Oxford, 1962).

J. Rilliet, *Zwingle*, (Paris, 1959).

C. Rogers, *Three Scottish Reformers*, (London, 1874).

J. Rondeau, *Les Calvinistes Châtelleraudais*, (Châtellerault, 1907).

M.P. Rooseboom, *The Scottish Staple in the Netherlands*, (Hague, 1910).

A. Ruchat, *Histoire de la Réformation de la Suisse*, (Nyon, 1836), III, IV.

E. Russell, *Maitland of Lethington*, (London, 1912), II.

P. Schaff, *History of the Christian Church*, (New York, 1916), VII.

Scots Peerage, J. Balfour Paul (Edinburgh, 1904–14), 9 vols.

B.H. Slichter van Bath, *The Agrarian History of Western Europe, 500–1850*, O. Ordish, tr. (London, 1963).

C.H. Smyth, *Cranmer and the Reformation under Edward VI*, (Cambridge, 1926).

Société d'Archeologie et Histoire de Gèneve, *Histoire de Genève*, (Geneva, n.d.)

J. Strype, *Ecclesiastical Memorials*, (London, 1822) II.

J. Strype, *The Life of Sir John Cheke*, (London, 1821).

J. Strype, *Memorials of Archbishop Cranmer*, (Oxford, 1840) I.

W. Thom, *History of Aberdeen*, (Aberdeen, 1811), I

G.M. Trevelyan, *A Shortened History of England*, (London, 1942).

H. Trevor-Roper, *Historical Essays*, (London, 1957).

E. Trocme et M. Delafosse, *La commerce rochelais de la fin du XV* siècle, (Paris, 1952).

P. F. Tytler, *England under the Reigns of Edward VI and Mary*, (London, 1839), 2 vols.

P. F. Tytler, *The History of Scotland*, (Edinburgh, 1864), III.

A. A. van Schelven, *Het Calvinisme Gedurende Zijn Bloeitijd*, (Amsterdam, 1943), 2 vols.

C. R. Warr, *Presbyterian Tradition*, (London, 1933).

H. Watt, *John Knox in Controversy*, (London, 1950).

L. Wencelius, *L'Esthétique de Calvin*, (Paris, n.d.)

ARTICLES

G. B. Beeman, "The Early History of the Strangers' Church, 1550–1561," *Proceedings of the Huguenot Society of London*, XV (1933–37).

M. Berengo, Review of *Nobilie Mercanti nella Lucca del Cinquecento*, (Torino, 1965), *Bibliothèque d'Humanisme et Renaissance*, 31 (Geneva, 1969).

P. Boissonade, "Le Mouvement Commercial entre la France et les Îles Britannique en le 16ème Siècle," *Révue Historique*, 134 (1920).

H. Bonar, "John Knox and Ranfurly," *Scottish Historical Review*, V (1908).

J. Bonneret, "Esquisse de la vie des routes au XVIe siècle," *Révue des Questions Historiques*, CXV (1931).

C. Bourgeaud, "Le 'Vrai Portrait' de John Knox," *Bulletin de la Société de l'Histoire du Protestantisme français*, LXXXIV (1935).

W. M. Bryce, "The Black Friars of Edinburgh," *The Book of the Old Edinburgh Club*, III (1910).

J. H. Burns, "The Political Background of the Reformation 1513–1625," *Essays on the Scottish Reformation*, D. McRoberts, ed., (Glasgow 1962).

P. Collinson, "The Role of Women in the English Reformation Illustrated by the Life and Friendships of Mrs. Anne Locke," *Studies in Church History*, II (1956).

G. Constant, "La Chute de Somerset et l'élévation de Warwick," *La Révue Historique*, 172 (1933).

H. Cowan, "When was Knox born?," *Records of the Scottish Church History Society*, I, (1926).

H. J. Cowell, "Sixteenth century English-speaking Refugee Congregations in Strasbourg, Basle, Aarau, Wesel, Emden," *Proceedings of the Huguenot Society of London*, XV (1933-7).

D. Davidson, "Influence of English Printers on the Scottish Reformation," *Records of the Scottish Church History Society*, I (1926).

G. Dickinson, "Instructions to the French Ambassador 30 March 1550," *Scottish Historical Review*, XXVI (1947).

G. Donaldson, " 'The Example of Denmark' in the Scottish Reformation," *Scottish Historical Review*, XXVII (1948).

G. Donaldson, "Foundations of Anglo-Scottish unity," *Elizabethan Government and Society*, S. T. Bindoff *et al.*, edd., (London, 1961).

G. Donaldson, "The Parish Clergy and the Reformation," *Essays on the Scottish Reformation*, D. McRoberts, ed., (Glasgow, 1960).

E. Dupont, "Les Prisonniers de Mont St. Michel," *Scottish Historical Review*, III (1903).

J. Durkan, "The cultural Background in Sixteenth Century Scotland," *Essays on The Scottish Reformation*, D. McRoberts, ed., (Glasgow, 1962).

"English Refugees in Germany and Switzerland," *Proceedings of the Huguenot Society of London*, IV (1891-3).

"Galley," *Encyclopaedia Britannica*, 11th ed. (1910).

C. P. Finlayson, "A Volume Associated with John Knox," *Scottish Historical Review*, XXXVIII (1959).

R. L. Greaves, "John Knox and the Covenant Tradition," *Journal of Ecclesiastical History*, XXIV (1973).

R. K. Hannay, "The Church Lands of the Reformation," *Scottish Historical Review*, XVI (1919).

R. K. Hannay, "The Earl of Arran and Queen Mary," *Scottish Historical Review*, XVIII (1921).

R. K. Hannay, "Letters of the Papal Legate in Scotland, 1543," *Scottish Historical Review*, XI (1914).

H. Hauser, "Le Capitalisme en France au XVIᵉ Siècle," *Révue des Cours et Conférences*, Paris, (1922).

F. Isaac, "Egedius van der Erve and English printed books," *The Library*, ser. 4, XII (1931-2).

Brother Kenneth, "The Popular Literature of the Scottish Reformation," *Essays on the Scottish Reformation*, D. McRoberts, ed., (Glasgow, 1962).

H. F. Kerr, "Cardinal Beaton's Palace: Blackfriars' Wynd," *Book of the Old Edinburgh Club*, XXIV (1942).

D. MacKay, "Parish Life in Scotland 1500–1600," *Essays on the Scottish Reformation*, D. McRoberts, ed., (Glasgow, 1962).

W. MacMillan, "The Anglican Book of Common Prayer in the Church of Scotland," *Records of the Scottish Church History Society*, IV (1932).

J. MacRae, "The Scottish Reformers and Public Worship," *Records of the Scottish Church History Society*, III (1929).

D. Mahoney, "The Scottish Hierarchy, 1513–1625," *Essays on the Scottish Reformation*, D. McRoberts, ed., (Glasgow, 1962).

J. U. Nef, "Industrial Europe at the time of the Reformation," *Journal of Political Economy*, XLIX (1941).

"Notes and Comments," *Scottish Historical Review*, I (1904).

J. Pannier, "Les résidences successives des étudiants écossais à Paris," *Association Franco-Ecossais Bulletin*, (1929).

G. T. Peck, "Sir John Hales and the Puritans during the Marian Exile," *Church History*, X (1941).

N. Pocock, "The conditions of morals and Religious Belief in the Reign of Edward VI," *The English Historical Review*, X (1895).

N. Pocock, "The Restoration settlement of the English Church," *The English Historical Review*, I, (1886).

C. A. Rahlenbeck, "Quelques notes sur les 'reformers' flamands et wallons de 16ᵉ siècle refugiés en Angleterre," *Proceedings of the Huguenot Society of London*, IV (1891–3).

W. S. Reid, "The Battle Hymns of the Lord: Calvinist Psalmody of the Sixteenth Century," *Sixteenth Century Essays and Studies*, II (1971).

W. S. Reid, "Clerical Taxation: The Scottish Alternative to Dissolution of the Monasteries, 1530–1560," *Catholic Historical Review*, XXXV, (1948).

W. S. Reid, "The Coming of the Reformation to Edinburgh," *Church History*, 42 (1973).

W. S. Reid, "The Ecumenicalism of John Calvin," *Westminster Theological Journal*, XI (1948).

W. S. Reid, "The Founding of the Genevan Academy," *Westminster Theological Journal*, XVIII (1955)

W. S. Reid, "John Knox's Attitude to the English Reformation," *Westminster Theological Journal*, XXVI (1963).

W. S. Reid, "The Lion Rampant in Sixteenth Century France," *Scottish Colloquium Proceedings*, (Guelph, Ontario: University of Guelph, 1970), III.

W. S. Reid, "The Lollards in Pre-Reformation Scotland," *Church History*, XI (1942).

W. S. Reid, "A Sixteenth Century Marriage Contract between Sir James Sandilands of Calder and Robert Barton of Over Barnton," *Scottish Historical Review*, XXVIII (1949).

W. M. Southgate, "The Marian Exiles and the Influence of John Calvin," *History*, XXVII (1942).

D. Shaw, "John Willock," *Reformation and Revolution*, D. Shaw, ed., (Edinburgh, 1967).

M. A. Simpson, "On the Troubles begun at Frankfurt, A.D. 1554," *Reformation and Revolution*, D. Shaw, ed., (Edinburgh, 1967).

R.L. Stevenson, "John Knox and his relations to women," *Familar Studies of Men and Books*, (London, 1963).

R.L. Stevenson, "The Foreigner at Home," *Memories and Portraits*, (London, n.d.)

T. Thomson, "Where was John Knox born?", *Proceedings of the Society of Antiquaries of Scotland*, (Edinburgh, 1862), III.

H. Trevor-Roper, "John Knox," *The Listener*, 80 (1968).

INDEX